PREFACE

Historically, education and training have always played a crucial role in the development of our societies. Nowadays, at a time marked by accelerating economic, technological, social and cultural change, the European Union must invest more than ever in knowledge and consequently increase its efforts in the area of education and training.

This investment will be one of the main keys to our competitiveness at a time of globalization of exchanges and with the advent of the information society.

The education provided from the very start of schooling must enhance the capacity of the greatest number of children to adapt to the rapid progress of both society and knowledge.

It is also by developing lifelong learning that we will ensure greater social cohesion.

Key data on education has appeared since 1994 and is now in its third edition. The first publication of its kind at European level, it aims to meet the increasing demand for reliable and varied data on all levels of education.

Building on the success of the earlier editions, this report includes some new indicators. This third edition has also opened its pages not only to the EFTA/EEA countries but also to the first six central and eastern European countries (CEECs) which are associated, under the preparatory measures, with the European Union's activities in the field of education, training and youth. Their inclusion in this reference work provides tangible proof of the eastward expansion of Community cooperation under the Socrates programme.

Finally, it should be said that this document is the product of close cooperation between the Eurydice network, as the source of the descriptive, qualitative information, and Eurostat, which has provided the statistics. In the interests of clarity and readability, the quantitative data and the qualitative analysis are closely interwoven. The report provides the reader with the most complete picture possible of the situation along with the explanations necessary to an understanding of the trends emerging in the field of education in Europe.

In parallel, and for the first time, the Commission has also published a version of *Key Data on Vocational Training* this year.

With the regular publication of quantitative and qualitative information on the way our education systems are organized and developing, the European Commission wishes to provide policy makers and all those involved in the education world with a comparative picture of the efforts being made in this field in Europe. It also hopes to encourage exchanges and strengthen mutual understanding within the Union. We hope that this document will thus be able to make a contribution to the development of education and training.

December 1997

Édith Cresson

Member of the Commission
responsible for Research, Innovation,
Education, Training and Youth

Yves-Thibault de Silguy

Member of the Commission
responsible for Economic,
Monetary and Financial Affairs
and the Statistical Office

CONTENTS

INTRODUCTION

GENERAL FRAMEWORK OF THE THIRD EDITION

In this, its third edition, *Key data on education in the European Union* retains its principal special feature — the presentation together of statistics and descriptive information on the education systems. Compared with the two earlier editions, however, this one covers a number of new aspects.

First, the information has been extended to include not only the three EFTA/EEA countries — Iceland, Liechtenstein and Norway — but also the first six associated countries of central and eastern Europe — Bulgaria, the Czech Republic, Hungary, Poland, Romania and Slovakia — which have been increasingly involved in the work of the Eurydice network since 1996. The inclusion of these countries in *Key data on education* is concrete evidence of the cooperation with these countries over the past two years in the context of the measures preparatory to their participation in Socrates, the European Union's education programme.

Each chapter includes new indicators as well as updated versions of those in the previous editions. Mention should be made of, amongst other things, the introduction of statistics on the opinion of young people on lifelong learning, and of information on the extent of the decision-making powers of schools, the main patterns of constituting groups and classes of children at both pre-primary and primary school level, and regulations on pupil:teacher ratios. A detailed diagram of the structures and fields of study in higher education has been drawn up for each country. Readers will also find information on the conditions of access to this level of education and the qualifications awarded. The main tasks and methods of recruitment of school heads are the subject of a separate analysis. Finally, there is a comparison of the norms used to define full-time and part-time teaching loads in the various countries.

This third edition also includes a new chapter on the education of children with special needs. This tries to shed light briefly on the current provision and historical development of special education in the education systems. Particular attention is given to the training of the adults responsible for these children. This represents a first effort which can be expanded on in future editions. In this context, a start is being made on cooperation between Eurydice and the European Agency for Development in Special Needs Education.[1]

Moreover, it is important to note that, in view of the number of countries which this report now covers, it does not include a thematic dossier as did the previous editions. In future, *Key data on education* will be published on a biennial basis. The general part dealing with the different levels of education will be published every other year, alternating with a *Thematic key data* on a topic of Community interest. The subject chosen for the 1998 publication is the allocation and management of financial resources for education.

As a result of this choice of subject, readers will find that the chapter dealing with the financing of education has been dropped from this edition as this information will be published on its own in the next edition, following in-depth study of the subject. On the other hand, some of the material included in the thematic dossier in the second edition, dealing with teachers, has been updated and is included in a separate chapter here.

---

[1] The European Agency for Development in Special Needs Education is a body set up in November 1996 at the initiative of the Danish government and supported by the governments of the Member States of the European Union. Its seat is in Denmark, at Teglgaardsparken 100, DK-5500 Middelfart.

This report contains another original feature, in that time series are included in most of the chapters and, in as far as the statistics were considered to be sufficiently reliable, regional data are presented. The aim is to bring out more clearly the trends and important changes that have appeared in relation to both access to and attendance at educational institutions at all levels in recent decades and also the regional disparities found in the operation of the education systems in certain countries. These make it possible to measure the efforts made by Member States in relation to education by placing the information in a historical and more dynamic perspective.

Key data on education deals exclusively with education systems in the strict sense. It therefore contains very little information on initial and continuing vocational training systems. Only four indicators on lifelong learning are included in the first chapter (Context). For more information on this sector of education and training, readers should consult the Commission's report *Key Data on Vocational Training* which has recently been published for the first time (1997, Office for Official Publications of the European Communities, Luxembourg).

*
* *

PRESENTATION AND METHODOLOGY

This publication is intended not only for policy makers but also to inform a very wide public about the diversity of the working of, and the major trends in, the education systems in the European Union, in the EFTA/EEA countries and in the six central and eastern European countries (CEECs). To make it accessible to the greatest possible number of people and to facilitate consultation, it contains many illustrations in the form of histograms, maps and diagrams. The document is constructed on the basis of alternating comparative graphs and comment bringing out the essentials revealed by the illustrations.

As far as possible, only statistics collected through a harmonized questionnaire have been used so as to ensure the highest degree of rigour and reliability in making comparisons. For this reason, priority has been given to the use of the statistics obtained annually from the joint Unesco/OECD/Eurostat (UOE) questionnaires and from the Labour force survey conducted by Eurostat. However, national statistics have had to be used for the EFTA/EEA countries and the six CEECs which are not yet covered by the Community surveys. Each time an indicator is constructed for a country on the basis of national sources, it is therefore shown in black and white to distinguish it from the harmonized statistics and alert the reader to this factor when making comparisons. All references to national sources used are mentioned in the annex.

The statistics relate to the academic year 1994/95. Exceptionally, where these statistics were not available, those for 1993/94 have been used, and such instances are indicated. All the indicators relating to descriptive information are for the academic year 1995/96. The necessary connections between the statistics and the organization of the education systems are therefore always included in the comments.

The statistics are constructed by level of education in accordance with the Unesco International Standard Classification for Education (ISCED). Where this classification does not match the actual structures in individual countries, readers are informed in a note below the graphs in question, and an explanation is given of the degree to which they are comparable. This is more particularly the case in relation to the statistics on primary and lower secondary education in countries with a single, continuous structure and no primary/secondary transition.

All the data relating to the Member States of the European Union are presented in such a way that they are clearly distinguished from those for the EFTA/EEA countries and the six central and eastern European countries. In the histograms, for example, the Member States of the European Union are always presented on the left-hand side and the other nine countries on the right. In the maps, the use of solid colours and coloured hatching also makes it easier to identify the Member States and the other associated countries.

The European averages which have been calculated for a large number of indicators are always presented separately to the left of the graphs and tables and these refer to the statistics of Member States of the European Union only.

To facilitate reading and make these illustrations easier to understand, a glossary of the codes and abbreviations used has been added, along with a readers' guide to the statistical tools and terminology used.

In the interests of presentational quality, all the numerical data are set out in the annexes. The tables there are arranged by chapter and numbered to match the graphs based on the raw data. On the other hand, the explanatory notes and individual explanations needed to understand the material appear immediately below the illustrations.

A list of some key Eurydice and Eurostat publications appears at the end of the document. These have been selected as offering useful supplementary information relevant to the subjects treated in this report.

*

* *

The indicators presented in this edition were chosen in consultations held in 1996 between members of the Eurydice network and Eurostat, on the basis of their previous experience. A joint meeting of these two networks was held in September 1996, during which the work was planned and cooperation between members of the networks strengthened. In addition to using already available statistics from surveys, specific questionnaires were drafted to obtain additional statistics. These questionnaires were tested in a trial run with some of the Eurydice national units and Eurostat national representatives.

We should particularly like to thank the Eurostat contacts in the Member State statistical services and the Eurydice national units for the provision of additional data and for checking the document as a whole. Despite the magnitude of the task, they have all contributed effectively to the collective final product.

By giving responsibility for editing and coordinating this periodical to the Eurydice European Unit, which has worked closely with Eurostat, the European Communities' statistical office, DG XXII (Education, Training, Youth) wished to have reliable information produced on the education systems in terms of both statistics and qualitative information.

Additional expertise in the preparation of this report has also been provided by the Service de Pédagogie Expérimentale of the University of Liège in Belgium and the Institut des Sciences Pratiques d'Éducation et de Formation of the Lumière University of Lyon in France. The task of writing and editing has been undertaken by the European Unit of Eurydice which carries full responsibility for the analysis and commentary and for the graphical presentation of the material.

GLOSSARY

ABBREVIATIONS

COUNTRY CODES AND ABBREVIATIONS

EU		European Union
B		Belgium
	B fr	Belgium – French Community
	B nl	Belgium – Flemish Community
	B de	Belgium – German-speaking Community
DK		Denmark
D		Germany
EL		Greece
E		Spain
F		France
IRL		Ireland
I		Italy
L		Luxembourg
NL		Netherlands
A		Austria
P		Portugal
FIN		Finland
S		Sweden
UK		United Kingdom
	E/W	England and Wales
	NI	Northern Ireland
	SC	Scotland
EFTA/EEA		European Free Trade Association/European Economic Area
IS		Iceland
LI		Liechtenstein
NO		Norway
CEEC		Central and Eastern European Countries
BG		Bulgaria
CZ		Czech Republic
HU		Hungary
PL		Poland
RO		Romania
SK		Slovakia

ABBREVIATIONS OF STATISTICAL TOOLS AND OTHER CLASSIFICATIONS

(e)	Estimate
Ø	Average
EUR15	European Union – 15 Member States
GDP	Gross domestic product
ILO	International Labour Organization
ISCED	International Standard Classification for Education
ISCO	International Standard Classification of Occupations
M	Male/Men
F	Female/Women
N/A	Not available
NUTS	Nomenclature of territorial units for statistics
ESA	European system of accounts
UOE	Unesco/OECD/Eurostat

NATIONAL ABBREVIATIONS IN THEIR LANGUAGE OF ORIGIN

AEA	Attestation d'études approfondies	F
AEI	Anotato Ekpaideftiko Idryma	EL
AHU	Année hospitalo-universitaire	F
BAC	Baccalauréat	F
BEP	Brevet d'études professionnelles	F
BTEC HNC	Business and Technology Education Council - Higher National Certificate	UK (E/W)
BTEC HND	Business and Technology Education Council - Higher National Diploma	UK (E/W)
BTS	Brevet de technicien supérieur	F, L
BUP	Bachillerato Unificado y Polivalente	E
CAP	Certificat d'aptitude professionnelle	F
CAPES	Certificat d'aptitude au professorat de l'enseignement secondaire	F
CAPSAIS	Certificat d'aptitude aux actions pédagogiques spécialisées d'adaptation et d'intégration scolaires	F
CESE	Curso de Estudos Superiores Especializados	P
COU	Curso de Orientación Universitaria	E
CPGE	Classes préparatoires aux grandes écoles	F
CS	Community school/Comprehensive school	IRL
CSCT	Certificat de synthèse clinique et thérapeutique	F
CSPOPE	Cursos Secundários Predominantemente Orientados para o Prosseguimento de Estudos	P
CT	Cursos Tecnológicos	P
CU	Centre universitaire de Luxembourg	L
DEA	Diplôme d'études approfondies	B fr, F
DES	Diplôme d'études spécialisées	B fr, F
DESS	Diplôme d'études supérieures spécialisées	F
DEUG	Diplôme d'études universitaires générales	F
DEUST	Diplôme d'études universitaires scientifiques et techniques	F
DipHE	Diploma of Higher Education	UK (E/W)
DNTS	Diplôme national de technologie spécialisé	F
DRT	Diplôme de recherche technologique	F
DUT	Diplôme universitaire de technologie	F
ETI	Education and Training Inspectorate	UK (NI)
EUD	Erhvervsuddannelse	DK
FPE	Formación Profesional Específica	E
GS	Grammar school	UK (E, NI)
HAVO	Hoger Algemeen Voortgezet Onderwijs	NL
HBO	Hoger Beroepsonderwijs	NL
HF	Højere Forberedelseseksamen	DK
HHX	Højere Handelseksamen	DK
HMI	Her Majesty's Inspector	UK
HTX	Højere Teknisk Eksamen	DK
IAP	Internationale Akademie für Philosophie	LI
IEES	Institut d'études éducatives et sociales	L
ISERP	Institut supérieur d'études et de recherches pédagogiques	L
IST	Institut supérieur de technologie	L
IUFM	Institut universitaire de formation des maîtres	F
IUP	Instituts universitaires professionnalisés	F
IUT	Instituts universitaires technologiques	F
LIS	Liechtensteinische Ingenieur Schule	LI
LOGSE	Ley Orgánica de Ordenación General del Sistema Educativo	E
MAVO	Middelbaar Algemeen Voortgezet Onderwijs	NL
MBO	Middelbaar Beroepsonderwijs	NL
MIAGE	Maîtrise d'informatique appliquée à la gestion économique	F
MSG	Maîtrise de Sciences de gestion	F
MST	Maîtrise de Sciences et techniques	F
OFSTED	Office for Standards in Education	UK (E)
OHMCI	Office of Her Majesty's Chief Inspector of Schools	UK (W)
PATES	Paidagogiki techniki scholi	EL
PGCE	Postgraduate Certificate in Education	UK (E/W)
PIC	Programme of interuniversity cooperation	EU
QTS	Qualified Teacher Status	UK (E/W)
SJNC	Scottish Joint Negotiating Committee	UK (SC)
STS	Sections de techniciens supérieurs	F
SV	Stredné vzdelanie	SK
TEI	Technologiko Ekpaideftiko Idryma	EL
TES	Techniki epaggelmatiki scholi	EL
UCAS	Universities and Colleges Admissions Service	UK
ULO	Universitaire eerstegraads lerarenopleiding	NL
ÚSV	Úplné stredné vzdelanie	SK
VBO	Voorbereidend Beroepsonderwijs	NL
VS	Vocational school	IRL
VWO	Voorbereidend Wetenschappelijk Onderwijs	NL
WO	Wetenschappelijk Onderwijs	NL

DEFINITIONS OF STATISTICAL TOOLS

THE UOE DATA COLLECTION

The UOE (UNESCO/OECD/EUROSTAT) data collection is an instrument through which these three organizations jointly collect internationally comparable data on key aspects of education systems on an annual basis using administrative sources. Data collected cover enrolments, new entrants, graduates, educational personnel, education institutions and educational expenditures. The specific breakdowns include level of education, sex, age, type of programme (general/vocational), mode (full-time/part-time), type of institution (public-private), field of study and country of citizenship. In addition, to meet the information needs of the European Commission, Eurostat collects enrolment data by region and on foreign language learning.

THE INTERNATIONAL STANDARD CLASSIFICATION FOR EDUCATION (ISCED)

In order to facilitate comparison between countries, the different levels of national education have been allocated the various ISCED categories as follows:
ISCED 0: pre-primary education
ISCED 1: primary education
ISCED 2: lower secondary education
ISCED 3: upper secondary education
ISCED 5, 6, 7: higher education.
Due to discrepancies in the allocation of data to the three ISCED levels comprising higher education, data in this report refer to the three levels combined. The three levels are:
ISCED 5: higher education programmes generally leading to an award not equivalent to a university first degree but admission to which requires at least the completion of upper secondary education.
ISCED 6: higher education programmes leading to a first degree or equivalent.
ISCED 7: higher education programmes leading to a post-graduate degree or equivalent.

EUROSTAT DEMOGRAPHIC DATABASE

The national demographic data are collected by Eurostat from responses to an annual questionnaire sent to the national statistical institutes of the Member States of the European Union and EFTA countries. The annual national population estimates are based either on the most recent census or on data extracted from the population register. Data at regional level are collected by Eurostat for the Member States of the European Union only.

THE NOMENCLATURE OF TERRITORIAL UNITS FOR STATISTICS (NUTS)

This was established by Eurostat to provide a single, uniform breakdown of territorial units for the production of regional statistics for the European Union. The NUTS is a five-level hierarchical classification (three regional levels and two local levels) which in most cases subdivides Member States into a number of NUTS 1 regions, each of which is in turn subdivided into a number of NUTS 2 regions and so on. For Sweden, the regional breakdown only begins at NUTS level 2, Ireland and Denmark at NUTS level 3 and Luxembourg at NUTS level 4. Education data are collected at NUTS levels 1 and 2 only.

THE COMMUNITY LABOUR FORCE SURVEY (LFS)

The LFS, which has been carried out annually since 1983, is the principal source of statistics on employment and unemployment in the European Union.
This survey is an inquiry directed at individuals and households. The questions cover mainly the characteristics of employment and job-seeking. It also includes questions on participation in education or training during the four weeks prior to the survey and information on the level of education attained.
The definitions are common for all Member States and are based in particular on the recommendations of the International Labour Organization.
For example, the definition of an unemployed person is someone who is without work, who is actively looking for work and who is available for work within the next 15 days.
The unemployment rate is defined as the number of persons unemployed as a percentage of the active population, i.e. the total of all persons employed and unemployed.

THE EUROBAROMETER SURVEY

The Eurobarometer opinion survey has been carried out twice a year since 1973 by the European Commission's Directorate General for Information, Communication, Culture and Audio-visual Affairs. An identical set of questions dealing with various areas of interest is put to a representative sample of the population aged 15 and over in each Member State. Supplementary questions can be added, and these change from year to year.

CONTEXT

FEWER AND FEWER YOUNG PEOPLE
IN THE POPULATION IN EUROPE

Since 1975, the number of young people under 30 years of age has been falling generally throughout the European Union.

FIGURE A1: INDEX OF THE NUMBERS OF 0- TO 9-YEAR-OLDS, 10- TO 19-YEAR-OLDS AND 20- TO 29-YEAR-OLDS IN THE EUROPEAN UNION, 1975-95 (1975 = 1)

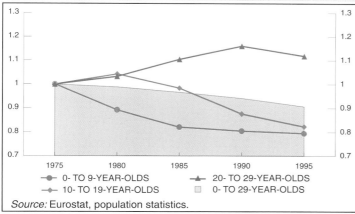

Source: Eurostat, population statistics.

The changes in the age groups within the population in the education age range are explained by the fall in the birth rate over at least the last 20 years.

Differences may be observed between the changes in the individual age groups: the proportion of the youngest, the 0- to 9-year-olds, has been declining steadily and that of the 10- to 19-year-olds started to fall in 1980. This decline in the proportion of the youngest age group is reflected in the 20- to 29-year-old group from 1990.

Portugal: Not included as data are not available for 1975 and 1980.

In 1995, there were 145 million young people under 30 years of age living in the 15 Member States of the European Union, representing 39% of the total population of the Union. But, as the following figure illustrates, a breakdown of these young people into the different age bands indicates that the over-20-year-olds are the most numerous. This is found in all the Member States except Ireland, where 10- to 19-year-olds form the largest proportion, and in Finland where the three age groups are about equal.

Of the EFTA/EEA countries, only Iceland departs from the general pattern, with an inversion of the distribution across the different age bands. This is explained in part by the considerable number of young people between 20 and 29 years old who have left Iceland in recent years, mainly to study abroad.

In all the Central and Eastern European countries (CEECs), contrary to the situation in the European Union, young people between 10 and 19 years of age constitute the largest proportion. Children under the age of 10 are also generally the least numerous there, except in Poland.

FIGURE A2: PERCENTAGES OF 0- TO 9-YEAR-OLDS, 10- TO 19-YEAR-OLDS AND 20- TO 29-YEAR-OLDS, 1995

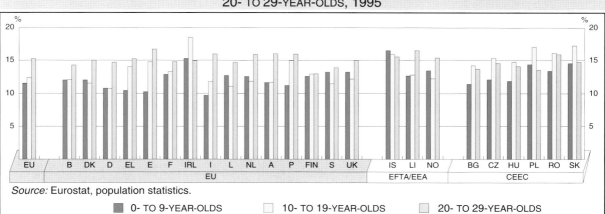

Source: Eurostat, population statistics.

■ 0- TO 9-YEAR-OLDS   □ 10- TO 19-YEAR-OLDS   □ 20- TO 29-YEAR-OLDS

EXPLANATORY NOTE
For the calculation of the changes in the numbers of young people in Figure A1, the base year is 1975. For example, the 1980 value is obtained by calculating the ratio of the numbers of young people found in 1980 and in 1975. For 1995, the percentages in Figure A2 of young people in the age groups 0 to 9, 10 to 19 and 20 to 29 years are obtained by calculating the ratio of the numbers in each of these individual groups to the numbers in the total population.

SIGNIFICANT REGIONAL VARIATIONS
IN THE PROPORTIONS OF YOUNG PEOPLE

In the European Union, the percentage of young people in relation to the total population reveals regional disparities. Large proportions of young people (more than 43%) are found in the south of Spain (and in the Canary Islands, not shown on the map), in the northern half of France, Ireland, the southern regions of Italy, the north of Portugal (and also in the Azores and Madeira, not shown on the map), the north of Finland and Northern Ireland.

The proportion of under-30's is, on the other hand, relatively small (less than 36%) in most of the regions of Germany and in the north of Italy.

In the EFTA/EEA countries and the CEECs, with the exception of Liechtenstein, Norway and Bulgaria, the percentage of young people between 0 and 29 years old is distinctly higher than the European Union average (39%). In the EFTA/EEA countries in 1995, for example, there were almost 2 million under-30-year-olds, representing 41% of the population, while in the CEECs there were over 42 million in this age group, or 44% of the total population.

FIGURE A3: PERCENTAGE OF 0- TO 29-YEAR-OLDS BY NUTS 1 AND 2 REGIONS, 1995

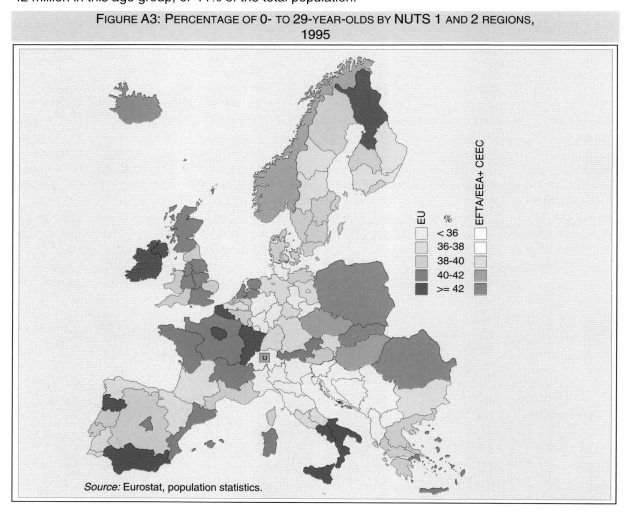

Source: Eurostat, population statistics.

EXPLANATORY NOTE

The nomenclature of territorial units for statistics (NUTS) is used in the European Union to provide a single and coherent breakdown of regional statistics. For most Member States, the nomenclature used here is that of the NUTS 1 level. NUTS 2 has been used for Portugal, Finland and Sweden. For the EFTA/EEA countries and the CEECs, only national statistics are included.
The division into bands is based on the distribution of the data. The method chosen leads to continuous series, each of which includes an equal percentage of values.

INCREASING NUMBERS OF YOUNG PEOPLE
───── HAVE BEEN STAYING ON IN EDUCATION ─────

For several decades, increasing numbers of young people have been remaining in education beyond the end of the upper secondary level. The percentage of the population leaving school without a qualification at this level is therefore progressively decreasing and the level of education of the population is rising.

In certain European Union Member States the pattern is different. In Denmark, Germany, the Netherlands and Austria, only small percentages of people are found without at least a final upper secondary school leaving qualification, whatever their age. In Spain, Italy, Luxembourg and, in particular, Portugal, the proportions of those without an upper secondary qualification are over 40%, even among the younger members of the population.

FIGURE A4: PERCENTAGE OF PEOPLE WITHOUT A FINAL UPPER SECONDARY SCHOOL LEAVING QUALIFICATION, BY AGE GROUP, 1995

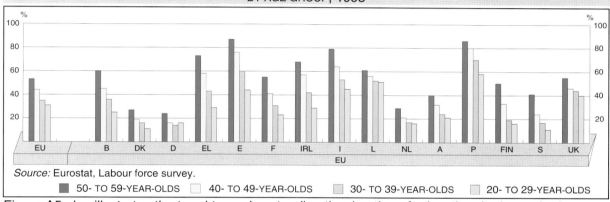

Source: Eurostat, Labour force survey.

■ 50- TO 59-YEAR-OLDS □ 40- TO 49-YEAR-OLDS ▨ 30- TO 39-YEAR-OLDS ▨ 20- TO 29-YEAR-OLDS

Figure A5 also illustrates the trend towards extending the duration of education. It shows the increase between 1987 and 1995 in the percentages of young people between 15 and 24 years old who are still in the education systems.

FIGURE A5: TREND IN THE PERCENTAGES OF STUDENTS (ALL PERSONS IN EDUCATION AND TRAINING) AMONG 15- TO 24-YEAR-OLDS, 1987 AND 1995

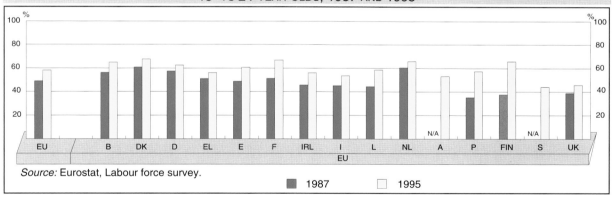

Source: Eurostat, Labour force survey.

■ 1987 □ 1995

Finland: National statistics for 1987.

In 1987, under 50% of 15- to 24-year-olds were still studying. The proportion was almost 60% in 1995. This increase is observed in all Member States for which data are available. It is especially marked in France, Luxembourg and, in particular, Portugal and Finland. The less pronounced change in Denmark, Germany and the Netherlands is explained by the fact that these Member States already had high participation rates in 1987.

EXPLANATORY NOTE

For each age group in Figure A4, the percentage is arrived at by calculating the ratio of the number of people who do not hold a final upper secondary school leaving qualification — at the ISCED 3 level or above — to the total number of people in the age group.

In the Labour force survey, a student (Figure A5) is defined as a person who has, during the previous four weeks, attended a school (general or vocational), university or apprenticeship-type sandwich course, full-time or part-time.

ALMOST 83 MILLION PUPILS AND STUDENTS
IN THE EUROPEAN UNION

During the academic year 1994/95, there were slightly under 83 million pupils and students in the European Union, representing about 22% of the total population.

In the same year, there were more than one million pupils and students in the EFTA/EEA countries, or 24% of the total population.

In the CEECs, the 21 million pupils and students represented 22% of the total population in 1994/95.

FIGURE A6: PUPILS AND STUDENTS (THOUSAND), 1994/95							
EUROPEAN UNION							
EU	B	DK	D	EL	E	F	IRL
82 969	2 534	1 145	16 324	1 980	9 733	14 679	1 012
I	L	NL	A	P	FIN	S	UK
10 681	65	3 586	1 616	2 351	1 143	1 978	14 142

Source: Eurostat, UOE.

Belgium: 1993/94.

EFTA/EEA		
IS	LI	NO
83	5	1 028

Source: Eurostat, UOE.

Liechtenstein: National statistics, 1993/94.

CEEC					
BG	CZ	HU	PL	RO	SK
1 432	2 256	2 062	9 552	4 595	1 307

National statistics.

From the total figure for all pupils and students, the under-30-year-old group was chosen to calculate the proportion that they represent of their age group in the population. Figure A7 shows these percentages.

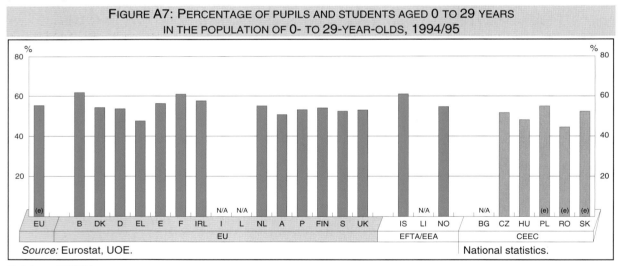

FIGURE A7: PERCENTAGE OF PUPILS AND STUDENTS AGED 0 TO 29 YEARS IN THE POPULATION OF 0- TO 29-YEAR-OLDS, 1994/95

Source: Eurostat, UOE.

National statistics.

Belgium: 1993/94.
Germany: The age breakdown of students aged 24 and over is an estimate.

In the European Union as a whole, over 55% of 0- to 29-year-olds are pupils or students. The highest percentages — over 60% — are found in Belgium and France. In Greece and Austria, on the other hand, less than 50% of the under-30s were pupils or students.

In the EFTA/EEA countries and the CEECs, the proportion of young people between 0 and 29 years of age in education is fairly close to the European Union average. The highest proportion (61%) is found in Iceland. The lowest education participation rate for this age group is found in Romania (45%).

The total numbers of pupils and students of compulsory school age and the percentages of the total population which they represent are indicated in Figure A8. The official ages for the beginning and end of compulsory education explain to some extent the differences between countries. Figure B1 (pages 16 to 18) illustrates *inter alia* when compulsory education starts and finishes in each of the education systems.

FIGURE A8: PUPILS OF COMPULSORY SCHOOL AGE IN THOUSANDS AND
AS A PERCENTAGE OF THE TOTAL NUMBER OF PUPILS AND STUDENTS, 1994/95

EUROPEAN UNION							
EU	**B**	**DK**	**D**	**EL**	**E**	**F**	**IRL**
41 128	1 457	501	10 484	1 139	5 013	7 749	574
57%	58%	44%	64%	58%	52%	53%	57%
I	**L**	**NL**	**A**	**P**	**FIN**	**S**	**UK**
N/A	48	2 366	846	1 326	578	915	8 130
N/A	74%	66%	52%	56%	51%	46%	57%

Source: Eurostat, UOE.

Belgium: 1993/94.
Luxembourg: Pupils in private non grant-aided schools are not included.

EFTA/EEA		
IS	**LI**	**NO**
42	4	471
51%	70%	46%

CEEC					
BG	**CZ**	**HU**	**PL**	**RO**	**SK**
N/A	1 258	1 288	5 023	2 726	803
N/A	56%	62%	53%	59%	61%

Source: Eurostat, UOE. National statistics.

Liechtenstein: National statistics, 1993/94.

Over the European Union as a whole, almost half of all pupils and students are of compulsory school age. In Denmark and Sweden, pupils of compulsory school age account for less than half of all pupils and students. This is due in part to the inclusion of nursery pupils in the total of all pupils and students and also to the huge numbers remaining in education beyond the minimum school leaving age.

In some countries, more than 60% of the total population in education consists of pupils of compulsory education age. This is the case in Germany and the Netherlands, where the proportion of pupils of compulsory education age is almost two thirds of the total population in education. In these two Member States, this phenomenon must be seen in the light of the lengthier duration of compulsory education. In Belgium, where the duration of compulsory education is comparable, the lower rate is attributable to the very high attendance at the pre-primary education level.

In the EFTA/EEA countries and the CEECs, with the exception of Iceland, Norway and Poland, the percentages of children of compulsory school age are well above the European average. In Liechtenstein, this high rate can be accounted for by the limited availability of structures providing education beyond the minimum school leaving age. In the CEECs, this is attributable in part to the large proportion of 10- to 19-year-olds in the population of these countries.

EXPLANATORY NOTE
The statistics in Figure A6 include pupils in special education and in pre-primary education under the Education Ministries. In previous editions, the latter category was not included in these statistics.
Figure A7 compares the number of pupils and students between 0 and 29 years old, whatever level of education they are attending, with the total population in that age group.
The numbers of pupils of compulsory school age in Figure A8 are calculated by adding up the numbers of children of statutory school age, whatever level of education they are attending.

HIGHER RATES OF UNEMPLOYMENT
AMONG 15- TO 24-YEAR-OLDS

In the European Union as a whole, more than one fifth of young people between 15 and 24 years of age on the labour market are unemployed. In all Member States except Germany, unemployment affects the younger members of the working population more.

However, the unemployment rates differ considerably between Member States in relation to both young people between 15 and 24 years of age (from 6 to 42%) and the working population as a whole (from 3 to 23%). In both categories, the highest unemployment rates are in Spain and Finland, where they are almost six times as high as those in Luxembourg and Austria, which have the lowest rates.

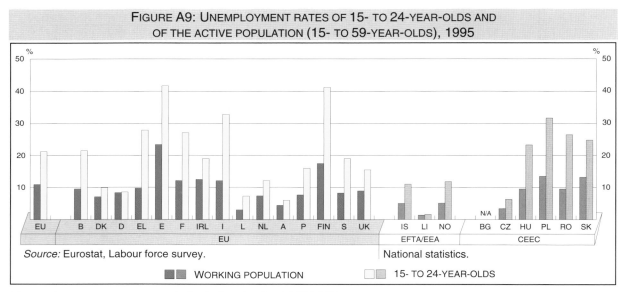

FIGURE A9: UNEMPLOYMENT RATES OF 15- TO 24-YEAR-OLDS AND OF THE ACTIVE POPULATION (15- TO 59-YEAR-OLDS), 1995

Source: Eurostat, Labour force survey. National statistics.

■ WORKING POPULATION ☐ 15- TO 24-YEAR-OLDS

Unemployment rates are relatively low in the EFTA/EEA countries, especially in Liechtenstein. These countries have proportionately more young people than adults out of work.

Of the CEECs, the Czech Republic has the lowest unemployment rates for both age groups (under 10%). In Poland, on the other hand, one third of young adults on the labour market are out of work and in the other countries slightly over 20% are in this situation.

EXPLANATORY NOTE
Unemployment is defined in accordance with the guidelines of the International Labour Organization (ILO). The unemployment rate is the ratio of the persons unemployed to the active population of the same age. The active population comprises all unemployed persons and those who are in work.

A HIGHER EDUCATION QUALIFICATION AND AGE
INCREASE THE CHANCES OF EMPLOYMENT

Figure A10 compares the unemployment rates and the levels of education of the population aged between 25 and 59 years. Generally speaking, unemployment rates are higher amongst people who have not been educated beyond lower secondary level. Two Member States deviate from this pattern. In Greece and to a lesser extent in Portugal, the unemployment rates of the least qualified are lower than those of people who hold an upper secondary education qualification. Conversely, in all Member States of the European Union, the best qualified are the least numerous in the ranks of the unemployed. This rate falls by half almost everywhere for those with a higher education qualification.

In the EFTA/EEA countries and the CEECs, a higher education qualification provides distinctly greater protection from unemployment than a primary or lower secondary school qualification. This difference is particularly marked in the Czech Republic, Romania and Slovakia.

FIGURE A10: UNEMPLOYMENT RATES IN THE POPULATION OF 25- TO 59-YEAR-OLDS, BY LEVEL OF EDUCATION, 1995

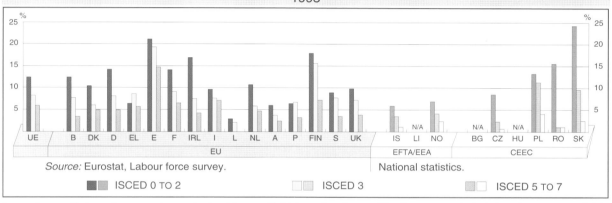

Luxembourg: Data on the unemployment rate of those with higher education qualifications are not included as they are not reliable due to the small sample.

Even among those with higher education qualifications, the unemployment rate of those aged between 25 and 34 years is higher overall than that of older graduates. In a majority of the Member States of the Union, people over 35 years of age therefore seem to be less exposed to the risk of unemployment. This is particularly marked in Greece, Spain and Italy, although different patterns are noted in certain Member States. In Denmark, for instance, a slight increase in unemployment is observed amongst higher education graduates over the age of 45. In Germany and the United Kingdom, age would appear to have less influence on unemployment amongst the most highly qualified.

In the EFTA/EEA countries and the CEECs, proportionately fewer people with higher education qualifications are unemployed than in the European Union. A higher unemployment rate is, however, noted among graduates under the age of 35 in Norway, Poland, Romania and Slovakia.

FIGURE A11: UNEMPLOYMENT RATES AMONG HIGHER EDUCATION GRADUATES, BY AGE GROUP, 1995

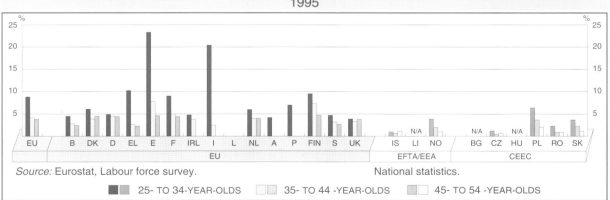

Ireland, Italy, Luxembourg, Austria and **Portugal**: Data on the unemployment rates of certain age groups are not included as they are not reliable due to the small sample.

YOUTH UNEMPLOYMENT SUSCEPTIBLE TO
ECONOMIC CONDITIONS

The fluctuations over time in unemployment rates across the whole active population and amongst those between 15 and 24 years old and those between 25 and 34 years old in the European Union are illustrated in Figure A12. The three graphs indicate broadly that unemployment rates have fallen during the second half of the 1980s, reaching their lowest point in 1990 then increasing, to fall again slightly in 1995. No single age group would appear to have benefited more than any other from the upturn of economic activity between 1987 and 1990. Similarly, the reduction in activity after 1990 would appear to have affected all three groups under consideration.

FIGURE A12: MOVEMENT IN THE UNEMPLOYMENT RATES OF 15- TO 24-YEAR-OLDS, 25- TO 34-YEAR-OLDS AND OVERALL UNEMPLOYMENT IN THE EUROPEAN UNION, 1987-95

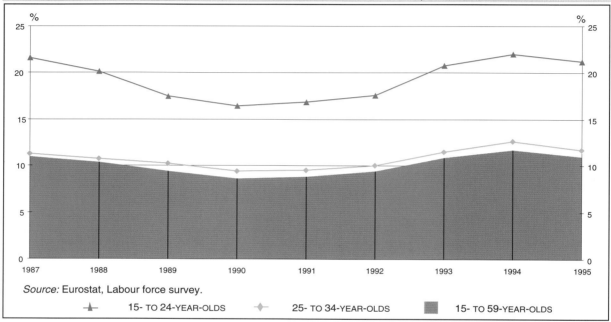

Source: Eurostat, Labour force survey.

▲ 15- TO 24-YEAR-OLDS   ◆ 25- TO 34-YEAR-OLDS   ■ 15- TO 59-YEAR-OLDS

The average rates of unemployment in the European Union conceal very different national situations. Figure A13 shows the movement in rates of unemployment in each of the present 15 Member States between 1987 and 1995. In general, it can be said that, since 1987, 15- to 24-year-olds have been affected proportionately more by unemployment than 25- to 34-year-olds. The unemployment rate of the former is often well above that of the latter. By contrast, the graph for the 25- to 34-year-olds, although slightly higher, always remains close to that of overall unemployment. This pattern is found everywhere except in Germany, and to a lesser extent in Denmark, where the rates remain close for all age groups.

EXPLANATORY NOTE
Unemployment rates are calculated on the basis of the 12 Member States of the European Union between 1987 and 1994. Since 1995, they have included the figures for the three new Member States, Austria, Finland and Sweden.

It appears that the movement in unemployment rates can be very different depending on the Member State concerned. For some Member States, the trend is close to the European Union average, with a fall in unemployment towards 1990, a subsequent increase and a slight fall since 1994 or 1995. This is found in Belgium, Spain, France, Ireland and the United Kingdom. The pattern in Greece and Portugal, which was close to that in these five Member States between 1987 and 1990, diverges, with a continued increase in unemployment since the beginning of the 1990s.

Finland and Sweden, which had relatively low rates of unemployment until 1990, have seen a steep increase since then.

Only Germany, Luxembourg and Austria have maintained relatively stable rates of unemployment since 1987, at under 10% for all age groups.

FIGURE A13: MOVEMENT IN THE UNEMPLOYMENT RATES OF 15- TO 24-YEAR-OLDS, 25- TO 34-YEAR-OLDS AND IN OVERALL UNEMPLOYMENT, BY MEMBER STATE, 1987-95

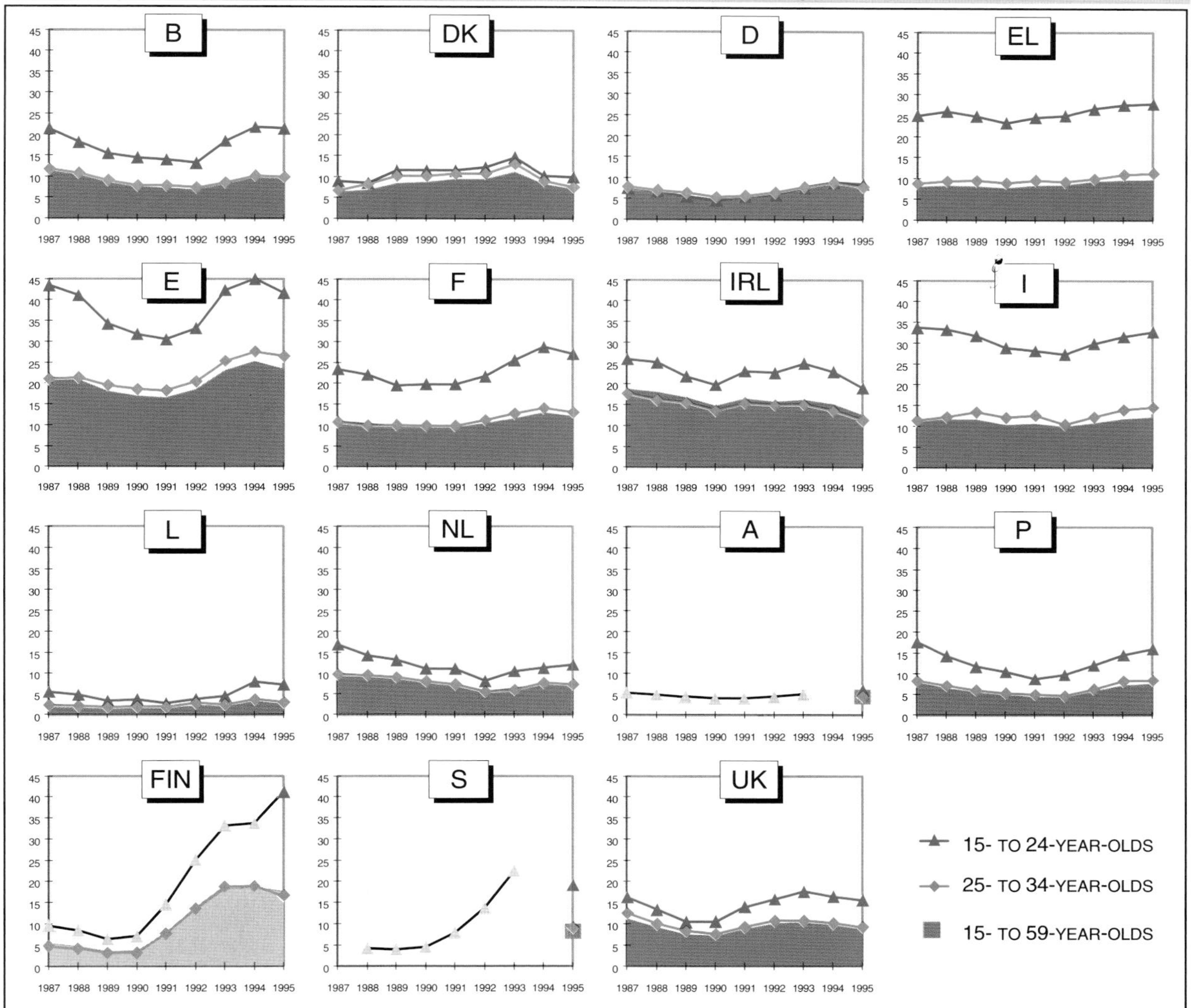

Source: Eurostat, Labour force survey.

Austria and **Sweden**: National statistics for 1987 to 1993.
Finland: National statistics for 1987 to 1994.

WITH THE SAME LEVEL OF EDUCATION,
—— PROPORTIONATELY MORE WOMEN THAN MEN ARE UNEMPLOYED ——

The increasing opportunities for women to remain in education and the growing numbers of women taking upper secondary and higher education qualifications have not completely eroded the differences between men and women in relation to employment. With equal qualifications, there are proportionately more women than men out of work.

This situation is found fairly generally throughout the European Union, and irrespective of the level of education, but generally more markedly in relation to those without a higher education qualification. The differences are particularly pronounced in Greece, Spain and Italy. As far as graduates are concerned, choices of different fields of study may partially explain disparities in rates of unemployment between men and women.

Some Member States are exceptions to this rule, with a female unemployment rate lower than that for men. These include Finland, Sweden and the United Kingdom, in relation to holders of both levels of qualification, and Portugal in relation to higher education graduates.

In those EFTA/EEA countries and CEECs for which data are available, the pattern is similar to that in the majority of the Member States of the European Union, with the exception of Norway in relation to higher education graduates.

FIGURE A14: UNEMPLOYMENT RATES OF 25- TO 59-YEAR-OLDS BY LEVEL OF EDUCATION AND BY SEX, 1995

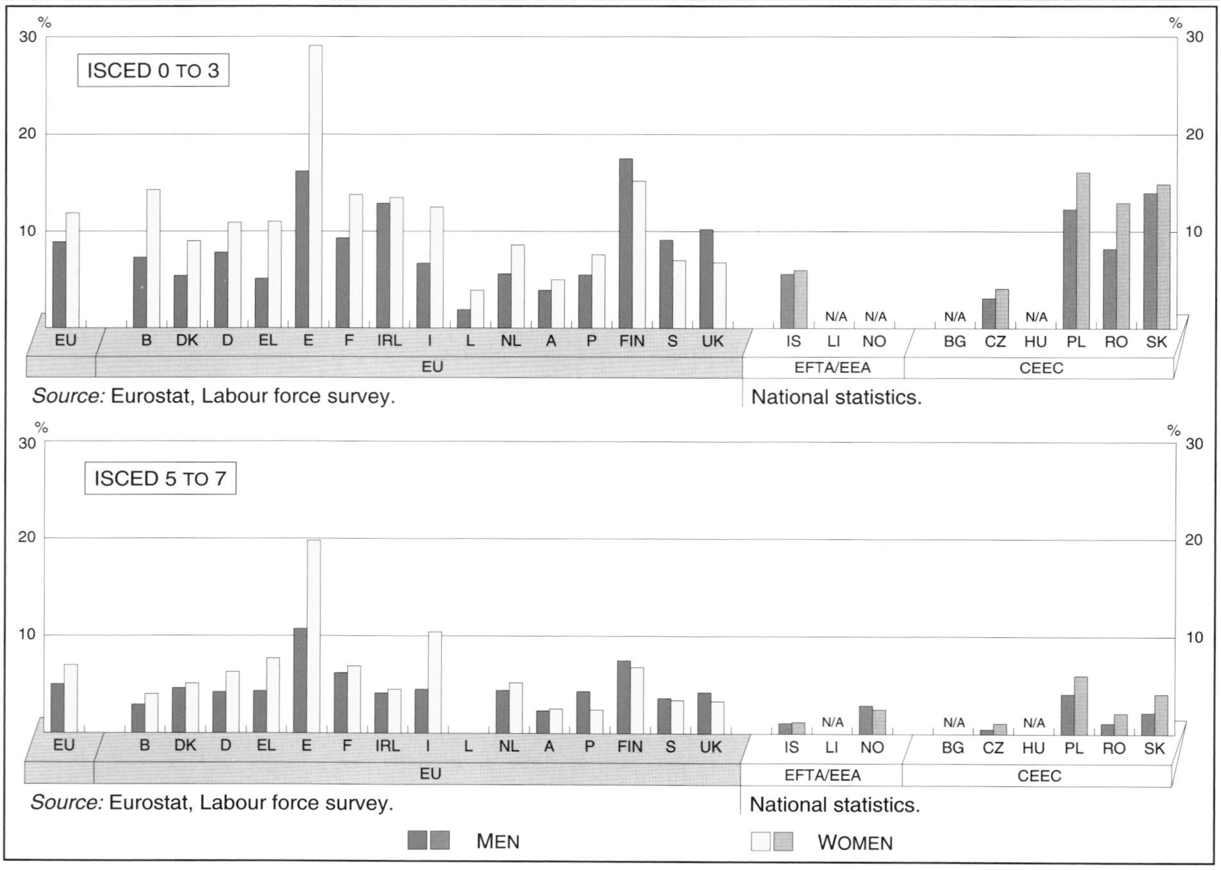

Source: Eurostat, Labour force survey. National statistics.

MEN   **WOMEN**

Luxembourg: Data on the unemployment rate of higher education graduates are not included as they are not reliable due to the small sample.
Norway: For ISCED 5 to 7 qualifications, the population is all 16- to 59-year-olds.

EXPLANATORY NOTE
The unemployment rates are broken down by sex and by whether the people between the ages of 25 and 59 have a higher education qualification.

SOME PEOPLE WITH HIGHER EDUCATION QUALIFICATIONS ARE OVER-QUALIFIED FOR THE JOBS THEY HOLD

In the labour market in the European Union, it would appear that having a higher education qualification is not sufficient to have a job commensurate with the level of one's education. In practice, while the majority of people with higher education qualifications are in responsible occupations, grouped together as professionals and managers in the International Standard Classification of Occupations, and about one fifth of them are working in a type of occupation classed as intermediate, a similar proportion is found in all the other categories combined. This is less the case with increasing age. In the professional and managerial category, some 65% of those between the ages of 35 and 59 have higher education qualifications and slightly more than half of those between 25 and 34. Conversely, the youngest people with higher education qualifications are found more frequently than their elders — 23% as against 15% — in occupational categories such as 'clerks, service and sales workers' and 'craft workers and machine operators'.

This is true of most of the Member States in the European Union. Portugal reveals a slightly different pattern — there are proportionately more 25- to 34-year-old people with higher education qualifications than older graduates there in posts with a high degree of responsibility.

FIGURE A15: OCCUPATIONS OF 25- TO 34-YEAR-OLD AND 35- TO 59-YEAR-OLD PEOPLE WITH HIGHER EDUCATION QUALIFICATION, 1995

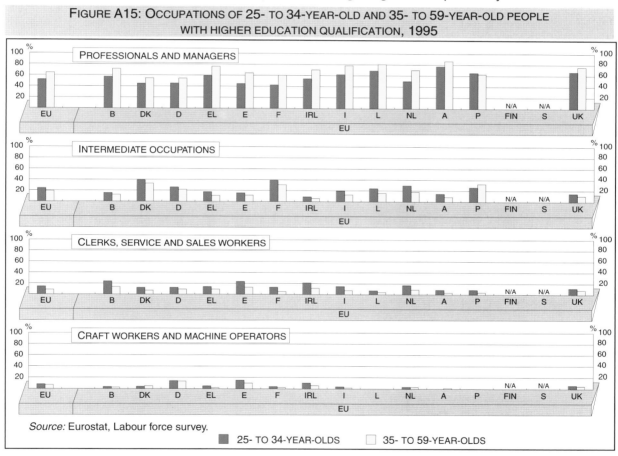

Source: Eurostat, Labour force survey.

■ 25- TO 34-YEAR-OLDS   ☐ 35- TO 59-YEAR-OLDS

EXPLANATORY NOTE

The International Standard Classification of Occupations (ISCO) was introduced by the International Labour Organization (ILO) and is used in the Labour force survey. At its highest level of aggregation, this distinguishes ten types of occupations which have been grouped together as follows:
1. Professionals and managers — liberal and academic professions;
2. Intermediate occupations;
3. Clerical occupations — service and sales staff;
4. Tradesmen and other workers — machine operators — unskilled workers etc.;
5. Other — detailed in table in annex; includes agriculture and fishery workers, the armed forces etc.

THE MOST EDUCATED EUROPEANS ARE THE MOST FAVOURABLE
———————— TO THE IDEA OF LIFELONG LEARNING ————————

When they are questioned about it, an overall majority of Europeans would like to be able to take part in lifelong learning. Differences, however, appear between Member States — Denmark, Greece and the United Kingdom give the highest rates of positive replies, while in Austria less than half the respondents expressed this desire.

FIGURE A16: PERCENTAGE OF PEOPLE WHO WOULD LIKE TO UNDERTAKE LIFELONG LEARNING, 1995							
EU	**B**	**DK**	**D**	**EL**	**E**	**F**	**IRL**
70%	63%	91%		83%	74%	79%	68%
I	**L**	**NL**	**A**	**P**	**FIN**	**S**	**UK**
65%	59%	67%	47%	68%	75%	76%	82%

Source: Eurobarometer 44.0 and 44.1.

Germany: Data are not included as the sample is not representative.

The pattern which appears from this sample is found irrespective of the age of those questioned. There is, however, a clear connection between a desire to take part in lifelong learning and level of education. In all the Member States of the European Union, fewer of those who left school before the age of 15 express such a desire than those who completed their education after the age of 20. This difference is a little more marked in the Netherlands than in the other Member States and less so in Denmark and the United Kingdom.

FIGURE A17: PERCENTAGE OF PEOPLE WHO WOULD LIKE TO UNDERTAKE LIFELONG LEARNING, BY AGE OF LEAVING EDUCATION, 1995

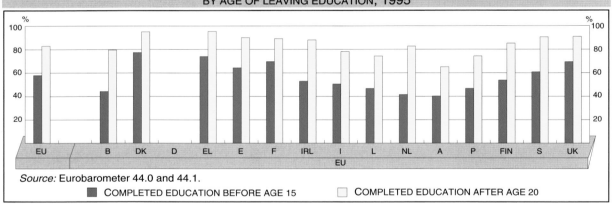

Source: Eurobarometer 44.0 and 44.1.

■ COMPLETED EDUCATION BEFORE AGE 15   ☐ COMPLETED EDUCATION AFTER AGE 20

Germany: Data are not included as the sample is not representative.

EXPLANATORY NOTE
In the context of the European Year of Lifelong Learning and at the request of the European Commission (Directorate General XXII: Education, Training and Youth), questions on this subject were included in the Eurobarometer survey of European attitudes (Eurobarometer 44.0 and 44.1, Autumn 1995). These questions were put in each Member State to a representative sample of the population aged 15 and over.
Lifelong learning aims at gaining new knowledge or updating knowledge obtained during initial training. It makes it possible to introduce innovations and/or to upgrade occupational skills.

CONTINUING TRAINING: NOT WIDESPREAD
———— AND LINKED TO THE DURATION OF EDUCATION ————

On average, just over 20% of Europeans had undertaken continuing training in the course of the past 12 months, as defined in the survey. There are substantial differences between Member States. In Denmark, almost half (45%) had undertaken training recently. The proportion is almost a third in the Netherlands, Finland, Sweden and the United Kingdom. In Greece and Portugal, however, less than 10% of people were found to have undergone continuing training during the previous year.

FIGURE A18: PERCENTAGE OF PEOPLE WHO HAD UNDERTAKEN TRAINING COURSES
DURING THE PAST 12 MONTHS, 1995

EU	B	DK	D	EL	E	F	IRL
22%	20%	45%		8%	19%	20%	15%
I	**L**	**NL**	**A**	**P**	**FIN**	**S**	**UK**
12%	18%	32%	24%	9%	33%	31%	31%

Source: Eurobarometer 44.0 and 44.1.

Germany: Data are not included as the sample is not representative.

Again, there are significant differences in the replies depending on when the persons interviewed had left school, whatever the Member State. More of those who had completed their education after the age of 20 had undergone training during the previous 12 months than of those who had left school before the age of 15.

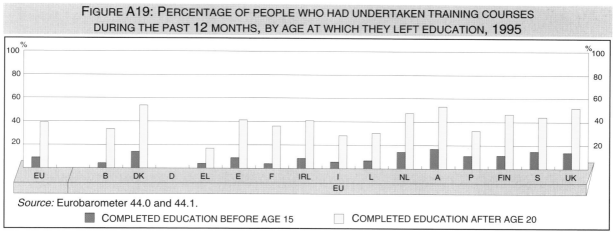

FIGURE A19: PERCENTAGE OF PEOPLE WHO HAD UNDERTAKEN TRAINING COURSES
DURING THE PAST 12 MONTHS, BY AGE AT WHICH THEY LEFT EDUCATION, 1995

Source: Eurobarometer 44.0 and 44.1.

■ COMPLETED EDUCATION BEFORE AGE 15   ☐ COMPLETED EDUCATION AFTER AGE 20

Germany: Data are not included as the sample is not representative.

Finally, and still according to the survey undertaken in the context of the European Year of Lifelong Learning, the majority of those who have undertaken continuing training courses are, throughout the European Union, under-40-year-olds.

EXPLANATORY NOTE
In the specific Eurobarometer survey, the past 12 months are defined as the period preceding the data collection, i.e. between November 1994 and October 1995.
Further information can be obtained from the Labour force survey regarding participation in training courses during the four weeks prior to the survey.

STRUCTURES AND SCHOOLS

A WIDE VARIETY OF EDUCATION SYSTEMS

Figure B1 highlights the similarities and differences between the structures of the European education systems. The diagrams illustrate only provision which is educational in the strict sense. An overview of all types of pre-primary institutions, both school and non-school, is presented in Chapter C. Special education organized separately is also excluded from these diagrams and can be found in Chapter H.

In half of the Member States of the European Union, children enter the school system at the age of 3 or 4 years, but the youngest ones may have their first experience of school at age 2 in France and at 2½ in Belgium. Children are admitted to the school system at the age of 6 years in Germany, but some *Länder* have opened pre-primary classes *(Vorklassen)* for 5-year-olds whose parents wish them to have a preparation for entry to primary school. In Denmark, Austria, Finland and Sweden, they are admitted at the age of 6. Attendance at a pre-primary educational institution is optional in most Member States, parents being free to send their children if they so desire.

The start of compulsory education generally coincides with the point of entry to primary school, except in Ireland, Luxembourg and the Netherlands. In Ireland and the Netherlands, where the school systems do not include a pre-primary level, children can attend the primary school 'infant classes' and an optional year of *basisonderwijs*, respectively, from 4 years of age. In Luxembourg, attendance at the two years of pre-primary education *(Spillschoul)* has been made compulsory. Education is compulsory from the age of 6 in nine of the European Union Member States, but begins earlier in some of them — at age 4 in Luxembourg and Northern Ireland (UK) and at age 5 in the Netherlands and Great Britain. In the Nordic Member States (Denmark, Finland and Sweden), education is not compulsory until the age of 7.

The pattern of education is generally the same for all children until the end of lower secondary school, i.e. up to the age of 14 or 15 years. A common core curriculum is followed until age 16 in Denmark, Spain, Finland, Sweden and the United Kingdom. In Germany and Austria, pupils are faced with choices regarding their direction of study at the beginning of lower secondary education at the age of 10 and in Luxembourg at age 12.

In most Member States, the end of compulsory education coincides with the transition from lower to upper secondary education. In France and Austria, however, lower secondary education ends one year before the end of compulsory education. In Belgium and the United Kingdom (except Scotland), it ends two years before the end of full-time compulsory education.

Full-time compulsory education lasts until at least age 16 in most Member States, but in Greece, Ireland, Luxembourg, Austria and Portugal it ends at 15. In Germany, it ends at age 15 or 16 and in Italy it ends at 14. In most Member States, full-time compulsory education lasts 9 or 10 years. In Italy, it lasts 8 years, whereas in Luxembourg and United Kingdom (England, Wales and Scotland), it lasts 11 years and in the Netherlands and Northern Ireland as long as 12 years. In the Netherlands, full-time compulsory education starts at age 5 and ends at age 16, but all pupils must complete at least 12 years of full-time education.

Compulsory education continues at least part-time for two years beyond age 16 in Belgium and the Netherlands and for three years beyond the age of 15 or 16 in Germany. In these Member States, the end of compulsory education coincides with the end of upper secondary education.

The Spanish school system is currently in a transition phase, following the passing in October 1990 of the organic act on the general organization of the education system (LOGSE). The process of implementing this act, initially intended to be brought in over a 10-year period, is currently going ahead at different rates in the various Communities. This reform provides for bringing together all early childhood education under the Ministry of Education. The diagram shows the post-reform situation, although the new organization of secondary education is not yet fully in place.

In Italy, it is intended to introduce a complete reform of the organization of the education system, from pre-primary to upper secondary, in autumn 1997.

FIGURE B1: ORGANIZATION OF THE EDUCATION SYSTEMS, 1995/96

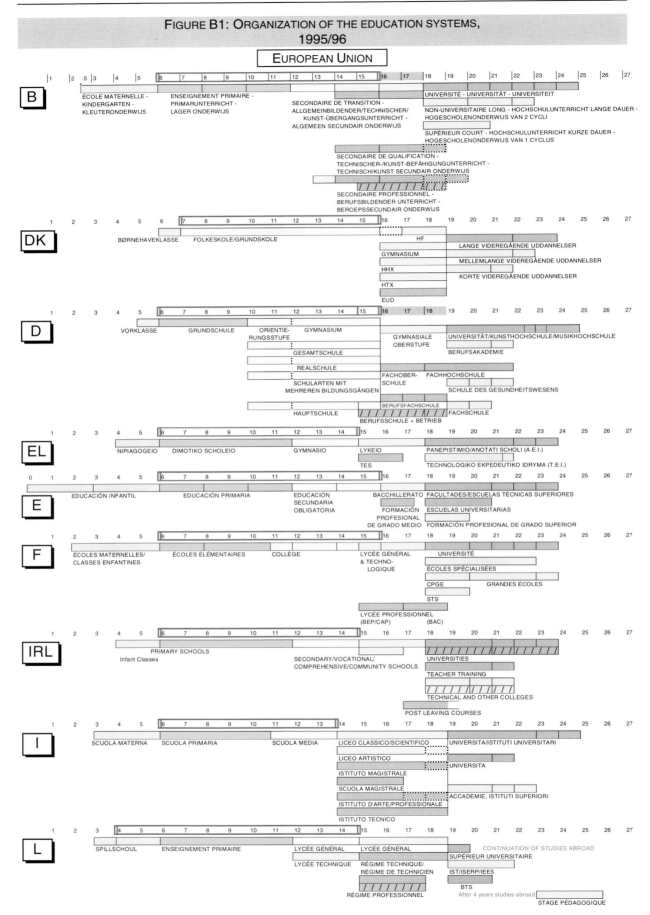

EUROPEAN UNION

Source: Eurydice.

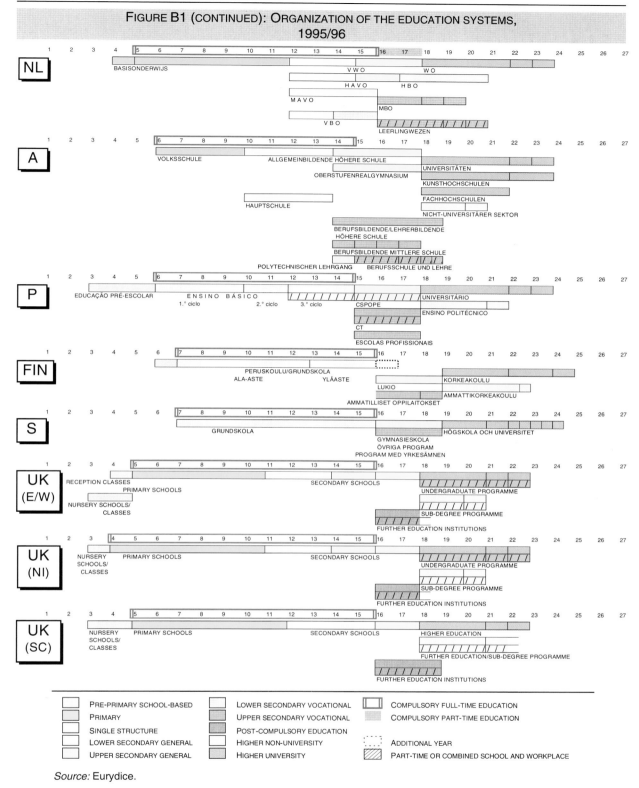

FIGURE B1 (CONTINUED): ORGANIZATION OF THE EDUCATION SYSTEMS, 1995/96

Source: Eurydice.

Denmark: Since 1995, the HHX and HTX courses have been considered to be upper secondary general education.

Portugal: Evening classes equivalent to the third stage of *ensino básico* and upper secondary education (CSPOPE and CT) are gradually being replaced by courses of recurrent education organized in transferable course credits.

United Kingdom (E/W and **NI)**: Further education institutions offer both general and vocational post-compulsory education to students of any age. There is wide variation in the nature, duration and content of courses.

FIGURE B1 (CONTINUED): ORGANIZATION OF THE EDUCATION SYSTEMS, 1995/96

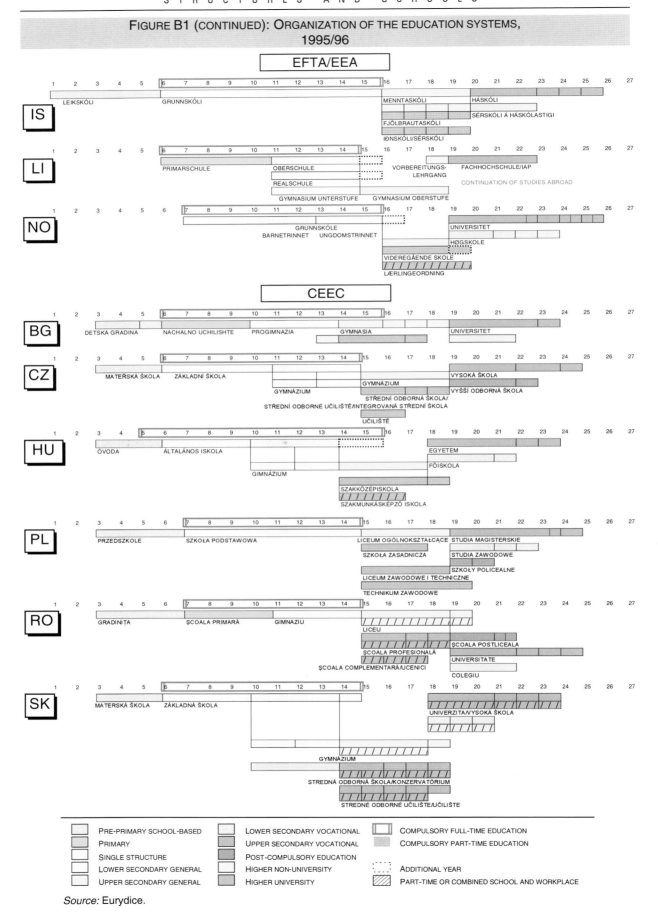

Source: Eurydice.

In upper secondary education, a vocational or technical branch is often available to pupils parallel to the general branch. In Sweden, since the 1994 education reform, vocational and general courses have both been delivered by the same schools, as modular upper secondary education. In the United Kingdom, pupils in post-compulsory education can take a qualification in general subjects, in a vocational field or in a combination of the two.

Entry to higher education is usually possible from age 18, except in Luxembourg, Finland and Sweden, where it is later. The age of entry varies in Germany (at age 18 or 19) and the Netherlands, depending on the type of course chosen.

To take a first higher education qualification, students in a majority of the Member States of the European Union have to study for a minimum of 2 years. The minimum is 3 years in Belgium, Portugal and Finland, 3½ years in Greece and 4 years in the Netherlands. This applies only to the minimum duration of study. In many Member States, students are free to complete their courses over a longer period or to opt to study part-time.

Luxembourg provides a certain number of non-university higher education courses. It is also possible for students to follow a one-year university-level course before continuing their studies abroad.

In Sweden, it is not possible to distinguish between programmes leading to a university first qualification or an equivalent qualification and programmes not leading to such a qualification. To obtain a qualification regarded as a university degree or equivalent in this Member State, it is necessary to take a course lasting at least 3 years. The distinction between a first university or non-university qualification is purely dependent on the duration of the course.

In the EFTA/EEA countries, young children enter the school system at the age of 6 or 7 years except in Iceland, where they can enter the *leikskóli* from the age of one year if their parents so desire and there are places available. The start of compulsory education coincides with the start of primary education. It lasts 9 years in Liechtenstein and Norway and 10 years in Iceland.

Pupils' schooling is organized in a single, continuous structure up to the end of compulsory education in Iceland and Norway. In Liechtenstein, pupils make a first choice regarding their direction of study at the age of 11 years, at the end of their primary education.

Entry to higher education is normally possible from the age of 19 in Norway and 20 in Iceland. In Liechtenstein, only non-university studies are available at higher education level, and students there wishing to undertake university studies have to do so abroad.

In the six CEECs, children can attend schools from the age of 3.

Education is compulsory from 6 years of age except in Hungary, where it starts at age 5, and in Poland and Romania, where it starts at age 7. Its duration varies, depending on the country — from 8 years in Poland and Romania to 11 in Bulgaria and Hungary.

With the exception of Bulgaria and Romania, where the primary level of education is quite separate from lower secondary, the other four countries' systems are organized in a single structure very similar to that found in the Nordic countries. In the Czech Republic, Hungary and Slovakia, however, pupils can proceed to separate lower secondary education at about 10 or 11 years of age. Vocational courses can be entered only at upper secondary level in the majority of these countries. Before then, only general education is provided.

In these six countries, higher education includes both university and non-university education. Students can normally start higher education courses at the age of 18 in Hungary and Slovakia and at 19 in the other countries.

EXPLANATORY NOTE
The ages given here represent the 'normal' ages of admission to courses and their duration. Neither early or late starts nor extended duration resulting from pupils having to repeat years are taken into account in these illustrations and explanations.

MOST PUPILS' EDUCATION FINANCED BY THE PUBLIC SECTOR

The education of the majority of pupils is financed by public authorities because the majority of pupils in all the countries under review attend schools in the public or the private grant-aided sector.

In the European Union, the education of all Belgian, Danish, German, Luxembourg, Finnish and Swedish pupils at primary and secondary level is financed by public authorities. There are generally more pupils in the public sector than in the private grant-aided sector except in Belgium and more particularly in the Netherlands, where there are proportionately more pupils in the private grant-aided sector.

Attendance at non-grant-aided independent schools is rare. According to the statistics available, a maximum of 4% are found in Greece and 6% in the United Kingdom.

FIGURE B2: PERCENTAGE OF PUPILS IN PUBLIC AND PRIVATE EDUCATION (PRIMARY AND SECONDARY), 1994/95

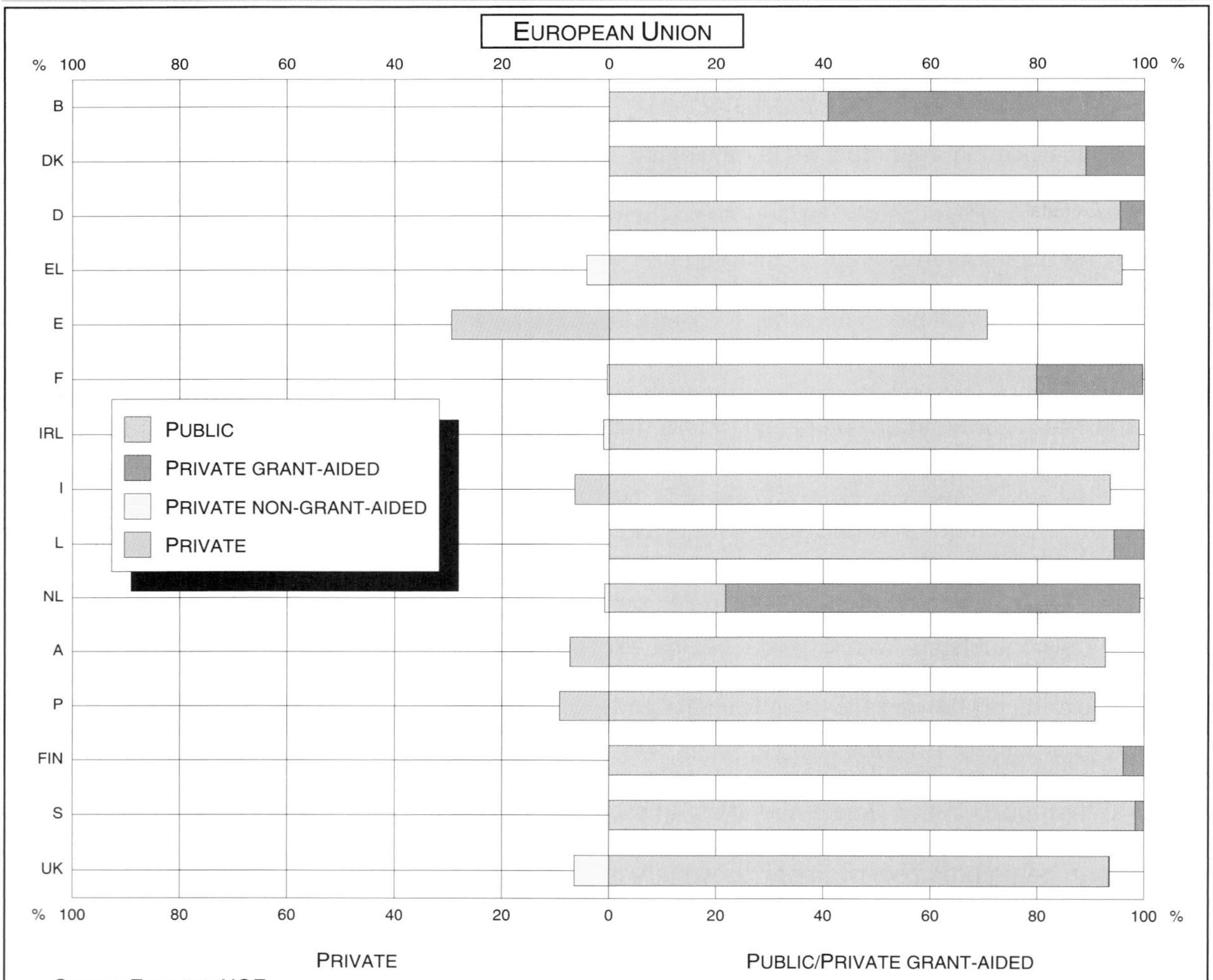

EUROPEAN UNION

Legend:
PUBLIC
PRIVATE GRANT-AIDED
PRIVATE NON-GRANT-AIDED
PRIVATE

PRIVATE — PUBLIC/PRIVATE GRANT-AIDED

Source: Eurostat, UOE.

Belgium: 1993/94.
Spain: A national estimate indicates that most of the pupils in private education are enrolled in private grant-aided schools.
Netherlands: Equal funding of public and private grant-aided schools is a constitutional right.
United Kingdom: Figures do not include further education institutions which provide post-compulsory general and vocational education.

In the EFTA/EEA countries and the CEECs, pupils whose education is financed by public authorities are also very largely in the majority. In Iceland and the Czech Republic, all are in this category.

The proportion of pupils in private sector schools (grant-aided or not) does not exceed 4% in any of these countries. Practically all pupils attend public sector schools in Bulgaria, Romania and Poland.

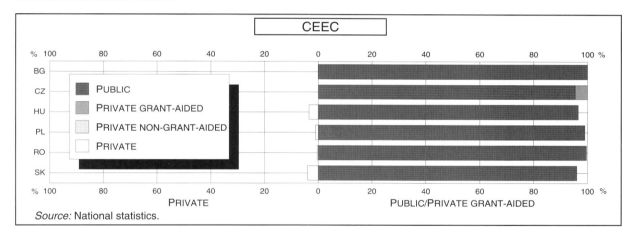

FIGURE B2 (CONTINUED): PERCENTAGE OF PUPILS IN PUBLIC AND PRIVATE EDUCATION (PRIMARY AND SECONDARY), 1994/95

Iceland: Full-time.
Liechtenstein: National statistics.

EXPLANATORY NOTE

Pupils may be divided into two categories depending on whether they attend:
— public-sector schools, provided and controlled directly by public authorities;
— private schools, provided and controlled by non-government bodies.
Private schools are further distinguished as between those that are grant-aided and those that are not. Private schools are said to be grant-aided if they receive more than 50% of their finance from the public sector. Private non-grant-aided schools receive less than 50% of their finance from the public sector. It is not possible to distinguish between pupils attending private grant-aided or non-grant-aided schools in Spain, Italy, Austria and Portugal; Norway; Bulgaria, Hungary, Poland, Romania and Slovakia.
Where data were available, the most accurate possible form of classification has been used. Figure B2 shows by Member State the percentage of pupils attending primary and secondary schools, public and private (grant-aided or not) (ISCED 1, 2 and 3).

PUBLIC SECTOR SCHOOLS: FROM CONSIDERABLE AUTONOMY
────── TO VERY LIMITED DECISION-MAKING POWERS ──────

From amongst the main functions involved in the organization of the school system, four lines of analysis are pursued here — the definition of school time, management of teaching staff, the use of financial resources and pedagogical matters, or teaching as such. Information has been gathered on the freedom that public-sector schools have in relation to a number of parameters in these four areas. The parameters are presented in the following schema. The four areas are represented by different symbols. Each cell relates to one of the parameters examined. In view of the variety of management situations, depending on whether the school comes under a private body or not, only public-sector schools at primary and lower secondary level are included in the analysis.

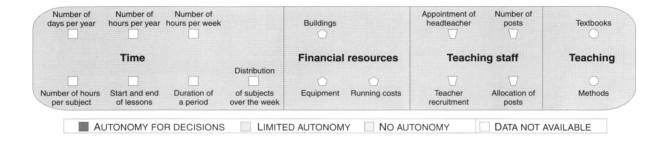

Depending on the function and the parameters concerned, a school's autonomy can be limited to a greater or lesser degree. Three main modes of decision making have been defined:
— the school has full powers and autonomy;
— the school takes decisions in consultation with the authority responsible and/or within limits set by the latter, and its autonomy is limited; or
— the school does not intervene in the decision-making process and has no autonomy.

Figures B3 and B4 are based on this schema and present the 'control panels' operated by public-sector schools at two levels of compulsory education — primary and lower secondary — in each Member State.

EXPLANATORY NOTE
The school is considered as a whole, represented either by its headteacher or by a management body. The attribution of responsibility for decisions on internal matters is not taken into consideration.
'Public-sector school' is taken to mean schools provided and controlled directly by public or government authorities. Schools controlled by private or non-government authorities are excluded, even when they are financed entirely from public funds.
The authority responsible at the level above the school can, depending on the situation, be a public authority at local, regional or central level. For more information on the authorities responsible, see School Heads in the European Union, *Eurydice, 1996.*
For secondary education, insofar as the teachers are specialized by subject, the parameter 'allocation of posts' relates to fixing the number of teaching posts established for teachers of the compulsory subjects and options.

FIGURE B3: CONTROL PANELS OF PUBLIC-SECTOR PRIMARY SCHOOLS, 1995/96

EUROPEAN UNION

(Control panel diagrams for: B fr, B nl, DK, D, EL, E, F, IRL, I, L, NL, A, P, FIN, S, UK (E/W), UK (NI), UK (SC))

EFTA/EEA

(Control panel diagrams for: IS, LI, NO)

CEEC

(Control panel diagrams for: BG, CZ, HU, PL, RO, SK)

Legend:

Time				Financial resources		Teaching staff		Teaching
Number of days per year	Number of hours per year	Number of hours per week		Buildings		Appointment of headteacher	Number of posts	Textbooks
Number of hours per subject	Start and end of lessons	Duration of a period	Distribution of subjects over the week	Equipment	Running costs	Teacher recruitment	Allocation of posts	Methods

■ AUTONOMY FOR DECISIONS   ▨ LIMITED AUTONOMY   ☐ NO AUTONOMY   ☐ DATA NOT AVAILABLE

Source: Eurydice.

Luxembourg: In primary schools, there are no headteacher posts. The function is carried out on behalf of the state by the primary education inspector who is responsible for several schools and on behalf of the commune by the communal council.

Portugal: First stage of *ensino básico* only.

United Kingdom (E/W and NI): Voluntary schools are not included in this analysis. They have differing degrees of autonomy according to their individual status.

FIGURE B4: CONTROL PANELS OF PUBLIC-SECTOR LOWER SECONDARY SCHOOLS, 1995/96

EUROPEAN UNION

(B fr, B nl, DK, D, EL, E, F, IRL, I, L, NL, A, P, FIN, S, UK (E/W), UK (NI), UK (SC))

EFTA/EEA

(IS, LI, NO)

CEEC

(BG, CZ, HU, PL, RO, SK)

Legend:

Number of days per year	Number of hours per year	Number of hours per week
Time		
Number of hours per subject	Start and end of lessons	Duration of a period
		Distribution of subjects over the week

Buildings	
Financial resources	
Equipment	Running costs

Appointment of headteacher	Number of posts
Teaching staff	
Teacher recruitment	Allocation of posts

Textbooks
Teaching
Methods

■ AUTONOMY FOR DECISIONS ▪ LIMITED AUTONOMY ▫ NO AUTONOMY ☐ DATA NOT AVAILABLE

Source: Eurydice.

Portugal: Second and third stages of *ensino básico*.
United Kingdom (E/W and NI): Voluntary schools are not included in this analysis. They have differing degrees of autonomy according to their individual status.

24

Overall, looking at all the Member States of the European Union, it is in the Netherlands and the United Kingdom (England, Wales and Northern Ireland) that schools have the greatest degree of autonomy at primary and lower secondary level. For most of the areas of decision making under consideration here, they have total autonomy. In relation to only a few parameters are decisions taken in consultation with the authority responsible or within limits that it has laid down. Only a very small number of decisions are taken solely by the authority responsible at a higher level.

The schools with the most limited autonomy in decision making, on the other hand, are to be found in Germany, Greece and Luxembourg, where at lower secondary level only the timetabling of subjects over the week is left entirely in the hands of the school.

In Belgium (Flemish Community), Denmark, Finland and Sweden, where the authorities responsible are very decentralized and represented by the local authorities, most of the decisions are taken at school level, but in agreement with a higher level, responsible authority or within limits it has laid down.

Generally, within any given Member State, few differences are found between the two levels of education as regards the decision-making powers given to schools. In France, however, the parameters for which the schools have or do not have decision-making powers differ greatly according to the level of education in question.

In the EFTA/EEA countries, school autonomy is fairly limited, although a small number of decisions are taken at school level in Iceland and Norway and most decisions are taken in consultation with the authority responsible in Liechtenstein.

In the CEECs, the levels of decision making vary depending on the area concerned. Schools have the greatest degree of autonomy in the Czech Republic, while in Poland the number of decisions taken at school level in consultation with the authority responsible is the greatest.

In all the EFTA/EEA countries and the CEECs, the scope of schools' decision-making powers varies little between the two levels of education under consideration.

——— DIFFERENT DEGREES OF FREEDOM IN DIFFERENT AREAS ———

A more detailed analysis of this first overview shows that the levels of autonomy depend to a great extent on the areas under consideration and, within these, the parameters to which the decisions relate. We thus find fairly generally that schools at both primary and lower secondary level usually have full powers in pedagogical matters, that is to say, the **choice of textbooks and teaching methods**. In Austria, there is a list of textbooks, but this does not amount to a legal constraint on schools. In only three countries — Germany, Spain and Luxembourg (lower secondary) — is the autonomy of schools limited in this area. Teachers at both primary and lower secondary level have to choose their textbooks from a list or on the basis of criteria set by the authorities responsible. Moreover, in these Member States, teaching methods are laid down on the basis of recommendations and suggestions made by the authorities responsible. This is also the case in Greece in lower secondary education.

In the EFTA/EEA countries, schools have limited freedom in the choice of textbooks. This is also the case as regards teaching methods in Liechtenstein.

In all of the CEECs, methods are decided on at school level. In the majority of these countries, however, the choice of textbooks is made in consultation with the authority responsible, except in Bulgaria, where the school has no autonomy in this respect, and conversely in Poland, where the school has complete freedom of choice.

As regards the **use of financial resources**, in Germany, France (primary), Luxembourg (primary) and Portugal (in the first stage of *ensino básico)* schools have no autonomy. In those Member States in which schools have a certain degree of freedom in relation to the use of their financial resources, the more the expenditure involves large amounts of money, the more the decisions are taken by the authorities responsible. Schools are therefore more often autonomous in relation to the use of revenue expenditure than capital, in particular for buildings. Only schools in Belgium (Flemish Community), Greece, Spain and Austria can take decisions in relation to capital expenditure on buildings in consultation with the authority responsible.

The same trend is found in Iceland and Norway, whereas in Liechtenstein, all of the decisions are taken in consultation with the authorities responsible. In the CEECs, schools in Hungary, Romania and Slovakia have no decision-making powers in relation to the use of financial resources. In Bulgaria (with the exception of capital expenditure on buildings) and in Poland, these decisions are taken in consultation between the school and the authority responsible. The Czech Republic is the only one of the CEECs in which schools enjoy complete freedom in the disbursement of their revenue expenditure.

SCHOOLS HAVE GREATER AUTONOMY TO ARRANGE THEIR TIMETABLES THAN TO DETERMINE THE AMOUNT OF TIME ALLOCATED TO TEACHING

As regards decisions linked to the management of school time, schools are seldom free to decide how much time they will devote to teaching. Thus, the number of days and hours of teaching time per year is often set by the authorities responsible. In Sweden, these questions are subject to decision taken in consultation with the authority responsible; schools even enjoy complete autonomy to set the annual number of hours of teaching. In Germany and Austria, while schools have limited freedom to decide on the number of days per year, they play no part in setting the overall volume of annual teaching time.

On the other hand, when it comes to the arrangement of lesson periods over the week or the day, schools have more autonomy practically everywhere in the European Union. More specifically, the placing of subjects in the timetable is left to the school in all Member States, except in Belgium (Flemish Community) and, in primary schools, in Ireland and Luxembourg.

The same trend can be observed in the EFTA/EEA countries except Liechtenstein, where schools have limited or no autonomy in these matters. In the CEECs, decisions on teaching time (number of days per year and number of hours per year and per week) are usually taken by the authorities responsible, whereas the organization of the school day is left to the school itself.

FIGURE B5: AUTONOMY OF PUBLIC-SECTOR SCHOOLS FOR DECISIONS RELATING TO TEACHING TIME, 1995/96

	NUMBER OF DAYS OF TEACHING PER YEAR	NUMBER OF HOURS OF TEACHING PER YEAR	NUMBER OF HOURS OF TEACHING PER WEEK	NUMBER OF HOURS PER SUBJECT PER YEAR	DURATION OF A PERIOD	FIXING OF START AND END OF LESSONS EACH DAY	DISTRIBUTION OF SUBJECTS OVER THE WEEK OR DAY
EUROPEAN UNION							
B fr							
B nl							
DK							
D							
EL							
E							
F							
IRL							
I							
L							
NL							
A							
P							
FIN							
S							
UK (E/W)							
UK (NI)							
UK (SC)							
EFTA/EEA							
IS							
LI							
NO							
CEEC							
BG							
CZ							
HU							
PL							
RO							
SK							

■ AUTONOMY FOR DECISIONS   □ LIMITED AUTONOMY   ▨ NO AUTONOMY   □ DATA NOT AVAILABLE

Source: Eurydice.

Where cells are shared, the information in the left-hand cell relates to primary education and that in the right to lower secondary.

EXPLANATORY NOTE
The authority responsible at a level above that of the school can be a public authority at local, regional or central level, depending on the situation.

MANAGEMENT OF TEACHING STAFF
—————— RARELY A FUNCTION OF SCHOOLS ——————

Whether at primary or lower secondary level, as far as the management of teaching staff is concerned, the most common model is one in which schools have little or no autonomy. In only a few Member States — Denmark, Ireland, Finland, Sweden and part of the United Kingdom (Scotland) — are most decisions on staffing matters taken by the school in consultation with the authorities responsible. The Netherlands and the United Kingdom (England, Wales and Northern Ireland) are exceptions, in that schools there enjoy full or extensive powers in relation to the selection and management of staff. In Finland and Sweden, teachers are employed by the municipalities. Frequently, the task of recruiting teachers there, and thus the determination of the number of teaching posts in the different subjects, falls to the headteacher, even though this function lies within the competence of the municipalities.

Similarly, the appointment of headteachers is generally subject to decision at a level above that of the school, except in the Netherlands where they are appointed by the *bevoegd gezag*. In Portugal they are elected by the *conselho de escola* or by the staff of the school. In Belgium (Flemish Community), Spain, Ireland and the United Kingdom (England, Wales and Northern Ireland), they are appointed following agreement between the schools and the authorities responsible.

Finally, the power to fix the total number of teaching posts often goes hand in hand with the allocation of posts to class teachers or to specialized subject teachers at primary school level and with the fixing of the number of teachers required for the compulsory subjects or for optional subjects in lower secondary schools.

In the EFTA/EEA countries, it is more specifically in relation to the allocation of posts that primary and lower secondary schools have a degree of freedom in taking decisions, although such freedom is always limited.

In the majority of the CEECs, schools are completely autonomous as regards staff recruitment and the allocation of posts. As in the EFTA/EEA countries, appointments to headships are made by authorities at a higher level, except in Poland.

FIGURE B6: AUTONOMY OF PUBLIC-SECTOR SCHOOLS IN MATTERS RELATING TO THE MANAGEMENT OF TEACHING STAFF, 1995/96

	APPOINTMENT OF HEADTEACHER	FIXING THE NUMBER OF TEACHING POSTS	RECRUITMENT OF TEACHING STAFF	ALLOCATION OF POSTS TO EITHER CLASS TEACHERS OR SPECIALIST TEACHERS (PRIMARY LEVEL)	FIXING THE NUMBER OF TEACHERS (COMPULSORY/ OPTIONAL SUBJECTS) (SECONDARY LEVEL)
EUROPEAN UNION					
B fr					
B nl					
DK					
D					
EL					
E					
F					
IRL					
I					
L					
NL					
A					
P					
FIN					
S					
UK (E/W)					
UK (NI)					
UK (SC)					
EFTA/EEA					
IS					
LI					
NO					
CEEC					
BG					
CZ					
HU					
PL					
RO					
SK					

AUTONOMY FOR DECISIONS   LIMITED AUTONOMY   NO AUTONOMY   DATA NOT AVAILABLE

Source: Eurydice.

Where cells are shared, the information in the left-hand cell relates to primary education and that in the right to lower secondary.

OVERSIGHT OF SCHOOLS:
FROM A NATIONAL INSPECTORATE TO THE SHARING OF RESPONSIBILITIES
BY SEVERAL ADMINISTRATIVE BODIES

The mechanisms for the administrative and pedagogical oversight of primary and secondary schools vary greatly from one Member State to another. Two main models are found, depending on whether there is a school inspectorate.

In Spain, there is an inspectorate at regional level, constituted on hierarchical lines. The inspectors are responsible for all of the oversight of schools, both administrative and pedagogical. In Italy, two separate inspectorates share these tasks, one being more concerned with the administrative aspects and the other with the pedagogical aspects.

At the opposite end of the scale, Denmark, Finland and Sweden have no inspectorates and the municipal authorities undertake administrative oversight. On the educational aspects, subject consultants in Denmark give teachers help and advice, while in Finland the municipal authorities oversee the activities of the headteacher and give help and advice to teachers in collaboration with the National Board of Education. In Sweden, every municipal authority has to monitor and evaluate the education system at local level. The National Agency for Education is responsible for national inspection of the education system. In Finland and Sweden, headteachers are responsible for the pedagogical supervision of teaching staff.

All the other Member States come somewhere between these two extremes, with responsibility for the oversight of schools being shared between a national inspectorate and the administrative departments of the education authorities.

In some Member States, the different tasks are clearly allocated. As well as supervising pedagogical matters, the inspectors check on compulsory school attendance in Belgium (French and German-speaking Communities). In Germany, supervision of schools lies with the *Länder* and includes both pedagogical matters and responsibility for staffing issues. The supervision is exercised by the lower and middle-tier school supervisory authorities *(untere und mittlere Schulaufsichtsbehörden)*. In Greece, in addition to their administrative tasks, the education authorities inspect the work of headteachers. In Austria, inspectors carry out for the most part tasks requiring their presence in schools (visiting classrooms, checking the state of equipment, and so on) and the different school authorities are responsible for all other tasks in relation to the schools for which they are responsible. In Portugal, the powers of the general inspectorate of education include the evaluation and inspection of the pedagogical, administrative and financial aspects of schools in collaboration with other branches of the Ministry of Education and more particularly the Institute for Innovation in Education, which has the task of designing systems for assessing pupils' educational attainments and studying their results.

In the other Member States, the tasks are shared between the inspectorate and education authorities. In the Netherlands, oversight of education is undertaken by the education inspectorate at the request of the Ministry of Education, Culture and Science. This covers compliance with the legal requirements and evaluation of the quality of education. The inspectors check that the prescribed curriculum is being taught and that such teaching is satisfactory. In England, Wales and Northern Ireland, responsibility for the quality of education provided by individual schools is shared between the school governing bodies and national and local bodies. The national inspectorates in England and Wales (OFSTED and OHMCI) focus on the educational standards achieved, the quality of education provided, the spiritual, moral, social and cultural development of pupils, and the efficient use of financial resources. In Northern Ireland, the Education and Training Inspectorate (ETI) has a similar role. In Scotland, the inspectors (HMI) carry out programmes of educational inspection as well as checking the state of buildings and equipment in collaboration with the local authorities.

In primary education in Luxembourg, where there are no headteachers, the inspectors carry out all the functions in relation to the supervision of teachers, ensure that the law on compulsory school attendance is complied with and also fulfil the role of headteacher. The local authority (mayor, communal council and schools committee) has functions in relation to the running and organization of primary schools. In secondary education, the opposite is the case — there is no inspectorate, and the administrative departments of the Ministry carry out directly the inspection of schools and their heads as well as the pedagogical supervision of teaching staff.

FIGURE B7: DISTRIBUTION OF EDUCATIONAL AND ADMINISTRATIVE INSPECTION BETWEEN INSPECTORATES AND ADMINISTRATIVE DEPARTMENTS, 1995/96

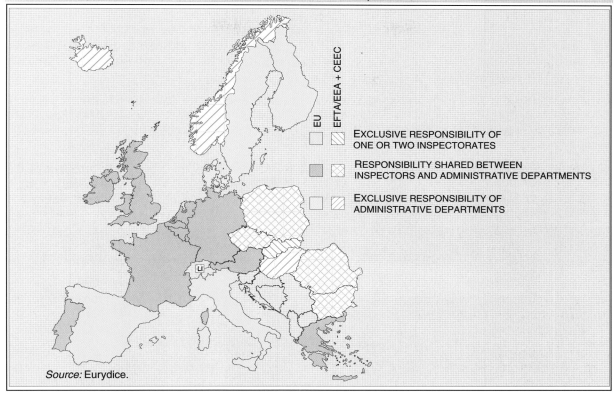

Source: Eurydice.

Luxembourg: Primary education only.
Poland: Primary education only.

In Iceland and Norway, there are no inspectorates. National and/or local authorities undertake the administrative and pedagogical monitoring of schools. In Liechtenstein, the inspectors carry out these different tasks, except in the *Gymnasium*.

In most of the CEECs, the inspectors and the administrative departments share the tasks of educational and administrative oversight. In the Czech Republic, the inspectors evaluate the teaching process, its outcome, the staff, technical and material conditions and the effectiveness of the use of financial resources and ensure, on behalf of the state, that the statutory regulations are being enforced. The inspection of secondary schools in Poland is a matter exclusively for the inspectorate. In Slovakia, the inspectors are responsible for the inspection of education, the supervision of headteachers and the external evaluation of schools. In Hungary, on the other hand, there is no inspectorate.

LOWER AND UPPER SECONDARY EDUCATION:
————— MOST OFTEN PROVIDED IN SEPARATE SCHOOLS —————

In some Member States of the European Union, lower and upper secondary education are provided in the same school. This arrangement is available to all pupils in Ireland and the United Kingdom. Practically all schools in Belgium and Luxembourg also combine these two levels of secondary education in a single school.

On the other hand, throughout Greece, France and Sweden and in the great majority of cases in Denmark, Spain and Finland, pupils have to transfer to another institution when they move to upper secondary education. This is also the case on a fairly large scale in Germany, the Netherlands and Austria.

In general, these situations are independent of the structure of secondary education. Both models are found as frequently in Member States with a single, continuous structure up to age 16 as in those in which secondary education is organized either on a common core basis or in separate streams after the end of primary education.

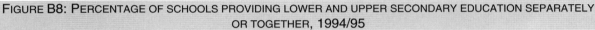

FIGURE B8: PERCENTAGE OF SCHOOLS PROVIDING LOWER AND UPPER SECONDARY EDUCATION SEPARATELY OR TOGETHER, 1994/95

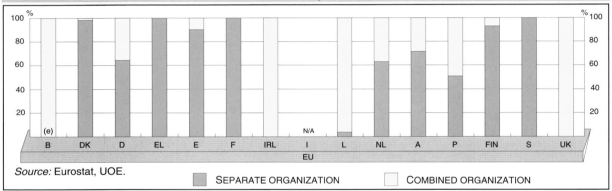

Source: Eurostat, UOE.

Belgium: The percentage is overestimated as a small number of schools provide only one of these levels of education. Their number is not known as the registration of this characteristic is carried out only at the school level.
Denmark: A few private schools provide primary and lower and upper secondary education together.
Sweden: Schools providing adult education at ISCED levels 1, 2 and 3 are excluded.
United Kingdom: The further education institutions which provide post-compulsory general and/or vocational education are not included.

EXPLANATORY NOTE
Secondary schools have been classified into two categories:
— *those providing lower secondary education (ISCED 2) separate from upper secondary education (ISCED 3);*
— *those providing both levels of education (ISCED 2 and 3) together.*
The fact that primary education may also be provided in certain secondary schools is not taken into account in the classification used.
The distributions shown in Figure B8 have been calculated on the basis of the relationship between the number of schools providing both levels of secondary education (ISCED 2 and 3) and the total number of schools in which at least lower secondary education is provided (ISCED 1 and 2, ISCED 1, 2 and 3, ISCED 2 and 3 and ISCED 2).

PRE-PRIMARY EDUCATION

───────── **CONTINUING RISE IN PRE-PRIMARY ENROLMENT RATES** ─────────

At the present time, in some Member States of the European Union, practically all 4-year-old children are attending a school or non-school education-oriented institution. Such attendance has even become compulsory in Luxembourg and the United Kingdom (Northern Ireland). Enrolment rates remain low, however, in Finland, where less than one third of 4-year-olds attend an institution, and they barely exceed 50% in Greece, Ireland and Portugal.

A time series starting in 1950 illustrates the movement in 4-year-olds' enrolment rates in pre-primary institutions in the European Union. The trend is clear — in all countries for which data are available, increasing numbers of 4-year-old children are attending pre-primary institutions. It should be noted that participation rates have been high in Belgium, France and the Netherlands since the beginning of the 1970s. With the exception of Ireland, a clear increase can be seen in the 1980s in those countries in which attendance by 4-year-olds was not already widespread.

FIGURE C1: TREND IN THE PARTICIPATION RATES OF 4-YEAR-OLDS IN EDUCATION-ORIENTED PRE-PRIMARY PROVISION, 1950-94

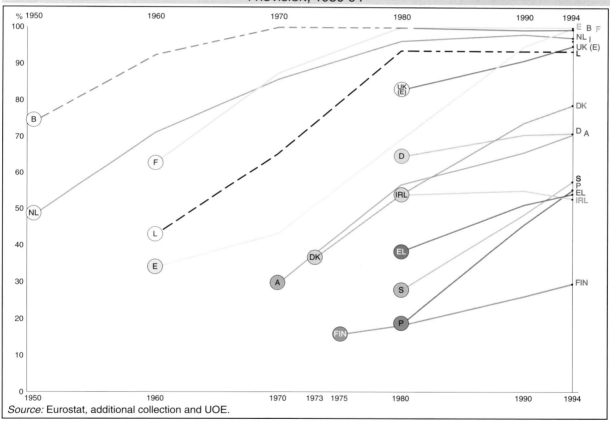

Source: Eurostat, additional collection and UOE.

Belgium: The data prior to 1980 are shown as a dotted line as they are available only in respect of all children in nursery schools (*écoles maternelles/kleuteronderwijs*). The rates for each of these three years have therefore been calculated for children aged 3, 4 and 5 years.
Germany: The data for 1994 include the new *Länder*.
Greece: This includes only children between 3½ and 4½ years old in public sector nursery schools.
Ireland: Not all children in private schools are included.
Italy: Data are available only for 1994.
Luxembourg: The data are shown as a dotted line as the percentages include both 4- and 5-year-olds in schools.
United Kingdom (E): The percentages include children in nursery schools and in nursery and infant classes in primary schools, special schools and independent schools.

A WIDE RANGE OF PROVISION
IN PRE-PRIMARY EDUCATION

There is a wide range of institutions which children in Europe may attend before entering primary school. Further details of them, with their names in the original languages, can be found in Figure C2. The criterion adopted for classification purposes is the qualification of the staff recruited to take charge of the children. In institutions coming under the schools administration as such, staff responsible for children's education always have specialized qualifications in education. On the other hand, in the non-school institutions (day nurseries, playgroups or day care centres) which generally come under authorities or ministries other than those responsible for education, the staff are not required to hold a qualification in education. There are, however, exceptions, such as the *Kindergärten* in Germany and Austria, the *børnehaver* in Denmark and the *jardins de infância* in Portugal, where the non-school institutions must employ staff with a qualification in education. (Assistants may be employed in addition.) In Finland and Sweden, all institutions catering for young children employ staff qualified in education.

Attendance at a pre-primary institution is voluntary in all Member States of the European Union with the exception of Luxembourg, where the *Spillschoul* is compulsory from the age of 4. In Northern Ireland (United Kingdom), compulsory primary education starts at age 4.

In three Member States of the European Union — Belgium, France and Italy — schools are the only form of provision for children from the age of 3 years. A range of educational provision is available in the other Member States. There are pre-primary classes for 6-year-olds in Denmark and Finland. In Germany, some *Länder* have introduced pre-primary classes *(Vorklassen)* for 5-year-olds who have not yet reached compulsory school age but whose parents wish them to have a preparation for the primary school. In most of the German *Länder*, in Denmark and in Sweden, school provision starts with compulsory primary education. In the last two Member States, parents may opt to enrol their children in, respectively, the *folkeskole* and the *grundskola* from age 6.

A similar diversity is also found in the EFTA/EEA countries and the CEECs. Many of these, however, share a common characteristic in that there is only one type of institution for children of a given age. This may be a playgroup, a non-school education-oriented institution or a school.

In all these countries, attendance at an institution is also voluntary, depending on the wishes of the parents and the provision available.

In Iceland, the only provision for pre-primary children is in the *leikskóli*. In Liechtenstein and Norway, there is no school provision for children before they start primary school at, respectively, 6 and 7 years of age. The non-school education-oriented institutions in these two countries are, however, required to recruit staff with qualifications in education.

In all the CEECs, under-3-year-olds are provided for in crèches and day nurseries except in Hungary, where there are non-school education-oriented institutions. For children over 3 years of age, schools constitute the only provision available. In Hungary, attendance at the *óvoda* is compulsory for children aged 5.

FIGURE C2: ORGANIZATION OF PRE-PRIMARY INSTITUTIONS, 1995/96

EUROPEAN UNION

Scale: 0 YEARS | 3 months | 6 months | 9 months | 1 YEAR | 2 YEARS | 3 YEARS | 4 YEARS | 5 YEARS | 6 YEARS | 7 YEARS

B
- CRÈCHES/KINDERDAGVERBLIJF/KRIPPEN
- ENSEIGNEMENT MATERNEL/KLEUTERONDERWIJS/KINDERGARTEN

DK
- VUGGESTUER
- ALDERSINTEGREREDE INSTITUTIONER
- BØRNEHAVER
- BØRNEHAVEKLASSE

D
- KRIPPEN
- KINDERGARTEN
- VORKLASSEN (SOME LÄNDER ONLY)

EL
- IDIOTIKI VREFONIPIAKI STATHMI
- KRATIKI STATHMI
- NIPIAKA TMIMATA
- IDIOTIKI PAIDIKI STATHMI, KRATIKI PAIDIKI STATHMI
- NIPIAGOGEIA

E
- GUARDERÍAS   and other institutions
- CENTROS DE EDUCACIÓN INFANTIL/ESCUELAS DE EDUCACIÓN INFANTIL

F
- CRÈCHES
- ÉCOLES MATERNELLES/CLASSES ENFANTINES

IRL
- DAY CARE / DAY NURSERIES
- PLAYGROUPS
- TRAVELLER CHILDREN CENTRES
- NATIONAL SCHOOLS (Infant Classes)

I
- ASILO NIDO
- SCUOLA MATERNA

L
- FOYERS DE JOUR
- Classes enfantines   SPILLSCHOUL

NL
- PEUTERSPEELZALEN
- KINDERDAGVERBLIJVEN/HALVEDAGOPVANG
- BASISONDERWIJS

A
- KRIPPEN
- KINDERGARTEN

P
- CRÈCHES
- JARDINS DE INFÂNCIA
- JARDINS DE INFÂNCIA

FIN
- PÄIVÄKOTI/DAGHEM
- PERUSKOULU /GRUNDSKOLA

S
- DAGHEM
- DELTIDSGRUPPER

UK

E/W
- DAY NURSERIES / NURSERY CENTRES
- PLAYGROUPS
- NURSERY SCHOOLS/CLASSES
- RECEPTION CLASSES

NI
- DAY NURSERIES
- PLAYGROUPS
- NURSERY SCHOOLS/CLASSES

SC
- DAY NURSERIES
- PLAYGROUPS
- NURSERY SCHOOLS/CLASSES

EFTA/EEA

Scale: 0 YEARS | 3 months | 6 months | 9 months | 1 YEAR | 2 YEARS | 3 YEARS | 4 YEARS | 5 YEARS | 6 YEARS | 7 YEARS

IS
- LEIKSKÓLI-PRIMARY SCHOOL

LI
- TAGESSTÄTTE
- KINDERHORT
- KINDERGARTEN/SONDERSCHULKINDERGARTEN/WALDORFKINDERGARTEN

NO
- ÅPNE BARNEHAGER/VANLIGE BARNEHAGER/FAMILIEBARNEHAGER

CEEC

Scale: 0 YEARS | 3 months | 6 months | 9 months | 1 YEAR | 2 YEARS | 3 YEARS | 4 YEARS | 5 YEARS | 6 YEARS | 7 YEARS

BG
- DETSKA YASLA
- DETSKA GRADINA
- PODGOTVITELNA GRUPA

CZ
- DENNI JESLE
- MATEŘSKÁ ŠKOLA

HU
- BÖLCSŐDE
- ÓVODA

PL
- ŻŁOBKI
- PRZEDSZKOLE
- ODDZIAŁY PRZEDSZKOLNE

RO
- CREŞA
- GRADINIŢA

SK
- MATERSKÁ ŠKOLA

Legend:
- NURSERIES/DAY CARE/PLAYGROUPS — Public and private
- NON-SCHOOL INSTITUTIONS WITH EDUCATIONAL ORIENTATION — Public and private
- SCHOOLS — Public and private

Source: Eurydice.

Spain: The *centros de educación infantil* are private institutions recognised as schools. The education law (LOGSE) provides for the *escuelas de educación infantil* to admit children from the age of 3 months and to provide the first stage of education (for children of 3 months to 3 years), the second stage (for 3- to 6-year-olds) or both.

Bulgaria: Children may enter the *podgotvitelna grupa* (one-year preparatory classes) at the age of 5 or 6 if their parents so desire.

Netherlands: *Basisonderwijs* is compulsory from 5 years of age, but children are admitted from the age of 4.

Poland: In small towns, the *oddziały przedszkolne* can accept children between the ages of 3 and 6 years.

Slovakia: In some cases, the *materská škola* can accept children under 3 and over 6 years of age.

A GENERALLY INCREASING TREND TOWARDS ATTENDANCE AT AN INSTITUTION AT AGE 4

Two main trends appear from a reading of Figure C3 which sets out by country and by age the percentages of children in schools (pre-primary or primary) and non-school education-oriented institutions.

— In one group of Member States, there is a very high level of attendance at schools from 3 years of age (Belgium, France and Italy) or from 4 years of age (Spain, Luxembourg and the Netherlands).

— In the other Member States of the EU, attendance at an institution (school or other) is more gradual. With increasing age, children attend education-oriented institutions in increasing numbers.

FIGURE C3: PARTICIPATION RATES IN EDUCATION-ORIENTED PRE-PRIMARY PROVISION BY AGE, 1994/95

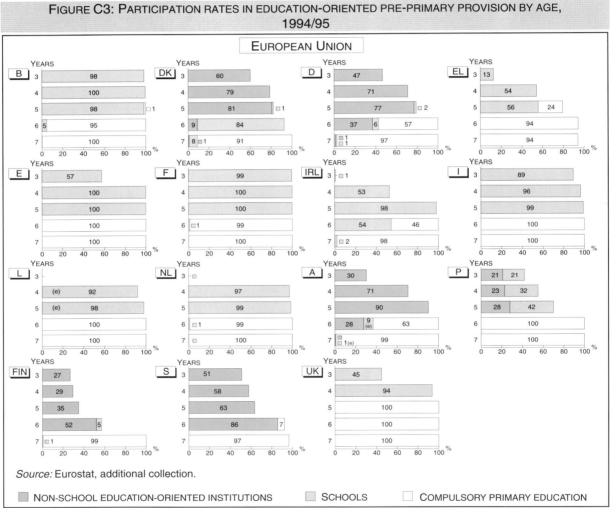

Source: Eurostat, additional collection.

NON-SCHOOL EDUCATION-ORIENTED INSTITUTIONS   SCHOOLS   COMPULSORY PRIMARY EDUCATION

Greece: Only children attending the *nipiagogeia* (public sector nursery schools) are included.
Ireland: Pupils attending certain private schools are not included.
Netherlands: Four-year-olds attend the non-compulsory year of *basisonderwijs*. Compulsory primary education starts at age 5, but for the purposes of international statistics, 5-year-olds are included under ISCED 0.
United Kingdom: The graph presents undifferentiated data for the United Kingdom as a whole. It therefore conceals disparities between the component parts. Northern Ireland differs in particular in having compulsory education starting at age 4. The figures include pupils in nursery schools, nursery and infant classes in primary schools, special schools and independent schools.

MOST PROVISION IS IN SCHOOLS

From the age of 3 years, even when the participation rates are low, children in the majority of Member States attend school provision. In Portugal, there are about equal numbers of children in school institutions and in non-school education centres. In Denmark, Germany, Austria, Finland and Sweden, children of this age attend non-school education-oriented institutions.

In the EFTA countries and the CEECs, there are constantly increasing participation rates of 3- to 7-year-olds in school and non-school institutions. In Liechtenstein, however, there is a mass entry of all 5-year-olds to the *Kindergarten*. Under that age, there are few children in this category. In Poland, barely a quarter of children are at school between the ages of 3 and 5 years. Mass attendance at the pre-primary school starts with 6-year-olds in the class before the first year of compulsory education.

FIGURE C3 (CONTINUED): PARTICIPATION RATES IN EDUCATION-ORIENTED PRE-PRIMARY PROVISION BY AGE, 1994/95

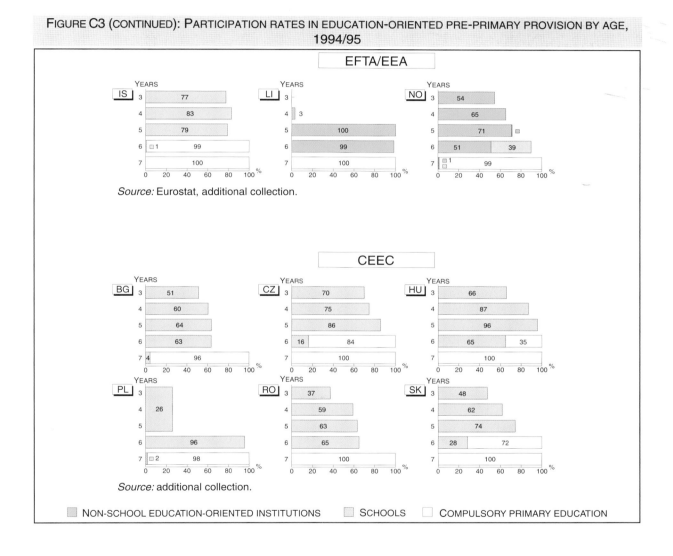

EXPLANATORY NOTE
The participation rate for a given age is the ratio of enrolments in the institutions concerned to the population of children of that age.
Rates below 1% are not given but are indicated by a coloured square.

— REGIONAL VARIATIONS IN PROVISION FOR THE YOUNGEST CHILDREN —

Belgium, France and Italy are strongholds of institutionalised pre-primary education for 3-year-olds, with high rates of participation in all regions. Considerable regional variations are found in the United Kingdom whose national rate is under 50%.

A similar map of participation at 4 years of age would show not only an increase in the rate in most countries but also a trend towards the mean in the regions.

FIGURE C4: PARTICIPATION RATES OF 3-YEAR-OLDS IN EDUCATION-ORIENTED PRE-PRIMARY PROVISION, BY NUTS 1 AND 2 REGIONS, 1994/95

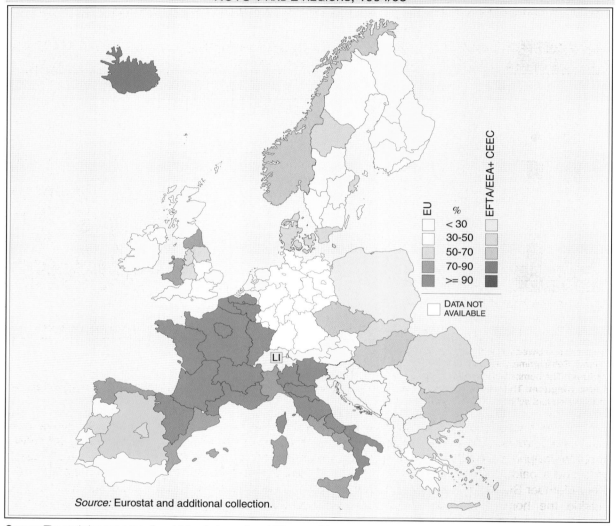

Source: Eurostat and additional collection.

Greece: The statistics group together children between 3 and 4½ years old.
Ireland: Public primary schools only.
United Kingdom: The statistics group together children attending nursery schools, nursery classes and infant classes in primary schools, special schools and independent schools.

EXPLANATORY NOTE

For most Member States, the nomenclature used here is that of NUTS 1. NUTS 2 is, however, used for Portugal, Finland and Sweden. For the EFTA/EEA countries and the CEECs, only national data are provided. The division into classes in this map is based on the distribution of the statistics. The method chosen tends to produce a continuous series, each element of which includes the same percentage of values.

MOTHERS IN PAID EMPLOYMENT
AND PARTICIPATION OF YOUNG CHILDREN
IN EDUCATION-ORIENTED PRE-PRIMARY INSTITUTIONS

It has been considered for quite some time that the increase in the uptake of pre-primary provision is related to the child-care needs of mothers who go out to work. However, analysis of the current situation in the European Union shows that the phenomenon is more complex. Nowadays, the importance of pre-primary education is recognised by everyone. Attending an educational institution is regarded as conducive to the young child's development and socialisation. As illustrated in Figure C5, there is no direct connection between the participation rates of 3-year-olds in education-oriented institutions and the percentages of mothers who have a 3-year-old child and are in paid employment.

FIGURE C5: PERCENTAGE OF MOTHERS WITH A 3-YEAR-OLD CHILD AND IN EMPLOYMENT AND PARTICIPATION OF 3-YEAR-OLDS IN EDUCATION-ORIENTED PRE-PRIMARY PROVISION, 1994/95

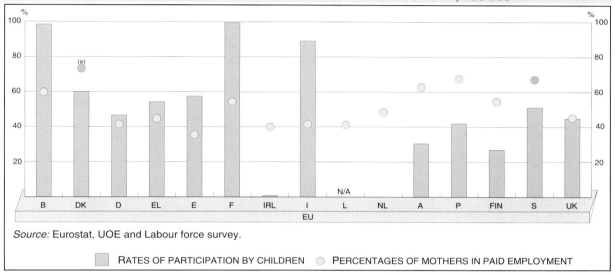

Source: Eurostat, UOE and Labour force survey.

RATES OF PARTICIPATION BY CHILDREN   PERCENTAGES OF MOTHERS IN PAID EMPLOYMENT

Denmark and **Sweden**: National statistics.
Ireland: Public primary schools only.
Portugal: The numbers of children in non-school education-oriented institutions is an estimate.
United Kingdom: The figures include children in nursery schools, nursery and infant classes in primary schools, special schools and independent schools.

This graph shows clearly that, in the three Member States in which there is full coverage of educational provision (Belgium, France and Italy), the percentage of 3-year-olds attending education-oriented pre-primary institutions is very much higher than the percentage of mothers with a 3-year-old child and a paid job. The situation is similar in Spain, but to a lesser degree. In the majority of the other Member States, however, the percentage of mothers who have a 3-year-old child and who work outside the home is greater than that of 3-year-olds attending education-oriented pre-primary institutions. In these Member States, the numbers of places in education-oriented provision are limited, and for this reason there is either a network of child-care centres and playgroups or family day-care for 3-year-olds.

EXPLANATORY NOTE
The data on mothers with a 3-year-old child and in employment are drawn from the 1995 Eurostat Labour force survey. The percentage of mothers who have a 3-year-old child and who are in employment is the ratio of the number of mothers who have a 3-year-old child and who are in employment to the total number of mothers with a 3-year-old child, multiplied by 100.
The pre-primary rates refer to 3-year-olds in schools or other education-oriented institutions. Data are taken from the UOE questionnaires.

BETWEEN ONE AND THREE YEARS OF PRE-PRIMARY
PROVISION, DEPENDING ON THE COUNTRY

The average duration of participation in pre-primary education depends on various factors: the minimum age of admission to educational provision, the starting age of compulsory primary education and the participation rates of children in pre-primary institutions. Thus, a short average period of attendance can be found for different reasons — either because the official provision extends to only a few years or because attendance at such schools or other institutions is not widespread.

The official availability of provision is calculated here from the age of 3 years, which in most Member States is the minimum age of entry, except in Belgium, Denmark, Spain, France, Finland and Sweden in the European Union, and in Iceland and Norway in the EFTA/EEA countries.

Those Member States with the shortest average duration of pre-primary education (only one year) are also those whose compulsory primary education starts earliest — the Netherlands and the United Kingdom, where it starts at age 5 (and even at age 4 in Northern Ireland). Four other Member States have an average of less than two years of attendance in pre-primary education. In Greece and Luxembourg this is because the educational structures take children only from 4 years of age. In Portugal and Finland, where provision is in theory sufficient to offer children three and four years respectively of pre-primary education from the age of 3, the short average duration is explained by the low percentage of participation.

The other EU Member States have an average duration of two or three years of pre-primary attendance. This coincides with the official duration of provision, as in Belgium, France, Ireland and Italy.

FIGURE C6: AVERAGE DURATION OF ATTENDANCE AT AN EDUCATION-ORIENTED PRE-PRIMARY INSTITUTION, 1994/95

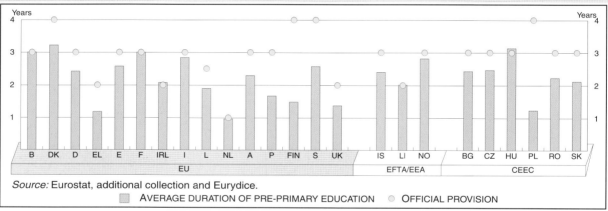

Source: Eurostat, additional collection and Eurydice.

AVERAGE DURATION OF PRE-PRIMARY EDUCATION   OFFICIAL PROVISION

Greece: Only children enrolled in the public sector nursery schools (*nipiagogeia*) are included.
Ireland: The calculation includes some 6- and 7-year-olds who are of compulsory school age but who are in the infant classes.
Netherlands: Only the optional first year of *basisonderwijs* is regarded as a pre-primary year.
Austria: The number of children in the pre-primary level of schools is an estimate.
United Kingdom: The figures include children in nursery schools, nursery and infant classes in primary schools, special schools and independent schools.

In most of the EFTA/EEA countries and the CEECs which officially provide their children with three years of pre-primary education, an average duration of participation of between two and three years is found. In Liechtenstein, the official availability matches the average duration (two years). On the other hand, in Poland, where the official availability is the longest, the average duration of attendance is shortest, owing to the low attendance rates of children under 6 years of age.

EXPLANATORY NOTE
The average duration of children's attendance at an education-oriented institution is obtained by adding together the attendance rates for the different age groups from the age of 3 years. For example, in Belgium the pre-primary rate for children aged 3 years is 98.5%, at 4 years it is 99.5% and at 5 years it is 98.3%, plus 4.7% of 6-year-olds and 0.1% of 7-year-olds. The duration of pre-primary education therefore equals (0.985+0.995+0.983+0.047+0.001) x 1year = 3.01 years. The official duration of provision corresponds to the number of years — starting at the age of 3 years — during which the pre-primary institution can take children prior to their entry into primary school.

GROUPING OF CHILDREN:
AGE GROUPS OR 'FAMILY GROUPS'

In education-oriented institutions which cater for children before they enter the compulsory primary school, the groups of children are formed following one of two main models.

— The first anticipates the pattern of organisation in classes that is used in primary schools, the children being grouped according to age. This pattern is called the 'school model'.

— The second is closer to the pattern of the family, children of different ages being placed in the same group. This is the 'family model'.

In schools in Greece, Spain, France, Ireland and the United Kingdom, the tendency is to make up classes of children of the same age, following the school model. This situation is also found in the pre-primary classes which take children at the age of 6 years in Denmark and Finland. On the other hand, in the non-school institutions for children under 6 years old in Denmark, Germany, Finland and Sweden, children of different ages are grouped together, rather on the family model. In Luxembourg, in the *Spillschuol*, the family model is also the most common. In Luxembourg, Finland and Sweden, still in the spirit of the family model, there is a tendency to group together children of the same family.

In the other Member States, institutions may adopt either model. This is the case in the schools in Belgium, Italy and the Netherlands, in the *Kindergärten* in Austria and in the *jardins de infância* in Portugal.

FIGURE C7: PRINCIPAL METHODS OF GROUPING CHILDREN
IN EDUCATION-ORIENTED PRE-PRIMARY INSTITUTIONS, 1995/96

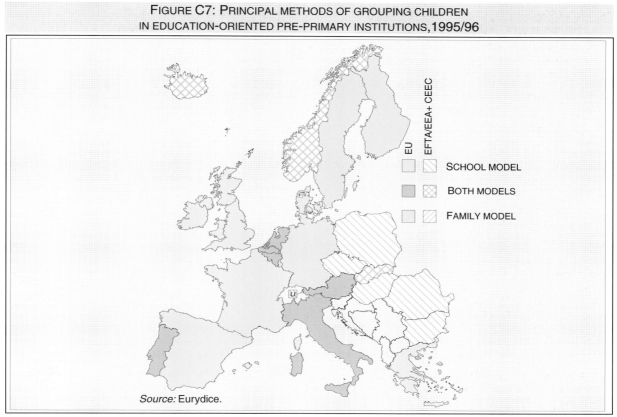

Source: Eurydice.

Sweden: There are no regulations; the school model is sometimes followed.

In the EFTA/EEA countries, institutions catering for children before they start primary school organize groups on both the school and the family models, although in Liechtenstein the *Kindergärten* usually place 4- and 5-year-olds together.

In the CEECs, the most common pattern is the school model. Only in Slovakia are both models found.

NUMBER OF CHILDREN PER ADULT: OFTEN SUBJECT TO REGULATIONS BUT WITH DIFFERENT NORMS

The majority of the EU Member States have regulations prescribing the maximum and/or minimum numbers of children in a class or group of children in education-oriented institutions, whether these are schools or not. These norms in relation to class sizes vary widely from one Member State to the other and even within the same one, depending on the ages of the children.

Member States which have no regulations on class or group sizes operate in a variety of ways. In some of them, the number of teachers in an institution is fixed on the basis of the total number of pupils enrolled. This is the case in Belgium and the Netherlands (in *basisonderwijs*), as well as in Sweden where the norms also differ according to the ages of the children. The basis of the calculation is, however, very different from one Member State to the other. In France, the *Inspecteur d'Académie* determines annually the average number of pupils per class in that area and can also set the maximum number of pupils in a class according to criteria unique to that *Académie*. In the United Kingdom (England, Wales and Northern Ireland), an indication is given as to the minimum number of adults to be provided for a given group of children.

All the EFTA/EEA countries and the CEECs have regulations which prescribe the maximum size of a group of children. In Liechtenstein, the maxima are recommended by the inspectors. In Norway, there are no regulations on the size of groups but there are on the number of children per teacher.

Figure C8 shows the maximum numbers of children for which each adult is responsible, and not the sizes of the groups. This means that, in those countries in which two adults work together routinely, the maximum number of children in the group is divided by two. In several countries, the maxima differ according to the ages of the children. The numbers shown here are therefore those prescribed for 4-year-olds. The comparison shows that the norms are relatively high in a number of Member States in the European Union, in particular those in which the children are in schools (except in Austria).

In most of the EFTA/EEA countries and the CEECs, the permitted numbers are high (between 20 and 25 children per adult). The norms appear more favourable in Iceland, Norway and Bulgaria (under 10 children per adult).

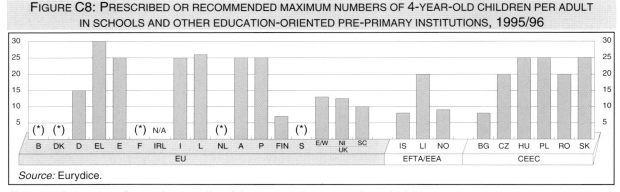

FIGURE C8: PRESCRIBED OR RECOMMENDED MAXIMUM NUMBERS OF 4-YEAR-OLD CHILDREN PER ADULT IN SCHOOLS AND OTHER EDUCATION-ORIENTED PRE-PRIMARY INSTITUTIONS, 1995/96

Source: Eurydice.

(*): no regulations regarding maximum and/or minimum group sizes, or numbers of adults per group.

Germany: A group should have between 15 and 30 children with at least one person with a qualification in education and usually an assistant.
France: The average number of pupils per class can be 25 in nursery schools in educational priority areas.
Finland: The law prescribes the number of qualified staff in relation to the numbers of children — one adult for every 4 children under 3 years old and one adult for every 7 children over 3 years old.
United Kingdom (E/W): Government guidance on the law recommends a minimum of two adults per group of 26 pupils in nursery classes and per group of 20 pupils in nursery schools.
United Kingdom (NI): A maximum number of 25 pupils is recommended on the basis of the size of the classroom.
United Kingdom (SC): Legislation requires a minimum staff/child ratio of 1:10 in local authority nursery schools and classes.
Czech Republic: Decisions on class sizes are taken by school heads after consultation with the school's organizing body and the responsible local authority.

STAFFING ARRANGEMENTS:
—————— ONLY ONE ADULT PER GROUP OR MORE? ——————

Staffing arrangements in schools or other education-oriented institutions differ from one Member State to the other. Two main patterns can be identified: one single adult with a group of children, and two or more adults working together with the same group at the same time.

In the first case, one adult is frequently responsible for the group all week (Belgium, Spain, France, Ireland and the Netherlands). In some countries, that person is replaced by others for specific activities (Greece and Luxembourg); in others, this pattern is found but not systematically (Belgium — German-speaking Community and Portugal).

In the second case, there is usually a team consisting of one person who is in charge and an auxiliary (Germany and the United Kingdom), while in some countries such help is available but again not on a systematic basis (Austria, Portugal).

In the non-school institutions in Denmark, Finland and Sweden, two or three adults work together with the same group of children at the same time. In Italy, two teachers take the class alternately, but for some hours in the day they both work with the class at the same time. In Belgium, there are examples of several teachers working together in certain classes which include children of different ages. It should however be noted that these three situations are not comparable since there are considerable differences in the adult/child ratios.

FIGURE C9: STAFFING ARRANGEMENTS IN PRE-PRIMARY SCHOOLS AND OTHER EDUCATION-ORIENTED INSTITUTIONS, 1995/96

ONE ADULT ALL WEEK OR SEVERAL ADULTS IN TURN	ONE ADULT AND AN AUXILIARY OR SEVERAL ADULTS AT THE SAME TIME	TWO PATTERNS
EUROPEAN UNION		
Belgium, Greece, Spain, France, Ireland, Luxembourg, Netherlands	Denmark, Germany, Finland, Sweden, United Kingdom	Italy, Austria, Portugal
EFTA/EEA		
Liechtenstein	Iceland, Norway	
CEEC		
Bulgaria, Czech Republic, Hungary, Poland, Romania, Slovakia		

Source: Eurydice.

Italy: Two teachers are present together for some hours each day.
Austria: An auxiliary is present in many cases (not always).
Portugal: One auxiliary is present for two classes (a total of 40/50 pupils).

In the EFTA/EEA countries, in Liechtenstein there is one adult in charge of the children for the whole week. Two adults work together in Iceland (both educators) and in Norway (one in charge and one auxiliary).

In the CEECs, the patterns of working are quite varied. In the Czech Republic and Poland, one adult is responsible for the class; in Hungary and Slovakia, several adults are involved in turn; in Romania, one adult is responsible for the group throughout the whole week, sometimes replaced by others for specific activities.

FEE-PAYING IS MORE FREQUENT
IN THE PRIVATE SECTOR THAN IN THE PUBLIC SECTOR

FIGURE C10: FEE-PAYING/FREE ADMISSION TO EDUCATION-ORIENTED PRE-PRIMARY INSTITUTIONS AND PERCENTAGE OF FEE-PAYING CHILDREN, 1995/96

	FREE OF CHARGE		FEE-PAYING		PERCENTAGE OF FEE-PAYING CHILDREN
	PUBLIC	PRIVATE	PUBLIC	PRIVATE	
EUROPEAN UNION					
B	*Enseignement maternel, kleuteronderwijs, Kindergarten*	*Enseignement maternel, kleuteronderwijs, Kindergarten*			0%
DK	*Børnehaveklasse*		*Aldersintegrerede institutioner, Børnehaver*	*Aldersintegrerede institutioner, Børnehaver, Børnehaveklasse*	72%
D	*Vorklassen, Schulkindergärten*		*Kindergärten* (with some exceptions)	*Kindergärten* (with some exceptions), *Vorklassen, Schulkindergärten*	N/A
EL	*Nipiagogeia*			*Idiotika nipiagogeia*	4%
E	*Escuelas de educación infantil*	*Centros de educación infantil*	*Escuelas de educación infantil* (some)	*Centros de educación infantil*	27%
F	*Écoles maternelles Classes enfantines*			*Écoles maternelles Classes enfantines*	12%
IRL	Traveller children centres National schools			Private schools	2%
I	*Scuola materna*			*Scuola materna*	N/A
L	*Classes enfantines, Spillschuol*				0%
NL	*Basisonderwijs*	*Basisonderwijs*			0%
A			*Kindergärten* (with some exceptions)	*Kindergärten* (with some exceptions)	N/A
P	*Jardins de infância* (ME)		*Jardins de infância* (MSSS)	*Jardins de infância*	N/A
FIN	*Peruskoulu/Grundskola*	*Peruskoulu/Grundskola*	*Päiväkoti/Daghem*	*Päiväkoti/Daghem*	96%
S	*Deltidsgrupper*		*Daghem*	*Daghem/Deltidsgrupper*	88%
UK (E/W)	Nursery schools/classes/ Reception classes	Nursery schools/classes/ Reception classes (voluntary schools)		Nursery schools/classes (independent schools)	N/A
UK (NI)	Nursery schools/classes	Nursery schools/classes (maintained schools)		Nursery schools/ classes (independent schools)	N/A
UK (SC)	Nursery schools/classes		Pre-school centres	Pre-school centres	N/A
EFTA/EEA					
IS			*Leikskóli*	*Leikskóli*	100%
LI	*Kindergärten*	*Sonderschulkindergärten*	*Kinderhort*	*Tagesstätte, Waldorf-Kindergärten*	2%
NO			*Åpne barnehager, Vanlige barnehager*	*Åpne barnehager, Vanlige barnehager, Familiebarnehager*	100% (e)
CEEC					
BG	*Poludnevna detska gradina*	*Detska gradina*			0%
CZ	*Mateřská škola*		*Mateřská škola*		N/A
HU	*Óvoda, Bölcsőde*	*Óvoda, Bölcsőde*	*Óvoda, Bölcsőde*	*Óvoda, Bölcsőde*	N/A
PL	*Przedszkole*		*Przedszkole*	*Przedszkole*	N/A
RO	*Gradinita*			*Gradinita*	0%
SK			*Materská škola*	*Materská škola*	100%

Source: Eurydice.

Ireland: Children enrolled in private pre-primary institutions are not included in the calculation of the percentage of children paying enrolment fees.

In most Member States of the European Union, admission to public sector pre-primary schools and other institutions is free of charge. On the other hand, in the private sector, parents often have to make a financial contribution. In four countries — Denmark, Austria, Finland and Sweden — where the only form of provision is non-school institutions, both sectors are fee-paying and this applies to all, or nearly all, children. In Belgium and the Netherlands, all children are guaranteed admission free of charge, even in the private grant-aided sector.

The same pattern is found in the EFTA/EEA countries and the CEECs. In Iceland, Norway and Slovakia, however, the pre-primary institutions are always fee-paying. In Liechtenstein, the Czech Republic, Hungary and Poland, pre-primary institutions in the public sector may be fee-paying. In Bulgaria and Romania, all institutions are free of charge.

EXPLANATORY NOTE

'Fee-paying' means that parents are required to pay fees other than charges for meals or certain optional, specific or additional activities.

PRIMARY EDUCATION

A SEPARATE LEVEL OF EDUCATION OR PART OF A SINGLE, CONTINUOUS STRUCTURE

In eleven Member States, primary education is a separate level of education. In most of these, it lasts six years. The shortest duration (four years) is found in the majority of the *Länder* in Germany and in Austria. In four Member States (Denmark, Portugal, Finland and Sweden), compulsory education is organized in a single, continuous structure with no division between a primary and a lower secondary stage. The information presented in this chapter refers to the first six years of the single structure in these Member States.

Primary education is divided into three stages in Belgium (French and German-speaking Communities) and Spain and into two in France and the United Kingdom (England, Wales and Northern Ireland). The single structures in Portugal and Finland are divided into three and two stages respectively.

In Figure D1, the names of the different structures and the corresponding stages of education are given in the original languages.

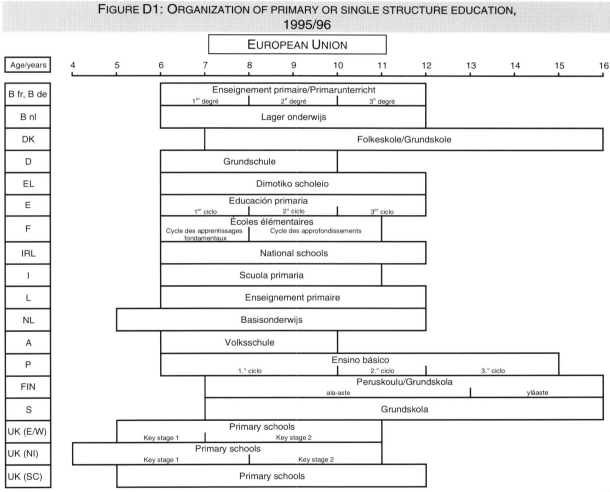

FIGURE D1: ORGANIZATION OF PRIMARY OR SINGLE STRUCTURE EDUCATION, 1995/96

Source: Eurydice.

Denmark: The name *folkeskole* is used only for schools coming under the municipalities.
Germany: The *Grundschule* lasts 4 years in 14 *Länder*. It lasts 6 years in Berlin and Brandenburg.
Netherlands: *Basisonderwijs* lasts 8 years. Compulsory education starts at age 5. Most children start *basisonderwijs* at age 4. Children who start at age 5 spend 7 years in *basisonderwijs*.
United Kingdom (E/W): Where a three tier system is in operation, pupils transfer from 'first' to 'middle' school at age 8 or 9 and from 'middle' school to secondary school at age 12 or 13.

EXPLANATORY NOTE
The diagram shows the age of pupils from the beginning of compulsory primary education to the end of primary education or the single structure. In most Member States, children can, under certain circumstances and if their parents so desire, start school before they reach compulsory school age.

In the EFTA/EEA countries, primary education in Liechtenstein consists of a separate level lasting five years. In Norway and Iceland, compulsory education is organized in a single structure as in the other Nordic countries. Iceland has one continuous stage running from age 6 to age 16. In Norway, this phase is of nine years divided into two stages, the first of which — *barnetrinnet* — takes in the first six years.

Amongst the CEECs, Bulgaria and Romania are exceptions to the rule, having four years of primary education and a separate secondary level of education. In the other four countries, compulsory education consists of a single structure which is divided into two stages.

FIGURE D1 (CONTINUED): ORGANIZATION OF PRIMARY OR SINGLE STRUCTURE EDUCATION, 1995/96

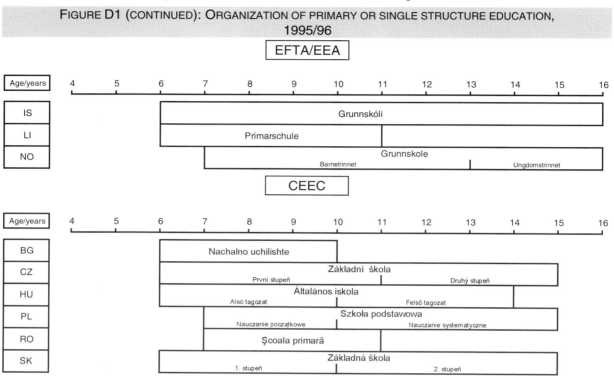

Source: Eurydice.

Hungary: The second stage of compulsory education (ages 10 to 14) is also provided in secondary education schools. This school — the *gimnázium* — provides 8 or 6 years of education from the age of either 10 or 12 years.

Slovakia: After the eighth year of compulsory education, pupils can continue their education in a secondary school.

EXPLANATORY NOTE

The diagram shows the age of pupils from the beginning of compulsory primary education to the end of primary education or the single structure. In most Member States, children can, under certain circumstances and if their parents so desire, start school before they reach compulsory school age.

PUPILS MOSTLY GROUPED BY AGE

The predominant model for forming classes in primary education is grouping children by age. In some Member States, however, mixed age classes are also found — in small schools in Belgium, Ireland, Portugal and Austria; in some mountain villages and on small islands in Italy; in the Netherlands, Finland, Sweden and the United Kingdom. In Denmark, schools may combine the pre-primary class and the first two years of the *folkeskole*.

Moreover, mixed classes seem to be the rule generally except in Ireland, where a quarter of all schools have single-sex classes, and in Finland, where sport is taught in single-sex groups from the third year.

Other criteria are sometimes used for constituting classes. In several Member States, classes are altered according to the educational activities being undertaken. In France, classes can be brought together for some subjects. In Finland and Sweden, pupils can also be grouped according to the subjects they have chosen. In these two Member States and in the Netherlands, some schools group together children of the same age for some activities and children of different ages for others. Finally, ability grouping is found in France and the Netherlands.

The EFTA/EEA countries and the CEECs organize their classes on lines fairly close to those followed in the European Union Member States. Pupils are usually grouped by age, although there are classes with children of different ages in some schools in Iceland and Norway. In Iceland, the Czech Republic and Hungary, there are ability groups in some schools. In Poland, in the second stage of compulsory education, girls and boys are separated for some activities, such as sport.

FIGURE D2: MAIN CRITERIA USED FOR CONSTITUTING PRIMARY CLASSES OTHER THAN BY AGE 1995/96		
MIXED AGES	ABILITY GROUPS	SINGLE-SEX GROUPS
EUROPEAN UNION		
Belgium, Ireland, Italy, Netherlands, Austria, Portugal, Finland, Sweden, United Kingdom	France, Netherlands	Ireland, Finland (sport, from the third year)
EFTA/EEA		
Iceland, Norway	Iceland	
CEEC		
	Czech Republic, Hungary	Poland (sport, second stage of compulsory education)

Source: Eurydice.

The extent and nature of regulations on class organization in primary schools vary from one Member State to another. Some countries, such as the Netherlands, Sweden and the United Kingdom, do not have statutory provisions for the composition of classes, whereas others such as Germany, Spain, Italy, Austria and Portugal legislate widely. The aspects most frequently subject to regulation are methods of grouping pupils by age and sex, the allocation of classes to teachers, and class sizes. Conversely, the possibility of grouping pupils according to criteria other than age are rarely provided for in the legislation. This would rather appear to be an educational option left to the school.

In the EFTA/EEA countries, the age criterion is the subject of regulations. Iceland and Norway also set maximum class sizes. Within the CEECs, Hungary and Bulgaria frequently resort to regulations whereas Romania and Slovakia do not.

EXPLANATORY NOTE
The table shows the methods used for constituting classes. It does not refer to the constitution of smaller groups within each class for particular activities. In countries in which pupils may be required to repeat the year, this table does not cover the situation of pupils who are behind or in advance of their age group.

─────── **CLASS SIZE NORMS: MAXIMA OF 25 TO 35 PUPILS** ───────

Most of the European Union Member States have regulations stipulating the maximum and/or minimum number of pupils in a class or group. The norms for maximum class sizes vary considerably from one Member State to another.

Where norms are defined, the maximum never exceeds 35, as in Ireland. However, there and in Greece, more favourable norms can be set for special situations such as the inclusion of several age groups or of disadvantaged pupils in the class. In some countries, a minimum number of pupils is also required to establish a class. This is lowest in Austria (10) while in Italy and Portugal the minimum is 20. In Greece, the minimum number of pupils can be less than 15 in one- and two-teacher schools.

In those Member States with no regulations on class sizes, individual schools have the power to decide how classes are made up. They generally do this taking into account educational guidelines and classroom sizes. In France, however, the *Inspecteur d'Académie* can set both the average number of pupils per class for that area and also the maximum number according to the specific criteria of that *Académie*.

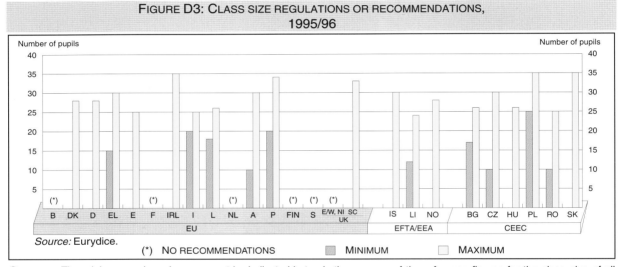

FIGURE D3: CLASS SIZE REGULATIONS OR RECOMMENDATIONS, 1995/96

Source: Eurydice.

(*) NO RECOMMENDATIONS   ▦ MINIMUM   ☐ MAXIMUM

Germany: The minimum and maximum cannot be indicated but only the average of the reference figures for the class size of all *Länder*.
Portugal: The minima and maxima are 26 and 34 respectively for 40 square metre classrooms, and 20 and 26 for classrooms between 35 and 40 square metres.
Czech Republic: In exceptional cases, there can be more than 30 pupils in a class.
Hungary: Regulations prescribe an average number of pupils per class (20) as well as a maximum.

In all the EFTA/EEA countries and the CEECs, the maximum number of pupils per class is prescribed in regulations, and varies from 35 in Poland and Slovakia to 25 in Romania. The maxima can be lower in composite classes with pupils of different ages or at different stages (in Iceland and Norway) or at the start of primary education (in Iceland and Slovakia). In some countries, minimum class sizes are also laid down. In the Czech Republic and Romania, the statutory minimum is 10 pupils while in Poland it is 25.

ONE TEACHER PER CLASS,
——— BUT OFTEN REPLACED FOR SOME SPECIALIZED SUBJECTS ———

In primary education throughout the European Union and in the first years of the single structure, one teacher is usually responsible for the class. These teachers teach most subjects and are sometimes replaced by other teachers for certain specialized activities, such as physical education and sport, music and religious education. In Denmark, however, each subject is taught by a different teacher. In Italy, two or three teachers routinely share the teaching of all subjects. They take the class in turns and also have a spell of some hours in the day where they work together. In Germany, Ireland, Finland and the United Kingdom (England, Wales and Northern Ireland), a single teacher is usually responsible for the class for the whole week. Finally, in France, the Netherlands and Sweden, several patterns of dividing up the teaching amongst the teachers are found at the same time.

In the EFTA/EEA countries, various patterns of organization are found in Iceland and Norway, while in Liechtenstein one teacher is responsible for the class except for some specialized activities.

In the CEECs, 7-year-olds usually have a number of teachers, one of whom is responsible for the class while the others teach subjects such as sport and music. Only in Poland is there one teacher with sole responsibility for all subjects.

In view of the extent of variation in the organization of teaching amongst the teachers, the situations described above and in Figure D4 refer exclusively to children of about 7 years of age. These variations are related in particular to the pupils' progress through the school. Thus in Belgium (German-speaking Community) and Sweden, differences in organization are found between the beginning and the end of primary education. In Germany and Finland, pupils are gradually introduced to subject teachers from the third year so as to prepare them for the transition to the secondary school where they will have only subject teachers. In Portugal, in the second stage of *ensino básico*, different teachers are each responsible for a group of subjects. In the United Kingdom (England, Wales and Northern Ireland), at the very beginning of primary education, reception class teachers have the help of a classroom assistant.

FIGURE D4: MAIN MODELS FOR DIVIDING TEACHING AND SUBJECTS AMONGST THE TEACHERS (AROUND AGE 7), 1995/96

EU   EFTA/EEA + CEEC

☐ ☐ ONE TEACHER WITH SOLE RESPONSIBILITY FOR ALL SUBJECTS

▨ ▨ SEVERAL METHODS

▓ ▨ ONE TEACHER ROUTINELY REPLACED BY OTHERS FOR SPECIALIZED ACTIVITIES AND/OR A NUMBER OF TEACHERS WORKING TOGETHER

Source: Eurydice.

Denmark: Each subject is taught by a different teacher.

FROM 525 TO 950 HOURS A YEAR OF TEACHING
FOR 7-YEAR-OLDS

In most Member States, pupils attend school five days a week. They attend six days a week in Luxembourg and in some regions of Italy. In Germany, Austria and Portugal (in the second stage of *ensino básico*), teaching can be provided on five or six days a week. The number of hours spent in class in any day also varies according to the Member State, the day of the week and pupils' ages. Given the wide variations in the organization of time in schools, an indicator showing the **total annual taught hours** has been calculated to permit comparison. Variations — sometimes considerable — may be observed in the annual number of taught hours across the Member States.

Figure D5 shows the annual course load of pupils around the age of 7 years. At this age, they are at very different points in their education, depending on the education system that they are in. While Danish, Finnish and Swedish children are in their first year of compulsory education, others (in the Netherlands and the United Kingdom (England, Wales and Scotland)) are starting their third year, or even their fourth year, for those in Luxembourg and the United Kingdom (Northern Ireland).

There are less marked differences in the school experience of children in the EFTA/EEA countries and the CEECs, where at age 7 they are all in the first or second year of compulsory education.

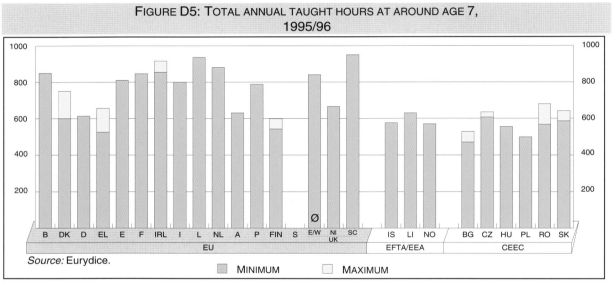

FIGURE D5: TOTAL ANNUAL TAUGHT HOURS AT AROUND AGE 7, 1995/96

Source: Eurydice.

Italy: The calculation takes into account a deduction of 30 minutes a day for breaks, although the duration of such breaks is not officially set, but left to the teacher's discretion. The official annual load comes to 900 hours, including breaks.
Finland: This is based on periods of 45 minutes each. The law also authorizes 50-minute periods.
Sweden: The new timetable introduced in 1995/96 represents 6 665 hours of teaching. The schools are free to divide up these hours over the 9 years of the *grundskola*, whilst ensuring that the children attain certain targets at the end of the fifth and ninth years.
United Kingdom (E/W): The annual number of taught hours is an average. The figures exclude time spent on registration and the daily act of worship.
Bulgaria: If the three additional non-mandatory hours per week (often spent on foreign languages, sport or art subjects) are taken into account, the annual load varies from a minimum of 533 hours to a maximum of 600 hours.

EXPLANATORY NOTE
The taught time presented in this graph does not represent the teacher's work-load but that of the pupil. Annual taught time is calculated by taking the average daily load, multiplied by the number of school-days in the year. Breaks of all types (recreation or other) and time spent on optional extra courses are excluded from the calculation. The tables showing the method of calculation appear in the annex.

MORE TAUGHT HOURS AT AROUND AGE 10

Figure D6 shows the annual course load of pupils around the age of 10 years. At this age, children in some Member States are in their last year of primary education (in Germany, France, Italy, Austria and the United Kingdom (England, Wales and Northern Ireland)).

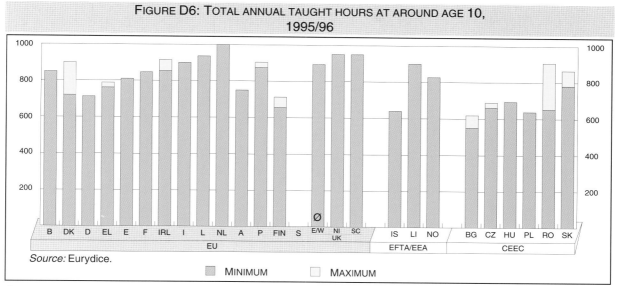

FIGURE D6: TOTAL ANNUAL TAUGHT HOURS AT AROUND AGE 10, 1995/96

Source: Eurydice.

MINIMUM   MAXIMUM

Germany and **Austria**: Data refer to the age of 9 years (fourth and final year of primary school).

Italy: The calculation takes into account a deduction of 30 minutes a day for breaks, although the duration of such breaks is not officially set, but left to the teacher's discretion. The official annual load amounts to 1 000 hours, including breaks.

Finland: This is based on periods of 45 minutes each. The law also authorizes 50-minute periods.

Sweden: The new timetable introduced in 1995/96 represents 6 665 hours of teaching. The schools are free to divide up these hours over the 9 years of the *grundskola*, whilst ensuring that the children attain certain targets at the end of the fifth and ninth years.

United Kingdom (E/W): The annual number of taught hours is an average. The figures exclude time spent on registration and the daily act of worship.

Bulgaria: If the four additional non-mandatory hours (often spent on foreign languages, sport or art subjects) are taken into account, the annual load varies from a minimum of 638 hours to a maximum of 718 hours.

Comparison of the annual load of pupils aged 7 and 10 years shows that more than half of all Member States have adopted a slightly reduced timetable for younger children at the start of their primary education. This reduction can range from 50 to over 100 hours and is particularly marked in the United Kingdom (Northern Ireland).

In the three EFTA/EEA countries and all the CEECs, the same pattern appears, with the annual taught time of pupils being less at the start of primary education than at around 10 years of age. It increases considerably at the age of 10 in Liechtenstein.

FIGURE D7: MINIMUM ANNUAL HOURS OF TAUGHT TIME AT ABOUT AGE 7 AND AGE 10, 1995/96

	EUROPEAN UNION							
	B	**DK**	**D**	**EL**	**E**	**F**	**IRL**	**I**	**L**
About age 7	849	600	613	525	810	846	854	800	936
About age 10	849	720	712	761	810	846	854	900	936

	NL	**A**	**P**	**FIN**	**S**	**UK (E/W)**	**UK (NI)**	**UK (SC)**
About age 7	880	630	788	542	not applicable	840	665	950
About age 10	1 000	750	875	656	not applicable	893	950	950

	EFTA/EEA			CEEC					
	IS	**LI**	**NO**	**BG**	**CZ**	**HU**	**PL**	**RO**	**SK**
About age 7	576	630	570	470	607	555	499	567	586
About age 10	640	900	827	550	662	694	638	652	781

Source: Eurydice.

COMPULSORY SUBJECTS:
——————— A COMMON BASIS BUT DIFFERENCES IN EMPHASIS ———————

In some Member States, the curricula and official directives give teachers or schools freedom to determine how much time to allocate to different subjects or when to introduce a specific subject. This is the case in the Netherlands, Portugal (first stage of *ensino básico*), Sweden and the United Kingdom. In Denmark, the municipalities are free to follow the Ministry recommendations or not. When the curricula prescribe the timetabling of the various subjects, it is possible to compare the relative amount of time devoted to each of these subjects.

In primary education, at about 7 years of age, major disparities are observed in the time allocated to the teaching of the mother tongue. Thus, whereas nearly half of the teaching hours are devoted to this in Denmark, only 4% of time is spent on it in Luxembourg. This very small percentage is explained by the fact that teaching is mainly in French and German (both being national languages) while Letzeburgesch — the mother tongue — is essentially a vernacular language.

Differences in the amount of time devoted to the teaching of mathematics and sport show a little less variation from one Member State to the other, ranging from 11 to 22% and from 5 to 15% respectively. The importance given to arts and science subjects, however, varies considerably. Thus in Spain, nearly 20% of time is spent on science subjects and 13% on artistic activities. The reverse is the case in Ireland.

In the EFTA/EEA countries and the CEECs, for children of around 7 years of age, the mother tongue has a major place in the curriculum, along with mathematics and art. These three subjects take up at least 55% of the timetable and as much as 80% in the Czech Republic, Hungary and Poland.

FIGURE D8: DISTRIBUTION OF ANNUAL HOURS OF TEACHING OF COMPULSORY SUBJECTS
AT AROUND AGE 7, 1995/96

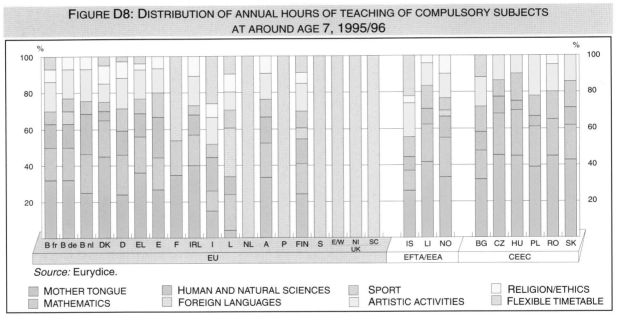

Source: Eurydice.

■ MOTHER TONGUE   ■ HUMAN AND NATURAL SCIENCES   ■ SPORT   □ RELIGION/ETHICS
■ MATHEMATICS   ▨ FOREIGN LANGUAGES   □ ARTISTIC ACTIVITIES   ■ FLEXIBLE TIMETABLE

Denmark: Figures stem from Ministry's guidelines for the distribution of lessons.
Germany: The calculation of the annual hours of teaching in each subject is based on the half-day school (*Halbtagsschule*) with a five-day school week and 7-year-olds in the second year of primary school. Other subjects are included under the heading 'flexible timetable'.
Spain: The percentages shown here are those for schools coming under the Ministry of Education and Culture. In the Autonomous Community of the Balearic Islands, which comes under the Ministry of Education and Culture, and in the Autonomous Communities with full powers in education, the timetabling may vary slightly within the same overall total.
France: The flexible timetable is divided into 130 hours of 'discovery of the world and civic education', 195 hours of art, physical education and sport, and 65 hours of supervised homework. Some 32 hours of modern language teaching can be taken from the mother tongue timetable.
Ireland: 'Mother tongue' refers to English (18%) and Irish (22%).
Finland: Within the limits of the national curriculum, schools can decide when a subject should be introduced and how to distribute the subjects over the 6 years of the first stage of the *peruskoulu*. The figures are estimates based on the minima given for the whole 6 years of the first stage.
Sweden: Schools are free to decide when to introduce a topic and how to distribute the teaching hours over the 9 years of the *grundskola*, provided the pupils reach certain targets at the end of the fifth and ninth years.
Czech Republic: Since 1993/94, there has been an experiment with a new, more flexible 'general curriculum' *(obecná škola)*.

At around age 10, the relative volume of mother tongue teaching drops in almost all Member States of the European Union. Only in France does it still occupy about one third of the timetable.

At this age, compulsory foreign language learning tends to be a general phenomenon in a majority of the Member States. The sciences also become more important.

In the CEECs, a greater range of subjects is provided around the age of 10 and this is at the expense of the mother tongue in particular.

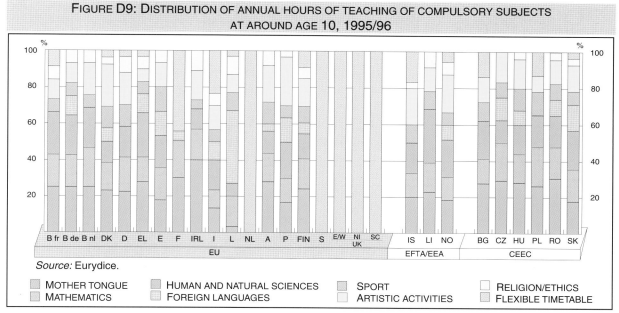

FIGURE D9: DISTRIBUTION OF ANNUAL HOURS OF TEACHING OF COMPULSORY SUBJECTS AT AROUND AGE 10, 1995/96

Source: Eurydice.

░ MOTHER TONGUE	▒ HUMAN AND NATURAL SCIENCES
░ MATHEMATICS	░ FOREIGN LANGUAGES

▓ SPORT	☐ RELIGION/ETHICS
☐ ARTISTIC ACTIVITIES	░ FLEXIBLE TIMETABLE

Denmark: Figures stem from Ministry's guidelines for the distribution of lessons.

Germany: The calculation of the annual hours of teaching in each subject is based on the half-day school (*Halbtagsschule*) with a five-day school week and 9-year-olds in the fourth year of primary school. Nine-year-olds have the opportunity to learn a foreign language as a separate subject in only 2 *Länder*. In the other *Länder*, foreign language learning is integrated with other subjects. Other subjects are included under 'flexible timetable'.

Spain: The percentages shown here are those for schools coming under the Ministry of Education and Culture. In the Autonomous Community of the Balearic Islands, which comes under the Ministry of Education and Culture, and in the Autonomous Communities with full powers in education, the timetabling may vary slightly within the same overall total.

France: A maximum of 47 hours are set aside for learning a modern language out of the 254 hours allocated to mother tongue learning. The flexible timetable is divided into 130 hours of 'history, geography, civic education and science and technology', 178 hours of art, physical education and sport and 65 hours of supervised homework.

Ireland: 'Mother tongue' refers to English (18%) and Irish (22%).

Portugal: Technology is included under 'artistic activities'. The number of hours of sport depends on the availability of staff and facilities. Lessons in religion and ethics are optional: pupils can choose to study 'personal and social development' instead.

Finland: Within the limits of the national curriculum, schools can decide when a subject should be introduced and how to distribute the subjects over the 6 years of the first stage of the *peruskoulu*. The figures are estimates based on the minima given for the whole 6 years of the first stage.

Sweden: Schools are free to decide when to introduce a topic and how to distribute the teaching hours over the 9 years of the *grundskola*, provided the pupils reach certain targets at the end of the fifth and ninth years.

Czech Republic: Since 1994/95, there has been an experiment with a new, more flexible 'civil curriculum' *(obcanská škola)*.

EXLANATORY NOTE

The graphs show the relationship between the annual time to be allocated to the various compulsory subjects and the total minimum number of hours of teaching in the year. Figures expressed as hours of teaching and as a proportion of taught time are contained in the annex.

In the interest of clarity, some subjects have been grouped together. This is the case, for example, with human and natural sciences which include subjects such as 'school life and culture', environmental studies, technology, social and political instruction, and handwork.

THE FIRST CONTACT WITH A FOREIGN LANGUAGE
TAKES PLACE INCREASINGLY EARLY

A real start is being made on foreign language teaching at primary level in most Member States of the European Union. When this is compulsory, it generally starts from the third year of primary school, or even later. Only Luxembourg is an exception, with German being introduced from the start of the first year of primary school and French from the second year. These two national languages, regarded as foreign languages, are used for teaching the various subjects instead of the mother tongue, Letzeburgesch, as pupils progress in their schooling. In France, an introduction to foreign languages is gradually being established for children in primary school (ages 7 to 9). This has the aim of introducing generally the teaching previously provided on an experimental basis.

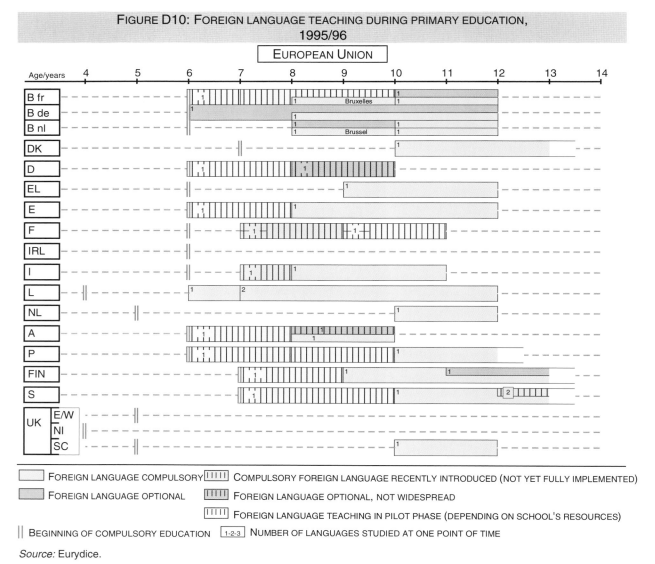

FIGURE D10: FOREIGN LANGUAGE TEACHING DURING PRIMARY EDUCATION, 1995/96

EUROPEAN UNION

Source: Eurydice.

Finland: The graph shows the most common practice. Both compulsory and optional languages can be started earlier or later, depending on the school.

Sweden: English and a second foreign language are compulsory. All pupils learn English from the fourth year at the latest. Schools themselves decide when to introduce foreign language lessons, but all children must have reached set levels of competence in English at the ages of 11 and 15 years. In place of a second foreign language, pupils can choose to extend their knowledge of English, sign language or Swedish (for pupils with another mother tongue).

United Kingdom (E/W): A foreign language is taught in some primary schools, but this practice is not widespread.

United Kingdom (SC): Foreign language teaching is not formally compulsory but the local authorities are strongly encouraged to ensure that all pupils are taught at least one foreign language at the end of primary education.

In a good number of Member States, the early learning of a foreign language also appears from the beginning of compulsory education in the form of experiments (Belgium (French Community), Germany, Spain, Austria, Portugal, Finland and Sweden) or on an optional basis (Belgium (German-speaking Community)).

In Ireland and the United Kingdom (England, Wales and Northern Ireland), the compulsory curriculum does not include foreign languages.

In the EFTA/EEA countries, foreign language teaching is compulsory in Iceland, from the age of 11 years, and in Norway, from the age of 9 years. In Liechtenstein, it was introduced in September 1996 in all primary schools.

In a majority of the CEECs, optional foreign language teaching is provided from the beginning of compulsory education. This is compulsory in the Czech Republic and Romania from the ages of 9 and 8 respectively.

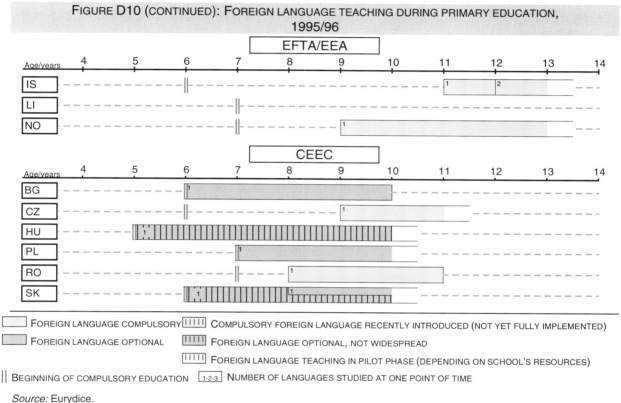

FIGURE D10 (CONTINUED): FOREIGN LANGUAGE TEACHING DURING PRIMARY EDUCATION, 1995/96

Source: Eurydice.

Liechtenstein: Since the start of the 1996/97 school year, all pupils in the third year of primary school have one English lesson per week. This is not explicitly set-out in the curriculum, however, and it is provisionally being given in the place of one of the other subjects.

Poland: Optional foreign languages can be introduced at any time during primary education, depending on the school's budget. The graph refers to state public schools. In the other schools, foreign language teaching can be introduced on a compulsory basis. Foreign language learning becomes compulsory at age 11, in the second stage of the single structure.

Slovakia: In the *základná škola*, providing specialized foreign language teaching, a foreign language is compulsory from age 8.

EXPLANATORY NOTE

The graph presents only languages regarded as modern and foreign. Consequently, Irish, Letzeburgesch and regional languages are excluded, although provision is made for them in certain Member States.

ENGLISH: THE MOST TAUGHT FOREIGN LANGUAGE
IN PRIMARY SCHOOLS

The two figures below show the percentages of primary school pupils learning English and/or French in the course of 1994/95. The data refer to foreign languages being learned by each pupil during the school year 1994/95 as opposed to those learned throughout primary education. A low percentage may thus be explained either by the fact that teaching of the foreign language starts late in the pupils' school career or because it is not compulsory and therefore involves only a few pupils.

In the European Union, the most taught foreign language in primary schools is English. It is learned by 26% of non-Anglophone European pupils. Those pupils who learn English the most are the Spanish and Finnish.

Of all the other foreign languages taught, French is in second place with an average of 4% in the European Union as a whole. The proportions of pupils concerned do not exceed a small percentage, except in the Flemish Community in Belgium and in Luxembourg, where all pupils learn French from the fifth and the second year of primary school respectively. In both these cases, French is one of the national languages of the country.

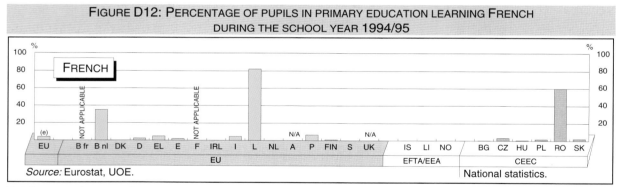

FIGURE D11: PERCENTAGE OF PUPILS IN PRIMARY EDUCATION LEARNING ENGLISH DURING THE SCHOOL YEAR 1994/95

Source: Eurostat, UOE.

National statistics.

Belgium: 1993/94.
Czech Republic, Romania and **Slovakia**: Data refer to 'basic' education (primary and lower secondary).
Poland and **Slovakia**: 1993/94.

FIGURE D12: PERCENTAGE OF PUPILS IN PRIMARY EDUCATION LEARNING FRENCH DURING THE SCHOOL YEAR 1994/95

Source: Eurostat, UOE.

National statistics.

Belgium: 1993/94. In the German-speaking Community, all pupils learn French from the first year primary.
Czech Republic, Romania and **Slovakia**: Data refer to 'basic' education (primary and lower secondary).
Poland and **Slovakia**: 1993/94.

Many Norwegian primary pupils learn English (66%) while in Iceland the corresponding figure is 15%. No children are taught French in these countries.

In the CEECs, the highest percentages of pupils learning English are found in the Czech Republic and Romania, with 48% and 35% respectively. In the CEECs for which data are available, the percentage of pupils learning French is small, except in Romania (60%).

EXPLANATORY NOTE
The data refer to foreign languages being studied by each pupil at one point of time, as opposed to those studied throughout their schooling.

———— FEW PUPILS LEARN TWO OR MORE FOREIGN LANGUAGES ————

As seen in Figure D10 above, foreign language teaching is either available to or compulsory for primary pupils in most European countries. In certain Member States of the European Union, it is even possible to learn two languages (in Luxembourg, Austria, Finland and Sweden). Figure D13 enables an estimate to be made of the proportion of pupils taking such courses. It shows the percentages of primary pupils learning one, two or no foreign languages in 1994/95. The percentages are calculated over the total primary school population of each country. The most frequently learned languages differ from country to country and languages other than English and French are therefore taken into account here.

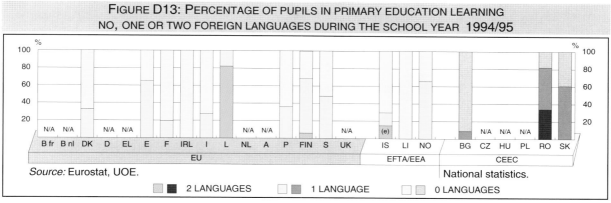

FIGURE D13: PERCENTAGE OF PUPILS IN PRIMARY EDUCATION LEARNING NO, ONE OR TWO FOREIGN LANGUAGES DURING THE SCHOOL YEAR 1994/95

Source: Eurostat, UOE.

National statistics.

Sweden: 1993/94. Pupils in the first 6 years of the *grundskola*.
Romania: Data refer to 'basic' education (primary and lower secondary).
Slovakia: 1993/94. Data refer to the number of children learning one or more foreign languages in 'basic' education (primary and lower secondary).

In all Member States for which data are available, a fairly large percentage of primary pupils were learning no foreign language in 1994/95 except in Luxembourg, which is distinguished by the fact that all pupils are taught two national languages as foreign languages, German from the first year and French from the second. This is the explanation for the 80% of primary school pupils who learn two foreign languages simultaneously. In Finland, the corresponding percentage was 6%.

In Spain and Finland, more than half of all primary pupils are learning one foreign language. In Denmark, France, Italy and Sweden, the proportions range from 19 to 48%.

In Ireland, foreign language teaching is not provided in primary schools.

The EFTA/EEA countries reveal three contrasting patterns. In primary education, 70% of Icelandic pupils learn no foreign language, the other 30% being equally divided as between those who learn one foreign language and those who learn two. In Norway, two thirds of pupils at this level of education are learning a foreign language. No primary pupils are shown as learning languages in Liechtenstein, such teaching having been introduced there in September 1996.

EXPLANATORY NOTE
The data refer to foreign languages being studied by each pupil at one point of time, as opposed to those studied throughout their schooling.

PROMOTION TO THE NEXT CLASS: ——————— AUTOMATIC OR SUBJECT TO REPEATING THE YEAR ———————

The management of pupils' learning difficulties varies from one Member State to the other. In half of the Member States, pupils who have not acquired an adequate mastery of the curriculum at the end of the year are made to repeat the year. Repeating is however imposed only in exceptional circumstances in Greece, Portugal (since 1992) and Finland. The decision to keep a child in one stage of education can be taken only at the end of each stage in Spain and France. Denmark, Ireland, Sweden and the United Kingdom have opted for automatic promotion from class to class throughout compulsory education and they provide other educational support measures for pupils in difficulty.

Two of the EFTA/EEA countries, Iceland and Norway, also have automatic promotion throughout compulsory education. Repeating a year is possible in Liechtenstein, but exceptional.

The practice of making pupils with difficulties repeat a year each year is a feature of the six CEECs.

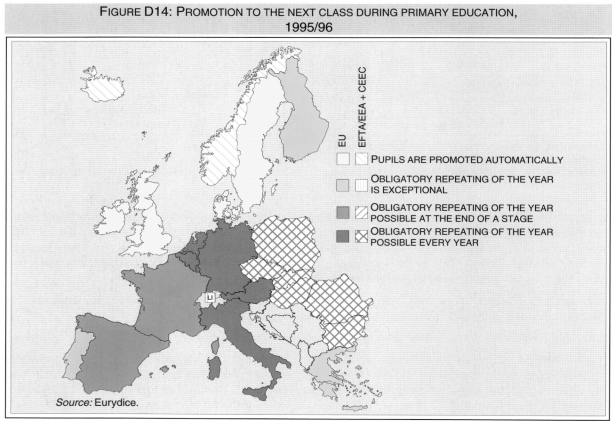

FIGURE D14: PROMOTION TO THE NEXT CLASS DURING PRIMARY EDUCATION, 1995/96

Source: Eurydice.

Belgium (B fr): Repeating a year is possible, but this is only allowed once or twice throughout the 6 years of primary school.
Germany: All pupils move automatically from the first to the second year of the primary school. As a rule, from the second year of the primary school onwards, each pupil is assigned to a suitable class, depending on his/her level of attainment, either by being promoted to the next year or by repeating a year.
Spain: Repeating a year at the end of a stage *(ciclo)* can only take place once during primary education.
Austria: All pupils move automatically from the first to the second year of the primary school.
Portugal: Since 1992, repeating is exceptional in the first stage *(ciclo)*. Since 1994, at the end of the second stage, pupils can be made to repeat the year if they are severely behind in more than three subjects, including Portuguese and mathematics.
Bulgaria: Repeating a year is possible, except in the first year of primary school where summer courses are organized for those in difficulty.

CHOICES AT THE END OF PRIMARY EDUCATION

Requiring pupils to choose their direction of study in one of several possible branches at the beginning of lower secondary education is a relatively rare pattern of organization nowadays in the Member States of the European Union. This pattern is found in Belgium, Germany, Luxembourg, the Netherlands and Austria. In some of these Member States (Belgium, Germany and the Netherlands), there is a first year or stage common to all pupils in order to delay the moment of specialization.

FIGURE D15: MAIN PATTERNS OF ORGANIZATION OF COURSES AT THE BEGINNING OF LOWER SECONDARY EDUCATION, 1995/96

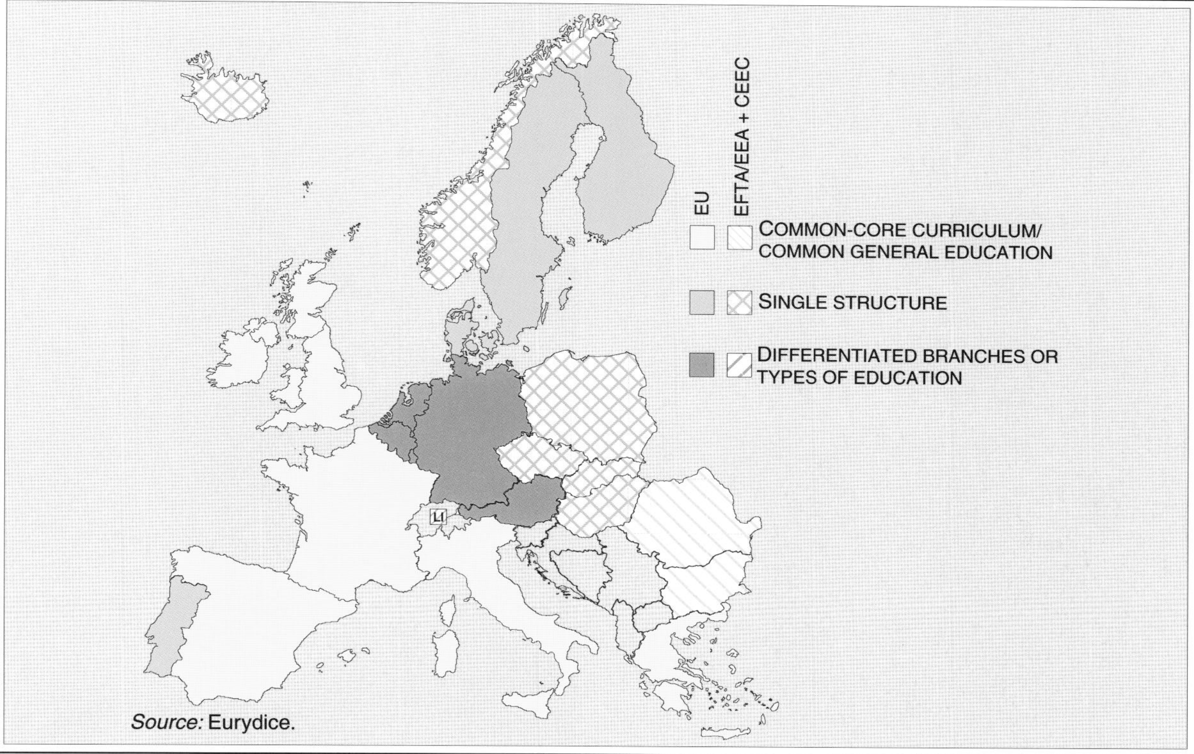

COMMON-CORE CURRICULUM/ COMMON GENERAL EDUCATION

SINGLE STRUCTURE

DIFFERENTIATED BRANCHES OR TYPES OF EDUCATION

Source: Eurydice.

Czech Republic, Hungary and **Slovakia**: There is also a possibility of entering secondary school around the age of 10 or 11, parallel to continuing studies in the single structure.

In the Nordic countries (Denmark, Finland and Sweden) and in Portugal, pupils follow a rather different path, as their choice of direction is made at around age 16, at the end of compulsory education which is organized as a continuum, with no transition from a primary to a lower secondary stage. Between the two extremes, a third model is found for the transition to secondary education. This consists of a single general course, usually known as the 'common core' curriculum during the first three or four years of secondary education. This model, which also tends to delay specialization until the end of lower secondary education, is found in the southern Member States of the Union (Greece, Spain, France and Italy) and also in Ireland and the United Kingdom.

Of the EFTA/EEA countries, it is only in Liechtenstein that pupils have to choose their direction of study at the end of primary education. Norway and Iceland, like the other Nordic countries, have a single, continuous structure throughout compulsory education.

In the six CEECs, there are two patterns of transition. Lower secondary education with a common core curriculum is found in Bulgaria and Romania. The single structure extends without a break from primary into secondary education for Czech, Hungarian, Polish and Slovak pupils.

EXPLANATORY NOTE
The existence of a choice between differentiated branches or types of education reflects either distinctions between general, technical and vocational secondary education, or the existence of an academic hierarchy within general education.

SECONDARY EDUCATION

THE END OF COMPULSORY EDUCATION OFTEN COINCIDES ── WITH THE END OF LOWER SECONDARY EDUCATION ──

The way in which secondary education is organized differs from one Member State to another, but it usually comprises two stages of varying length or even a three stage division. The end of the first stage and the end of the single structure system often correspond to the minimum school leaving age.

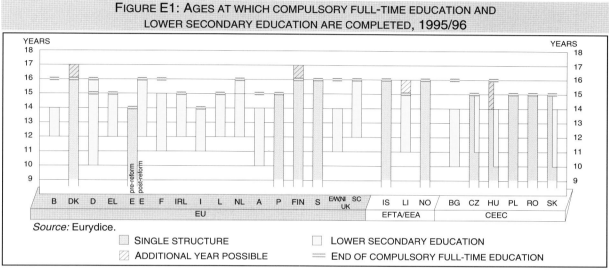

FIGURE E1: AGES AT WHICH COMPULSORY FULL-TIME EDUCATION AND LOWER SECONDARY EDUCATION ARE COMPLETED, 1995/96

Source: Eurydice.

☐ SINGLE STRUCTURE   ☐ LOWER SECONDARY EDUCATION
▨ ADDITIONAL YEAR POSSIBLE   ═ END OF COMPULSORY FULL-TIME EDUCATION

Belgium: Secondary education is divided into 3 two-year stages. The first 2 years correspond to lower secondary education.
Germany: Full-time compulsory education lasts 9 years in 12 *Länder* and 10 years in 4 *Länder*. It therefore finishes at age 15 or 16.
Czech Republic, Hungary and **Slovakia**: In parallel to the single structure which ends at age 15 or 16, depending on the country, lower secondary education can be started from the age of 10 or 11 years.

The age at which pupils start secondary education in the European Union varies from one Member State to another. It is generally set at age 11 or 12, the earliest start being in Germany and Austria, from age 10. The first stage of secondary education is in most cases either three or four years long, except in Germany, where it is five or six years, and in Belgium, where it is only two years. In Denmark, Spain (pre-reform), Portugal, Finland and Sweden, there is no separate lower secondary education, compulsory education being organized in one single, continuous structure over nine years.

In the EFTA/EEA countries, the end of compulsory education coincides with the last year of the single structure in Iceland and Norway, while in Liechtenstein, 15-year-old pupils at the end of lower secondary education are no longer subject to compulsory education.

In three of the CEECs the Czech Republic, Poland and Romania, the end of lower secondary education or the single structure coincides with the minimum school leaving age, whereas compulsory education continues for one more year for pupils attending the *gymnázium* in Slovakia and for two more years for pupils in Bulgaria and Hungary.

EXPLANATORY NOTE
According to the ISCED classification, the last three years of educación general básica (in Spain pre-reform), of the folkeskole (in Denmark), of ensino básico (in Portugal), of the peruskoulu/grundskola (in Finland), and of the grundskola (in Sweden) are classified as lower secondary education (ISCED 2). The same applies to the last three years of the single structure in Iceland and Norway amongst the EFTA/EEA countries.

EDUCATIONAL PATHWAYS ACROSS THE MEMBER STATES:
FROM A SINGLE COURSE TO SPECIALIZED BRANCHES

Figure E2 shows the organization of the secondary education structures by country. Different branches of education, their duration and their position in this level of education are indicated.

FIGURE E2: ORGANIZATION OF SECONDARY EDUCATION STRUCTURES, 1995/96

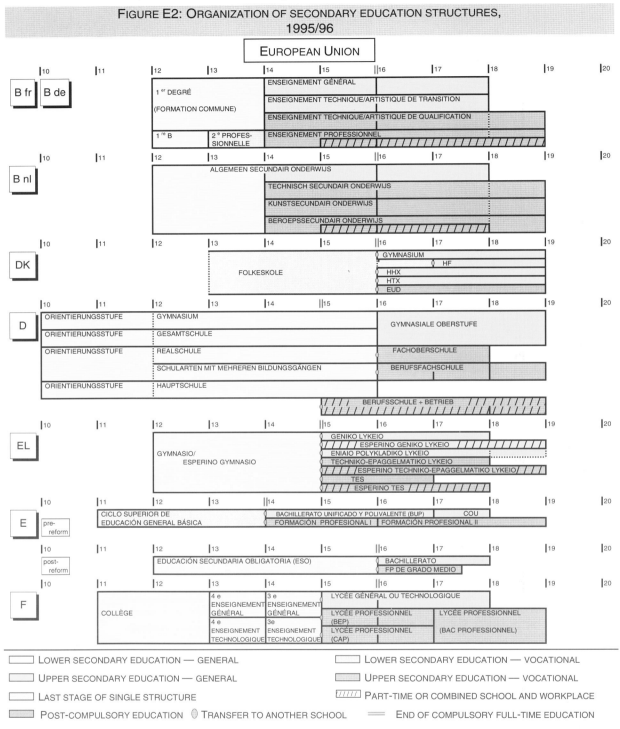

Source: Eurydice.

Germany: The first 2 years of secondary education can be provided in separate organizational units independent of the standard school types. Compulsory education normally comprises 9 years of full-time education (10 years in 4 *Länder*). Once pupils have completed their full-time compulsory education, those who do not continue in full-time general upper secondary or vocational education must attend part-time education, normally for 3 years, in accordance with the duration of training for recognised occupations for which formal training is required *(anerkannter Ausbildungsberuf)*.

Spain: The pre-reform structure is shown because the post-reform structure is not yet complete (LOGSE).

FIGURE E2 (CONTINUED): ORGANIZATION OF SECONDARY EDUCATION STRUCTURES, 1995/96

EUROPEAN UNION (CONTINUED)

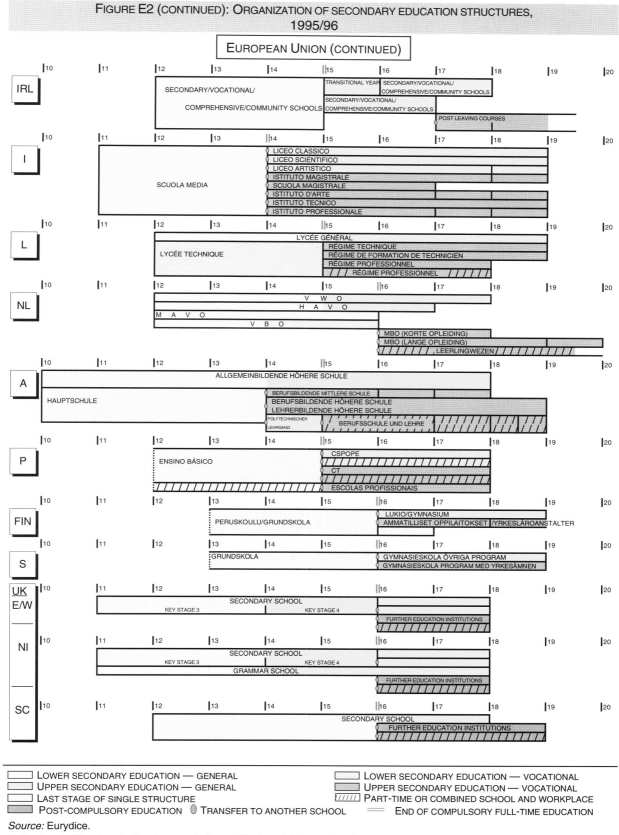

LOWER SECONDARY EDUCATION — GENERAL
UPPER SECONDARY EDUCATION — GENERAL
LAST STAGE OF SINGLE STRUCTURE
POST-COMPULSORY EDUCATION ⊙ TRANSFER TO ANOTHER SCHOOL

LOWER SECONDARY EDUCATION — VOCATIONAL
UPPER SECONDARY EDUCATION — VOCATIONAL
PART-TIME OR COMBINED SCHOOL AND WORKPLACE
END OF COMPULSORY FULL-TIME EDUCATION

Source: Eurydice.

Netherlands: Vocational education was to be modified as of 1 August 1997.

Portugal: Evening classes equivalent to the third level of *ensino básico* and upper secondary education (CSPOPE and CT) are gradually being replaced by a system of course credit units.

United Kingdom (E/W): Where a three-tier system is in operation, pupils transfer from 'first' to 'middle' school at age 8 or 9 and from 'middle' school to secondary school at age 12 or 13.

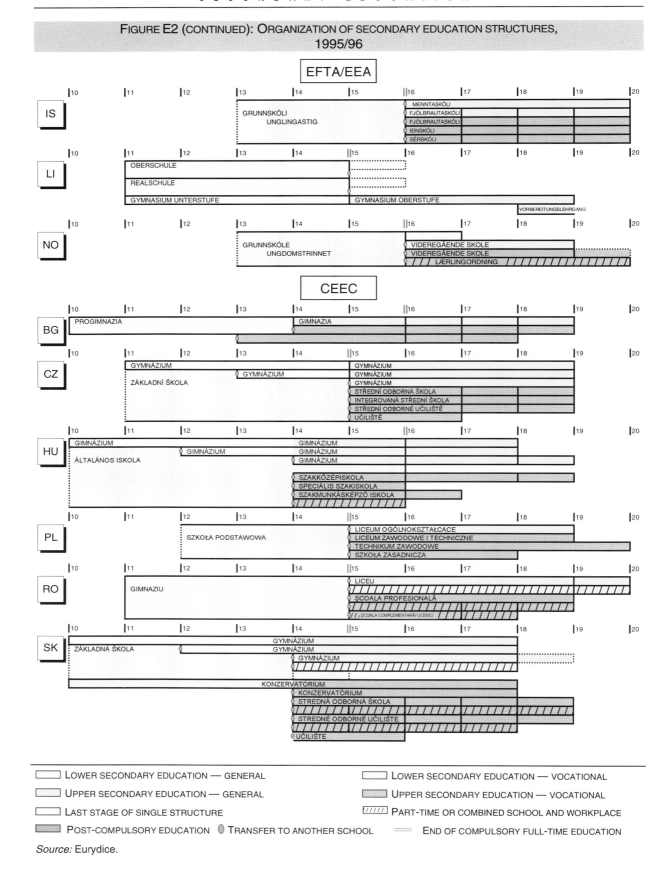

FIGURE E2 (CONTINUED): ORGANIZATION OF SECONDARY EDUCATION STRUCTURES, 1995/96

Source: Eurydice.

The majority of Member States have 'integrated' structures in lower secondary education, with all pupils following a common curriculum of general education. Only a few Member States have different types of course at the lower secondary stage. In upper secondary education, differentiated courses of education are provided in all the European Union Member States. Leaving aside differences of name, it is possible to distinguish two major categories: general, providing education leading to entry to higher education, and vocational, providing qualifications both in preparation for working life and for pursuing further studies.

In Denmark, Portugal, Finland and Sweden, 'secondary education' refers to what other countries regard as upper secondary education. Lower secondary education is not found there as such, the nine years of compulsory education being provided in a single, continuous structure.

In Greece, France and Italy, the two levels of secondary education are provided in different schools. The first level is referred to as 'integrated', meaning that all pupils receive exactly the same curriculum of general education. (In France, however, it is possible to choose a more technical type of course in the last two years of the lower secondary *collège*.) At upper secondary level in these three Member States, a range of types of course is available to pupils, who choose their school according to the kind of course they wish to take.

Belgium, Spain, Ireland and the United Kingdom all aim to give all pupils a common educational foundation in the first years of secondary education. Except in Belgium, those common courses continue until the end of compulsory education. Moreover, in Belgium, Spain and Ireland, and in some schools in the United Kingdom, pupils can complete their full secondary education in the same school, although a change of school may be necessary at the end of lower secondary education or of compulsory education for pupils wishing to enter vocational education.

In Germany, the Netherlands and Austria, all pupils receive general education at lower secondary level but at different academic levels depending on the type of school. There are, however, 'harmonized' curricula in the first years preparatory to decisions being taken regarding pupils' directions of study. In Germany and the Netherlands, these do not lead to equivalent qualifications. Some types of school provide only lower secondary education while others cover both lower and upper secondary education. Luxembourg has two distinct streams — general and technical — from the beginning of secondary education.

In the EFTA/EEA countries, pupils in Liechtenstein are selected for separate streams at the end of primary education. In upper secondary schools, only general education is provided. Vocational courses alternate between school and workplace — pupils participate in practical in-company training in Liechtenstein and attend theory classes in a neighbouring country. In Iceland and Norway, pupils remain in compulsory education within the single, continuous structure up to age 16. In upper secondary education, both general and vocational streams are provided.

In the CEECs, two types of structure coexist. In the Czech Republic, Hungary and Slovakia, pupils can either continue their education under the single structure until the age of 15 or 16, or opt to transfer to a secondary school at age 10 or 11. In Bulgaria and Romania, all pupils enter lower secondary education at the end of their four years of primary education and follow a common curriculum of general education. In Poland, as in the Nordic countries, the last stage of education in the single, continuous structure corresponds to the lower secondary level. The six CEECs reveal a great diversity of upper secondary structures and provide both general and vocational education.

MORE PUPILS IN VOCATIONAL THAN IN GENERAL EDUCATION AT UPPER SECONDARY LEVEL

Figure E3 depicts, for each country, the distribution of upper secondary pupils between general and vocational education. In the European Union as a whole, there are more pupils in vocational upper secondary education than in general education. This pattern is found in most Member States but is particularly pronounced in Germany and Austria, where more than three quarters of pupils are in the vocational stream. In Greece, Spain, Ireland and Portugal, on the other hand, more pupils are to be found in general education.

FIGURE E3: PERCENTAGE OF PUPILS IN GENERAL AND VOCATIONAL UPPER SECONDARY EDUCATION (ISCED 3),1994/95

Source: Eurostat, UOE.   National statistics.

GENERAL   VOCATIONAL

Belgium: In the French Community of Belgium, pupils in transitional secondary technical and art education are included with pupils in vocational education.
Greece and **Netherlands**: 1993/94.
Sweden: Includes mature students.
United Kingdom: For international statistical purposes, all pupils in schools are classified as following general programmes. All students on further education courses, some of which are academic, are classified as following vocational programmes. The majority of these students are also over 'traditional' school age.
Iceland: Full-time only.
Liechtenstein: National statistics. General education takes into account only the upper section of the *Gymnasium (Oberstufe)*. Vocational courses alternate between school and workplace — pupils participate in practical in-company training in Liechtenstein and attend theory classes in a neighbouring country.
Slovakia: 1993/94. Data expressed in full-time equivalents, excluding special education.

In the majority of the EFTA/EEA countries and in the CEECs, the proportion of pupils in vocational secondary education is also greater than that of pupils in the general stream. It is above 70% in most of these countries. In Norway also, there are proportionately more pupils in vocational than general education, but to a less marked degree. Iceland and Bulgaria are exceptions, having respectively 64% and 53% of upper secondary pupils in general education.

EXPLANATORY NOTE
In Figure E3, the distribution of pupils between the two types of education is based on the total number of pupils enrolled in educational institutions. From the data available, it is not possible to take into account students undertaking in-company vocational training.

SECONDARY EDUCATION

PREDOMINANCE OF GENERAL EDUCATION
IN CERTAIN COUNTRIES AND REGIONS

Figure E4 shows for each region pupils in general upper secondary education as a percentage of all pupils in upper secondary education.

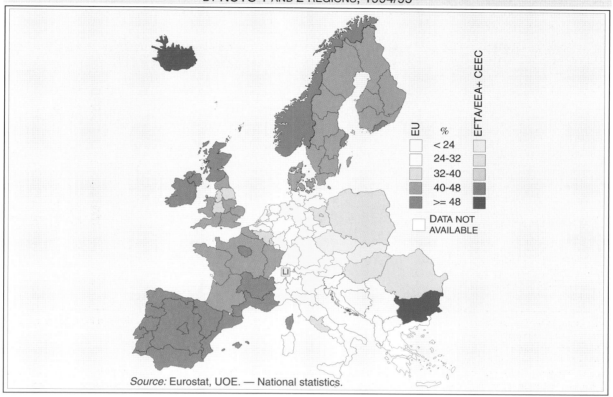

FIGURE E4: PROPORTION OF UPPER SECONDARY PUPILS (ISCED 3) IN GENERAL EDUCATION BY NUTS 1 AND 2 REGIONS, 1994/95

Source: Eurostat, UOE. — National statistics.

Belgium: In the French Community of Belgium, pupils in transitional secondary technical and art education are included with pupils in vocational education.
Belgium, France and **the Netherlands**: 1993/94.
Sweden: Excluding adult education and distance learning.
United Kingdom: For international statistical purposes, all pupils in schools are classified as following general programmes. All students on further education courses, some of which are academic, are classified as following vocational programmes. The majority of these students are also over 'traditional' school age.
Iceland: Full-time only.
Liechtenstein, Bulgaria, Czech Republic, Hungary, Poland, Romania and **Slovakia**: National statistics.
Slovakia: 1993/94.

Most Member States have some regions in which the distribution of pupils between general and vocational education is the opposite to that found at national level. In Belgium, the highest percentage of students in general upper secondary education is found in the Brussels and Wallonia regions. In Germany, the highest percentages of pupils in the general branch are found in Berlin and Brandenburg. In Italy, only the Nord Est and Emilia-Romagna regions have under 24% in the general branch of upper secondary education. In Finland, two regions stand out – Uusimaa, with a very high rate, and the Åland Islands with a much lower rate of participation in the general branch of upper secondary education. In Sweden, Stockholm has the largest proportion of pupils in the general stream. In the United Kingdom, Scotland and Northern Ireland have large proportions of pupils in general upper secondary education.

EXPLANATORY NOTE
For most of the Member States, the nomenclature used here is that of NUTS 1, which is the largest of the regional units. NUTS 2 is, however, used for Portugal, Finland and Sweden. For the EFTA countries and the CEECs, only national data are presented.
The division into bands is based on the distribution of the data. The method chosen leads to continuous series, each of which includes an equal percentage of values.

MORE GIRLS THAN BOYS
——— IN GENERAL UPPER SECONDARY EDUCATION ———

Figure E5 shows country by country the trend since 1985 in the numbers of girls for every 100 boys in each of the branches of upper secondary education.

In the majority of Member States, there are currently more girls than boys in general education. On the other hand, boys outnumber girls in vocational secondary education. The reverse is the case in the United Kingdom. These situations have been fairly stable since 1985.

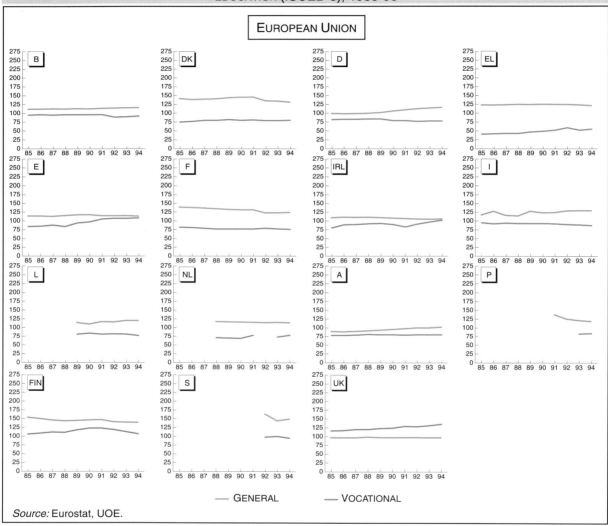

FIGURE E5: TREND IN THE NUMBER OF GIRLS PER 100 BOYS IN GENERAL AND VOCATIONAL UPPER SECONDARY EDUCATION (ISCED 3), 1985-95

Source: Eurostat, UOE.

Belgium: In the French Community of Belgium, pupils in transitional secondary technical and art education are included with pupils in vocational education.
Denmark: From 1993, figures have been reallocated between general and vocational education.
Germany: Data for years up to 1990 refer to the former Federal Republic of Germany.
Sweden: Includes mature students.
United Kingdom: For international statistical purposes, all pupils in schools are classified as following general programmes. All students on further education courses, some of which are academic, are classified as following vocational programmes. The majority of these students are also over 'traditional' school age.

Finland has had the highest ratio of girls to boys in general upper secondary education since the beginning of the series. In 1995, Sweden had the highest ratio of girls, with 149 girls for every 100 boys enrolled. The ratios were fairly similar in Denmark and Italy. In Ireland, Austria and the United Kingdom, however, there are about equal numbers of girls and boys in general upper secondary education.

The trend in the ratio of girls to boys in vocational education shows greater variation. In Finland, the numbers of girls have consistently exceeded those of boys for more than 10 years, despite some fluctuations. This branch has also seen an increase in female participation over the last few years in Spain and Ireland. In the other Member States, there are fewer girls than boys in vocational education and this is particularly marked in Greece.

In Spain and Finland, there are fewer boys than girls in education beyond the minimum school leaving age. There are in fact more girls than boys in both vocational and general education.

FIGURE E5 (CONTINUED): TREND IN THE NUMBER OF GIRLS PER 100 BOYS IN GENERAL AND VOCATIONAL UPPER SECONDARY EDUCATION (ISCED 3), 1985-95

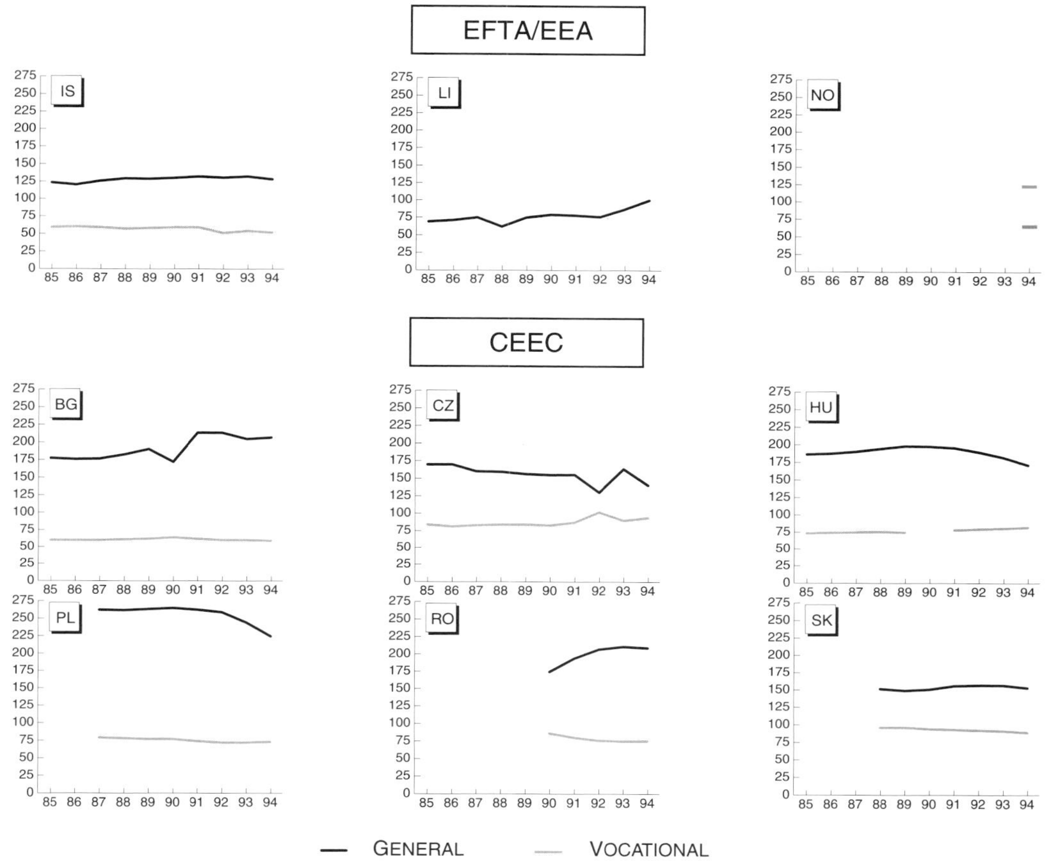

EFTA/EEA

CEEC

— GENERAL   — VOCATIONAL

Source: National statistics.

Iceland: Full-time only.
Norway: Eurostat UOE data. Data available only for 1994.
Slovakia: Full-time equivalents, excluding special education.

In Iceland and more particularly in the CEECs, girls have for a number of years been distinctly more numerous than boys in general upper secondary education. Developments in recent years indicate a slight narrowing of the gap in the Czech Republic, Hungary and Poland. In these countries, as in the European Union, boys are predominant in vocational upper secondary education. This pattern is a little less pronounced in the Czech Republic and Slovakia, where there are almost as many girls as boys in the vocational branch of secondary education.

EXPLANATORY NOTE
The number of girls per 100 boys is calculated by dividing the total number of girls by the total number of boys and multiplying the result by 100.

SECONDARY EDUCATION

PUPILS RECEIVE DIFFERENT AMOUNTS OF TEACHING ACCORDING TO MEMBER STATE, COURSE AND YEAR OF STUDY

There are wide variations between Member States of the European Union in the organization of school time, as illustrated in Figures E6 and E7 for lower and general upper secondary education respectively. In most Member States, at lower secondary level, the annual number of taught hours varies between a compulsory minimum which applies to all pupils, and a maximum. In some Member States, variations result from pupils having subject options, as in Belgium, Spain, France and Italy. In other Member States, such as Denmark, Germany, Greece (until September 1996), Spain and Austria, the number of lesson periods increases as pupils progress in their school careers. In those Member States with no set maximum, variations exist between schools. In most of these countries, particularly Finland, Sweden and the United Kingdom, schools have substantial freedom in setting the timetable. For Finland, the figure illustrates a notional average and for England and Wales (UK) it illustrates an average derived from an annual census of schools. Luxembourg and the Netherlands are the only Member States in which all lower secondary general pupils follow the same number of lesson periods per year.

At this level of education, Ireland and the Netherlands have the highest annual minimum load – over 1 000 hours. In Italy, some pupils have classes for more than 1 200 hours per year. (This maximum is calculated taking into account the hours of optional language lessons.) Young Danes and Germans, on the other hand, receive an annual minimum of about 800 hours of teaching.

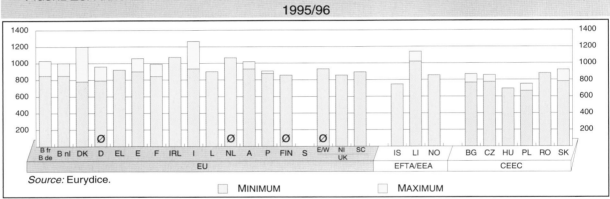

FIGURE E6: ANNUAL NUMBER OF HOURS OF TAUGHT TIME IN GENERAL LOWER SECONDARY EDUCATION, 1995/96

Source: Eurydice.

NB: Notes on individual countries' arrangements can be found in the annex.

In the EFTA/EEA countries, the lowest minimum annual lesson time is 747 hours in Iceland, but the municipal authorities there are free to increase this time. In Liechtenstein, the minimum is over 1 000 hours a year.

In the CEECs, the annual hours of lesson time are fairly close. The least hours are found in Hungary and Poland, where they are under 700 hours a year.

EXPLANATORY NOTE
The last three years of the folkeskole *(in Denmark), of* ensino básico *(in Portugal), of the* peruskoulu/grundskola *(in Finland), and of the* grundskola *(in Sweden) are classified as lower secondary education. The same applies to the last three years of the single structure in Iceland and Norway amongst the EFTA/EEA countries.*
The annual load of teaching is calculated by taking the average daily load, which is multiplied by the number of days of teaching in the year. Tables giving the detailed method of calculation appear in the annex.

68

As illustrated in Figure E8, in three Member States, Greece, Italy and Portugal, the minimum annual number of hours of teaching is less in general upper secondary education than in lower secondary. It is the same in Belgium, Luxembourg and Northern Ireland (UK), and in England and Wales (UK), the average taught time is broadly the same. The minimum taught hours are more in Denmark, Germany, Spain, France and Austria. In all Member States, the annual lesson load differs from one pupil to the other, even in those for which the graph shows no set maximum. In such cases, schools have considerable freedom in distributing the number of lesson hours over the years. The graph therefore shows the average of these. In upper secondary education, differences can mainly be explained by the numerous options available to pupils (languages, mathematics, sciences, literature etc.) in the different branches.

In the EFTA/EEA countries, the minimum annual taught time is the same in lower and upper secondary education. There is a minimum and a maximum in Liechtenstein and Norway. The minimum in Liechtenstein exceeds the potential maximum in Iceland and Norway.

In the CEECs, pupils' annual lesson load is greater at upper secondary level than at lower secondary, except in Romania.

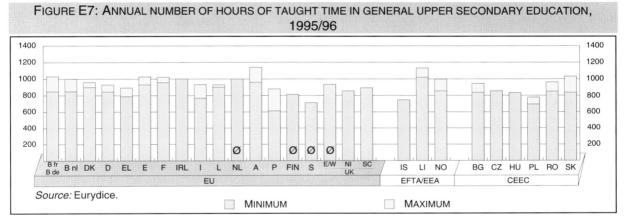

FIGURE E7: ANNUAL NUMBER OF HOURS OF TAUGHT TIME IN GENERAL UPPER SECONDARY EDUCATION, 1995/96

Source: Eurydice.

☐ MINIMUM   ☐ MAXIMUM

NB: Notes on individual countries' arrangements can be found in the annex.

FIGURE E8: MINIMUM ANNUAL HOURS OF TAUGHT TIME IN SECONDARY EDUCATION, 1995/96

	EUROPEAN UNION								
	B	**DK**	**D**	**EL**	**E**	**F**	**IRL**	**I**	**L**
LOWER SECONDARY (GENERAL)	849	780	790	919	898	842	1 074	933	900
UPPER SECONDARY (GENERAL)	849	900	846	788	931	957	1 002	767	900

	NL	**A**	**P**	**FIN**	**S**	**UK (E/W)**	**UK (NI)**	**UK (SC)**
LOWER SECONDARY (GENERAL)	1 067	930	875	855	not applicable	931	855	893
UPPER SECONDARY (GENERAL)	1 000	960	613	812	712	935	855	893

	EFTA/EEA			CEEC					
	IS	**LI**	**NO**	**BG**	**CZ**	**HU**	**PL**	**RO**	**SK**
LOWER SECONDARY (GENERAL)	747	1 020	855	765	773	694	666	878	781
UPPER SECONDARY (GENERAL)	747	1 020	855	837	856	833	694	850	837

Source: Eurydice.

AT AROUND AGE 13, THE SAME COMPULSORY SUBJECTS, BUT DIFFERENT TIMETABLE LOADS

In some Member States, schools are free to determine the amount of time they allocate to the various subjects in the timetable. These countries are shown as having a flexible timetable. Insofar as curricula indicate the number of hours allocated to each subject, the amount of time devoted to the various compulsory subjects can be compared. Figures E9 and E10 show the proportions of the annual timetable allocated to each of the compulsory subjects, at around ages 13 and 16.

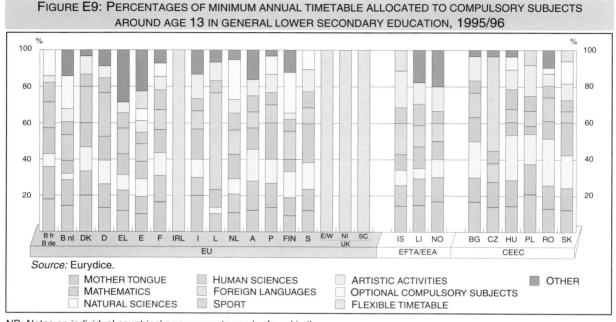

FIGURE E9: PERCENTAGES OF MINIMUM ANNUAL TIMETABLE ALLOCATED TO COMPULSORY SUBJECTS AROUND AGE 13 IN GENERAL LOWER SECONDARY EDUCATION, 1995/96

Source: Eurydice.

- MOTHER TONGUE
- MATHEMATICS
- NATURAL SCIENCES
- HUMAN SCIENCES
- FOREIGN LANGUAGES
- SPORT
- ARTISTIC ACTIVITIES
- OPTIONAL COMPULSORY SUBJECTS
- FLEXIBLE TIMETABLE
- OTHER

NB: Notes on individual countries' arrangements can be found in the annex.

At about age 13, in general education, all pupils are taught the same compulsory subjects. However, the proportion of time allocated to each of these subjects varies from one Member State to another. At this level of education, the mother tongue, mathematics and a foreign language are relatively the most important subjects in the majority of Member States.

Thus, the time devoted to mother tongue teaching represents one fifth of the time in Denmark and Italy. In Spain, the Netherlands and Finland, the compulsory minimum amount of time allocated to this subject represents 10% of the total timetable. In Luxembourg, at this age, Letzeburgesch is no longer included in the curriculum. This is explained by the fact that this language is essentially oral. Pupils in Luxembourg have the greatest number of hours of foreign language courses which include, in addition to English, both German and French, which are also used in the teaching of other subjects. Belgium (French Community) has the greatest proportion of the compulsory timetable allocated to the teaching of mathematics (18%).

In some Member States, 13-year-old pupils must include some optional subjects in their timetables. The proportion of the timetable set aside for such subjects is fairly high in the Netherlands and Finland (22%). The amount of time allocated to 'other' subjects is large in Greece (29%) and Spain (23%). In Greece, this is largely accounted for by the compulsory teaching of ancient Greek. In Spain, the high percentage is a result of the time spent on technology. In most of the other Member States, this category mainly includes the teaching of religion.

In the EFTA/EEA countries, the distribution of the compulsory subjects is notable for the importance given to artistic subjects and the absence of time allocated to compulsory options. The amount of time allocated to the subjects grouped under the heading 'other' is quite considerable in Liechtenstein and Norway.

Of the CEECs, Hungary and Romania are notable for the importance given to the natural sciences – more than a quarter of the timetable. In Poland, pupils devote almost 40% of their taught time to the mother tongue and mathematics. Bulgaria and Romania allocate 13% of the taught time of 13-year-olds to foreign language teaching. In the Czech Republic, more than half of the timetable is organized in a flexible manner.

AT AROUND AGE 16, DIFFERENT COMPULSORY SUBJECTS IN THE SCIENCE SECTION OF UPPER SECONDARY EDUCATION

In view of the diversity of the streams and courses at the upper secondary level, the science section of general education has been selected so as to make comparison possible.

FIGURE E10: PERCENTAGES OF MINIMUM ANNUAL TIMETABLE ALLOCATED TO COMPULSORY SUBJECTS AROUND AGE 16 IN THE SCIENCE SECTION OF GENERAL UPPER SECONDARY EDUCATION, 1995/96

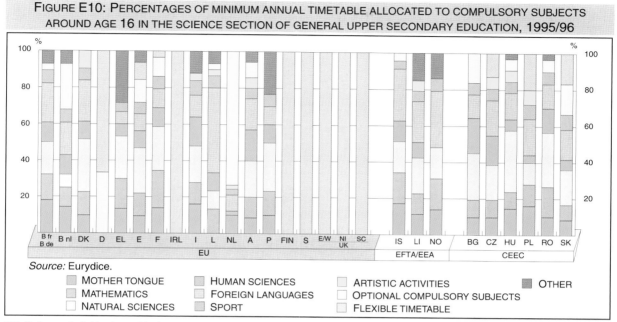

Source: Eurydice.

MOTHER TONGUE · HUMAN SCIENCES · ARTISTIC ACTIVITIES · OTHER
MATHEMATICS · FOREIGN LANGUAGES · OPTIONAL COMPULSORY SUBJECTS
NATURAL SCIENCES · SPORT · FLEXIBLE TIMETABLE

NB: Notes on individual countries' arrangements can be found in the annex.

At about the age of 16, considerable differences are found in timetables in the science section of general education. At this point in their school careers, pupils do not necessarily all have the same compulsory subjects. In this section of general upper secondary education, the teaching of the mother tongue, mathematics and foreign languages usually retains a fairly important relative position in the majority of Member States. However, where the curriculum has not become flexible, according to the individual choices of pupils, the proportion of time devoted to science has increased considerably compared with that at age 13 and this has fairly generally been one of the most important subjects, the time devoted to it sometimes even exceeding the minimum compulsory time given to mathematics. In those Member States in which art and sport activities are still included in the compulsory curriculum, they are allocated less time than in lower secondary, except in Denmark. More time is often allocated to foreign languages at this age. The flexible timetable is a feature of Germany, Ireland, Finland, Sweden and the United Kingdom. In Germany, subjects are taught in basic and advanced courses (*Grundkurse* and *Leistungskurse*) according to pupils' aptitudes and attainments. The curriculum includes compulsory subjects (2/3) plus others obligatorily chosen from given fields (1/3). The proportion of time allocated to compulsory elective subjects is particularly large in the Netherlands, taking up over 70% of the timetable.

In the EFTA/EEA countries, the amount of lesson time spent on mathematics and the mother tongue is more or less the same as at age 13. Artistic activities have, however, disappeared from the compulsory curriculum and foreign languages are very important.

In the CEECs, artistic activities are retained in the compulsory curriculum at age 16 in the Czech Republic, Hungary and Poland. Almost everywhere, the amount of time allocated to mathematics and mother tongue lessons is less than at the age of 13.

EXPLANATORY NOTE
The proportion of time allocated to each subject is calculated on the basis of the ratio of the minimum number of class hours to be allocated to each compulsory subject to the total minimum number of class hours at ages 13 and 16. These are set out in the annex.
Subjects have been grouped together as follows: human sciences includes history and geography; natural sciences takes in biology, physics and chemistry; the 'other' category includes religious education, Latin and Greek, technology and computer science.

WIDESPREAD LEARNING OF FOREIGN LANGUAGES

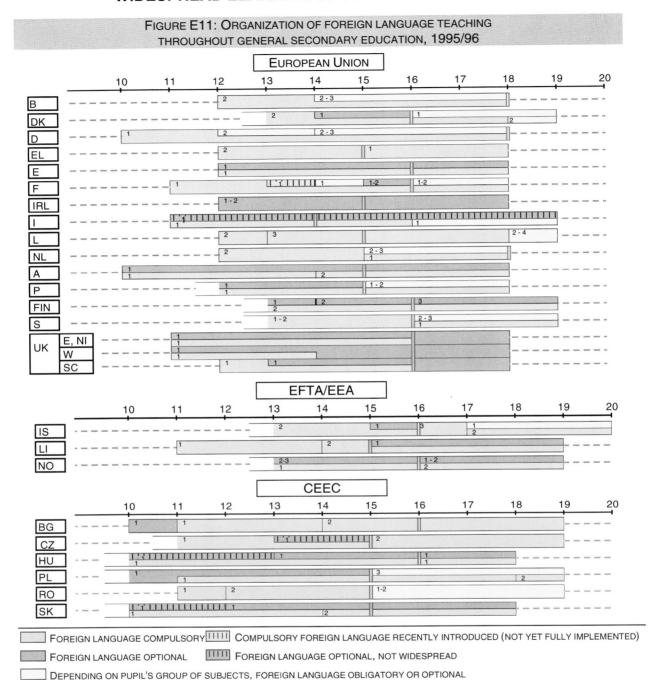

FIGURE E11: ORGANIZATION OF FOREIGN LANGUAGE TEACHING THROUGHOUT GENERAL SECONDARY EDUCATION, 1995/96

Source: Eurydice.

France: In the framework of the *Nouveau contrat pour l'école*, learning a second foreign language will become compulsory in the third year of secondary education (at around age 13) for pupils who entered the *collège* in 1996.

Luxembourg: In the classics section, English is started at age 14 instead of 13.

Portugal: In upper secondary education, a second foreign language is compulsory for pupils who have taken only one foreign language in *ensino básico*.

United Kingdom (E/W, and NI): At least one foreign language is compulsory for 11- to 16-year-olds in England and Northern Ireland, and for 11- to 14-year-olds in Wales (where Welsh as a compulsory subject is being phased in). Schools may elect to offer pupils one or more additional foreign languages at any time. Students choose individual subjects after age 16.

United Kingdom (SC): While foreign language learning is not a statutory requirement, local authority education departments are strongly encouraged to require this of their schools. This means that, in practice, foreign language teaching is compulsory in lower secondary education.

Slovakia: In the specialized foreign language schools, two foreign languages are compulsory, from the age of 10 years (in the *základná škola*) and from age 12 (in the eight-year *gymnázium*).

At general lower secondary level, learning several foreign languages is compulsory except in Ireland, where foreign languages are only offered as options. In some countries, two foreign languages are included in the compulsory curriculum (Belgium, Denmark, Greece, Netherlands, Finland and Sweden) or even three (Luxembourg). The possibility of learning one or more additional foreign languages is available to pupils in a majority of the Member States on an optional basis.

In general upper secondary education, most Member States continue to teach at least one foreign language on a compulsory basis in all branches. In the United Kingdom (England, Northern Ireland and Scotland), the compulsory teaching of a foreign language stops at the end of compulsory education. Some Member States have made two foreign languages compulsory up to the minimum school leaving age — Belgium, Denmark, Greece, Luxembourg, Austria, Finland and Sweden. In a number of Member States, the possibility of learning additional languages increases, depending on either the branch of study chosen or the choice of optional courses available.

In the EFTA/EEA countries, the lower secondary curriculum provides for the compulsory learning of foreign languages — one in Norway and two in Iceland — and options can be added to these. After the end of compulsory education, in general upper secondary education, all pupils in the EFTA/EEA countries must study at least two foreign languages and in Iceland three.

All of the CEECs prescribe the learning of a foreign language throughout lower secondary education and maintain this obligation in general upper secondary education, except Romania, where this obligation depends on the pupil's chosen branch of study. In Bulgaria, the Czech Republic and Poland, compulsory learning of two languages is part of the upper secondary curriculum. In addition to this compulsory curriculum, options are available throughout secondary education in Hungary, Poland and Slovakia and during part of it in the Czech Republic and Romania.

All education systems give pupils an opportunity to learn at least one foreign language. Figure E12 shows the average number of foreign languages learned per pupil in general secondary education. The languages most commonly learned vary from country to country, and for this reason all the available possibilities are taken into account, beyond the languages most commonly studied in the European Union as a whole.

FIGURE E12: AVERAGE NUMBER OF FOREIGN LANGUAGES PER PUPIL IN GENERAL SECONDARY EDUCATION, DURING THE SCHOOL YEAR 1994/95

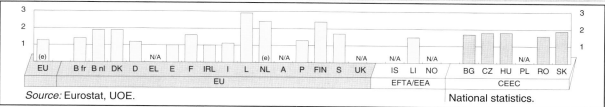

Source: Eurostat, UOE. National statistics.

Belgium and **Sweden**: 1993/94.
Ireland, Netherlands and **Portugal**: Full-time pupils only.
Czech Republic and **Slovakia**: Excluding the second stage of the single structure system.
Slovakia: 1993/94.

The average number of foreign languages studied per pupil during the course of general secondary education in those European Union Member States for which data are available is 1.3. The average varies widely from one Member State to another and is equivalent to one language in Spain and Ireland. The highest figures are for Luxembourg (2.9 languages per pupil) and the Netherlands and Finland (2.4). The high figure for Luxembourg is a consequence of the compulsory teaching of two of the official languages of the country as foreign languages.

In the EFTA/EEA countries and the CEECs, the average number of foreign languages learned per pupil is generally above the European Union average, varying from 1.5 in Liechtenstein to 1.9 in Slovakia.

EXPLANATORY NOTE

This graph presents only languages regarded as modern and foreign. Consequently, Irish and Letzeburgesch and regional languages are excluded, although provision may be made for them in certain Member States. In the general secondary education curricula, one or more foreign languages are often included among the compulsory subjects. In addition to these courses, which are compulsory for all pupils, foreign language courses are sometimes available as options or compulsory in some branches only. Figure E12 illustrates the various possibilities.

ENGLISH:
THE MOST TAUGHT FOREIGN LANGUAGE

The following figures present the percentages of pupils in general secondary education learning in 1994/95 any one of the four most taught languages discussed here. This is an average calculated over all pupils in general secondary education and not over a population of pupils of a specific age.

English is by far the most taught foreign language at secondary level. The other official languages of the European Union feature less in the curriculum and are selected less often by pupils. Thus, on average in 1994/95 in the whole of the European Union, 89% of pupils in general secondary education were learning English whereas 32% studied French, 18% German and only 8% Spanish. This is also the pattern in the EFTA/EEA countries and the CEECs.

FIGURE E13: PERCENTAGE OF PUPILS LEARNING **ENGLISH**
IN GENERAL SECONDARY EDUCATION (ISCED 2 AND 3), DURING THE SCHOOL YEAR 1994/95

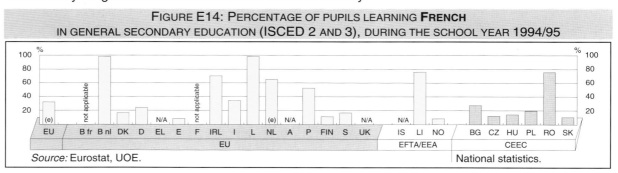

Source: Eurostat, UOE. National statistics.

Belgium (B fr and **B nl)** and **Sweden**: 1993/94.
Netherlands and **Portugal**: Full-time pupils only.
Czech Republic, Poland and **Slovakia**: Excluding the second stage of the single structure system.
Poland and **Slovakia**: 1993/94.

The extent to which English is taught is comparable in all Member States where it is not the mother tongue. In several countries, over 90% of pupils learn this language. It is in Belgium, Italy, and, to a lesser extent, Luxembourg and Portugal that the proportion is lowest (between 60 and 76%).

The percentages in the EFTA/EEA countries and the CEECs are fairly close to those in the European Union. They range from 56% in Romania to 100% in Norway.

FIGURE E14: PERCENTAGE OF PUPILS LEARNING **FRENCH**
IN GENERAL SECONDARY EDUCATION (ISCED 2 AND 3), DURING THE SCHOOL YEAR 1994/95

Source: Eurostat, UOE. National statistics.

Belgium (B nl) and **Sweden**: 1993/94.
Belgium (B de): All pupils in general secondary education learn French.
Ireland, Netherlands and **Portugal**: Full-time pupils only.
Czech Republic, Poland and **Slovakia**: Excluding the second stage of the single structure system.
Poland and **Slovakia**: 1993/94.

French is the second most taught foreign language in the European Union as a whole, but with greater variations between Member States. Thus, it is the most taught foreign language in the Flemish Community of Belgium (98%), Ireland (70%) and Luxembourg (98%).

In the Netherlands and Portugal, during the school year 1994/95, just over half of the pupils studied French. Of the Member States for which information is available, the lowest rates are to be found in Spain and Finland.

In Liechtenstein and Romania, three quarters of pupils were studying French in that year. However, in the other EFTA/EEA countries and the CEECs for which figures are available, the percentages are relatively low – under 30% everywhere.

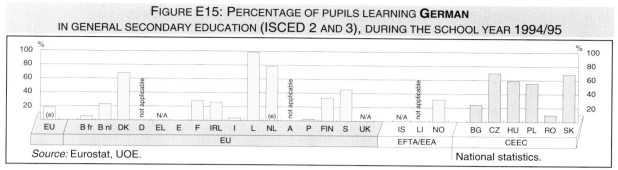

FIGURE E15: PERCENTAGE OF PUPILS LEARNING **GERMAN**
IN GENERAL SECONDARY EDUCATION (ISCED 2 AND 3), DURING THE SCHOOL YEAR 1994/95

Source: Eurostat, UOE.

National statistics.

Belgium and **Sweden**: 1993/94.
Ireland, Netherlands and **Portugal**: Full-time pupils only.
Czech Republic, Poland and **Slovakia**: Excluding the second stage of the single structure system.
Poland and **Slovakia**: 1993/94.

The numbers of pupils learning German also vary greatly from one Member State to another. In Luxembourg, this national language, which is taught as a foreign language, is obligatorily learned by all pupils. Of the four languages under consideration here, it is in second place in some countries (in the Netherlands, Denmark, Sweden and Finland) with respectively 78, 68, 45 and 33% of pupils involved. In the French Community of Belgium, Spain, Italy and Portugal, in 1994/95, very few pupils studied German.

In the CEECs, German has a relatively important place in the teaching of foreign languages in the Czech Republic, Hungary, Poland and Slovakia with between 55 and 70% of pupils learning this language at secondary level. On the other hand, it is learned by less than 10% of Romanian pupils.

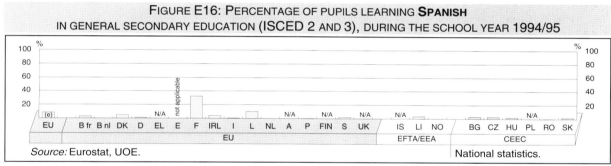

FIGURE E16: PERCENTAGE OF PUPILS LEARNING **SPANISH**
IN GENERAL SECONDARY EDUCATION (ISCED 2 AND 3), DURING THE SCHOOL YEAR 1994/95

Source: Eurostat, UOE.

National statistics.

Belgium and **Sweden**: 1993/94.
Ireland, Netherlands and **Portugal**: Full-time pupils only.
Czech Republic, Poland and **Slovakia**: Excluding the second stage of the single structure system.
Poland and **Slovakia**: 1993/94.

In France, one third of pupils in general secondary education were learning Spanish in 1994/95. In Luxembourg, the figure was 10%. In the remaining Member States, figures for pupils learning Spanish did not exceed 5% and in some of them they were nil.

In the EFTA/EEA countries and the CEECs, the teaching of Spanish is even more marginal. The greatest proportion of pupils learning this language is found in Liechtenstein and Bulgaria (3%).

EXPLANATORY NOTE
The data refer to foreign languages being studied by each pupil at one point of time, as opposed to those studied throughout their schooling.

A CONSIDERABLE PROPORTION OF YOUNG PEOPLE HAVE COMPLETED ——— THE UPPER SECONDARY LEVEL OF EDUCATION ———

Figure E17 shows the percentage of young people aged 22 who had completed the upper secondary level of education in 1995. In the European Union as a whole, 71% of young people had completed upper secondary education, taking into account all branches of study. Two Member States depart from this overall pattern — Luxembourg, in which slightly more than half of all 22-year-olds had completed this level, and Portugal with 46%.

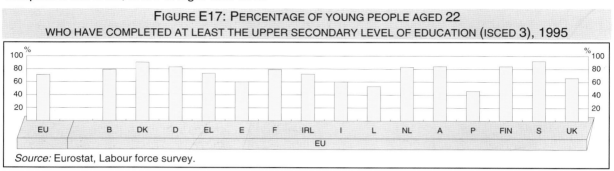

FIGURE E17: PERCENTAGE OF YOUNG PEOPLE AGED 22
WHO HAVE COMPLETED AT LEAST THE UPPER SECONDARY LEVEL OF EDUCATION (ISCED 3), 1995

Source: Eurostat, Labour force survey.

Luxembourg: Most young people taking higher education courses are abroad. They have all completed at least the upper secondary education level. The percentage in Figure E17 is therefore an under-estimate.

United Kingdom (E/W and NI): The General Certificate of Secondary Education (GCSE) taken at the end of compulsory schooling at the age of 16 is treated as a lower secondary qualification.

MORE GIRLS THAN BOYS QUALIFYING FROM ——— GENERAL UPPER SECONDARY EDUCATION ———

It is estimated that over 4 million pupils obtained a general upper secondary education qualification in the Member States of the European Union in 1995. In all Member States for which data are available, more girls than boys obtained a general upper secondary education qualification.

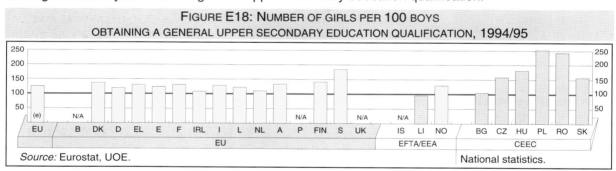

FIGURE E18: NUMBER OF GIRLS PER 100 BOYS
OBTAINING A GENERAL UPPER SECONDARY EDUCATION QUALIFICATION, 1994/95

Source: Eurostat, UOE.

National statistics.

Liechtenstein: 1993/94.

This phenomenon is a little more marked in Denmark and Finland than in the other EU Member States, while in Ireland and the Netherlands, the ratio comes closest to 100, indicating that there is little difference between the numbers of girls and boys.

In most of the CEECs, far more girls than boys obtained general upper secondary education qualifications. In Poland and Romania, more than two thirds of those qualifying at this level were girls.

EXPLANATORY NOTE

In the Eurostat Labour force survey, all vocational training in schools (excluding sandwich courses) has been allocated to ISCED 3. This may explain a relative over-estimate of the numbers completing ISCED 3 in Denmark, Germany, France and, in particular, the Netherlands, in Figure E17.
For figure E18, the number of girls per 100 boys is calculated by dividing the total number of girls by the total number of boys and multiplying the result by 100.

F

HIGHER EDUCATION

——————————— HIGHER EDUCATION STRUCTURES ———————————

Higher education in Europe has traditionally been characterized by a division between university and non-university education. This binary divide is, however, becoming less and less clear-cut. In recent years, there have been varying degrees of rapprochement between university and non-university education in many Member States.

As Figure F1 shows, higher education institutions in several Member States have become part of the university sector and award university-level qualifications, e.g. the Spanish *Escuelas Técnicas Superiores* and the Austrian *Kunsthochschulen.*

In Germany, the various higher, or tertiary, education institutions include those which award university-level qualifications (*Universitäten, Universitäten-Gesamthochschulen, Technische Hochschulen, Technische Universitäten, Theologische Hochschulen, Pädagogische Hochschulen, Kunsthochschulen, Musikhochschulen* and *Fachhochschulen*). Non-university education at tertiary level is provided by *Fachschulen, Schulen des Gesundheitswesens* and *Berufsakademien/ Fachakademien.*

In some Member States, the distinction between university and non-university courses refers only to the institutions and not to the level of qualification. In France, for example, the non-university *grandes écoles* award high-level qualifications and therefore form part of *enseignement supérieur long* (long courses of higher education) while the IUTs, although linked to the universities, provide *enseignement supérieur court* (short courses of higher education). In Ireland, the technological institutions and colleges provide university-level courses but are not part of the university system.

In other Member States, higher education institutions offer courses at different levels and the distinction between university and non-university courses has disappeared. In the United Kingdom, for example, students may study for a degree in a non-university institution, while not all courses of study offered by universities lead to a degree.

Evidence of this movement to remove the barriers between university and non-university institutions is also shown by other indicators. In several Member States, admission to doctoral studies can be gained after non-university higher education courses. This is the case in Belgium (Flemish Community), Greece, France, Ireland, the Netherlands and Austria. In Ireland and Portugal, the names given to some qualifications awarded in university and non-university higher education are similar.

At the same time, in many Member States, the distinction between non-university higher education and upper secondary education is becoming increasingly blurred. Teaching for some non-university higher education qualifications such as the *Brevet de Technicien Supérieur* in France and Luxembourg is provided by secondary-level institutions. Vocational training, which was previously delivered at upper secondary level, is also appearing at higher non-university level. This is the case, for example, in the *formación profesional de grado superior* in Spain.

The EFTA/EEA countries reveal different patterns with regard to the division between the university and non-university sectors. In Liechtenstein, all courses are of university level. In Iceland and Norway there is a distinction between university and non-university institutions. In Norway, movement between state colleges (non-university) and universities is very common — many students enrolled in undergraduate courses have undertaken the first part of their studies in a state college.

In contrast, in the CEECs, the distinction between university and non-university courses remains. Non-university institutions award either qualifications from short higher education courses or post-secondary qualifications. However, some non-university higher education courses can be extended with specific complementary courses which are of university level.

—————— A VARIETY OF UNIVERSITY PATHWAYS ——————

The organization of university studies also varies from one Member State to another. In some Member States, the stages of study are relatively short, with a degree or other qualification at the end of each one. In others, the first level of university education is longer, with no subdivisions or intermediate qualifications, but then leads directly to doctoral studies.

In France, for example, apart from some specific courses, the university path is characterized by a succession of one- or two-year courses, each of which leads to a qualification (DEUG, *Licence, Maîtrise,* DEA, etc.). The passage from one qualification to another is often subject to specific admission procedures. However in Denmark, Germany, Greece, Austria and Portugal, students must study for at least four years before they can obtain their first qualification.

The organization of university post-graduate studies also differs from one Member State to another. In Greece, Ireland and Portugal, a one- or two-year course following on from the undergraduate programmes precedes the doctorate. In most of the other Member States, students may undertake such courses first or proceed direct to doctoral studies.

Similarities exist between the names given to qualifications awarded in the different European Union Member States. However, as Figure F1 shows, similar names such as *Maîtrise/Magister/*Master's or even *licence/licenciado/lisensiaatti* cover entirely different courses. Awarded at the end of undergraduate courses in some Member States, these qualifications are not delivered elsewhere until the end of post-graduate studies. The number of years of study that they require also differs.

In the EFTA/EEA countries, undergraduate studies are made up of one or two successive stages. All these courses can be followed by a doctorate.

In the CEECs, undergraduate studies often take the form of a course running over several years, with no intermediate qualification. Post-graduate studies usually lead to a doctorate. In Bulgaria, Hungary and Romania, post-graduate courses other than the doctorate are also available.

———— THE DURATION OF STUDIES: FROM TWO TO SIX YEARS ————

The notional duration of higher education studies depends on the course chosen and the mode of provision, many students now being able to choose more flexible options such as part-time study. In addition, in some Member States, modular or credit-based courses are available which allow studies to be completed over a very long period if desired. In other Member States, students are, however, obliged to complete their studies within a prescribed period. This may correspond to the notional length of the course or a one or two-year extension may be permitted.

Within most European Union Member States, the longest first degree courses (usually in medicine) are designed to last for six years of full-time study, while in many Member States, the shortest university or non-university course lasts two years. In Greece, Portugal and Finland, it lasts three years. In Luxembourg, courses of study provided within the country last a maximum of three years. However, places are limited and the great majority of students pursue their studies abroad.

The shortest higher education courses in the EFTA/EEA countries last for three years in Iceland and Norway. In Liechtenstein, where the number of places is limited, the courses provided in the country are of four years' duration.

In the CEECs, the longest courses are designed to last for six years of full-time study. The minimum period of study is three years, except in Poland and Romania where one- or two-year courses are offered in the non-university sector.

OPPORTUNITIES FOR PART-TIME STUDY

Although higher education courses in most Member States are usually designed for full-time students, there are also opportunities for studying part-time. These courses allow students who have either professional or family obligations to pursue higher education. These are offered in particular by distance learning systems such as the Open University in the United Kingdom.

Some higher education institutions also make specific arrangements for part-time study. This form of provision is particularly well-developed in the United Kingdom, where most higher education institutions admit part-time students to some of their courses. This is also true of some university and non-university courses in the Netherlands. In Luxembourg, the *éducateur gradué* course can be followed while working. In other Member States, possibilities for part-time study exist within the conventional full-time higher education structures.

In Norway, part-time studies are quite common, since the organization of courses of study is often flexible. It is possible to obtain most levels of qualification through part-time study in most higher education institutions.

In Romania, evening classes or courses requiring no formal attendance are offered for most university courses. The length of these courses is one year longer than for full-time study. In Slovakia, classes for part-time courses may be concentrated into one week, or given on Saturdays.

EXPLANATORY NOTE
Figure F1 includes all higher education courses which require at least an upper secondary qualification or its equivalent. Any additional admission requirements are shown by a red line to the left of the diagram. The starting ages shown in the figure are the notional ages for students who have neither repeated a year nor been individually promoted to a higher class and do not indicate the students' real ages. It is, in fact, possible to enroll in higher education at any age, as long as the admission requirements are met. The figure shows only full-time education structures.
A distinction is made between a first level of higher education (ISCED levels 5 and 6) and a second level (ISCED 7). For the first level, the length of each cell represents the notional duration of full time studies. The distinction between non-university and university programmes refers to institutions and not to any level of qualification. University courses are here taken to include all courses offered by universities or university-type institutions, whatever the level of qualification awarded. Non-university institutions offer courses which may be at a high level (ISCED 6). For the second level, the lengths of the programmes are shown in brackets in the relevant cells.
The names of institutions (shown in the top left-hand part of the cell) and the names of the qualifications awarded (bottom right-hand part), in italics, are in the original languages.
In most countries, the category 'other programmes' includes the majority of higher education courses such as languages, most sciences and theology where these have not been mentioned elsewhere in the diagram.

FIGURE F1: ORGANIZATION OF HIGHER EDUCATION STRUCTURES, 1995/96

EUROPEAN UNION

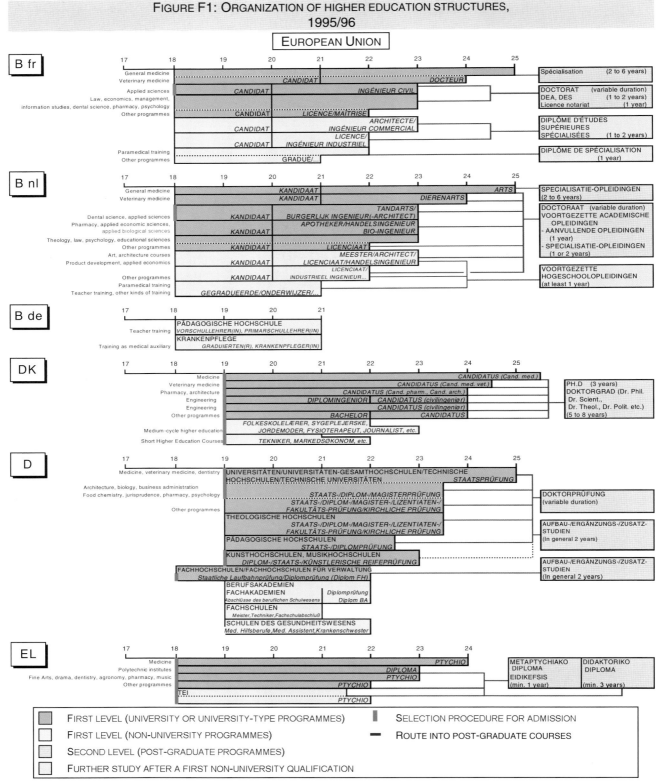

Legend:
- ▨ FIRST LEVEL (UNIVERSITY OR UNIVERSITY-TYPE PROGRAMMES)
- ☐ FIRST LEVEL (NON-UNIVERSITY PROGRAMMES)
- ▨ SECOND LEVEL (POST-GRADUATE PROGRAMMES)
- ☐ FURTHER STUDY AFTER A FIRST NON-UNIVERSITY QUALIFICATION
- ▌ SELECTION PROCEDURE FOR ADMISSION
- — ROUTE INTO POST-GRADUATE COURSES

Source: Eurydice.

Germany: In some *Länder*, colleges of art and music *(Kunst- und Musikhochschulen)* have the right to award doctorates if they provide academic courses in their specific fields of study in addition to applied arts courses. In other *Länder*, these rights can be invested in them by the ministry on application. In some training courses at *Berufsakademien*, a qualification comparable to the vocational school leaving certificate can be obtained after only 2 years on the basis of a state examination or an examination administered by a chamber of commerce, industry etc.

The duration of study indicated refers to the standard period of study *(Regelstudienzeit)* which is fixed in the examination regulations *(Prüfungsordnungen)* for each course. On average, however, students take one or 2 years longer to finish, depending on the type of higher education institution they attend.

FIGURE F1(CONTINUED): ORGANIZATION OF HIGHER EDUCATION STRUCTURES, 1995/96

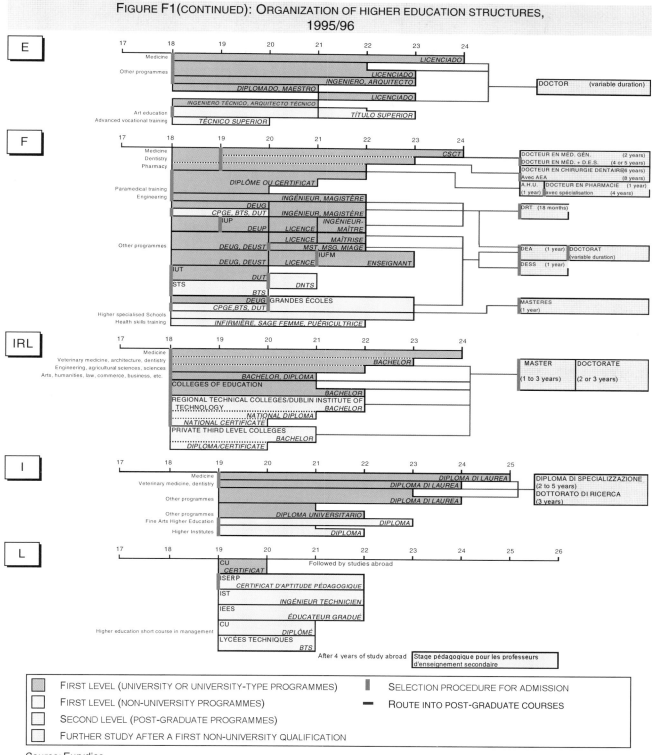

■	FIRST LEVEL (UNIVERSITY OR UNIVERSITY-TYPE PROGRAMMES)	▌ SELECTION PROCEDURE FOR ADMISSION
□	FIRST LEVEL (NON-UNIVERSITY PROGRAMMES)	▬ ROUTE INTO POST-GRADUATE COURSES
□	SECOND LEVEL (POST-GRADUATE PROGRAMMES)	
□	FURTHER STUDY AFTER A FIRST NON-UNIVERSITY QUALIFICATION	

Source: Eurydice.

Spain: To gain access to some branches of university education, students with the corresponding secondary education certificate should theoretically not have to pass through a selection process. However, for most courses in most institutions, the number of places available is less than the number of students applying and students who have passed the university entrance examination have priority over the others.

The cell off-set to the right leading to the *licenciado* qualification corresponds to the second cycle of studies which students enter from a first cycle of study established by law.

France: The *mastères* are open not only to graduates of the *grandes écoles* but also in some cases to university post-graduates, engineers, doctors and pharmacists.

Luxembourg: From the 1997/98 academic year, courses at the IST will be extended to 4 years and the final qualification will be that of industrial engineer.

FIGURE F1 (CONTINUED): ORGANIZATION OF HIGHER EDUCATION STRUCTURES, 1995/96

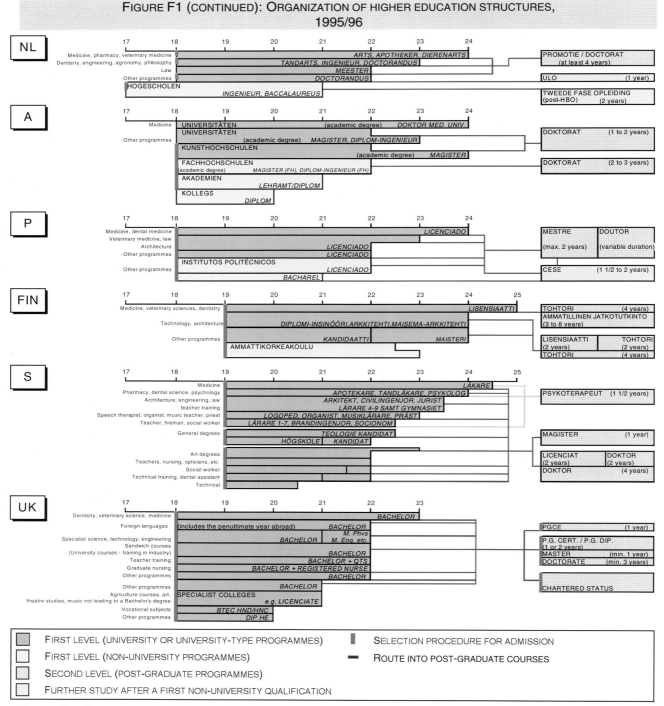

Source: Eurydice.

Austria: From the winter semester 1997/98 onwards, it will be possible to take a second doctorate in medicine (called *Doktor med. univ. et scient. med.*), which will take an additional 2 years.

Finland: The university system was reformed during the 1990s. In the old system, the *maisteri* qualification was called the *kandidaatin tutkinto*. There are still terminological variations. For example, in legal sciences the qualification is still called a *kandidaatti*. Vocational higher education is provided in the *ammattikorkeakoulu* which combine the old post-secondary education and vocational higher education systems.

United Kingdom: In England, Wales and Northern Ireland, most first degree courses are of 3 years' duration, although there are some 4-year courses. The award of an Honours degree at first (Bachelor's) level indicates a greater depth of study than an Ordinary degree. In Scotland, the Ordinary degree course comprises 3 years of studies. The Honours degree is a 4-year course involving more in-depth study. Scottish higher education studies may begin at age 17. Universities do not usually provide professional training, although they do provide a range of professionally accredited degree courses including engineering, accountancy and teacher training. Qualifications specific to a profession and (sometimes) required for its practice are more often obtained through successfully completing examinations set or accredited by professional institutes and institutions. In England, Wales and Northern Ireland, a Post-graduate Certificate of Education (PGCE) which leads to QTS (Qualified Teacher Status) can follow any first degree, except for the Bachelor + QTS path.

FIGURE F1 (CONTINUED): ORGANIZATION OF HIGHER EDUCATION STRUCTURES, 1995/96

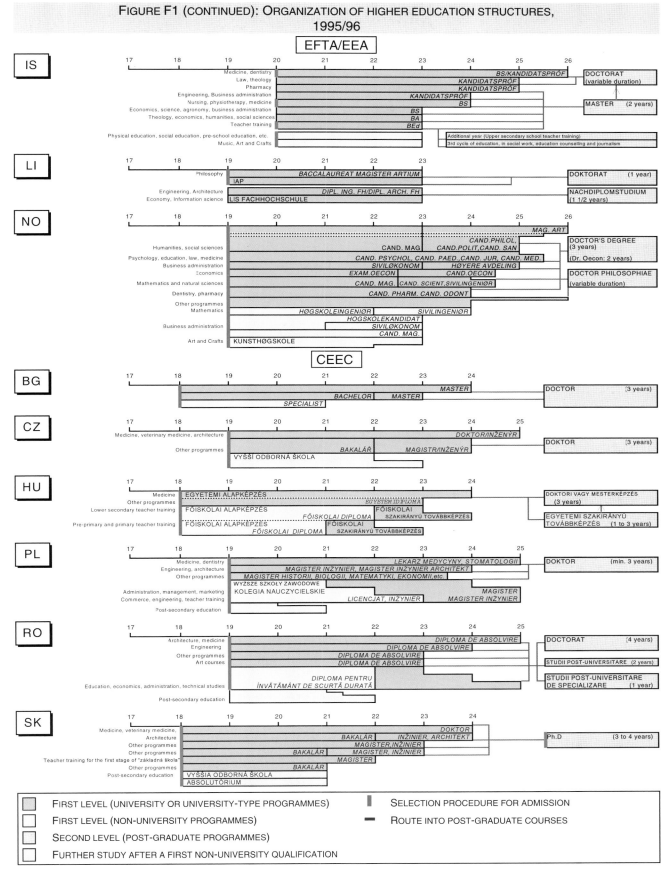

EFTA/EEA

CEEC

FIRST LEVEL (UNIVERSITY OR UNIVERSITY-TYPE PROGRAMMES)

FIRST LEVEL (NON-UNIVERSITY PROGRAMMES)

SECOND LEVEL (POST-GRADUATE PROGRAMMES)

FURTHER STUDY AFTER A FIRST NON-UNIVERSITY QUALIFICATION

SELECTION PROCEDURE FOR ADMISSION

ROUTE INTO POST-GRADUATE COURSES

Source: Eurydice.

Iceland: The programme for medicine or dentistry lasts 6 years and leads to the *Kandidatspróf*. After 4 years of study, students can, however, obtain a BS degree in medicine which is an academic, rather than a professional qualification.

Liechtenstein: From 1997, the *LIS Fachhochschule* has been renamed the *Fachhochschule Liechtenstein*.

Norway: Links and transfers between university and non-university education are common.

ACCESS TO COURSES:
—— THERE ARE NEARLY AS MANY SYSTEMS AS MEMBER STATES ——

In all the Member States of the European Union, the minimum requirement for gaining access to higher education is generally an upper secondary certificate or equivalent. Other admission procedures may be added to this, such as passing an entrance examination or competition, submitting a personal record of achievement, or attending an interview. Such procedures are usually used to limit the number of admissions, either because the number of candidates is greater than the capacity of the institution or because of a national *numerus clausus* system.

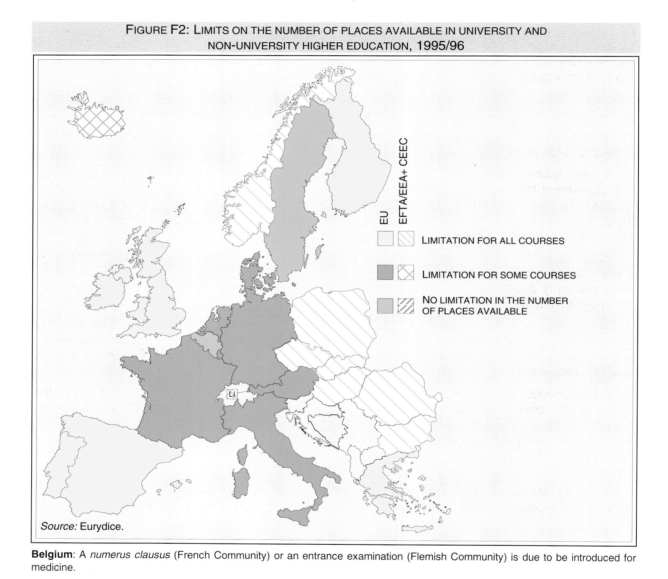

FIGURE F2: LIMITS ON THE NUMBER OF PLACES AVAILABLE IN UNIVERSITY AND NON-UNIVERSITY HIGHER EDUCATION, 1995/96

Source: Eurydice.

Belgium: A *numerus clausus* (French Community) or an entrance examination (Flemish Community) is due to be introduced for medicine.

In Greece, all higher education courses have a restricted number of places available. This number is decided centrally and accompanied by an entrance examination which is also set centrally. In Spain, sitting the national university entrance examination is in principle not compulsory for all courses. However, the capacity of the institutions is lower than the demand for places and priority is therefore given to those students who have passed the entrance examination. In Portugal, selection is based on the candidate's results in secondary school and on higher education aptitude tests arranged centrally. From 1997/98, only the results obtained in secondary school subjects will be taken into account. In the public sector in Portugal, students choose six institutions and courses in order of preference and can be directed towards other courses if they are not admitted to any of those chosen.

In three other Member States, there are also limits on the numbers of places available for all courses, but the limits are always set by the institutions themselves. In Finland, the institutions limit the numbers of places available and set their own admission procedures. These are based either on

passing an examination or on the student's personal record of achievement. In the United Kingdom, for most courses of study, the institution determines the number of places and the admission requirements. In their last year of secondary education, applicants may make up to six choices of institution and course on a single application form which includes details of their educational record. This form is sent to each of the institutions concerned via the Universities and Colleges Admissions Service (UCAS) which processes applications on behalf of all United Kingdom universities and most colleges of higher education. Each institution makes its own decision on an offer of a place. This offer is usually conditional. The final decision is made in August on receipt of the applicant's results in the examinations at the end of upper secondary school. Applicants who fail to secure a place, or who apply late, can then reapply for those courses which still have vacancies. In Ireland, there is a similar system of admissions. The institution determines the number of places and the admission requirements, and application for almost all full-time undergraduate courses is made through a Central Applications Office. Applicants can apply for up to 20 courses and offers are made on the basis of grades achieved in the examinations at the end of upper secondary school. Mature students and non-standard entry students apply directly to the appropriate institution.

In the other Member States, limits on the number of places available and the admission procedures vary according to the course chosen and can be decided at national level, institutional level, or both.

In Denmark, the restrictions on access which apply to certain courses are determined by the individual higher education institutions.

In Germany, access to courses is via a supra-regional selection procedure which is based on an inter-state agreement between the *Länder* on the allocation of study places. The courses subject to this selection procedure can vary from one semester to another depending on the available places. The limitation in admissions to certain courses offered by higher education institutions depends only on the capacity of the institution.

In France, general university courses are not selective. For the selective courses (IUT, preparatory classes for the *grandes écoles*) the selection procedures are usually determined by the institutions. Some university courses incorporate national competitive examinations in which students must be successful during the course.

In Italy, the universities decide on the faculties which will offer either open or limited access. In higher non-university education, access to courses is systematically based on admission procedures defined by the institutions themselves. In Luxembourg, only access to pre-primary and primary teacher training is limited on the basis of a decision taken at national level.

In the Netherlands, all branches of higher education have open access in principle. However, the number of admissions can be limited at national level when the number of people with a qualification exceeds the labour market needs. Such a decision can also be taken by the institution when the number of applicants exceeds the places available. For some courses, the Minister can impose a requirement that candidates must have studied one or two specific subjects during secondary education.

In Austria, admission procedures exist in some higher university and non-university institutions (e.g. *Fachhochschul-Studiengänge* and *Kunsthochschulen*) and these are determined at institutional level.

In Belgium, there is no limit on the number of places available, and access to higher education is usually open. Only applied sciences and, in the Flemish Community, dentistry require a pass in the entrance examination set by the institution. In Sweden also, there is no limit in the number of places available, but unlike in Belgium, all courses have admission procedures which are defined by the institutions.

In the EFTA/EEA countries, in Iceland, the number of places available may be limited depending on the course: nearly all university courses are open access. In Norway, the number of places is limited for most courses and the decision on the number of places available each year is taken at national level.

In the CEECs, courses usually have limited numbers of places available. Decisions are taken at national level in Bulgaria and Romania (public sector), and at institution level in the other countries.

OVER 11 MILLION STUDENTS IN THE UNION

During the academic year 1994/95, there were more than 11.7 million students in higher education, comprising 14% of all pupils and students in education in the European Union.

FIGURE F3: STUDENTS IN HIGHER EDUCATION, IN THOUSANDS AND AS A PERCENTAGE OF THE TOTAL POPULATION IN EDUCATION, 1994/95

EU	B	DK	D	EL	E	F	IRL
11 777	353	170	2 156	296	1 527	2 073	122
14%	14%	15%	13%	15%	16%	14%	12%

I	L	NL	A	P	FIN	S	UK
1 792	2	503	234	301	205	246	1 813
17%		14%	14%	13%	18%	12%	13%

Source: Eurostat, UOE.

Luxembourg: The very small number of students in higher education within the country is explained by the fact that the majority of students study abroad.

EFTA/EEA		
IS	LI	NO
7	0.3	173
9%		17%

CEEC					
BG	CZ	HU	PL	RO	SK
223	166	116	682	300	82
13%	8%	6%	8%	6%	8%

Source: Eurostat, UOE.   National statistics.

Iceland: Figures include only full-time students.
Liechtenstein: The very small number of students in higher education within the country is explained by the fact that the majority of students study abroad.

In the European Union, the proportion of students studying in higher education in their home country as a percentage of all those in education varies from 12 to 18%, depending on the Member State. These variations reflect different patterns of organization, such as varying course lengths, the numbers of places available and the numbers of people in education, which is linked to demographic changes.

The number of students in relation to the number of pupils and students in education is particularly high in Norway (17%). In Iceland and the CEECs, this proportion is under 10%, except in Bulgaria where it reaches 13%.

EXPLANATORY NOTE

The different types of higher education analysed in this chapter correspond to ISCED levels 5, 6 and 7. At present, these are treated globally in the statistics available from Eurostat, with full-time and part-time, university and non-university higher education being regarded as a whole.

The proportion of students in higher education as a percentage of the total population in education is calculated by dividing the number of students in higher education by the total number of pupils and students. The total figure for all pupils and students (ISCED levels 0 to 7) includes pupils in pre-school institutions. In the previous edition of this document (1995), ISCED level 0 was not included.

The European Union figure is calculated by dividing the total number of students enrolled in higher education by the total number of pupils and students in the European Union, all Member States combined.

F

HIGHER EDUCATION

STUDENTS ARE UNEVENLY DISTRIBUTED
——— ACROSS THE DIFFERENT REGIONS ———

The proportion of students in relation to the total population in education varies from one region to another in the European Union.

The highest percentages of students in higher education are found in the Brussels region of Belgium (24%), in the German *Länder* of Berlin (21%), Bremen (21%) and Hamburg (23%), in the Madrid region of Spain (21%), in Italy in the regions of Emilia-Romagna (26%), Centro (22%) and Lazio (24%), in Eastern Austria (20%) and in the Uusimaa region of Finland (25%). These are regions with large cities, probably well-endowed with higher education institutions and facilities.

Relatively high proportions of students are also found in the northern European regions and around the Mediterranean basin.

FIGURE F4: HIGHER EDUCATION STUDENTS AS A PERCENTAGE OF ALL PUPILS AND STUDENTS, BY NUTS 1 AND 2 REGIONS, 1994/95

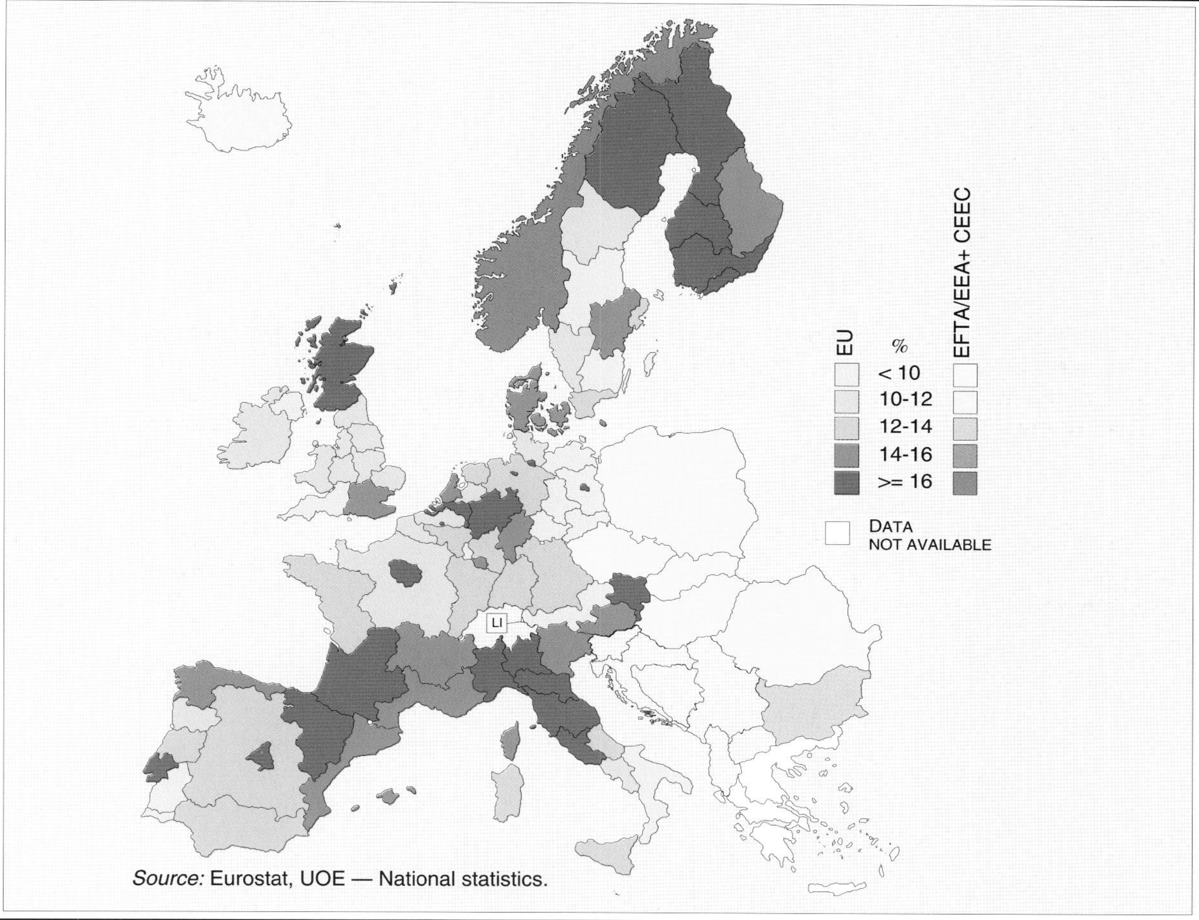

EU %
EFTA/EEA+ CEEC
< 10
10-12
12-14
14-16
>= 16

DATA NOT AVAILABLE

LI

Source: Eurostat, UOE — National statistics.

Belgium and **Netherlands**: 1993/94.
Spain: Figures exclude distance learning students.

EXPLANATORY NOTE
For most of the Member States, the nomenclature used here is that of NUTS 1, which is the largest of the regional units. NUTS 2 is, however, used for Portugal, Finland and Sweden. For the EFTA/EEA countries and the CEECs, only national data are presented.
The division into classes is based on the distribution of the data. The categories created make up a continuous series each containing the same percentage of values.

STUDENT NUMBERS ON THE INCREASE
OVER THE LAST TWENTY YEARS

Figure F5 illustrates the steady rise in the number of students enrolled in higher education in each of the Member States since 1975. This rise is shown in terms of an index of the growth in student numbers based on the reference year 1975.

In the European Union as a whole, the number of students in higher education has nearly doubled over the last twenty years.

The Member States which show the greatest growth in student numbers are Portugal (3.4 times) and Spain (2.8 times).

FIGURE F5: TRENDS IN THE NUMBERS OF STUDENTS IN HIGHER EDUCATION (ISCED LEVELS 5 TO 7) BETWEEN 1975 AND 1994

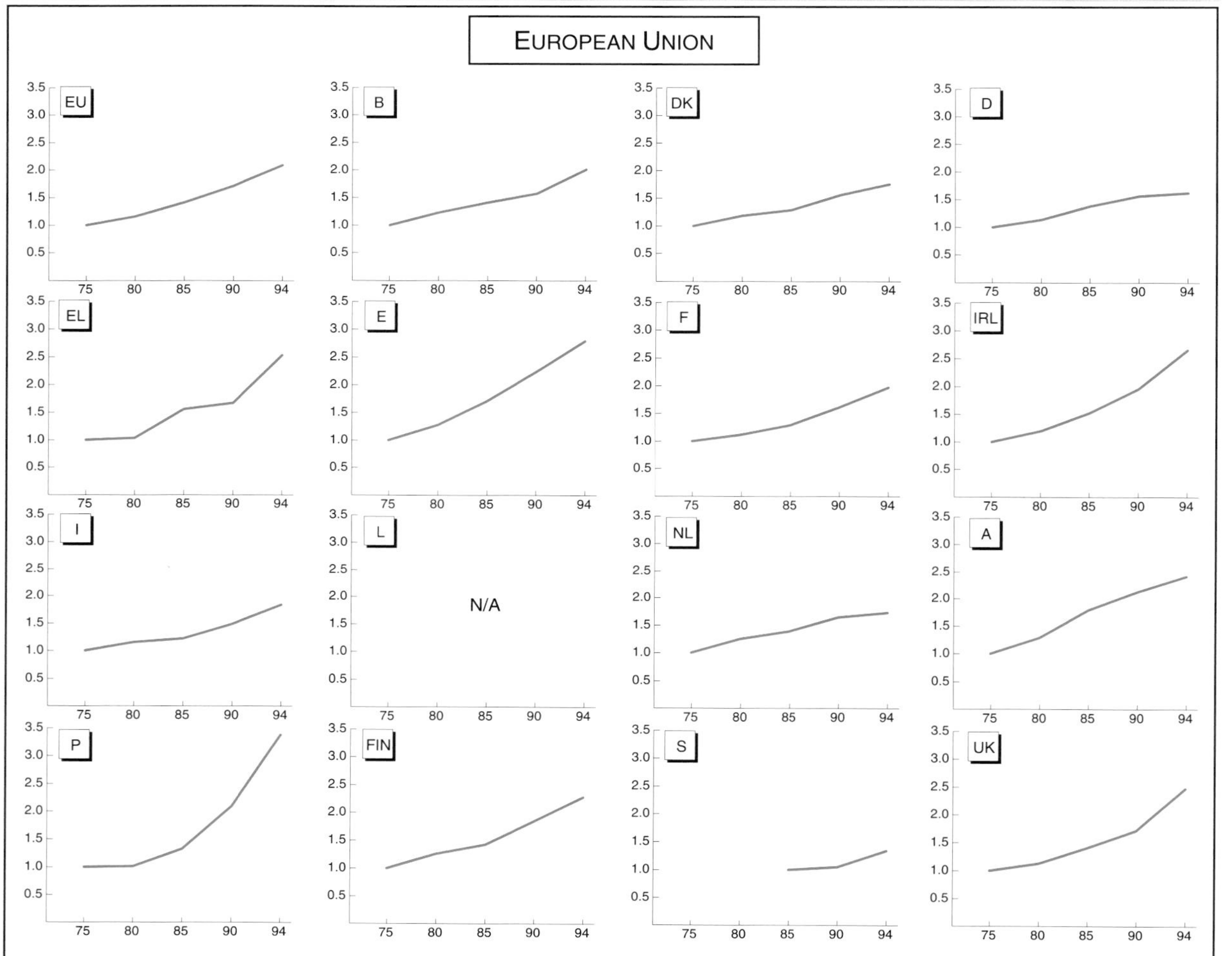

Source: Eurostat, UOE.

Sweden: The reference year is 1985.
United Kingdom: Data for years prior to 1982 do not include nursing and paramedical students.

In Iceland there has been a steady increase in the number of students since 1975/76. The CEECs show different trends over the two decades. During the early 1980s, the number of students decreased in most countries, though this decrease took place earlier in Bulgaria. Since 1985, however, the number of students has increased in all countries.

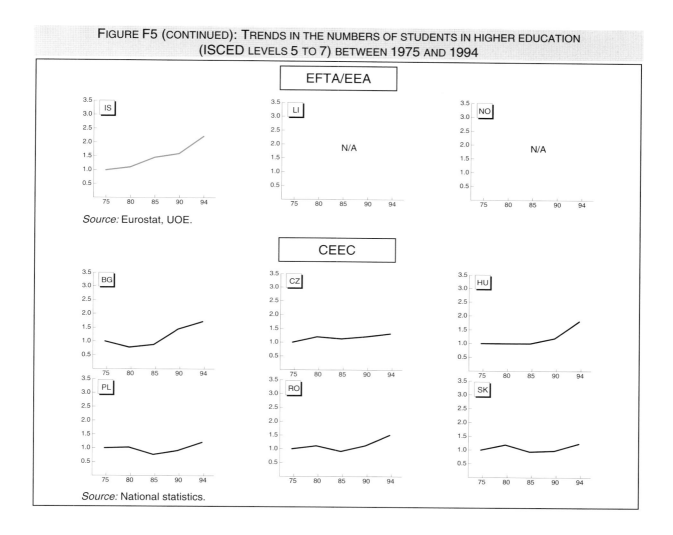

FIGURE F5 (CONTINUED): TRENDS IN THE NUMBERS OF STUDENTS IN HIGHER EDUCATION (ISCED LEVELS 5 TO 7) BETWEEN 1975 AND 1994

EXPLANATORY NOTE

The growth index is obtained by dividing the number of students each year by the number in the 1975 reference year. The European Union values are estimates.

PARTICIPATION IN HIGHER EDUCATION:
A WIDE AGE RANGE

The ages of students in higher education vary greatly from one Member State to another. In Belgium, Greece, France, Ireland and the United Kingdom, the participation rate is high at the age of 18. The participation rates peak between 19 and 20 and drop sharply from the age of 21. Conversely, in Denmark and Germany, the highest participation rates are at the age of 23 or 24. It is also in these Member States that students study longest.

FIGURE F6: PARTICIPATION RATES IN HIGHER EDUCATION BY AGE AND BY SEX, 1994/95

EUROPEAN UNION

— MEN   — WOMEN

Source: Eurostat, UOE.

Denmark: Excluding adult education.
Germany: The breakdown by age is estimated for students aged 24 and over.
Ireland: Data for the numbers of male and female students at ages 25 to 29 years are not available.

Male and female participation rates in higher education at different ages follow a similar pattern. They are initially higher for women than for men, though with increasing age the rates for men catch up or even pass those for women in some Member States. This tendency is particularly marked in Germany (partly due to compulsory military or civil service for men).

The pattern in Iceland and Norway is similar to that in the northern Member States of the European Union. Participation rates increase gradually between ages 18 and 21 and are still relatively high at the age of 26. The participation rate of women is higher than that of men from age 21 to 26 in Iceland and from 19 to 24 in Norway.

In the CEECs for which information is available, participation rates tend to be lower than in the European Union and few students study after the age of 26.

FIGURE F6 (CONTINUED): PARTICIPATION RATES IN HIGHER EDUCATION
BY AGE AND BY SEX, 1994/95

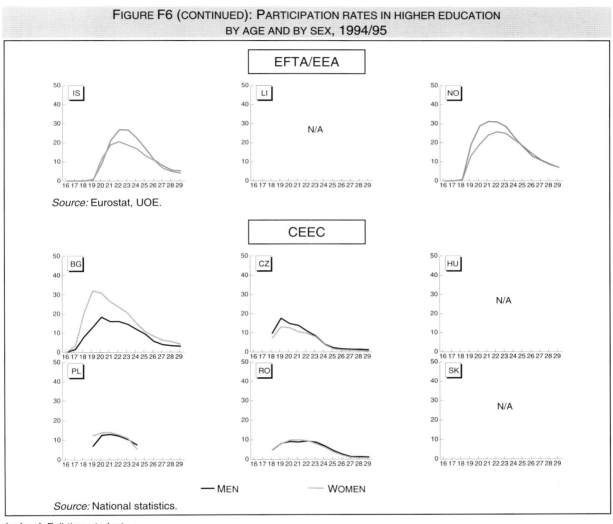

Iceland: Full-time students.
Poland: Data for the numbers of male and female students at ages 25 to 29 years are not available.

EXPLANATORY NOTE
Participation rates by age in higher education are calculated by dividing the number of young people of a particular age enrolled in higher education by the total number of people of this age. The rates are calculated separately for men and women.
The European Union rates are calculated by dividing the numbers of young people by age and by sex enrolled in higher education, by the total number of people of the same age/sex. The figures are estimates.

F

HIGHER EDUCATION

PROPORTION OF WOMEN STUDENTS
CONSTANTLY INCREASING

In tandem with the overall increase in student numbers since 1975, there has also been a marked increase in the proportion of women students in higher education.

FIGURE F7: TRENDS IN THE NUMBER OF WOMEN PER 100 MEN ENROLLED IN HIGHER EDUCATION (ISCED LEVELS 5 TO 7) BETWEEN 1975 AND 1994

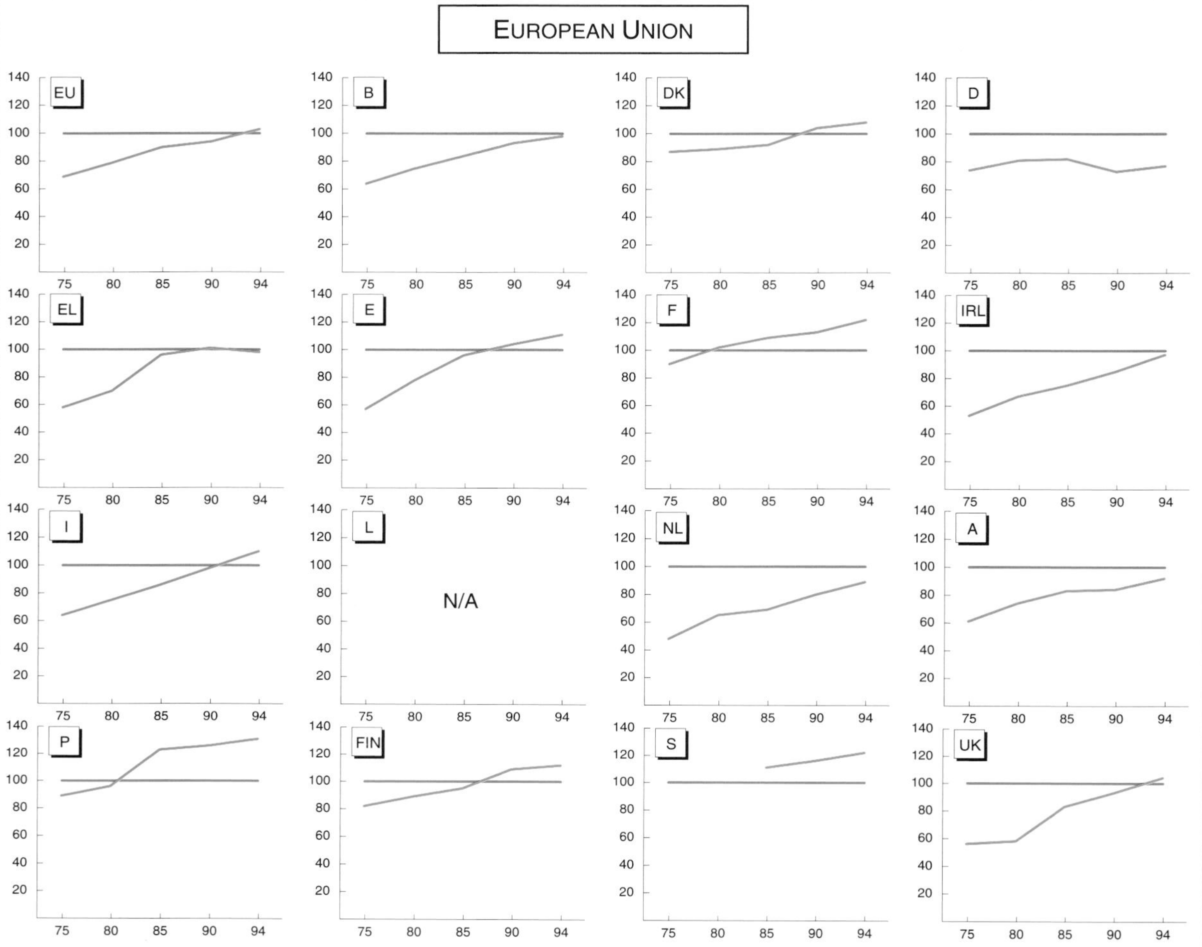

EUROPEAN UNION

Source: Eurostat, UOE.

Sweden: From 1992, data include adult education.
United Kingdom: Data for years prior to 1982 do not include nursing and paramedical students.

Twenty years ago, women were in the minority in higher education in every Member State. Over time, the proportion of women has increased and they are now in the majority in many of them. There have been more women than men in higher education since the early 1980s in France and Portugal and women students now outnumber men in Denmark, Spain, Italy, Finland and the United Kingdom. Although all countries show an increase in the proportion of women students, women remain in the minority in Germany, the Netherlands and Austria.

EXPLANATORY NOTE
The number of women per 100 men enrolled in higher education is calculated by dividing the number of female students by the number of male students and then multiplying the result by 100. The European Union values are estimates.

In Iceland the participation rates of women students grew steadily until 1990 when women became the majority.

The CEECs show contrasting patterns. In Bulgaria and Poland, women have been in the majority in higher education since 1975. On the other hand, although the numbers of women students have increased in the Czech Republic, Romania and Slovakia, they are still outnumbered by men. In Hungary the male/female balance has remained about equal.

FIGURE F7 (CONTINUED): TRENDS IN THE NUMBER OF WOMEN PER 100 MEN ENROLLED IN HIGHER EDUCATION (ISCED LEVELS 5 TO 7) BETWEEN 1975 AND 1994

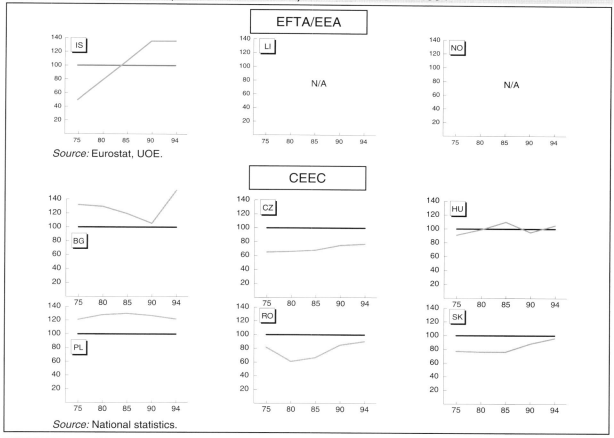

FIGURE F8: NUMBERS OF WOMEN PER 100 MEN ENROLLED IN HIGHER EDUCATION (ISCED LEVELS 5 TO 7), 1994/95

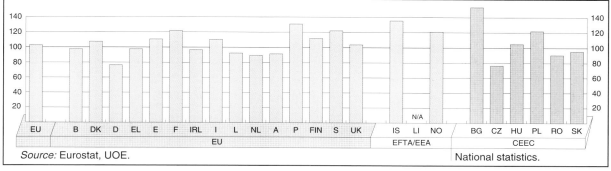

Iceland: Full-time students only.

In the European Union as a whole, the proportion of women is slightly higher than that of men, with 103 women to every 100 men enrolled in higher education. This overall rate, however, conceals disparities between Member States. Although female students outnumber male students in more than half of the Member States, this is not true in all of them. There are 131 women for 100 men in Portugal, but only 77 in Germany and 89 in the Netherlands.

ERASMUS:
A SUCCESSFUL STIMULUS TO STUDENT MOBILITY

Since 1976, the European Community has been encouraging students to enrich their education by undertaking part of their course of study outside their own Member State. With this in view, the ERASMUS programme for the mobility of students in higher education was introduced in 1987. Since 1995, this activity has been included as part of the SOCRATES programme.

As Figure F9 shows, the number of participants in this exchange programme organized by the European Union has increased eight-fold in six years.

FIGURE F9: TREND IN THE NUMBERS OF EUROPEAN UNION STUDENTS SELECTED TO TAKE PART IN AN ERASMUS EXCHANGE PROGRAMME (THOUSANDS), 1988-95

Source: Erasmus, Time series statistics 1988/89 to 1995/96.

Austria, Finland and **Sweden**: Participation from 1992/93.

As Figure F10 shows, this is a general trend which is found in all Member States of the European Union, but to differing degrees. Some of them saw a very marked increase in their numbers of participants at the start of the period and the growth appears to be slowing down. Others have seen a slower but more steady increase.

FIGURE F10: NUMBERS OF STUDENTS SELECTED TO PARTICIPATE IN AN ERASMUS EXCHANGE PROGRAMME (THOUSANDS), 1988, 1992, 1995

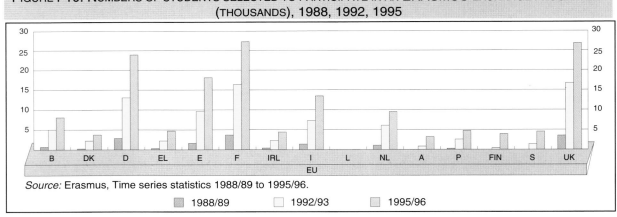

Source: Erasmus, Time series statistics 1988/89 to 1995/96.

■ 1988/89   □ 1992/93   □ 1995/96

Luxembourg: The number of students is too small to show in this graph. Full data appear in the annex.
Austria, Finland and **Sweden**: Did not participate in 1988/89.

Aside from the proportion of home students taking part in this programme, it is also interesting to examine whether and, if so, the extent to which, certain Member States send more students abroad under the Community programme than they receive from the others. Figure F11 shows for each of the Member States the percentage of home students sent abroad with a SOCRATES exchange scholarship and the corresponding percentage of non-national students received by their higher education institutions in 1994/95. In most Member States, the proportions of non-national students received by their higher education institutions and of students sent to other Member States taking part in the Community programme are roughly the same.

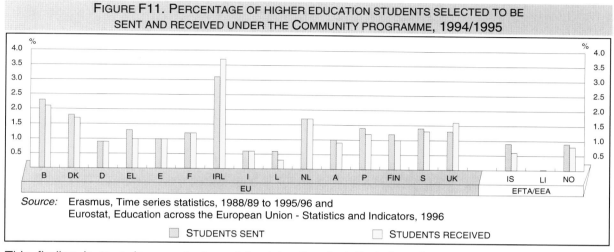

FIGURE F11. PERCENTAGE OF HIGHER EDUCATION STUDENTS SELECTED TO BE SENT AND RECEIVED UNDER THE COMMUNITY PROGRAMME, 1994/1995

Source: Erasmus, Time series statistics, 1988/89 to 1995/96 and
Eurostat, Education across the European Union - Statistics and Indicators, 1996

STUDENTS SENT   STUDENTS RECEIVED

This finding is to a large extent explained by the fact that that these exchanges are arranged bilaterally between institutions. The number of students received is therefore often relatively close to the number of students sent abroad.

The attraction of the English-speaking Member States is however evident as Ireland, in particular, and the United Kingdom stand out as those which have a net inflow of foreign students. In Belgium, Greece, Luxembourg, Portugal and Finland of the EU Member States, and in Iceland of the EFTA/EEA countries, the situation is the reverse. They receive fewer students under the SOCRATES programme than they send to higher education institutions abroad. Luxembourg and Liechtenstein are particular cases in that neither has its own university system.

EXPLANATORY NOTE

Between 1990 and 1994, some of the students moving under the Inter-university Cooperation Programmes (ICP) were financed under Action II of the LINGUA programme. This action implemented in 1990 aimed to promote foreign language learning at higher education level and involved, in particular, future teachers of modern languages. The application and management arrangements in relation to these scholarships were identical to those introduced for ERASMUS students.

All the statistics provided in this note are for the numbers of students included in the ICPs approved by the European Commission and therefore eligible for an ERASMUS (or Lingua Action II) travel scholarship.

In Figure F11, the percentages are calculated by taking, on the one hand, the ratio of the number of home students selected to go abroad under the Community programme to the total number of higher education students in the Member State and, on the other hand, by calculating the same ratio for non-national students selected to be received in the Member State under the same scheme.

YOUNG PEOPLE STUDYING
OUTSIDE THEIR OWN COUNTRY

Figure F12 presents for each nationality the percentages of students pursuing their higher education in another EU Member State or in an EFTA/EEA country.

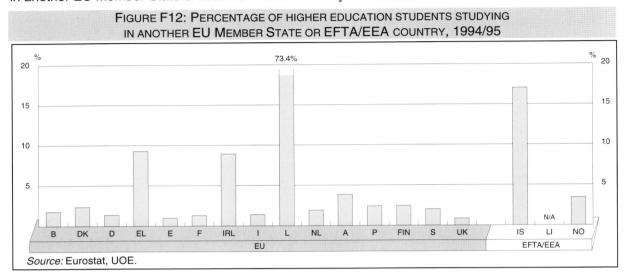

FIGURE F12: PERCENTAGE OF HIGHER EDUCATION STUDENTS STUDYING IN ANOTHER EU MEMBER STATE OR EFTA/EEA COUNTRY, 1994/95

Source: Eurostat, UOE.

Within the European Union, a proportionately greater number of Greek and Irish students go abroad to pursue their higher education in another Member State or in an EFTA/EEA country. The case of Luxembourg is unusual — there is only limited higher education provision in that Member State, and students are therefore obliged to study abroad. The number of students from Luxembourg studying abroad therefore far exceeds the number of students enrolled in Luxembourg. On the other hand, in the larger Member States, such as Germany, Spain, France, Italy and the United Kingdom, the vast majority of students pursue their studies in their own country.

In the EFTA/EEA countries for which information is available, the percentage of students leaving their country to study in an EU Member State or another EFTA/EEA country is particularly high in Iceland.

EXPLANATORY NOTE

Member States do not have details of the numbers of their home students studying abroad. For a given nationality, the number of students studying abroad (either in the EU or in an EFTA/EEA country) is calculated by summing the numbers provided for this nationality by the receiving Member States or EFTA/EEA countries. The number is then divided by the total number of students of this nationality. The lack of data on the distribution of students by nationality for some Member States or EFTA/EEA countries has repercussions for nearly all of the values shown: these are generally under-estimated.

SOCIAL SCIENCES:
THE MOST POPULAR AREA OF STUDY

The largest proportion of higher education students in the European Union as a whole (26%) are studying social sciences, including business administration and mass communication and documentation. The next most popular subject group is 'engineering and architecture' (17%), followed by 'humanities, applied arts and theology' (13%), and medical sciences (11%).

The social sciences group attracts the largest proportion of students in most Member States. This field is particularly popular in the Netherlands and Portugal, where it is chosen by over one third of students. The field of 'engineering and architecture' is the second most popular in most Member States, whereas it is the most popular in Finland.

A relatively high percentage (about 20%) of Danish and Irish students turn to 'humanities, applied arts and theology', whereas proportionately more Spanish and Italian students choose to study law. Finland and the United Kingdom have the highest proportions of those studying 'medical science', which includes the training of nurses.

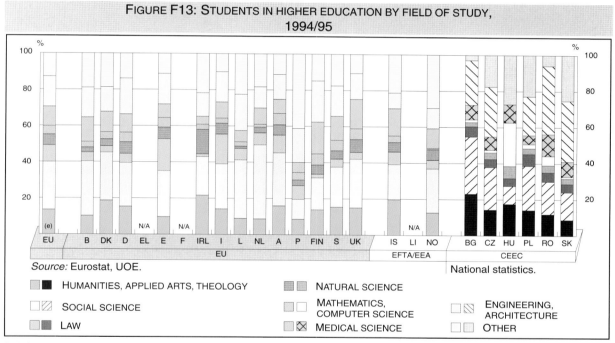

FIGURE F13: STUDENTS IN HIGHER EDUCATION BY FIELD OF STUDY, 1994/95

Source: Eurostat, UOE. National statistics.

Belgium: 1993/94.
Italy: Data under the heading 'Other' all refer to ISCED level 5.
Luxembourg: Data relate only to the higher education institutions in Luxembourg.
Bulgaria: The 'Other' category includes students at the military training schools.
Hungary: Technical education is included under 'mathematics and computer science'. 'Social science' includes only economics.

In Iceland, the 'humanities, applied arts and theology' group is very popular. In Norway, as in most Member States, the social sciences attract a large proportion of students. The social sciences also appear to attract a large proportion of students in the CEECs. However, the classification used in these countries does not always correspond to that used by Eurostat and the data should be interpreted with caution.

EXPLANATORY NOTE
Using the ISCED definitions of fields of study, Eurostat classifies subjects into eight groups in the following terms: humanities, applied arts and theology; social science (including business administration and mass communication and documentation); law; natural science; mathematics and computer science; medical science (including nursing); engineering and architecture (including trade, craft and industrial programmes); other and unspecified (including education science and teacher training; agriculture; home economics and service trades).

WOMEN PREFER ARTS AND MEDICAL SCIENCES

Some subject areas are more often chosen by women than others. Throughout the European Union, more women than men choose the medical sciences, which include nursing, and 'humanities, applied arts and theology'.

The large proportion of women in the medical sciences can be clearly seen in Denmark (80%), Finland (84%) and the United Kingdom (77%). However, in Italy, where the balance of men to women on these courses is equal, more women tend to choose 'humanities, applied arts and theology'.

Women tend to be underrepresented in 'mathematics and computer science' and in 'engineering and architecture' in all Member States. However, the proportion of women enrolling on courses in these subjects is relatively higher in Spain, Italy and Portugal than in the other Member States.

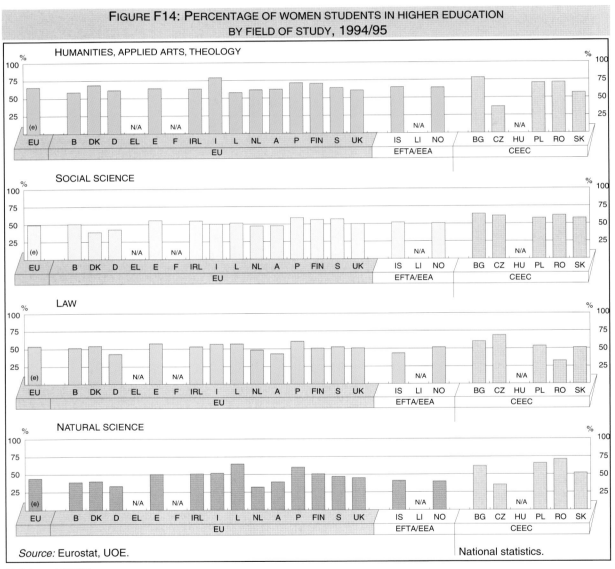

FIGURE F14: PERCENTAGE OF WOMEN STUDENTS IN HIGHER EDUCATION BY FIELD OF STUDY, 1994/95

Source: Eurostat, UOE. National statistics.

Belgium: 1993/94.

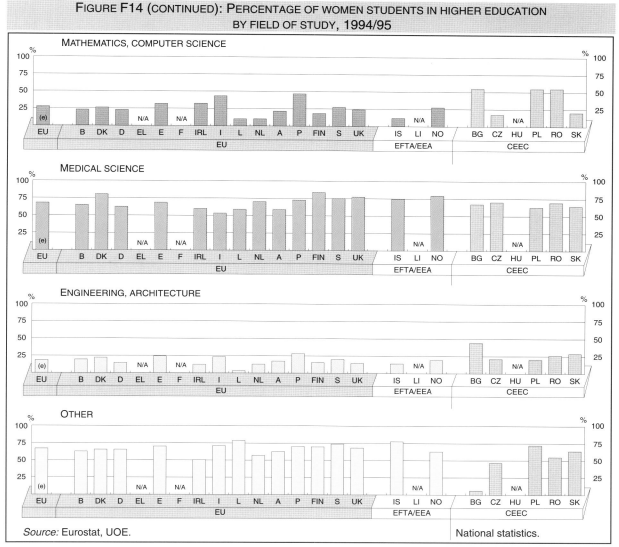

FIGURE F14 (CONTINUED): PERCENTAGE OF WOMEN STUDENTS IN HIGHER EDUCATION BY FIELD OF STUDY, 1994/95

Source: Eurostat, UOE. National statistics.

Belgium: 1993/94.

In the EFTA/EEA countries, there are also more women than men on courses in the medical sciences (over 75%) and in 'humanities, applied arts and theology'. They are less represented in 'mathematics and computer science' and 'engineering and architecture'.

EXPLANATORY NOTE

Using the ISCED definitions of fields of study, Eurostat classifies subjects into eight groups in the following terms: humanities, applied arts and theology; social science (including business administration and mass communication and documentation); law; natural science; mathematics and computer science; medical science (including nursing); engineering and architecture (including trade, craft and industrial programmes); other and unspecified (including education science and teacher training; agriculture; home economics and service trades).

A rate is calculated for each study area and the European Union rate is calculated by dividing the total number of female students by the total student population for all Member States, and multiplying the result by 100.

AMONG 35- TO 60-YEAR-OLDS, THE YOUNGER PEOPLE ARE BETTER QUALIFIED

FIGURE F15: PROPORTION OF PEOPLE BETWEEN THE AGES OF 35 AND 60 WITH HIGHER EDUCATION QUALIFICATIONS, BY AGE GROUP, 1995

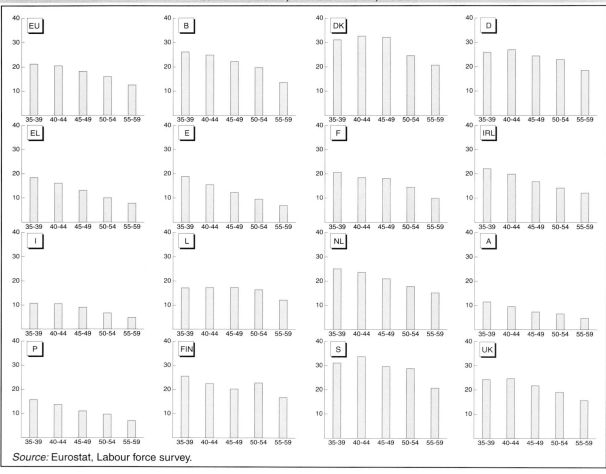

Source: Eurostat, Labour force survey.

Younger Europeans are more likely to have a higher education qualification than their elders. Whereas 20% of EU citizens aged between 35 and 39 have a higher education qualification, the rate for those between 55 and 59 years is 12.5%.

This trend is apparent throughout the European Union and is particularly strong in Belgium, Greece, Spain, France, Ireland, Austria and Portugal where there are twice as many qualified people in the youngest as in the oldest age group. In other countries, the age-based differences are less marked since the percentage of people with higher education qualifications in the 55- to 59-year age group is relatively high. In Italy and Austria, the proportions of those with qualifications are relatively small across all the age groups considered.

EXPLANATORY NOTE
The percentage of people with higher education qualifications is calculated by dividing the number of those with higher education qualifications by the population figures, for a given age. The European Union figure is calculated by dividing the total number of qualified people by the European Union population figures, all Member States combined.

ONE YOUNG PERSON IN FIVE HOLDS
A HIGHER EDUCATION QUALIFICATION

In the European Union, more than 20% of young adults between 30 and 34 years old hold a higher education qualification. However, this percentage conceals major disparities between Member States. In Belgium and Sweden, over 30% of those in this age band have a qualification at this level while in Italy, Austria and Portugal, the proportions with such qualifications are distinctly smaller.

FIGURE F16: PERCENTAGE OF YOUNG PEOPLE BETWEEN THE AGES OF 30 AND 34 WITH HIGHER EDUCATION QUALIFICATIONS, 1995.

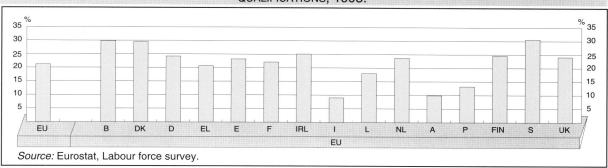

Source: Eurostat, Labour force survey.

Denmark: The figures are a slight underestimate due to the method of calculation.

EXPLANATORY NOTE
The European Union percentage is obtained by dividing the total number of those with qualifications by the European Union population figures, all Member States combined.

MORE WOMEN HAVE HIGHER EDUCATION QUALIFICATIONS

FIGURE F17: NUMBER OF WOMEN WITH HIGHER EDUCATION QUALIFICATIONS PER 100 MEN, 1994/95

Source: Eurostat, UOE. | National statistics.

Ireland: 1993/94. Some students with a vocational qualification at ISCED level 5 are excluded. Students in private independent colleges are also excluded, as are those in nursing schools who obtained their qualification after 3 or 4 years of in-hospital training.

In the European Union as a whole, more women than men have higher education qualifications. This is true in most Member States, except Germany, Ireland and the Netherlands. Portugal has the highest ratio of women to men with higher education qualifications, whereas in Germany, there are only 83 women for every 100 men with a higher education qualification.

In Norway, more women than men have higher education qualifications. In the CEECs for which figures are available, it appears that slightly more women than men obtain a higher education qualification in the Czech Republic. However, in Poland and Hungary, although women students are in the majority, fewer women than men obtain qualifications.

EXPLANATORY NOTE
The European Union figure is calculated by dividing the total number of women with higher education qualifications by the total number of men with higher education qualifications in all Member States, and multiplying the result by 100.

NEARLY A QUARTER OF THOSE WITH HIGHER EDUCATION QUALIFICATIONS HAVE STUDIED SOCIAL SCIENCES

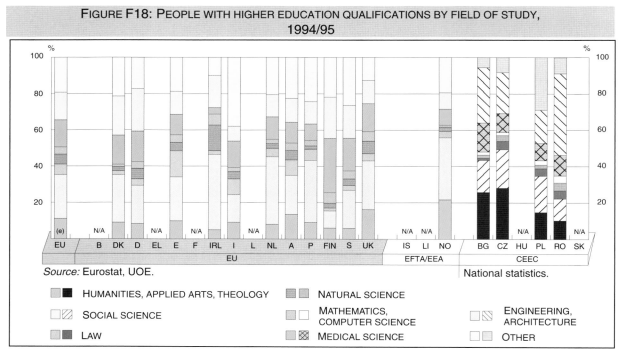

FIGURE F18: PEOPLE WITH HIGHER EDUCATION QUALIFICATIONS BY FIELD OF STUDY, 1994/95

Source: Eurostat, UOE.

National statistics.

Ireland: 1993/94. The total number of those with higher education qualifications is included here, including those with two qualifications (about 4 000). Some students with a vocational qualification at ISCED level 5 are excluded. Students in private independent colleges are also excluded, as are those in nursing schools who obtained their qualification after 3 or 4 years of in-hospital training.

In the European Union as a whole, nearly a quarter (24%) of those obtaining a higher education qualification in 1994/95 completed social sciences courses (including business administration and mass communication and documentation). The next largest percentage of qualifications (19%) is in the 'other' category which includes teacher education and training. This is followed in popularity by medical sciences and 'engineering and architecture' (both 15%).

The social sciences produce the greatest proportion of those with higher education qualifications in Denmark, Spain, Ireland, the Netherlands, Portugal and the United Kingdom. In Italy, Austria and in Sweden, the highest proportion of qualifications is in the 'other' category, whereas in Germany, the most popular field is 'engineering and architecture' and in Finland medical sciences.

In Norway, the social sciences category predominates and the largest proportion of people with qualifications in 'humanities, applied arts and theology' is also found there.

The classification used in the CEECs does not always match that used by Eurostat and the figures must therefore be interpreted with caution.

EXPLANATORY NOTE

Using the ISCED definitions of fields of study, Eurostat classifies subjects into eight groups in the following terms: humanities, applied arts and theology; social science (including business administration and mass communication and documentation); law; natural science; mathematics and computer science; medical science (including nursing); engineering and architecture (including trade, craft and industrial programmes); other and unspecified (including education science and teacher training; agriculture; home economics and the service trades).

HIGHER EDUCATION PARTICIPATION RATES
IN RELATION TO PARENTS' LEVEL OF EDUCATION

FIGURE F19: PARTICIPATION RATE OF 19- TO 24-YEAR-OLDS IN HIGHER EDUCATION
BY EDUCATIONAL LEVEL OF PARENTS, 1995

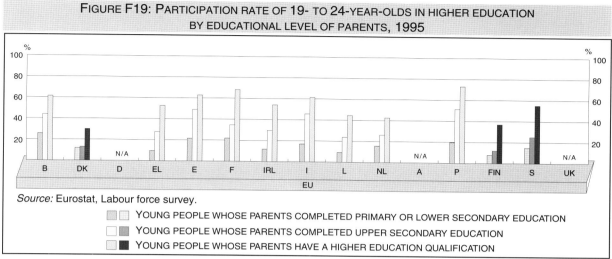

Source: Eurostat, Labour force survey.

■□ YOUNG PEOPLE WHOSE PARENTS COMPLETED PRIMARY OR LOWER SECONDARY EDUCATION
□■ YOUNG PEOPLE WHOSE PARENTS COMPLETED UPPER SECONDARY EDUCATION
□■ YOUNG PEOPLE WHOSE PARENTS HAVE A HIGHER EDUCATION QUALIFICATION

Denmark: National surveys of 18- to 24-year-olds. Note that a relatively high proportion of this age group is still in upper secondary education.
Finland: National survey of 20- to 24-year-olds.
Sweden: National survey of 26- and 27-year-olds.

Figure F19 compares for each Member State the rates of participation in higher education of three groups of young people: those whose parents completed primary or lower secondary education; those whose parents completed upper secondary education; and those whose parents have a higher education qualification.

In the European Union as a whole, the higher education participation rates for 19- to 24-year-olds increase as their parents' educational level increases. The same pattern emerges whichever Member State is considered: a greater proportion of young people participates in higher education from families in which the head of household has a higher education qualification and proportionately fewer from families in which the head of household has completed only primary or lower secondary education.

EXPLANATORY NOTE
The Labour force survey (LFS) *enables the connection between parents and children to be analysed to the extent that they live in the same household. This causes problems in those Member States in which a large number of students live away from their family and are heads of households themselves. Where the estimated participation rate for the whole LFS sample was too far from the actual participation rate (UOE data), the survey data were considered to be unreliable and were not used. This was the case for Germany, Austria and the United Kingdom. For some countries, national surveys have been used to help determine the parents' (father's or mother's) level of education.*
The 19- to 24-year-olds in the study sample are assigned to one of three categories depending on the educational level of the head of household — A: young people from families in which the head of household completed either primary or lower secondary education (ISCED 1 or 2); B: young people from families where the head of household completed upper secondary education (ISCED 3); C: young people from families where the head of household has a higher education qualification (ISCED 5, 6 or 7). The indicator establishes the higher education participation rates by dividing the number of students in each category by the number of young people in each of these categories.

TEACHERS

INCREASING TREND TOWARDS UNIVERSITY-LEVEL EDUCATION AND TRAINING

In the European Union today, the education and training of teachers working in primary and secondary schools is generally provided at higher education level, either in universities or in non-university institutions of higher education. In Italy, however, the reform measure passed in 1990 providing for the university training of primary teachers has not yet been implemented and those teachers are still being trained in the *istituti magistrali* at upper secondary level.

The education and training of pre-primary teachers is at higher education level except in Germany, where it is provided at upper secondary level for the adults *(Erzieher)* responsible for children in the *Kindergärten,* and in Italy, where pre-primary teachers are still trained in the *scuole magistrali,* pending the implementation of the 1990 reform which aims to provide training at university level for these teachers. In Austria, their preparation takes place at either upper secondary or higher education level.

In more than half of the Member States (Denmark, Germany, Greece, Spain, France, Ireland, Finland, Sweden and the United Kingdom), initial teacher training for the primary and secondary levels of education takes place in university-level institutions. Almost everywhere, the higher the level of education, the more common is university-level education and training. To teach in lower secondary schools, teachers are trained in university-level institutions in all Member States, except Belgium, the Netherlands and Austria (for teachers in the *Hauptschulen).* For teaching at upper secondary level, training is provided at university level everywhere. In some Member States, it is also possible to follow another non-university route.

The professional and practical training of teachers is provided either at the same time as their general (degree) course (**the concurrent model**) or following the general course, for instance at post-graduate level (**the consecutive model**). The entrance requirement for admission to teacher education and training following the concurrent model is the school-leaving certificate awarded at the end of upper secondary education, and also, in some cases, a certificate of aptitude for higher education. Under the consecutive model, students who have already obtained a first higher education qualification (university or non-university) in a particular discipline train for the teaching profession by taking a post-graduate university or non-university course.

The concurrent model is more common in preparation for primary teaching, except in France, where all primary teacher education and training follows the consecutive model. In the United Kingdom, both models coexist but the concurrent model is the more common. Conversely, the consecutive model is more common for secondary teacher training.

More particularly, in Germany, the education and training of teachers for both primary and secondary levels is in two stages — first, study at a higher education institution which includes integrated professional training and theory from the start, then a second stage of training involving a programme of practical training in the form of preparatory service *(Vorbereitungsdienst).* During this period, future primary and secondary teachers are remunerated and usually have the status of temporary civil servants. In France, professional experience in a school setting is also required at the end of training. Those who have been successful in the open competition have, during their second year in the *Instituts universitaires de formation des maîtres* (IUFM), the status of paid student teachers. In Denmark, professional training for upper secondary teachers is available only to university graduates who have been recruited to schools. The training course lasts six months and consists of seminars on educational theory. This training is assessed by way of written tests and supervised practice. In Luxembourg, admission to practical training for secondary school teachers is dependent on success in a national open entrance competition. This training is undertaken in school. During this professional training placement, student teachers are remunerated. In these four Member States, the period of practical training in school is an integral part of students' training and has to be completed before they receive their diplomas.

FIGURE G1: DURATION AND LEVEL OF THE INITIAL EDUCATION AND TRAINING OF PRE-PRIMARY TEACHERS, 1995/96

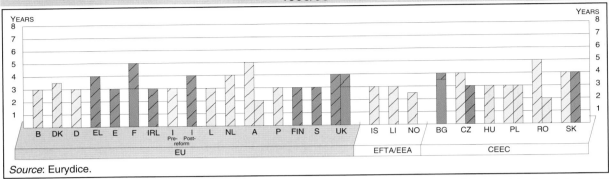

Source: Eurydice.

Germany: The figure refers to qualified 'educators' (*Erzieher*), who have neither the training nor the status of teachers. Intending students must have 2 years' vocational training or experience in addition to the lower secondary school leaving certificate to be admitted to training in the *Fachschule für Sozialpädagogik*.

France: Applicants to the open competition for primary school teachers *(professeurs des écoles)* must hold a full degree *(licence)* or one of the equivalent qualifications, of which a list is prescribed in a decree, awarded after at least 3 years of post-secondary education in another Member State of the European Union.

Ireland: No distinction is made between pre-primary education and primary education, children of 4 to 6 years being integrated in the primary schools in the 'Infant Classes'. The graph therefore presents the initial training of primary teachers.

Italy: According to the law passed in 1990, the initial training of pre-primary and primary school teachers should be at university level, but this has not yet been implemented. The duration of the course has been set at 4 years.

Netherlands: Children aged 4 to 6 years are integrated in primary schools. The figure presents the training of primary teachers. Initial training takes place over 4 years (full-time study) or 6 years (part-time study).

Finland: Since 1995, pre-primary teacher training takes place at university.

United Kingdom: Teacher training is the same as that for primary teachers. The concurrent model is the most common.

United Kingdom (E/W and NI): There are several routes to 'qualified teacher status', including part-time training.

Bulgaria: Training can last 4 or 5 years.

Poland: There are 3 possible training routes. The 2 most common models are shown here. Training at university level is also possible.

Romania: Pre-primary education can be delivered by the *educatoare* who follow a 5-year training course at upper secondary level or by the *institutori* who follow a 2- or 3-year training course in colleges of education at higher education level.

FIGURE G2: DURATION AND LEVEL OF INITIAL EDUCATION AND TRAINING OF PRIMARY TEACHERS, 1995/96

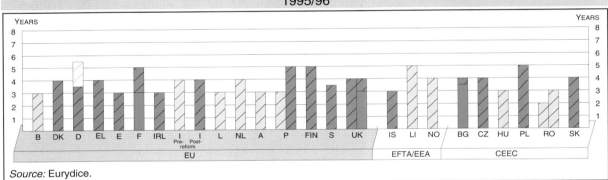

Source: Eurydice.

Germany: At least 7 semesters (three-and-a-half years) of university higher education, in a university *(Universität)* or a *Pädagogische Hochschule*, depending on the *Land*. The practical and professional training period (usually 2 years) is compulsory.

France and **Italy**: See notes to Figure G1.

Portugal: The first model shown corresponds to the training of teachers for the first level of *ensino básico*. The second model is one of the training possibilities for teachers for the second level of *ensino básico*. Two other training routes are also offered within higher non-university education.

Finland: Data refer mainly to class teachers in the first 6 years of the *peruskoulu/grundskola*.

Sweden: Data refer to teachers in the first seven years of the *grundskola*.

United Kingdom: The most common models are shown here. In England, Wales and Northern Ireland, there are several routes to 'qualified teacher status', including part-time training. In Scotland, in addition to the courses shown here, a 4-year university degree followed by one year of professional training is also possible.

Bulgaria: Training can last 4 or 5 years.

Hungary: The model presented here refers only to teachers for the first 4 years of compulsory education.

Slovakia: The course duration is fixed at 4 years for the first stage of *základná škola* and 5 years for the second stage.

GENERAL EDUCATION	GENERAL AND PROFESSIONAL TRAINING
UNIVERSITY-LEVEL EDUCATION	UNIVERSITY-LEVEL EDUCATION
NON-UNIVERSITY HIGHER EDUCATION	NON-UNIVERSITY HIGHER EDUCATION
PRACTICAL TRAINING IN SCHOOLS	NON-HIGHER EDUCATION

FIGURE G3: DURATION AND LEVEL OF INITIAL EDUCATION AND TRAINING OF TEACHERS
FOR LOWER SECONDARY SCHOOLS (GENERAL EDUCATION), 1995/96

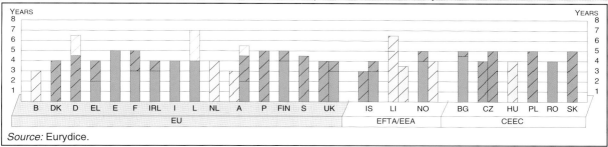

Source: Eurydice.

Germany: Seven to nine semesters (between three-and-a-half and four-and-a-half years) of university-level training at a university *(Universität)*, *Kunsthochschule, Musikhochschule* or *Pädagogische Hochschule*, depending on the *Land*. There is a compulsory 2-year period of teaching practice/professional training *(Vorbereitungsdienst)*.

Greece: Courses last from 4 to 6 years, depending on the university faculty. In faculties of education, professional and practical training takes the concurrent form. Future teachers who have studied in other faculties must obtain an education qualification from the teacher training school (PATES).

Spain: After taking a university qualification (4-, 5- or 6-year courses), it is necessary to take a teacher training course of a minimum of 300 hours.

France: Students who have been successful in the open competition for the *Certificat d'aptitude au professorat de l'enseignement secondaire,* (CAPES) are admitted to the year of professional training in the IUFM. As *professeurs certifiés* they may teach in lower and upper secondary schools *(collèges* and *lycées,* respectively).

Italy: The university qualification, obtained after a minimum of 4 years, certifies that the student has a command of the subjects studied, but it is not a qualification for teaching at secondary level. Currently, to obtain this qualification, the candidate must sit the examination called *abilitazione* on teaching norms, theories and methods. However, preparation for this examination is left to the candidate's own initiative. The reform envisages a professional qualification being obtained after a 2-year post-graduate course concluding with an examination

Netherlands: Candidates obtaining grade 2 may teach general subjects in lower secondary schools and vocational upper secondary schools. Initial training takes place over 4 years (full-time study) or 6 years (part-time study).

Portugal: This illustrates the training of teachers for the third stage of *ensino básico*. Some institutions offer training following the consecutive model over 5 or 6 years.

Finland: The information relates mainly to single-subject teachers in the last 3 years of the *peruskoulu/grundskola.* Training lasts 5 or 6 years.

Sweden: The information relates to teachers in the last 6 years of the *grundskola.* Depending on the subject chosen, training ranges from three-and-a-half to four-and-a-half years (the latter being more common).

United Kingdom (E/W and **NI)**: There are several routes to qualified teacher status. The most common models are shown here.

United Kingdom (SC): The most common model is a 4-year university degree followed by one year of professional training.

Liechtenstein: Training can also be undertaken in a university abroad.

Bulgaria, Romania and **Slovakia**: Training can last 4 or 5 years.

FIGURE G4: DURATION AND LEVEL OF INITIAL EDUCATION AND TRAINING OF TEACHERS
FOR UPPER SECONDARY SCHOOLS (GENERAL EDUCATION), 1995/96

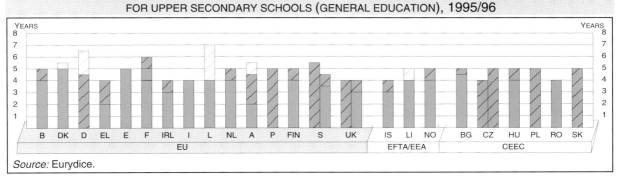

Source: Eurydice.

Belgium: Training usually lasts 4 years. Post-graduate teacher training may be undertaken either parallel to the university course (along with the *licence*, in one or 2 years, as the student chooses) or following the university course, in one year, or 2 years part-time.

Germany: At least 9 semesters (four-and-a-half years) at university *(Universität)* or in a college of art or music *(Kunsthochschule, Musikhochschule)*. Practical teaching experience and professional training generally lasting 2 years is obligatory *(Vorbereitungsdienst)*.

Greece, Spain, Italy and **United Kingdom**: See notes to Figure G3.

France: Two kinds of teacher may teach at this level — certificated teachers with the CAPES (see lower secondary, above) and teachers who have passed the *agrégation.* This graph represents the training of the latter. After taking the entrance competition, successful candidates undertake a year of professional training in the IUFM.

Netherlands: Non-university (HBO) training is also possible. All the practical courses can be taken on a part-time basis.

Portugal: Some institutions offer training following the consecutive model over 5 or 6 years.

Finland: Training can last 5 or 6 years.

Sweden: Training can last from four-and-a-half to five-and-a-half years depending on the subjects chosen.

Romania: Training can last 4 or 5 years.

In the EFTA/EEA countries, teacher education and training is provided at higher education level, whatever level of education the trainee teacher is aiming at. Three years of non-university training are required for pre-primary teaching. In Iceland, training is at university for all primary and secondary teachers. In Liechtenstein and Norway, on the other hand, training at university is available only to those intending to teach at lower secondary level and it is compulsory for the upper secondary level.

In the CEECs, initial training for primary and secondary teachers is also provided at higher education level. In these countries, the training of teachers responsible for children at pre-primary level is not yet provided at higher education level everywhere. This is the only form of training possible in Bulgaria and Hungary while in the other countries training is still provided at upper secondary level alongside higher education university training (in the Czech Republic and Slovakia) or higher education non-university training (in Poland and Romania).

In the EFTA/EEA countries and the CEECs generally, the concurrent model is the more common, whatever the level of education. In Iceland and Norway, however, the training of lower secondary teachers for the last stage of the single structure follows both models. The training of upper secondary teachers in the three EFTA/EEA countries is typically according to the consecutive model. In Romania, secondary teachers receive general education but no professional preparation.

ALMOST FOUR-AND-A-HALF MILLION TEACHERS IN THE EUROPEAN UNION

At the present time, the European Union has almost four-and-a-half million teachers in the primary and secondary levels of its education systems, quite apart from the thousands of young people intending to teach and who are attending initial teacher training institutions. In fact, it can be said that the teaching profession (excluding higher education) employs 2.6% of the active population in the Member States. The variations are however significant. Belgium appears as the country in which teachers make up the highest percentage (4.5%) while in Germany they account for the lowest (1.9%).

In these statistics, only teachers in post are taken into account. Staff allocated to duties other than teaching (inspectors, non-teaching heads, teachers on secondment etc.) are excluded. The numbers of such staff can vary considerably depending on the Member State. The definitions of teaching staff are not, however, always the same from one Member State to the other. It is also important to note that special education is included in these statistics.

Caution is therefore called for in comparing percentages between Member States. In practice, in view of the variety of situations across the Member States, a number of variables have to be taken into account in carrying out a comparative analysis of this sort. It is necessary, amongst other things, to take account of parameters such as the duration of compulsory education and the numbers of young people in the education systems as well as the magnitude of the ratio of the active population to the total population.

FIGURE G5: TEACHERS IN PUBLIC AND PRIVATE, PRIMARY AND SECONDARY SCHOOLS, IN RELATION TO THE TOTAL ACTIVE POPULATION, 1994/95.

	TOTAL ACTIVE POPULATION (in thousands)	PERCENTAGE ACTIVE POPULATION/TOTAL POPULATION	TEACHERS (FULL-TIME AND PART-TIME) (in thousands)	TEACHERS (FULL-TIME EQUIVALENTS) (in thousands)	PERCENTAGE TEACHERS/TOTAL ACTIVE POPULATION	PERCENTAGE PUPILS/TOTAL POPULATION
EUROPEAN UNION						
B	4 183	41	188	167	4.5	17.7
DK	2 796	54	83	76	3.0	14.8
D	40 162	49	755	644	1.9	14.6
EL	4 201	40	109	N/A	2.6	14.9
E	15 561	40	432	419	2.8	18.1
F	25 033	43	691	650	2.8	17.4
IRL	1 434	40	43	40	3.0	21.6
I	22 607	39	756	N/A	3.3	12.8
L	167	41	4	N/A	2.6	12.9
NL	7 304	47	152	124	2.1	17.5
A	3 842	48	116	N/A	3.0	14.5
P	4 753	48	142	N/A	3.0	18.8
FIN	2 429	48	63	N/A	2.6	16.5
S	4 498	51	148	105	3.3	16.5
UK	28 404	49	734	608	2.6	20.4
Total EU	167 374	45	4 416	N/A	2.6	16.5

Source: Eurostat, UOE.

Belgium and **Netherlands**: 1993/94.
Sweden: Teachers teaching in two levels of education are counted twice.

EFTA/EEA						
IS	147	55	5	N/A	3.4	22.2
LI	15	48	0.4	0.3	2.8	11.3
NO	N/A	N/A	N/A	N/A	N/A	15.8

Source: Eurostat, UOE.

Liechtenstein: National statistics, 1993/94. The percentage of pupils relates to ISCED levels 1 and 2.

CEEC						
BG	3 242	38	92	N/A	2.8	14.4
CZ	4 801	46	N/A	98	2.0	16.7
HU	4 325	42	163	N/A	3.8	15.1
PL	15 282	40	560	468	3.7	18.7
RO	9 493	42	237	N/A	2.5	19.3
SK	2 212	41	72	N/A	3.2	19.1

Source: National statistics.

EXPLANATORY NOTE
The ratio of teachers to active population has been calculated on the basis of the number of full-time and part-time teachers. Pupils include all those in primary and secondary education (ISCED 1, 2 and 3). The full-time equivalent number of teachers has been calculated by each Member State according to the criteria set out in the UOE questionnaire.

DEFINITION OF FULL-TIME AND PART-TIME TEACHING:
VERY DIFFERENT NORMS

In the majority of the Member States, the official regulations prescribing teachers' contracts of employment or conditions of service make reference only to the teaching time required of teachers, i.e. the time during which they give lessons. In some Member States, contracts also define teachers' obligations outside class contact time. In the Netherlands and the United Kingdom, only the overall working time is laid down, and no reference is made to the amounts of time teachers have to devote to different activities. It is the headteachers who decide on the allocation of the tasks expected of their teaching staff. Consequently, it is not possible to identify actual teaching time separately on the basis of the official regulations in force in these two Member States.

Analysis of the norms defining the weekly numbers of teaching periods required to constitute a full-time or part-time contract shows that the numbers of hours of teaching laid down as full-time or part-time reflect situations which can be very different from one level of education to another and from one Member State to another.

In the Member States of the European Union, three main patterns emerge for defining full-time and part-time teaching.

— Full-time may be defined as a fixed number of periods per week, represented by a circle in Figure G6. Depending on the level of education and the Member State, this fixed number can vary from 15 to 27 periods. Anything below this is regarded as part-time. This is the case in Denmark, Spain (in primary schools), the Netherlands, Austria (for teachers under contract), Finland and Sweden.

— Full-time and part-time may each be defined as a number of periods within a range. This pattern is represented in Figure G6 by a bar. There can be considerable variation in the differences between the minimum and maximum numbers of periods from one Member State to another — from two or three periods per week in Luxembourg up to six to eight periods.

— Full-time alone may be defined, and this as a number of periods falling between a minimum and a maximum, with no definition of part-time (Greece and Portugal).

In France, full-time is defined as a fixed number of periods which is different for teachers with different qualifications. Part-time varies between a minimum and a maximum. In the United Kingdom (England, Wales and Northern Ireland), the maximum annual working hours are fixed and part-time is defined as anything less than full-time.

These main types of definition of full-time and part-time are also found in the regulations in the EFTA/EEA countries. Norway defines only full-time, which is a fixed number of periods, while in Iceland and in secondary education in Liechtenstein, full-time and part-time vary between a minimum and a maximum number of periods.

The CEECs reveal two patterns. In Bulgaria in the main, in secondary education, and in Romania, the definition of full-time and part-time can vary between a minimum and a maximum. In the other countries, only a full-time contract is defined, this being a fixed number of periods ranging between 19 and 31 a week.

In the European Union, the higher the level of education, the more limited is the contractual teaching load. This is the case everywhere except in Denmark, the Netherlands and the United Kingdom.

In the EFTA/EEA countries and the CEECs also, the teaching load is less for teachers working in a higher level of education, except in Poland and Romania where the number of periods laid down is the same.

FIGURE G6: NUMBER OF CONTRACTUAL TEACHING PERIODS DEFINING FULL-TIME AND PART-TIME POSTS, BY LEVEL OF EDUCATION, 1995/96

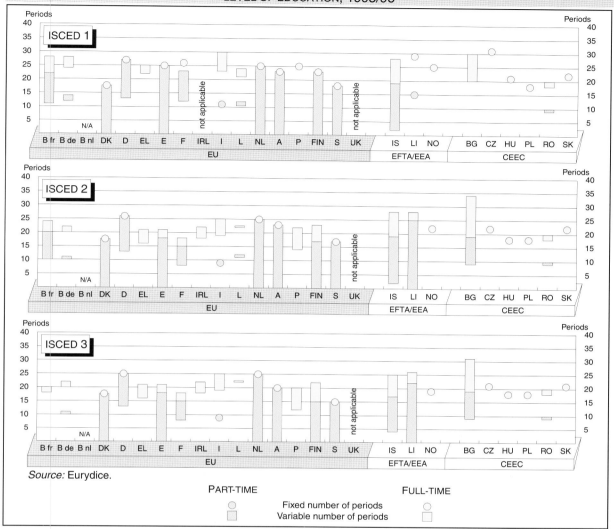

Source: Eurydice.

PART-TIME
○ Fixed number of periods
▭ Variable number of periods

FULL-TIME
○ Fixed number of periods
▭ Variable number of periods

Belgium (B fr): Data not available for the definition of part-time at the ISCED 3 level.

Denmark: Teachers' employment contracts are based on a 37-hour week. Teaching time is estimated at 45% of total working time. The data here have been calculated on this basis. A working week of less than 37 hours is considered as part-time.

Germany: This is an average. The minimum and maximum vary depending on the *Land*.

Greece: Certain hourly-paid teachers can teach less than 11 hours a week.

Spain: The number of periods for a part-time post is decided on an individual basis.

France: Full-time teaching time in secondary education varies depending on whether the teacher is *certifié* (18 hours a week) or *agrégé* (15 hours a week). In vocational education, it depends on whether the teacher takes theory classes (18 hours a week), practical classes (23 hours a week) or is in charge of a workshop (39 hours a week).

Ireland: At primary level, full-time status is defined by the number of hours worked per year, week and day. No formal definition of part-time exists.

Netherlands: The teacher's contract is based on a 38-hour week. Teaching time is estimated at 65% of working time in primary education and 60% in secondary education. The data here have been calculated on this basis.

Austria: The data are for contract teachers.

Portugal: At secondary level, teachers with a teaching load less than the set maximum are employed on a temporary basis. These posts are considered as being part-time.

Sweden: The number of periods per week has been calculated by dividing the annual number of periods by 36.

United Kingdom (E/W and NI): Teachers' contracts are based on a contract of 195 days or 1265 hours a year. Within this framework, headteachers decide the number of teaching hours for staff. A part-time teacher is any teacher who works less than full-time hours.

United Kingdom (SC): Full-time contracts are for 35 hours a week. Anything under this figure counts as part-time.

EXPLANATORY NOTE

The definitions of full-time and part-time are expressed as a number of periods per week. Depending on the country, a period can vary in length from 40 to 60 minutes. For the primary level, the data relate to class teachers responsible for all subjects.

PART-TIME WORK:
—— NOT A VERY COMMON PRACTICE IN TEACHING ——

The proportion of teachers working part-time varies considerably from one Member State to another. The highest percentages of part-time teachers are found in Germany (in primary education) and Sweden (in secondary education), with 50 and 63% respectively. On the other hand, under 10% of teachers work part-time in primary education in France and Ireland, and in both primary and secondary education in Spain, Italy and Finland. At primary level, there are no part-time teachers in Greece, while their numbers are insignificant in Spain and Italy.

The extent of part-time work also differs depending on the level of education. Thus in Belgium, France, Ireland, the Netherlands and Sweden, a higher percentage of part-time teachers is found at secondary level. The reverse is the case in Germany and the United Kingdom.

In Iceland, the only EFTA/EEA country for which data are available, the proportion of teachers working part-time represents overall one quarter of the teaching population and it is larger in primary than in secondary education.

FIGURE G7. PERCENTAGE OF TEACHERS WORKING PART-TIME, IN PRIMARY AND SECONDARY EDUCATION, 1994/1995.

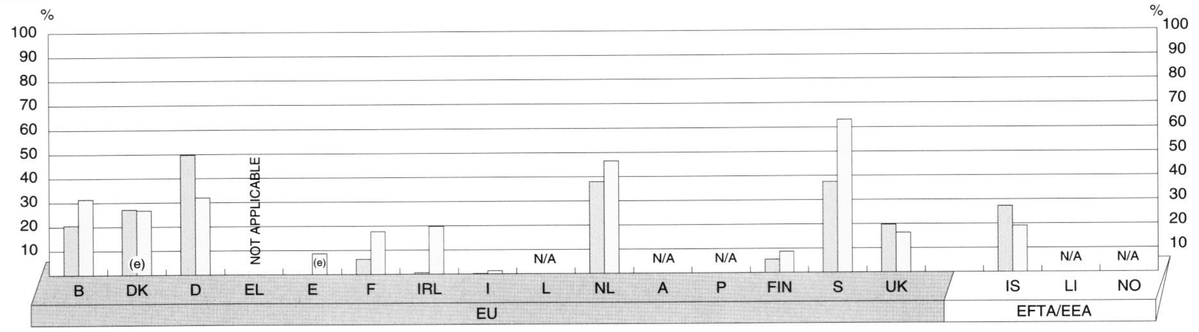

Source: Eurostat, UOE. PRIMARY SECONDARY

Belgium and **Netherlands**: 1993/1994.
Finland: The primary figures include ISCED 1 and 2 and those for upper secondary ISCED 3 and 5.
Iceland: The primary figures include ISCED 1 and 2 and those for upper secondary ISCED 3.
Poland and **Romania**: The data available are set out in the annex.

IN TEACHING, A GREATER PROPORTION OF WOMEN THAN MEN WORK PART-TIME

In primary education in most of the EU Member States for which data are available, the percentage of women teaching part-time is higher than that of men. This situation is particularly marked in Germany and the Netherlands, where more than half of all women teachers work part-time. In Denmark, the proportions of men and women teachers working part-time are about equal.

FIGURE G8: PROPORTIONS OF WOMEN AND MEN TEACHERS WORKING PART-TIME AT PRIMARY LEVEL, 1994/95

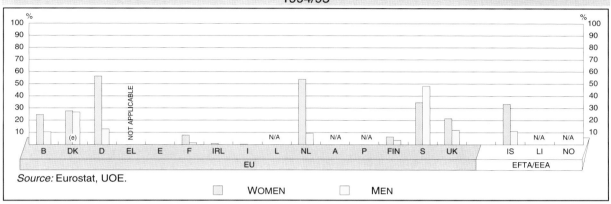

Source: Eurostat, UOE.

Belgium and **Netherlands**: 1993/94.
Finland: ISCED 1 and 2.
Poland and **Romania**: The data available are set out in the annex.

In secondary education in the Netherlands, more than 80% of women teachers work part-time while in Sweden 65% of women and 60% of men teachers work part-time.

In Denmark and Finland, the proportions of men and women teachers working part-time are about equal. Spain and Ireland have proportionately slightly fewer women than men working part-time in secondary education.

FIGURE G9: PROPORTIONS OF WOMEN AND MEN TEACHERS WORKING PART-TIME AT SECONDARY LEVEL, 1994/95

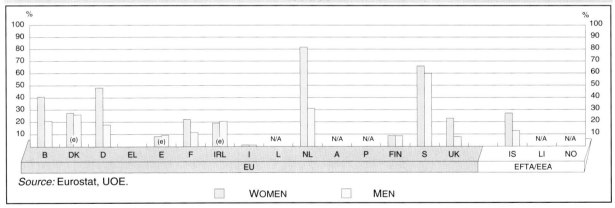

Source: Eurostat, UOE.

Belgium and **Netherlands**: 1993/94.
Greece: The number of teachers working part-time is negligible.
Ireland: The number of women working part-time is an underestimate.
Finland: ISCED 3 and 5.
Iceland: ISCED 3 only.
Poland, **Romania** and **Slovakia**: The data available are set out in the annex.

In Iceland, the proportion of women teachers working part-time is greater than that of men teachers in both primary and secondary education.

EXPLANATORY NOTE
For each level of education, the percentage of women teachers working part-time has been calculated by taking the ratio of the number of women teachers working part-time to the total number of women teachers. The percentage of men teachers has been calculated in the same way.

113

PREDOMINANCE OF WOMEN IN TEACHING:
———————— DIFFERENCES BETWEEN LEVELS AND COUNTRIES ————————

Primary teaching is a predominantly female profession in the European Union. In all Member States, women are in the majority at this level of education, the largest proportion of all being found in Italy (93%). In only a few Member States are the numbers of men and women approximately equal. This is the case in Denmark, Greece and Luxembourg, with between 55 and 58% of women.

The percentage of women in the teaching population is lower at secondary than at primary level, except in Greece.

At secondary level, the male/female ratio in the teaching profession is generally fairly evenly balanced. In a number of Member States, although women are in the majority, their percentage is not much over 50%. Two Member States stand out, however, with a particularly small proportion of women secondary teachers — Luxembourg and the Netherlands, with about one third.

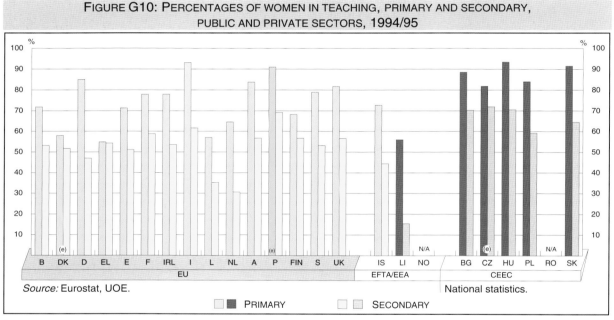

FIGURE G10: PERCENTAGES OF WOMEN IN TEACHING, PRIMARY AND SECONDARY, PUBLIC AND PRIVATE SECTORS, 1994/95

Source: Eurostat, UOE.

National statistics.

■ PRIMARY   ☐ SECONDARY

Belgium and **Netherlands**: 1993/94.
Finland: Data for primary education cover ISCED 1 and 2 and for secondary education ISCED 3 and 5.
Iceland: Data for primary education cover ISCED 1 and 2 and for secondary education ISCED 3.
Liechtenstein: National statistics, 1993/94.
Poland: Data for primary education cover primary and lower secondary education and those for secondary education cover upper secondary.
Slovakia: Including headteachers.

Of the EFTA/EEA countries, in Iceland and Liechtenstein, women constitute the majority of teachers in primary education but the minority in secondary.

In the CEECs for which data are available, there are proportionately more women than men at both levels of education. There is a particularly high proportion of women teachers in primary education — over 80%, and even over 90% in Hungary and Slovakia.

WOMEN ARE MORE OFTEN HEADTEACHERS
IN PRIMARY THAN IN SECONDARY SCHOOLS

At primary level, almost half of all headteachers are women in Ireland, Italy and Austria. They represent a little more than half in Sweden and the United Kingdom. The highest percentage is found in France (65%) while in Denmark barely 17% of *folkeskole* headships are occupied by women.

In secondary education, in most of the countries for which data are available, only between 21 and 30% of school heads are women. This rate is, however, very much higher in Sweden (over 40%) while in Luxembourg and Austria it scarcely reaches 19 and 18% respectively.

A similar trend appears in the EFTA/EEA countries. The largest proportion of women in headships in primary education is found in Iceland, at under one third. In secondary education, their percentage does not exceed 20% in any of the three countries.

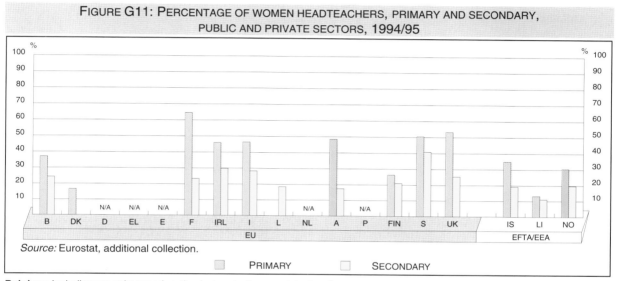

FIGURE G11: PERCENTAGE OF WOMEN HEADTEACHERS, PRIMARY AND SECONDARY, PUBLIC AND PRIVATE SECTORS, 1994/95

Source: Eurostat, additional collection.

PRIMARY   SECONDARY

Belgium: Including pre-primary education but excluding special education.
Denmark: The primary level includes the 9 years of the *folkeskole*. Data for the upper secondary level are not available.
France and **Austria**: Primary data also cover special education.
Ireland: Public sector only.
Luxembourg: The headteacher function does not exist at primary level.
Finland: Data for primary education cover ISCED 1 and 2 and for secondary education ISCED 3 (general).
United Kingdom: The primary level includes pre-primary. Secondary data relate only to general education.
Iceland: Data for primary education cover ISCED 1 and 2 and for secondary education ISCED 3.
Hungary: The data available are set out in the annex.
Slovakia: No data available for primary education; data on upper secondary education are set out in the annex.

——— HEADTEACHERS' TASKS AND SCOPE FOR DECISION-TAKING ———

The role and responsibilities of headteachers vary greatly from one Member State to another. They depend on the level of autonomy given to each school, and also on whether the school has its own management body.

In the Netherlands, where schools have a considerable degree of autonomy in the management of human and material resources, there is a body at school level responsible for such affairs. Headteachers work closely with these bodies and are responsible under their aegis for developing the curriculum. In the United Kingdom (except Scotland), the governing body determines the general conduct of the school while the detailed day-to-day management is the responsibility of the headteacher.

In Denmark, the headteacher is responsible to the school board and the municipal council for the administrative and educational management of the school. In Finland, the headteacher's role in management activities depends on the municipality. Headteachers are usually responsible for developing the curriculum. In Sweden, the headteacher's main role is to ensure that the school's results meet set national objectives as well as those of the educational project defined by the municipality.

In those countries where schools have more limited autonomy, the headteacher's role and scope for action vary greatly. In France, Spain, Italy and Scotland, the headteacher shares responsibility with a body responsible for certain functions (administrative, financial and/or educational). In Portugal, in accordance with the 1991 management model, the headteacher executes decisions made by several bodies responsible for the individual matters.

In Germany, Luxembourg (in secondary education) and Austria, the headteacher is responsible for all decisions taken at school level, but has assistance from an advisory body. In these Member States and also in Belgium, headteachers are also responsible for appraising teachers' work. In Greece, headteachers coordinate teachers' activities and enforce ministerial directives.

In the EFTA/EEA countries and the CEECs, the headteacher's role also varies. In Liechtenstein and in Poland and Slovakia, headteachers apply ministerial directives. They are responsible for the administrative and educational running of the school in Iceland and Norway, and in the Czech Republic and Hungary, while in Bulgaria they apply ministerial directives and are also responsible for the administrative and educational running of the school. In Romania, they share their responsibilities with an education committee and a management committee.

PROFESSIONAL EXPERIENCE AND
TRAINING OF HEADTEACHERS

In all Member States, teaching experience of, generally, between five and ten years is expected of applicants for headteacher posts. In most of those countries in which recruitment is decentralized (Denmark, Netherlands, Finland, Sweden and the United Kingdom), the length of such experience is not usually specified. In the Netherlands and the United Kingdom, management experience is also demanded. This is usually acquired during a period of service as a deputy head.

In addition to this professional experience, some Member States require applicants to have undertaken specific training in school management before taking up their post. This has been the case since 1995 in the French Community of Belgium, where candidates have to undergo training and pass an examination. In Spain, since 1996, teachers wishing to become headteachers have had to be recognised by the education administration, which requires them to have initial training. In France, applicants for the open competition for posts as *principal (collège)* or *proviseur (lycée)* receive initial training which takes place in two stages: the first, of 20 weeks, includes alternating professional courses (in theory, practice and methodology) and placements in companies, regional/local offices of the ministry and schools, while the second stage lasts a minimum of three weeks and covers additional professional training in administration and school management. In Portugal, according to the 1991 management model, applicants must have completed specific training in the administration and management of schools. In Finland, they have to hold a qualification in school administration.

In Italy and Luxembourg (at secondary level), programmes of preparation for headships are starting to be arranged on a sporadic and voluntary basis. In Austria and Sweden, various optional training programmes are arranged for newly appointed headteachers. In the United Kingdom, national professional qualifications for headteachers are being introduced.

In the EFTA/EEA countries and the CEECs, teaching experience is required everywhere. In Iceland, this must also be accompanied by administrative experience acquired in the course of a year's appointment on a provisional basis. No compulsory, specific training is required.

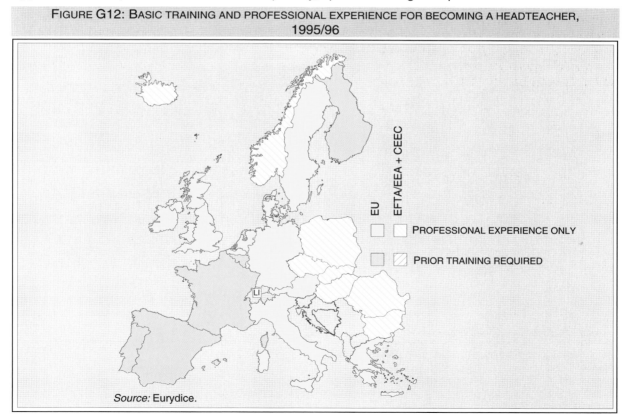

FIGURE G12: BASIC TRAINING AND PROFESSIONAL EXPERIENCE FOR BECOMING A HEADTEACHER, 1995/96

Source: Eurydice.

Austria: As of 1 September 1996, prior to being appointed, headteachers must successfully complete a training course in school management.

MOST TEACHERS ARE OVER 40 YEARS OLD

In the European Union as a whole, the majority of teachers are over 40 years old. The ageing of the teaching population is even more marked at secondary level, where more than two thirds of teachers are over 40 years old and more than a quarter are over 50 years old.

FIGURE G13: EUROPEAN UNION AVERAGE (12 MEMBER STATES) OF THE BREAKDOWN OF TEACHERS BY AGE BAND, PRIMARY AND SECONDARY, PUBLIC AND PRIVATE SECTORS, 1994/95

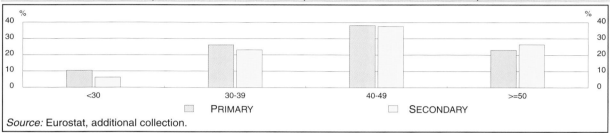

Source: Eurostat, additional collection.

In some Member States, the age distribution of teachers deviates from that of the European Union. In primary education, Belgium and Austria have relatively young teaching staff — more than half of all teachers there are under 40 years of age. Luxembourg has the greatest proportion of primary teachers who are under 30 years old (22%). On the other hand, in Denmark, the percentage of young teachers is very small — under 5%. In Denmark, Germany and Sweden, teachers over 40 years old account for more than 70% of primary teaching staff.

FIGURE G14: DISTRIBUTION OF TEACHERS BY AGE BAND, PRIMARY EDUCATION, PUBLIC AND PRIVATE SECTORS, 1994/95

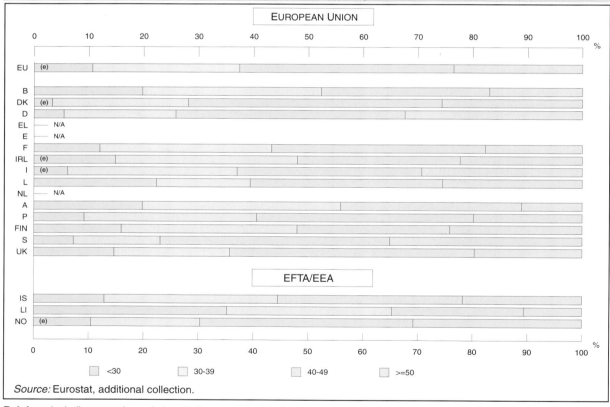

Source: Eurostat, additional collection.

Belgium: Including pre-primary but excluding special education.
France: Including pre-primary.
Ireland: Including school heads and guidance teachers.
Ireland and **Italy**: Teachers whose age is not known are not included in Figure G14.
Luxembourg and **Portugal**: Public sector only.
Finland: 1995/96.
Iceland and **Norway**: ISCED 1 and 2, public sector.
Liechtenstein: Public sector.
Norway: Teachers whose age is not known are not included in Figure G14.
Bulgaria: The data available are set out in the annex.

In secondary education, teachers are relatively young in Portugal, more than a quarter being under 30 years old. There and in Austria, more than half of all teachers are under 40 years old. On the other hand, in Denmark, Germany and Sweden, the percentage of teachers under the age of 30 is extremely low. It is also in these three Member States that the greatest proportions of teachers over the age of 40 are found. In Sweden, 43% of secondary teachers are over the age of 50.

In two of the EFTA/EEA countries, Iceland and Norway, the majority of teachers are over the age of 40. There are proportionately more of them in secondary than in primary education.

The ageing of the teaching population is no doubt explained in part by the fact that, in the 1960s, in most European countries, there was a very high birth rate which led to an increase in pupil numbers and consequently to a wide recruitment of teachers. In the 1980s, there was a fall in pupil numbers and little need to recruit new staff. As a result, the number of younger teachers entering the profession was restricted, causing an imbalance in the age structure of the profession. As the cohort of teachers recruited in the 1960s reaches retirement age in the coming years, it will be important to ensure that in all Member States the planning of teacher supply is effectively managed to avoid the risks of shortages.

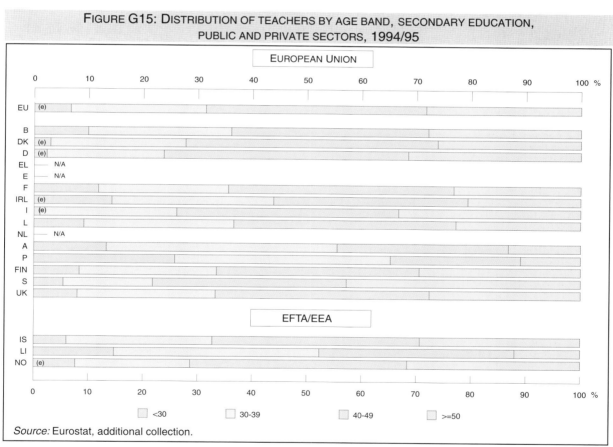

FIGURE G15: DISTRIBUTION OF TEACHERS BY AGE BAND, SECONDARY EDUCATION, PUBLIC AND PRIVATE SECTORS, 1994/95

Source: Eurostat, additional collection.

Belgium: Excluding special education.
Germany, Ireland and **Italy**: Teachers whose age is not known are not included in Figure G15.
Ireland: Including school heads and guidance teachers.
Luxembourg and **Portugal**: Public sector only.
Finland: ISCED 2 to 5, 1995/96.
Iceland and **Norway**: ISCED 3, public sector.
Liechtenstein: Public sector.
Norway: Teachers whose age is not known are not included in Figure G15.
Bulgaria: The data available are set out in the annex.

SENIORITY REMAINS THE MAIN SOURCE OF DIFFERENCES
IN TEACHERS' SALARIES

In order to illustrate teachers' financial position relative to the average standard of living in their respective countries, Figures G16 to G18 show teachers' salaries as percentages of the **per capita gross domestic product** (GDP) — an index of the general standard of living in the country. This indicator is obtained by dividing the GDP, which reflects the country's wealth, by the total population of the country. By systematically establishing the ratio of the salary of a teacher (in national currency) to the per capita GDP (at current prices in national currency), it is possible to make comparisons both within individual Member States and between them. Examination of this ratio provides an idea of the teacher's salary status.

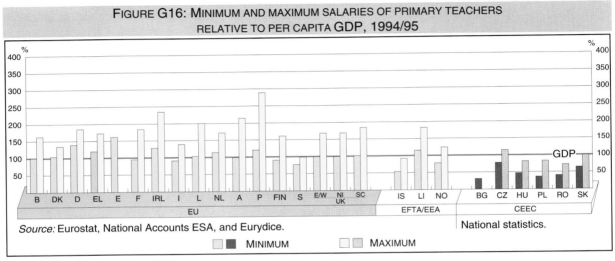

FIGURE G16: MINIMUM AND MAXIMUM SALARIES OF PRIMARY TEACHERS
RELATIVE TO PER CAPITA GDP, 1994/95

Source: Eurostat, National Accounts ESA, and Eurydice.

Spain: Maximum salary not available.
Portugal: Teachers in the first stage of *ensino básico* holding the *Bacharelato*.
United Kingdom: A considerable number of teachers have specific responsibilities and therefore receive higher salaries than those shown here.
Iceland: Only basic salaries are shown. Additional remuneration (for overtime, extra responsibility etc.) can be considerable in certain cases.
Bulgaria: Maximum salary not available.

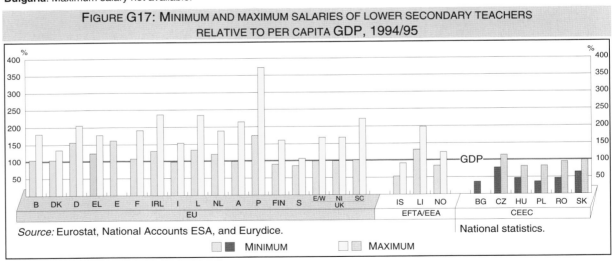

FIGURE G17: MINIMUM AND MAXIMUM SALARIES OF LOWER SECONDARY TEACHERS
RELATIVE TO PER CAPITA GDP, 1994/95

Source: Eurostat, National Accounts ESA, and Eurydice.

Spain and **United Kingdom**: See notes to Figure G16.
Austria: Data refer to teachers in the *Hauptschulen*.
Portugal: Teachers in the first stage of *ensino básico* holding the *Licenciatura em Ensino* or an equivalent qualification and teachers in the second and third stages of *ensino básico*.
Iceland: See notes to Figure G16.
Bulgaria: See notes to Figure G16.

Amongst the factors examined here, seniority is the main source of disparities in teachers' salaries. In only a few Member States are differences explained by the levels of education in which teachers are serving. In Germany and Portugal, salary differences are found mainly between the primary and secondary levels. In the French Community of Belgium, Denmark and Spain, on the other hand, the gap is more marked between upper secondary teachers' salaries and the others.

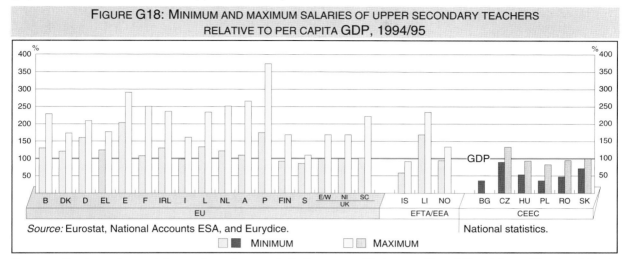

FIGURE G18: MINIMUM AND MAXIMUM SALARIES OF UPPER SECONDARY TEACHERS RELATIVE TO PER CAPITA GDP, 1994/95

Source: Eurostat, National Accounts ESA, and Eurydice.   National statistics.

MINIMUM   MAXIMUM

Germany: Teachers who are civil servants can be promoted in the course of their career if they fulfil certain conditions in relation to qualifications and results. This is not taken into account in this figure.
United Kingdom: See notes to Figure G16.
Iceland: See notes to Figure G16.
Bulgaria: See notes to Figure G16.

The following points are also established.

— In Belgium, Denmark, Italy, Austria and the United Kingdom, the minimum salaries of teachers at the start of their careers are close to the per capita GDP.

— In France and Italy, at primary level, and in Finland and Sweden at all levels of education, the starting salaries of teachers are below the per capita GDP of the Member State.

— In Spain, the minimum salaries of teachers are systematically more than one and a half times the per capita GDP. This is also the case in Germany and Portugal, but only in relation to teachers in secondary education.

— Finally, Portugal has the highest end-of-career salaries relative to per capita GDP.

In the EFTA/EEA countries, in Iceland and Norway starting salaries in both primary and secondary teaching are below the per capita GDP.

In the CEECs for which data are available, the minimum salaries of teachers, whatever level of education they are working in, are below the per capita GDP. They approach or reach the per capita GDP at the end of the teacher's career.

EXPLANATORY NOTE
The values appearing in this graph have been obtained by calculating the ratio of the gross annual salary (minimum and maximum) in national currency to the per capita GDP (at current prices in national currency) of the country concerned.
Gross annual salary *is defined as the amount paid by the employer in the year — including all bonuses, increases and allowances such as those for cost of living, end of year (if applicable), holiday pay etc. — less the employer's social security and pension contributions. This salary does not include any other financial benefits in respect of additional functions, further qualifications or specific responsibilities.*
The figures are based on the situation of a teacher who is (a) single and without children; and (b) living in the capital.
Minimum salary *is the salary received by teachers with the above profile who are starting teaching, having completed their education, initial training and probation.*
Maximum salary *is the salary received by teachers with the above profile who are at the end of their career, i.e. during the last year prior to retirement.*

SPECIAL EDUCATION

PROVISION OF PRIMARY AND SECONDARY EDUCATION
──────── FOR CHILDREN WITH SPECIAL EDUCATIONAL NEEDS ────────

Certain pupils are recognized as having special educational needs where they have either physical disabilities (for example, deafness or problems of vision) or severe learning problems or are maladjusted. The current trend in the different Member States of the European Union is towards the integration of children with special educational needs into mainstream schools, giving teachers varying degrees of support in terms of staff, materials and equipment.

Three main models are found: separate schools, completely independent of mainstream schools; separate classes, i.e. special classes integrated into mainstream schools; and fully integrated education, i.e. the inclusion of children with special educational needs with the other pupils in a mainstream class.

In the French Community of Belgium and in Germany, apart from some pilot projects, education is completely separate. In Italy, on the other hand, integration is general. In the other Member States of the European Union, these different structures exist side by side, providing children with different degrees of integration depending on their individual special educational needs.

In most of the EFTA/EEA countries and the CEECs, all three types of educational structure are found. In Norway, education is almost totally integrated. In Bulgaria and Romania, however, children with special educational needs attend separate schools.

FIGURE H1: MAIN PATTERNS OF PROVISION OF SPECIAL EDUCATION, 1995/96

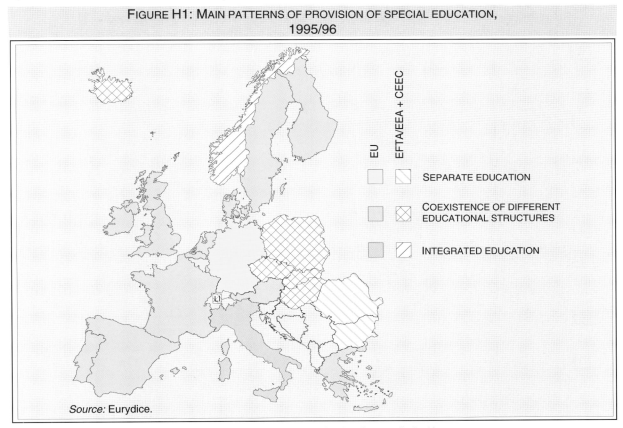

Source: Eurydice.

Belgium (B fr and **B de)**: There are some experiments with integration but they are limited in scope.
Germany: Since 1980, there have been some experiments with integration in the form of pilot schemes. In some *Länder*, integration is regulated under the schools legislation.
Spain: The integration of a pupil depends on the extent to which the official curriculum would have to be modified and the possibility of the pupil's social integration into mainstream education.
Italy: In general, pupils with special educational needs are integrated into mainstream schools. There are a few schools for blind and deaf and dumb children. The family decides where the child is placed.
Sweden: There are special schools for profoundly deaf children and one special school for children with speech problems. In other cases, pupils are integrated into mainstream education. There are, however, some special classes for children with severe learning difficulties.
Bulgaria: Whether a pupil is integrated or not depends on the disability.

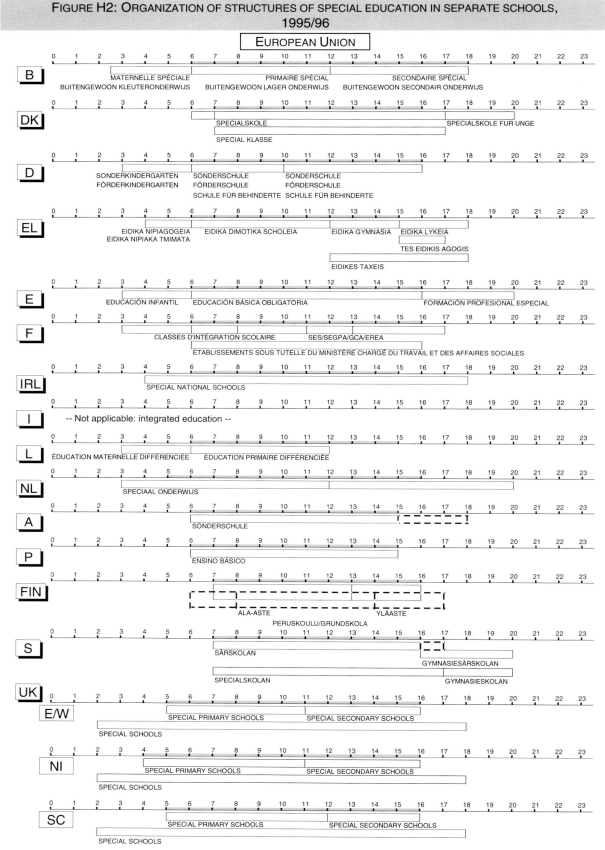

FIGURE H2: ORGANIZATION OF STRUCTURES OF SPECIAL EDUCATION IN SEPARATE SCHOOLS, 1995/96

EUROPEAN UNION

Source: Eurydice.

Germany: The terms vary depending on the *Länder* and the type of special education.

Finland: Special secondary education is also organized in special vocational institutions.

Sweden: All pupils of compulsory school age follow the same curriculum. There are, however, differences in the curricula for profoundly deaf children and those with severe learning difficulties.

FIGURE H2 (CONTINUED): ORGANIZATION OF STRUCTURES OF SPECIAL EDUCATION IN SEPARATE SCHOOLS, 1995/96

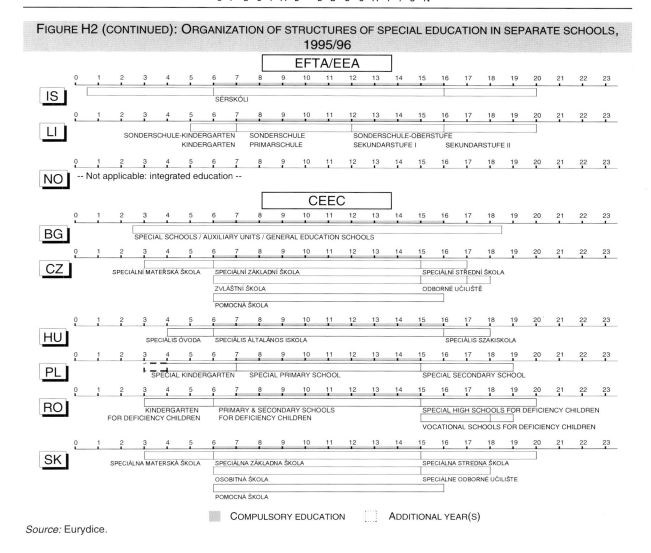

Source: Eurydice.

In all Member States which have parallel special education, its structure is similar to that of mainstream education. This structure is presented in Figure H2 which gives the names of the separate institutions providing special education. Differences from the structure of ordinary education appear in the duration of compulsory education. In the French Community of Belgium (in full-time education), and in Finland (in some cases), it is longer for children with special educational needs. In the Flemish Community of Belgium, primary education continues up to age 13 and secondary education to age 21.

In the EFTA/EEA countries and the CEECs, the structures of special education provided in separate schools are very close to those in mainstream education. The duration of compulsory education is the same for all children, whether they have special educational needs or not.

FROM SEGREGATION TO INTEGRATION

Special education developed in the course of the nineteenth century in order to guarantee the right to education of all children. Structures separate from mainstream education were provided in twelve Member States of the EU for the education of 'handicapped' children — now referred to more commonly as children with special educational needs. These were subsequently followed by other structures. The current trend is towards the integration of these children, in either special or ordinary classes in mainstream schools.

Generally speaking, the first form of integration consisted of the introduction of separate special classes in mainstream schools, with integration only coming later. This is the situation in Denmark, Spain, France, Ireland, Austria, Portugal, Finland, Sweden and the United Kingdom.

The integration of some children with special needs has been possible since the late 1940s in the United Kingdom (England and Wales and Northern Ireland) and more recently in the other Member States of the European Union.

In the present century, Belgium, Denmark and the United Kingdom (Scotland) were the first countries to consider opening special classes for children with special educational needs in mainstream schools. However, in Belgium this experiment has been suspended since 1970 and at the present time integration is only practised on a very limited basis there. In Italy, on the other hand, an increasingly integrated structure has gradually replaced the segregated structure.

In the EFTA/EEA countries, the development of education for children with special educational needs was marked by the provision of separate classes within mainstream education and then the relatively recent appearance of integration. In Iceland, there are parallel separate schools for profoundly disabled pupils. In Norway, the closure of many special schools in 1992 has resulted in a reduction in the number of pupils attending separate schools. There are still separate classes in mainstream schools, for mentally retarded pupils.

In the CEECs, in the Czech Republic, Poland and Slovakia, the provision of special education has followed the same pattern of development as in most of the European Union Member States. It was provided first in separate schools then also in separate classes and has finally very recently been integrated into mainstream education.

In Hungary, there have been separate special schools since the beginning of the century. Integration has been possible since 1973.

In Bulgaria and Romania, education for children with special educational needs is provided exclusively in special schools, although special classes were introduced between 1960 and 1980 in Bulgarian schools.

CONDITIONS REQUIRED FOR INTEGRATION

In most Member States of the European Union for which information is available, there are no legal limits on the integration of special needs children. Whether integration is widespread or on an experimental basis, certain preconditions have to be met, including:

— the agreement of a board comprising psychologists and/or educationists (Germany, Spain, France, United Kingdom (Scotland));

— the school's ability to cater for the needs of integrated pupils (Germany, Greece, Spain, Austria) and also concern for the efficiency of the education of the rest of the pupils in the class (Germany, United Kingdom (England, Wales and Northern Ireland));

— parents' views (Germany, Spain, Austria, United Kingdom).

The nature and degree of integration vary between Member States. For instance, in Greece and the United Kingdom, many deaf children are integrated while in Sweden they are in separate schools. Children with severe learning difficulties and maladjusted children are also in separate schools in Spain, France, Austria and Portugal. In Denmark, half of all special needs children are in mainstream schools and the other half in special schools.

In the EFTA/EEA countries and the CEECs, integration is sometimes subject to conditions. In Liechtenstein, the Czech Republic and Poland, the approval of the responsible authority and/or the parents is required. In Iceland, profound deafness and the use of sign language constitute limits to integration. In Norway, all pupils are integrated except the deaf, for whom separate schools have been retained.

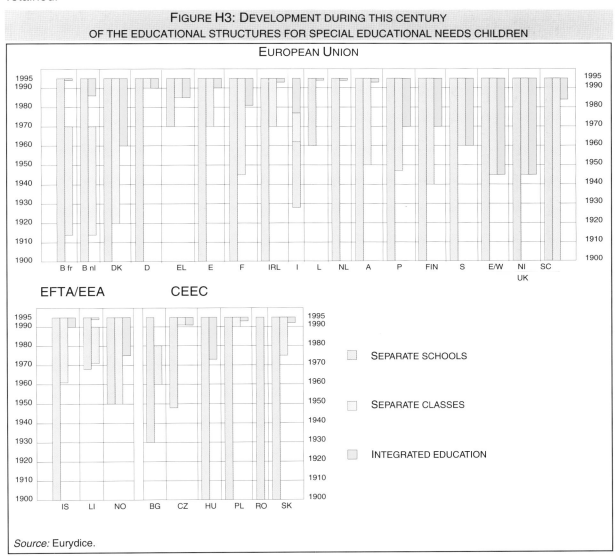

FIGURE H3: DEVELOPMENT DURING THIS CENTURY
OF THE EDUCATIONAL STRUCTURES FOR SPECIAL EDUCATIONAL NEEDS CHILDREN

Source: Eurydice.

Belgium (B fr and **B de)**: There are some experiments with integration but they are limited in scope.
Germany: Since 1980, there have been experiments with integration in the form of pilot schemes.
Spain: From 1985, an experimental programme of integration was introduced and since 1990 (LOGSE), the integration of pupils with special educational needs has been general.
Sweden: Since the end of the 1950s, increasing numbers of children have been integrated into mainstream education. Since 1 January 1996, the municipalities have been responsible for the education of children with severe learning difficulties. Nowadays, the aim is to achieve full integration, except for deaf children who remain in separate schools.
Bulgaria: Integration is in process of being introduced.

SPECIAL EDUCATION

VARIOUS SPECIALIZED TRAINING OPPORTUNITIES
FOR TEACHERS

FIGURE H4: TRAINING OF TEACHERS FOR WORKING SOLELY WITH PUPILS
WITH SPECIAL EDUCATIONAL NEEDS, 1995/96

	SPECIFIC INITIAL TRAINING	SUPPLEMENTARY TRAINING	IN-SERVICE TRAINING
EUROPEAN UNION			
B			
DK	2 years (3 years and 6 months since 1996)	1 year in the Royal Danish School of Educational Studies	1 year and 6 months - 3 years
D	9 semesters		
EL	4 years	2 years of post-graduate training or 5 years of experience in special education	Organized by special education schools
E	3 years (*escuelas universitarias de formación del profesorado*)		
F	2 or 3 years (CAPSAIS)		Takes the form of specialized *stages* (training placements)
IRL		1 year	
I	2 years (support teachers)		
L		1 year abroad	
NL		2 years part-time	
A	3 years		
P	2 years		Specialized placements
FIN	5 years (Master's degree in education)	1 year - 1 year and 6 months (after first qualification)	
S	1 year and 6 months (in addition to initial basic training)		
UK (E/W, NI)			
UK (SC)		After 2 probationary years	
EFTA/EEA			
IS		2 years	
LI	3 years part-time		
NO		6 months or 1 year	
CEEC			
BG	4 years		
CZ	4 - 5 years		
HU	4 years	4 semesters	
PL	3 or 5 years	2 semesters	3 semesters
RO	4 years (support teachers)		
SK	5 years (university course)	2 years maximum part-time (non-specialist teachers)	

COMPULSORY TRAINING	OPTIONAL TRAINING

Source: Eurydice.

Denmark, Netherlands and **Sweden**: All teachers receive initial training which includes an introduction to the education of children with special educational needs.

Germany: Those wishing to become special education teachers have to take either the specific initial training course (9 semesters) or, in certain *Länder*, an additional course of study (generally 4 semesters) after initial training for another type of teaching career. Both training schemes for special education teachers lead to a state examination.

Luxembourg: Reform of initial, supplementary and in-service training is in progress under the *Institut Supérieur d'Études et de Recherches Pédagogiques* (ISERP).

Austria: Supplementary training is compulsory if it leads to a further qualification as a specialized teacher for special educational needs (for instance, to entitle the teacher to teach blind children).

Finland: It is also possible to obtain a qualification with a specialization in special education in which case the additional training is not required.

Sweden: Teachers are free to choose an in-service training course from those on offer.

United Kingdom (E/W and **NI)**: Qualified teacher status equips staff to teach children with special educational needs; however, teachers of children with visual or hearing impairments, in special schools or units, are required to obtain a relevant approved special education qualification within 3 years of appointment, in addition to qualified teacher status.

Iceland and **Norway**: All teachers receive initial training which includes an introduction to the education of children with special educational needs.

Hungary: Only teachers dealing with mentally handicapped children can undertake specific initial training.

Slovakia: The additional training is compulsory for teachers who wish to work with special needs children and who have not undertaken the specific initial training.

The availability of, and obligation to undertake, specialized training differ considerably from one Member State to the other. Three models are found, depending on the country.

— Specific initial training is given to future teachers with a view to providing them with a qualification to teach certain or all children with special educational needs.

— Supplementary training additional to the initial training of teachers provides new skills for which further qualifications are awarded. This may make it possible to change direction professionally, more particularly by specializing in some specific disability.

— In-service training aims at updating the knowledge teachers have acquired during initial training. It also makes it possible for them to innovate and/or to improve their professional practice in relation to the specific needs of the children they are dealing with from day to day.

In Belgium, Ireland, Luxembourg, the Netherlands and the United Kingdom (Scotland), no specific initial training is provided and only supplementary training is possible or even obligatory. In Luxembourg, a reform of initial, supplementary and in-service training is in progress. In Scotland, teachers are encouraged to undertake additional special training once they have completed their two-year period of probation.

In Portugal, specific initial training is available as an option but there is no supplementary training. In Germany, Spain and France, specific initial training is obligatory for those wishing to teach children with special educational needs and this is not followed by supplementary training.

In Greece, Italy, Austria and Sweden, specific initial training is compulsory and is followed by supplementary training, which is optional in certain of these Member States. These courses of study vary in length from two to nine semesters (from one to four-and-a-half years). In Denmark, the Netherlands and Sweden, initial teacher training includes an introduction to the teaching of children with special educational needs. Ten weeks are devoted to this in Sweden. In Finland, two types of training are possible — either specific training or supplementary training following a first higher education qualification. In the United Kingdom (England, Wales and Northern Ireland), special needs training forms an element of all initial training. In both mainstream and special schools, in-service training for teachers is available. Teachers in special schools or units who work with children with visual and hearing impairments must obtain a relevant qualification.

As regards the EFTA/EEA countries, in Iceland and Norway all teachers receive initial training which includes an introduction to special needs education. This can be followed by a specialized course lasting two years in Iceland and 6 months or a year in Norway. In Liechtenstein, teachers working with special needs children have compulsory specific initial training.

In the CEECs, in Bulgaria, Hungary, Poland, Romania and Slovakia, specific initial training is compulsory and is followed by supplementary training. Only Slovakia has made this supplementary training compulsory. In the Czech Republic, specific initial training is compulsory for persons working with special needs children, but without supplementary training.

EXPLANATORY NOTE
Where the training of teachers for separate or integrated special education is the same as the basic initial training of teachers in general, it is not included here. It is described in the chapter on teachers.

ADDITIONAL STAFF
TO ASSIST CLASSROOM TEACHERS

Whatever the system, additional staff are provided in many Member States to help classroom teachers to cater for pupils with special educational needs. Three patterns may be observed.

— In Denmark and Sweden, only specialized teachers deal with the children.

— In Belgium and Luxembourg, where teachers do not have specific initial training, educational, medical and paramedical staff, psychologists and/or social workers assist in working with the children.

— In the other Member States of the European Union, additional non-teaching staff are associated with the teacher's work. These may include educationists, psychologists, speech and other therapists, nurses, classroom assistants and instructors. Teachers are also assisted by specialist teachers (specializing in one subject, one method or one type of handicap). In Italy, specialist teachers are responsible for all the pupils in the class in the same way as the other teachers.

In the EFTA/EEA countries and the CEECs, three patterns appear.

— In the Czech Republic, the children are taught only by specialized teachers.

— In Iceland, Liechtenstein and Norway, and in Bulgaria, Poland and Romania, teachers are assisted by specialist teachers and/or additional non-teaching staff.

— In Hungary, additional staff consist exclusively of speech therapists.

FIGURE H5: STAFF RESPONSIBLE FOR PUPILS WITH SPECIAL EDUCATIONAL NEEDS, 1995/96

	TEACHING TEAM	MEDICAL STAFF AND THERAPISTS	SOCIAL SERVICES
EUROPEAN UNION			
B	*Enseignants*	*Infirmiers, psychologues, logopèdes, kinésithérapeutes, puéricultrices, ergothérapeutes, orthopédagogues*	*Assistants sociaux*
DK	*Speciallærere, lærere*	*Psykologer, konsulenter, socialrådgivere*	*Sundhedsplejersker, socialpædagoger, socialrådgivere, psykologer*
D	*Sonderschullehrer*	Physiotherapists, speech therapists, occupational therapists, nurses	*Sozialpädagogen, Erzieher*
EL	*Daskalos eidikis agogis, kathigitis eidikis agogis*	Physiotherapists, speech therapists, occupational therapists, psychologists, assistants	Social workers
E	*Maestros con la especialidad de pedagogía terapéutica o educacion especial, maestros con la especialidad de audición y lenguaje*	*Psicológos, pedagogos, fisioterapeutas, auxiliares técnicos educativos (cuidadores), ayudantes técnicos sanitarios*	*Trabajadores sociales*
F	*Titulaires du CAPSAIS*	*Psychologues, psychiatres, rééducateurs*	*Assistants sociaux*
IRL	Class teachers, remedial teachers, visiting teachers, special needs assistants, special class teachers, resource teachers, Home-School-Community Liaison teachers, guidance teachers	Speech therapists, physiotherapists, occupational therapists, therapists, psychologists, counsellors, family doctors, nurses, dentists, psychiatrists	Social workers, special needs assistants, vocational officers, school attendance officers, junior liaison officers
I	Teachers and support teachers	Therapists, psychologists	Social workers
L	*Enseignants*	*Ergothérapeutes, orthophonistes, orthoptistes, psychorééducateurs, pédagogues curatifs*	*Éducateurs gradués ou diplômés*
NL	*Leraren speciaal onderwijs*	*Creatief therapeut, ergotherapeut, speltherapeut, fysiotherapeut, logopedist, psycholoog of psychodiagnostisch geschoolde orthopedagoog, psychologisch assistent, medisch specialist, audiloog, akoepedist*	*Maatschappelijk werker*
A	Support teachers, specialists	Therapists, medical staff	Nurses
P	Teachers and specialist teachers	Psychologists, therapists and speech therapists	Social workers
FIN	Special needs teachers, special class teachers	Psychologists, therapists and assistants, nurses	Social workers, residential care staff
S	Teaching team, special advisers and support staff		
UK	Teachers, support teachers, special needs coordinators, educational psychologists	Psychologists, nurses, speech and other therapists	Social workers
EFTA/EEA			
IS	Teachers, specialist teachers	Special needs coordinators, social therapists, assistants, psychologists	
LI	*Ergänzungslehrer*	Therapists, psychologists	
NO	Specialist teachers	Non-teaching staff, specialized and other assistants	
CEEC			
BG	Teachers, specialist teachers	Therapists, psychologists, instructors, speech and hearing therapists	
CZ	*Učitel na speciálních školách*		
HU		Speech therapists	
PL	Specialist teachers	Psychological assistance, nurses, speech and other therapists	Educational assistance, auxiliary staff
RO	Special needs teachers, special class teachers	Therapists, nurses, specialists in speech and hearing problems	
SK	Specialist teachers	Psychologists, therapists, nurses	Social workers

SPECIALIST TEACHERS

Source: Eurydice.

UNDER 2% OF CHILDREN ARE IN SPECIAL SCHOOLS IN THE EUROPEAN UNION

The data on which the graph below is based indicate only the proportion of children who are educated in separate special schools. The percentage of pupils with special educational needs in mainstream schools varies according to the extent of integration in the different countries and the policies in place in those countries.

In all countries, there is a percentage, sometimes very small, of pupils in special schools.

In Belgium, Germany, France and the Netherlands, this percentage is relatively high, between 2.6 and 4.3%. In the first two Member States, integration is partially at an experimental stage at the present time while in the Netherlands it has been introduced only very recently.

In the countries in which integration is more widespread, the proportion does not exceed 1%, as in Greece, Ireland and the United Kingdom. The lowest rates are found in Italy and Sweden (0.2 and 0.06% respectively).

Among the EFTA/EEA countries, a very small percentage (0.5%) is found in Iceland and Norway. Teaching in Norway is almost completely integrated.

In the CEECs, the policy of integration is relatively recent and the separate structures are still in existence. The percentage of children in special schools ranges from 1.1 to 3.8%.

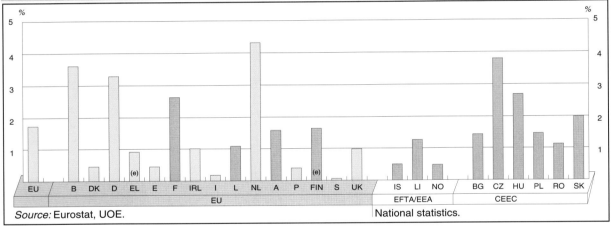

FIGURE H6: PUPILS WITH SPECIAL EDUCATIONAL NEEDS EDUCATED IN SEPARATE SCHOOLS AS A PERCENTAGE OF ALL PRIMARY AND SECONDARY PUPILS (ISCED 1, 2 AND 3), 1994/95

Source: Eurostat, UOE.   National statistics.

Belgium: 1993/94.
Denmark: Including pupils in all types of special school.
France, Luxembourg, Austria and **Finland**: National statistics.
Luxembourg and **Portugal**: ISCED 1 and 2.
Sweden: Excluding mature students.
Liechtenstein: ISCED 1 and 2.
Norway: Includes children with social and behavioural problems, mentally handicapped children, children in psychiatric hospitals and child-care institutions, deaf children and people educated in prison.
Czech Republic: Including pre-primary level.

EXPLANATORY NOTE
The percentages of children educated in separate special schools have been calculated in relation to the total numbers of children in education at ISCED levels 1, 2 and 3, including children in special education.

Annex

CONTEXT

CHANGES IN NUMBERS OF YOUNG PEOPLE AGED 0 TO 9 YEARS, 10 TO 19 YEARS AND 20 TO 29 YEARS
IN THE EUROPEAN UNION, 1975-95 (FIGURE A1)

(1 000)

EU (except P)	0 TO 9 YEARS	10 TO 19 YEARS	20 TO 29 YEARS	0 TO 29 YEARS
1975	52 599.4	54 017.3	49 156.9	155 773.6
1980	46 882.6	56 354.3	50 761.5	153 998.5
1985	43 138.0	53 167.6	54 291.5	150 597.1
1990	42 283.9	47 379.2	57 036.1	146 699.2
1995	41 760.5	44 521.8	54 972.2	141 254.5

B	0 TO 9 YEARS	10 TO 19 YEARS	20 TO 29 YEARS
1975	1 399.7	1 569.2	1 459.8
1980	1 265.2	1 530.9	1 548.8
1985	1 195.8	1 398.5	1 578.6
1990	1 195.4	1 275.7	1 547.9
1995	1 217.5	1 222.2	1 443.7

DK	0 TO 9 YEARS	10 TO 19 YEARS	20 TO 29 YEARS
1975	757.0	759.0	799.6
1980	684.7	787.6	746.5
1985	587.3	761.6	761.7
1990	556.9	690.3	798.1
1995	627.0	602.3	782.1

D	0 TO 9 YEARS	10 TO 19 YEARS	20 TO 29 YEARS
1975	10 683.0	12 272.0	10 374.3
1980	8 447.7	12 807.3	11 462.5
1985	8 066.2	10 756.5	12 576.6
1990	8 639.2	8 614.5	13 392.2
1995	8 799.6	8 752.0	11 964.3

EL	0 TO 9 YEARS	10 TO 19 YEARS	20 TO 29 YEARS
1975	1 451.9	1 404.6	1 244.5
1980	1 429.3	1 508.6	1 326.4
1985	1 384.3	1 481.7	1 413.9
1990	1 233.4	1 504.1	1 483.2
1995	1 091.0	1 461.9	1 587.0

E	0 TO 9 YEARS	10 TO 19 YEARS	20 TO 29 YEARS
1975	6 497.6	6 122.5	5 023.3
1980	6 465.3	6 397.6	5 495.7
1985	5 683.1	6 591.2	6 002.8
1990	4 643.1	6 395.7	6 443.2
1995	4 018.6	5 774.9	6 539.8

F	0 TO 9 YEARS	10 TO 19 YEARS	20 TO 29 YEARS
1975	8 360.4	8 527.6	8 416.6
1980	7 835.6	8 583.0	8 482.3
1985	7 508.5	8 583.4	8 531.2
1990	7 662.3	8 057.4	8 575.9
1995	7 465.4	7 705.6	8 579.2

IRL	0 TO 9 YEARS	10 TO 19 YEARS	20 TO 29 YEARS
1975	662.6	607.3	442.2
1980	696.3	658.4	511.3
1985	687.2	682.9	543.4
1990	616.7	670.7	513.1
1995	548.6	665.1	537.6

I	0 TO 9 YEARS	10 TO 19 YEARS	20 TO 29 YEARS
1975	8 936.3	8 529.5	7 804.6
1980	8 081.2	9 165.2	7 801.4
1985	6 740.8	9 018.3	8 464.1
1990	5 843.3	8 054.9	9 073.5
1995	5 564.5	6 752.3	9 134.7

L	0 TO 9 YEARS	10 TO 19 YEARS	20 TO 29 YEARS
1975	45.8	53.5	54.9
1980	42.6	54.1	57.2
1985	41.7	48.2	60.0
1990	44.5	43.3	61.2
1995	51.6	45.1	59.4

NL	0 TO 9 YEARS	10 TO 19 YEARS	20 TO 29 YEARS
1975	2 259.3	2 387.0	2 304.1
1980	1 961.4	2 470.4	2 338.1
1985	1 762.8	2 321.7	2 469.4
1990	1 814.5	2 007.7	2 555.0
1995	1 934.0	1 826.2	2 447.1

A	0 TO 9 YEARS	10 TO 19 YEARS	20 TO 29 YEARS
1975	1 131.2	1 223.0	1 027.0
1980	935.8	1 277.4	1 087.1
1985	885.7	1 145.6	1 241.4
1990	906.6	963.0	1 330.4
1995	935.7	938.6	1 285.0

P	0 TO 9 YEARS	10 TO 19 YEARS	20 TO 29 YEARS
1975	N/A	N/A	N/A
1980	N/A	N/A	N/A
1985	1 537.3	1 701.9	1 574.9
1990	1 255.4	1 647.9	1 518.3
1995	1 111.1	1 479.4	1 579.6

FIN	0 TO 9 YEARS	10 TO 19 YEARS	20 TO 29 YEARS
1975	657.2	788.4	872.8
1980	619.7	739.7	796.6
1985	650.0	657.8	766.3
1990	636.5	627.1	731.3
1995	641.6	658.5	660.9

S	0 TO 9 YEARS	10 TO 19 YEARS	20 TO 29 YEARS
1975	1 140.3	1 090.3	1 239.2
1980	1 050.4	1 149.8	1 145.6
1985	963.0	1 150.3	1 133.3
1990	1 023.0	1 065.4	1 204.6
1995	1 163.7	1 011.2	1 221.8

UK	0 TO 9 YEARS	10 TO 19 YEARS	20 TO 29 YEARS
1975	8 617.2	8 683.5	8 094.0
1980	7 367.5	9 224.3	7 961.8
1985	6 981.7	8 570.0	8 748.8
1990	7 468.7	7 409.5	9 326.5
1995	7 701.5	7 105.7	8 729.5

Source: Eurostat, population statistics.

135

NUMBER OF 0- TO 9-YEAR-OLDS, 10- TO 19-YEAR-OLDS AND 20- TO 29-YEAR-OLDS, 1995 (FIGURE A2)

(1 000)

	0 TO 9 YEARS	10 TO 19 YEARS	20 TO 29 YEARS	TOTAL POPULATION
EUROPEAN UNION				
EU	42 871.6	46 001.2	56 551.8	371 381.1
B	1 217.5	1 222.2	1 443.7	10 130.6
DK	627.0	602.3	782.1	5 215.7
D	8 799.6	8 752.0	1 1964.3	81 538.6
EL	1 091.0	1 461.9	1 587.0	10 442.9
E	4 018.6	5 774.9	6 539.8	39 177.4
F	7 465.4	7 705.6	8 579.2	58 020.4
IRL	548.6	665.1	537.6	3 594.7
I	5 564.5	6 752.3	9 134.7	57 268.6
L	51.6	45.1	59.4	406.6
NL	1 934.0	1 826.2	2 447.1	15 424.1
A	935.7	938.6	1 285.0	8 039.9
P	1 111.1	1 479.4	1 579.6	9 912.1
FIN	641.6	658.5	660.9	5 098.8
S	1 163.7	1 011.2	1 221.8	8 816.4
UK	7 701.5	7 105.7	8 729.5	58 294.4
EFTA/EEA				
IS	44.1	42.5	41.5	267.0
LI	3.9	3.9	5.1	30.6
NO	583.7	532.4	668.9	4 348.4
CEEC				
BG	962.8	1 195.9	1 153.3	8 427.4
CZ	1 249.5	1 586.5	1 502.8	10 333.2
HU	1 214.6	1 510.9	1 438.8	10 245.7
PL	5 539.9	6 577.5	5 214.8	38 580.6
RO	3 038.0	3 664.4	3 611.3	22 712.4
SK	778.1	924.4	788.8	5 356.2

Source: Eurostat, population statistics.

NUMBER AND PERCENTAGE OF 0- TO 29-YEAR-OLDS BY NUTS 1 AND 2 REGIONS, 1995 (FIGURE A3)

			TOTAL POPULATION (1 000)	POPULATION 0 TO 29 YEARS (1 000)	0 TO 29 YEARS (%)
		EUROPEAN UNION			
BE		**BELGIQUE — BELGIË**	10 130.6	3 883.4	38
	BE1	BRUXELLES — BRUSSEL	951.6	368.3	39
	BE2	VLAAMS GEWEST	5 866.1	2 221.6	38
	BE3	RÉGION WALLONNE	3 312.9	1 293.5	39
DK		**DANMARK**	5 215.7	2 011.5	39
DE		**DEUTSCHLAND**	81 493.3	29 515.9	36
	DE1	BADEN-WÜRTTEMBERG	10 266.6	3 856.6	38
	DE2	BAYERN	11 915.7	4 387.0	37
	DE3	BERLIN	3 469.5	1 229.4	35
	DE4	BRANDENBURG	2 535.7	936.6	37
	DE5	BREMEN	679.6	230.3	34
	DE6	HAMBURG	1 704.6	579.1	34
	DE7	HESSEN	5 977.3	2 117.1	35
	DE8	MECKLENBURG-VORPOMMERN	1 831.7	708.3	39
	DE9	NIEDERSACHSEN	7 710.7	2 824.2	37
	DEA	NORDRHEIN-WESTFALEN	17 805.9	6 406.8	36
	DEB	RHEINLAND-PFALZ	3 949.3	1 417.5	36
	DEC	SAARLAND	1 083.6	367.8	34
	DED	SACHSEN	4 581.7	1 590.2	35
	DEE	SACHSEN-ANHALT	2 758.0	984.0	36
	DEF	SCHLESWIG-HOLSTEIN	2 706.7	966.9	36
	DEG	THÜRINGEN	2 516.7	914.1	36
GR		**ELLADA**	10 442.9	4 139.8	40
	GR1	VOREIA ELLADA	3 369.6	1 342.4	40
	GR2	KENTRIKI ELLADA	2 584.9	992.7	38
	GR3	ATTIKI	3 485.4	1 396.5	40
	GR4	NISIA AIGAIOU. KRITI	1 003.0	408.3	41
ES		**ESPAÑA**	39 177.4	16 333.4	42
	ES1	NOROESTE	4 333.8	1 646.4	38
	ES2	NORESTE	4 049.0	1 535.4	38
	ES3	COMUNIDAD DE MADRID	5 004.4	2 097.1	42
	ES4	CENTRO (E)	5 273.0	2 098.1	40
	ES5	ESTE	10 689.8	4 345.6	41
	ES6	SUR	8 285.1	3 879.1	47
	ES7	CANARIAS	1 542.3	731.7	47

136

NUMBER AND PERCENTAGE OF 0- TO 29-YEAR-OLDS BY NUTS 1 AND 2 REGIONS, 1995 (FIGURE A3 CONTINUED)

			TOTAL POPULATION (1 000)	POPULATION 0 TO 29 YEARS (1 000)	0 TO 29 YEARS (%)
		EUROPEAN UNION (CONTINUED)			
FR	FRANCE		58 020.1	23 750.2	41
	FR1	ÎLE-DE-FRANCE	10 977.7	4 748.9	43
	FR2	BASSIN PARISIEN	10 453.9	4 326.0	41
	FR3	NORD-PAS-DE-CALAIS	3 994.8	1 811.3	45
	FR4	EST	5 114.6	2 136.5	42
	FR5	OUEST	7 605.7	3 050.8	40
	FR6	SUD-OUEST	6 079.5	2 242.0	37
	FR7	CENTRE-EST	6 884.6	2 829.0	41
	FR8	MÉDITERRANÉE	6 909.3	2 605.7	38
IE	IRELAND		3 597.6	1 758.9	49
IT	ITALIA		57 268.6	21 451.6	37
	IT1	NORD OVEST	6 080.1	1 923.2	32
	IT2	LOMBARDIA	8 910.5	3 130.9	35
	IT3	NORD EST	6 522.2	2 312.6	35
	IT4	EMILIA-ROMAGNA	3 922.6	1 203.3	31
	IT5	CENTRO (I)	5 789.5	1 873.4	32
	IT6	LAZIO	5 193.2	1 927.1	37
	IT7	ABRUZZO-MOLISE	1 599.8	599.7	37
	IT8	CAMPANIA	5 745.8	2 649.6	46
	IT9	SUD	6 762.6	2 950.4	44
	ITA	SICILIA	5 082.7	2 189.3	43
	ITB	SARDEGNA	1 659.5	692.1	48
LU	LUXEMBOURG (GRAND-DUCHÉ)		406.6	156.1	38
NL	NEDERLAND		15 424.1	6 207.3	40
	NL1	NOORD-NEDERLAND	1 622.4	652.5	40
	NL2	OOST-NEDERLAND	3 177.4	1 323.2	42
	NL3	WEST-NEDERLAND	7 218.0	2 891.6	40
	NL4	ZUID-NEDERLAND	3 406.3	1 339.9	39
AT	ÖSTERREICH		8 039.9	3 159.3	39
	AT1	OSTÖSTERREICH	3 382.3	1 250.5	37
	AT2	SÜDÖSTERREICH	1 764.9	694.1	39
	AT3	WESTÖSTERREICH	2 892.6	1 214.8	42
PT	PORTUGAL		9 912.1	4 170.1	42
	PT1	CONTINENTE	9 415.0	3 923.6	42
	PT11	NORTE	3 519.0	1 620.3	46
	PT12	CENTRO (P)	1 713.7	684.6	40
	PT13	LISBOA E VALE DO TEJO	3 308.8	1 297.0	39
	PT14	ALENTEJO	528.7	191.7	36
	PT15	ALGARVE	344.8	130.2	38
	PT2	AÇORES	240.5	120.0	50
	PT3	MADEIRA	256.6	126.5	49
FI	SUOMI (FINLAND)		5 098.8	1 961.1	38
	FI1	MANNER-SUOMI	5 073.6	1 951.5	38
	FI11	UUSIMAA	1 309.5	514.6	39
	FI12	ETELÄ-SUOMI	1 793.3	657.4	37
	FI13	ITÄ-SUOMI	707.5	264.1	37
	FI14	VÄLI-SUOMI	707.1	278.5	39
	FI15	POHJOIS-SUOMI	556.2	236.8	43
	FI2	AHVENANMAA/ÅLAND	25.2	9.6	38
SE	SVERIGE		8 816.4	3 396.7	39
	SE01	STOCKHOLM	1 708.5	662.9	39
	SE02	ÖSTRA MELLYEARSVERIGE	1 500.6	587.6	39
	SE03	SMÅLAND MED ÖARNA	795.5	306.5	39
	SE04	SYDSERIGE	1 259.0	479.7	38
	SE05	VÄSTSVERIGE	1 762.3	686.9	39
	SE06	NORRA MELLYEARSVERIGE	866.4	319.4	37
	SE07	MELLERSTA NORRLAND	396.6	145.8	37
	SE08	ÖVRE NORRLAND	527.4	207.9	39
UK	UNITED KINGDOM		58 500.2	23 533.7	40
	UK1	NORTH	3 097.6	1 221.1	39
	UK2	YORKSHIRE AND HUMBERSIDE	5 027.2	2 030.1	40
	UK3	EAST MIDLANDS	4 113.1	1 637.2	40
	UK4	EAST ANGLIA	2 114.0	824.9	39
	UK5	SOUTH EAST (UK)	17 929.4	7 263.8	41
	UK6	SOUTH WEST (UK)	4 812.6	1 811.8	38
	UK7	WEST MIDLANDS	5 300.7	2 150.8	41
	UK8	NORTH WEST (UK)	6 410.8	2 613.8	41
	UK9	WALES	2 914.9	1 139.9	39
	UKA	SCOTLAND	5 134.5	2 068.6	40
	UKB	NORTHERN IRELAND	1 645.3	771.6	47

NUMBER AND PERCENTAGE OF 0- TO 29-YEAR-OLDS BY NUTS 1 AND 2 REGIONS, 1995 (FIGURE A3 CONTINUED)

	TOTAL POPULATION (1 000)	POPULATION 0 TO 29 YEARS (1 000)	0 TO 29 YEARS (%)
EFTA/EEA			
ÍSLAND	267.0	128.0	48
LIECHTENSTEIN	30.6	12.9	42
NORGE	4 348.4	1 785.0	41
CEEC			
BĂLGARIJA	8 427.4	3 312.0	39
ČESKÁ REPUBLIKA	10 333.2	4 338.9	42
MAGYARORSZÁG	10 245.7	4 164.3	41
POLSKA	38 580.6	17 332.2	45
ROMÂNIA	22 712.4	10 313.7	46
SLOVENSKÁ REPUBLIKA	5 356.2	2 491.3	47

Source: Eurostat, population statistics.

PEOPLE WITHOUT A FINAL UPPER SECONDARY SCHOOL LEAVING QUALIFICATION, BY AGE GROUP, 1995 (FIGURE A4)

(%)

AGE	EU	B	DK	D	EL	E	F	IRL	I	L	NL	A	P	FIN	S	UK
20-29	31	25	11	16	29	44	23	29	45	51	16	21	58	16	11	40
30-39	35	36	16	14	43	60	31	42	53	52	17	24	70	19	17	44
40-49	44	45	19	16	58	76	41	57	64	56	21	32	80	33	24	46
50-59	53	60	27	24	73	87	55	68	79	61	29	40	86	50	41	55

Source: Eurostat, Labour force survey.

TREND IN THE PERCENTAGES OF STUDENTS (ALL PERSONS IN EDUCATION AND TRAINING) AMONG 15- TO 24-YEAR-OLDS, 1987 AND 1995 (FIGURE A5)

(%)

	EU	B	DK	D	EL	E	F	IRL	I	L	NL	A	P	FIN	S	UK
1987	49	56	61	57	51	49	51	46	45	44	61	N/A	35	38	N/A	39
1995	58	65	68	63	56	61	67	56	54	59	66	53	57	66	44	46

Source: Eurostat, Labour force survey.

UNEMPLOYMENT RATES OF 15- TO 24-YEAR-OLDS AND OF THE ACTIVE POPULATION (15- TO 59-YEAR-OLDS), 1995 (FIGURE A9)

(%)

	EUROPEAN UNION							
	EU	B	DK	D	EL	E	F	IRL
15- TO 59-YEAR-OLDS	11	10	7	8	10	23	12	13
15- TO 24-YEAR-OLDS	21	22	10	9	28	42	27	19

	I	L	NL	A	P	FIN	S	UK
15- TO 59-YEAR-OLDS	12	3	7	4	8	18	8	9
15- TO 24-YEAR-OLDS	33	7	12	6	16	41	19	16

Source: Eurostat, Labour force survey.

	EFTA/EEA				CEEC					
	IS	LI	NO		BG	CZ	HU	PL	RO	SK
15- TO 59-YEAR-OLDS	5	1	5		N/A	3	10	14	10	13
15- TO 24-YEAR-OLDS	11	2	12		N/A	6	23	32	27	25

Source: National statistics.

UNEMPLOYMENT RATES IN THE POPULATION OF 25- TO 59-YEAR-OLDS, BY LEVEL OF EDUCATION, 1995 (FIGURE A10)

(%)

	EUROPEAN UNION							
	EU	B	DK	D	EL	E	F	IRL
ISCED 0-2	12	12	10	14	6	21	14	17
ISCED 3	8	8	6	8	9	19	9	8
ISCED 5-7	6	3	5	5	6	15	7	4

	I	L	NL	A	P	FIN	S	UK
ISCED 0-2	10	3	11	6	6	18	9	10
ISCED 3	8	2	6	4	7	16	8	7
ISCED 5-7	7		5	2	3	7	4	4

Source: Eurostat, Labour force survey.

	EFTA/EEA				CEEC					
	IS	LI	NO		BG	CZ	HU	PL	RO	SK
ISCED 0-2	6	N/A	7		N/A	9	N/A	13	16	24
ISCED 3	4	N/A	4		N/A	2	N/A	11	1	10
ISCED 5-7	1	N/A	2		N/A	1	N/A	4	1	3

Source: National statistics.

PUPILS AND STUDENTS BY AGE, TOTAL, ISCED 0-7, 1994/95 (FIGURE A8)

(1 000)

	EUROPEAN UNION															EFTA/EEA		
	B	DK	D	EL	E	F	IRL	I	L	NL	A	P	FIN	S	UK	IS	LI	NO
TOTAL	2 534.0	1 144.9	16 324.4	1 979.9	9 732.7	14 678.8	1 011.7	10 680.6	52.7	3 586.3	1 616.5	2 351.3	1 143.4	1 978.5	14 142.4	82.9	5	1 027.7
UNDER 3 YEARS	50.0	0.0		0.0	63.9	258.4	0.0			0.0	1.2	0.0	0.0	0.0	47.9	2.8		0.0
3	123.5	39.0	398.5	13.2	225.8	743.5	0.5			0.2	29.0	48.1	17.6	64.2	355.4	3.5		33.6
4	122.9	50.7	668.1	57.7	393.3	762.0	29.1			195.3	66.1	59.5	19.5	72.7	731.7	3.9		40.2
5	121.4	51.3	736.8	85.9	411.8	772.1	53.6			190.4	83.2	69.3	22.4	74.2	771.4	3.5		42.9
6	119.5	58.1	829.6	104.0	425.2	776.1	55.2			188.6	92.3	125.3	37.0	77.1	781.8	4.6		52.8
7	118.6	57.2	927.2	106.5	435.2	773.7	58.5			189.5	90.7	119.3	60.4	105.9	759.9	4.2		54.6
8	115.4	56.7	906.0	112.7	450.1	779.9	61.0			188.7	93.0	122.9	61.4	108.3	745.5	3.8		53.1
9	117.0	55.4	878.5	118.6	467.9	770.3	61.0			183.1	93.0	126.5	63.4	106.0	741.5	3.9		52.1
10	118.0	53.4	878.8	129.2	487.2	761.7	62.7			179.6	92.6	145.5	65.7	100.9	716.9	4.1		51.2
11	120.5	52.4	875.7	147.4	510.4	741.9	64.9			173.4	92.2	132.1	67.5	97.6	718.1	4.3		51.0
12	124.1	54.2	900.2	143.8	537.6	791.1	68.7			175.6	96.5	149.6	67.0	98.3	717.3	4.3		52.2
13	124.5	54.5	899.4	141.1	562.8	803.5	70.1			182.0	100.0	143.5	64.4	99.2	728.0	4.3		51.9
14	123.5	57.9	900.7	135.7	575.0	798.7	71.9			185.6	96.2	129.9	64.0	101.7	734.2	4.5		52.3
15	126.8	59.5	854.6	130.6	561.9	752.1	68.9			180.0	86.6	131.7	64.1	97.3	716.0	4.5		52.8
16	126.4	59.8	833.7	120.8	514.8	723.7	63.2			180.0	83.6	111.8	60.1	94.8	580.5	3.6		50.4
17	122.8	52.0	799.2	85.6	481.4	703.7	55.4			169.5	78.8	118.8	59.8	96.5	486.6	3.1		47.4
18	104.4	48.1	714.5	73.9	413.7	619.4	47.5			153.5	57.5	96.1	54.4	90.9	363.2	2.7		45.7
19	90.9	40.4	543.9	70.0	352.7	535.2	29.3			132.5	34.9	79.8	27.1	38.6	318.4	2.7		28.5
20	80.4	30.9	388.5	57.0	332.4	452.9	22.6			119.1	26.3	64.1	26.7	35.5	289.2	1.8		26.4
21	62.2	29.3	297.7	46.1	265.8	361.0	11.6			99.9	23.3	77.8	27.6	35.6	257.1	1.7		25.7
22	49.3	27.8	410.1	27.4	226.9	270.0	8.9			86.9	20.6	41.7	25.8	35.6	180.5	1.7		25.1
23	35.2	25.0	223.3	20.4	164.9	183.9	7.3			73.0	20.1	34.8	23.7	33.4	149.7	1.3		22.7
24	26.3	20.5	208.8	12.5	114.2	112.0	5.7			58.3	150.4	26.9	20.3	28.2	126.6	1.0		18.0
25	19.3	17.1	211.1	13.2	78.9	77.6	33.9			44.0		34.7	17.3	23.8	114.4	0.8		14.9
26	15.7	14.4	195.8	9.4	54.5	55.0				35.8		13.2	14.8	20.9	107.0	0.6		11.3
27	13.9	12.0	174.3	7.9	43.7	40.5				25.7		9.2	12.6	18.9	102.1	0.4		9.0
28	17.2	10.0	133.0	3.5	34.3	33.6				21.5		7.6	10.5	16.7	97.8	0.3		7.3
29	10.3	7.9	105.1	2.6	27.8	27.7				19.2		6.3	8.6	14.8	94.8	0.3		5.9
30-34	128.9	22.8	423.0	1.6	91.3	197.6				68.2		24.0	31.2	56.9	429.4	1.0		18.6
35-39		11.8			44.2					40.1		14.7	20.1	42.8	327.6	0.6		12.0
40 AND OVER	5.0	14.8		1.6	39.5					47.1		22.7	28.2	75.2	851.9	0.8		18.0
AGE UNKNOWN			9.4		343.5						8.4	63.9	15.9					

Source: Eurostat, UOE.

Belgium: 1993/94.

Belgium, Germany and **France:** The figure for students aged 30 to 34 years is that for all students aged 30 years and over.

Ireland and **Portugal:** The figure for students aged 25 years is that for all students aged 25 years and over.

Austria: The figure for students aged 24 years is that for all students aged 24 years and over.

UNEMPLOYMENT RATES AMONG HIGHER EDUCATION GRADUATES, BY AGE GROUP, 1995 (FIGURE A11)

(%)

		B	DK	D	EL	E	F	IRL	I
ISCED 5-7	25-34	9	5	6	5	10	23	9	5
	35-44	4	3	4	5	3	8	5	4
	45-54	4	2	5	4	2	5	4	
	25-54	6	4	5	5	6	15	7	4

		L	NL	A	P	FIN	S	UK	EU
ISCED 5-7	25-34	20		6	4	7	10	5	4
	35-44	3		4			7	3	3
	45-54			4			5	3	4
	25-54	8		5	2	3	7	4	4

Source: Eurostat, Labour force survey.

		IS	LI	NO		BG	CZ	HU	PL	RO	SK
ISCED 5-7	25-34	1	N/A	4		N/A	1	N/A	6	2	4
	35-44	1	N/A	2		N/A	0	N/A	4	1	2
	45-54	1	N/A	1		N/A	1	N/A	2	1	1
	25-54	N/A	N/A	N/A		N/A	N/A	N/A	N/A	1,3	N/A

Source: National statistics.

MOVEMENT IN THE UNEMPLOYMENT RATES OF 15- TO 24-YEAR-OLDS, 25- TO 34-YEAR-OLDS AND OVERALL UNEMPLOYMENT IN THE EUROPEAN UNION, 1987-95 (FIGURE A12)

(%)

	1987	1988	1989	1990	1991	1992	1993	1994	1995
15- TO 59-YEAR-OLDS	11	10	9	9	9	9	11	12	11
15- TO 24-YEAR-OLDS	22	20	18	16	17	18	21	22	21
25- TO 34-YEAR-OLDS	11	11	10	9	10	10	12	13	12

Source: Eurostat, Labour force survey.

MOVEMENT IN THE UNEMPLOYMENT RATES OF 15- TO 24-YEAR-OLDS, 25- TO 34-YEAR-OLDS AND IN OVERALL UNEMPLOYMENT, BY MEMBER STATE, 1987-95 (FIGURE A13)

(%)

B

1987	1988	1989	1990	1991	1992	1993	1994	1995	
11	10	8	7	7	7	8	10	10	15-59
21	18	16	15	14	13	19	22	22	15-24
12	11	9	8	8	7	9	10	10	25-34

DK

1987	1988	1989	1990	1991	1992	1993	1994	1995
6	7	8	9	9	9	11	8	7
9	9	12	12	12	12	15	10	10
7	8	10	10	11	11	13	9	8

D

1987	1988	1989	1990	1991	1992	1993	1994	1995	
7	6	6	5	5	6	8	9	8	15-59
8	7	6	5	6	6	8	9	9	15-24
8	7	6	5	6	6	8	9	8	25-34

EL

1987	1988	1989	1990	1991	1992	1993	1994	1995
8	8	8	8	8	8	9	10	10
25	26	25	23	25	25	27	28	28
9	9	9	9	9	9	10	11	11

E

1987	1988	1989	1990	1991	1992	1993	1994	1995	
22	21	18	17	17	18	23	25	23	15-59
44	41	34	32	31	33	42	45	42	15-24
21	21	19	18	18	20	25	28	26	25-34

F

1987	1988	1989	1990	1991	1992	1993	1994	1995
11	10	10	10	9	10	12	13	12
23	22	20	20	20	22	26	29	27
11	10	10	10	10	11	13	14	13

IRL

1987	1988	1989	1990	1991	1992	1993	1994	1995	
19	18	17	15	16	16	16	15	13	15-59
26	25	22	20	23	23	25	23	19	15-24
18	16	15	14	15	15	15	14	11	25-34

I

1987	1988	1989	1990	1991	1992	1993	1994	1995
11	12	12	10	11	10	11	12	12
34	33	32	29	28	27	30	32	33
11	12	13	12	12	10	12	14	14

L

1987	1988	1989	1990	1991	1992	1993	1994	1995	
3	2	2	2	2	2	2	4	3	15-59
5	5	3	4	3	4	4	8	7	15-24
2	2	2	2	2	3	2	4	3	25-34

NL

1987	1988	1989	1990	1991	1992	1993	1994	1995
10	10	9	8	7	6	6	7	7
17	14	13	11	11	8	10	11	12
10	9	9	8	7	5	6	8	7

Movement in the unemployment rates of 15- to 24-year-olds, 25- to 34-year-olds and in overall unemployment, by Member State, 1987-95 (Figure A13 continued)

(%)

A

1987	1988	1989	1990	1991	1992	1993	1994	1995	
N/A	N/A	N/A	N/A	N/A	N/A	N/A	N/A	4	15-59
5	5	4	4	4	4	5	N/A	6	15-24
N/A	N/A	N/A	N/A	N/A	N/A	N/A	N/A	4	25-34

P

1987	1988	1989	1990	1991	1992	1993	1994	1995
8	6	6	5	4	4	6	7	8
18	14	12	10	9	10	12	15	16
8	7	6	5	5	5	6	8	8

FIN

1987	1988	1989	1990	1991	1992	1993	1994	1995	
5	5	4	4	8	13	18	19	18	15-59
10	8	6	7	15	25	33	34	41	15-24
5	4	3	3	8	14	19	19	17	25-34

S

1987	1988	1989	1990	1991	1992	1993	1994	1995
N/A	N/A	N/A	N/A	N/A	N/A	N/A	N/A	8
N/A	4	4	5	8	14	23	N/A	19
N/A	N/A	N/A	N/A	N/A	N/A	N/A	N/A	9

UK

1987	1988	1989	1990	1991	1992	1993	1994	1995	
11	9	7	7	9	10	10	10	9	15-59
16	13	10	10	14	16	18	16	16	15-24
12	10	8	7	9	11	11	10	9	25-34

Source: Eurostat, Labour force survey.

Austria, Finland and **Sweden**: Data for 1987-94 are from the national statistical offices.

Unemployment rates of 25- to 59-year-olds by level of education and by sex, 1995 (Figure A14)

(%)

		EUROPEAN UNION							
		EU	B	DK	D	EL	E	F	IRL
ISCED 0-3	M	9	7	5	8	5	16	9	13
	F	12	14	9	11	11	29	14	14
ISCED 5-7	M	5	3	5	4	4	11	6	4
	F	7	4	5	6	8	20	7	5

		I	L	NL	A	P	FIN	S	UK
ISCED 0-3	M	7	2	6	4	6	18	9	10
	F	13	4	9	5	8	15	7	7
ISCED 5-7	M	5		4	2	4	8	4	4
	F	10		5	3	2	7	3	3

Source: Eurostat, Labour force survey.

		EFTA/EEA				CEEC					
		IS	LI	NO		BG	CZ	HU	PL	RO	SK
ISCED 0-3	M	6	N/A	N/A		N/A	3	N/A	12	8	14
	F	6	N/A	N/A		N/A	4	N/A	16	13	15
ISCED 5-7	M	1	N/A	3		N/A	1	N/A	4	1	2
	F	1	N/A	3		N/A	1	N/A	6	2	4

Source: National statistics.

Occupations of 25- to 34-year-old and 35- to 59-year-old graduates, 1995 (Figure A15)

(%)

	EU		B		DK		D		EL		E		F		IRL	
	25-34	35-59	25-34	35-59	25-34	35-59	25-34	35-59	25-34	35-59	25-34	35-59	25-34	35-59	25-34	35-59
ARMED FORCES	1	1				1	1	0	4	2	0	1	1	1	6	5
LEGISLATORS AND MANAGERS	10	15	10	17	5	12	6	12	6	9	5	11	11	16	10	16
PROFESSIONALS	42	50	47	54	39	43	39	43	53	67	40	53	31	45	44	55
TECHNICIANS	24	19	15	12	39	33	26	22	17	10	15	11	39	31	9	6
CLERKS	10	6	20	11	7	4	7	6	9	7	16	9	11	4	14	6
SERVICE AND SALES WORKERS	4	3	4	2	5	3	5	4	5	2	8	4	2	1	7	5
AGRICULTURAL AND FISHERY WORKERS	1	1					1	1	1		1	1	1	1		2
CRAFT AND RELATED TRADES WORKERS	5	5	2	1	2	3	10	9	2	2	8	6	2	1	6	3
PLANT AND MACHINE OPERATORS	2	1	1	1		1	1	2	1		4	3	1	1	4	2
ELEMENTARY OCCUPATIONS	2	1	1	1	2	1	3	3	1		3	1	1	1		

Source: Eurostat, Labour force survey.

OCCUPATIONS OF 25- TO 34-YEAR-OLD AND 35- TO 59-YEAR-OLD GRADUATES, 1995 (FIGURE A15)

(%)

	I		L		NL		A		P		FIN		S		UK	
	25-34	35-59	25-34	35-59	25-34	35-59	25-34	35-59	25-34	35-59	25-34	35-59	25-34	35-59	25-34	35-59
ARMED FORCES						0				1	N/A	N/A	N/A	N/A	1	0
LEGISLATORS AND MANAGERS	5	10	9	15	9	17	9	21	8	12	N/A	N/A	N/A	N/A	20	22
PROFESSIONALS	57	68	59	65	41	53	68	66	58	51	N/A	N/A	N/A	N/A	47	54
TECHNICIANS	19	13	24	16	30	18	14	8	26,1	32,4	N/A	N/A	N/A	N/A	14,8	10,4
CLERKS	11	5	7	4	11	6	6	3	6	4	N/A	N/A	N/A	N/A	8	5
SERVICE AND SALES WORKERS	4	2			7	3	3			3	N/A	N/A	N/A	N/A	3	3
AGRICULTURAL AND FISHERY WORKERS		0									N/A	N/A	N/A	N/A	0	0
CRAFT AND RELATED TRADES WORKERS	2	0			1	1		1			N/A	N/A	N/A	N/A	4	3
PLANT AND MACHINE OPERATORS		1			1	1					N/A	N/A	N/A	N/A	1	1
ELEMENTARY OCCUPATIONS	2	1			2	2					N/A	N/A	N/A	N/A	1	1

Source: Eurostat, Labour force survey.

**PEOPLE WHO WOULD LIKE TO UNDERTAKE LIFELONG LEARNING,
BY AGE OF LEAVING EDUCATION, 1995** (FIGURE A17)

(%)

	EU	B	DK	D	EL	E	F	IRL
COMPLETED EDUCATION BEFORE AGE 15	58	44	77		74	64	70	53
COMPLETED EDUCATION AFTER AGE 20	83	80	95		95	90	90	89

	I	L	NL	A	P	FIN	S	UK
COMPLETED EDUCATION BEFORE AGE 15	51	47	42	40	47	54	61	69
COMPLETED EDUCATION AFTER AGE 20	78	74	83	65	74	85	91	91

Source: Eurobarometer 44.0 et 44.1.

**PEOPLE WHO HAD UNDERTAKEN TRAINING COURSES
DURING THE PAST 12 MONTHS, BY AGE AT WHICH THEY LEFT EDUCATION, 1995** (FIGURE A19)

(%)

	EU	B	DK	D	EL	E	F	IRL
COMPLETED EDUCATION BEFORE AGE 15	9	4	14		4	9	4	9
COMPLETED EDUCATION AFTER AGE 20	39	33	54		17	41	36	41

	I	L	NL	A	P	FIN	S	UK
COMPLETED EDUCATION BEFORE AGE 15	6	7	14	17	11	11	15	14
COMPLETED EDUCATION AFTER AGE 20	28	30	47	53	32	47	44	52

Source: Eurobarometer 44.0 et 44.1.

STRUCTURES AND SCHOOLS

PUBLIC AND PRIVATE EDUCATION.
NUMBER OF PUPILS (PRIMARY AND SECONDARY EDUCATION), 1994/95 (FIGURE B2)

(1 000)

	PUBLIC	PRIVATE	PRIVATE GRANT-AIDED	PRIVATE NON GRANT-AIDED	TOTAL
EUROPEAN UNION					
B	731.7	0.0	1 058.5	0.0	1 790.2
DK	688.9	0.0	84.6	0.0	773.6
D	11 339.8	0.0	539.7	0.0	11 879.5
EL	1 465.6	0.0	0.0	64.1	1 529.8
E	5 019.3	2 090.4	0.0	0.0	7 109.7
F	8 042.4	0.0	1 997.5	35.6	10 075.4
IRL	763.8	0.0	0.0	7.9	771.7
I	7 012.8	476.9	0.0	0.0	7 489.7
L	50.0	0.0	3.0	0.0	53.0
NL	587.0	0.0	2 088.6	22.1	2 697.8
A	1 082.8	84.8	0.0	0.0	1 167.5
P	1 694.0	171.6	0.0	0.0	1 865.6
FIN	809.3	0.0	32.7	0.0	842.0
S	1 428.2	0.0	23.8	0.0	1 451.9
UK	8 663.7	0.0	13.1	594.1	9 271.2
EFTA/EEA					
IS	57.0	0.0	2.4	0.0	59.4
LI	3.7	0.0	0.0	0.1	3.9
NO	659.5	25.5	0.0	0.0	685.0

Source: Eurostat, UOE.

	PUBLIC	PRIVATE	PRIVATE GRANT-AIDED	PRIVATE NON GRANT-AIDED	TOTAL
CEEC					
BG	247.5	0.2	0.0	0.0	247.6
CZ	1 653.4	0.0	78.6	0.0	1 732.0
HU	1 480.4	52.3	0.0	0.0	1 532.7
PL	7 329.9	72.0	0.0	0.0	7 401.9
RO	3 578.5	13.1	0.0	0.0	3 591.6
SK	963.5	39.7	0.0	0.0	1 003.2

Source: National statistics.

Liechtenstein: National statistics.

PRE-PRIMARY EDUCATION

TREND IN THE PARTICIPATION RATES OF 4-YEAR-OLDS IN EDUCATION-ORIENTED PRE-PRIMARY PROVISION 1950-94 (FIGURE C1)

(%)

	1950	1960	1970	1980	1990	1994
B	74	92	100	100	99	100
DK			(1973) 36	54	74	79
D				65	71	71
EL				38	51	54
E		34	43	69	95	100
F		63	87	100	100	100
IRL				54	55	53
I						96
L		43	65	94	94	94
NL	48	71	86	96	98	97
A			29	57	66	71
P				18	46	55
FIN			(1975) 16	18	26	30
S				28	48	58
UK				83	91	95

Source: Eurostat, UOE and additional collection.

PARTICIPATION RATES IN EDUCATION-ORIENTED PRE-PRIMARY PROVISION BY AGE AND TYPE OF INSTITUTION, 1994/95 (FIGURE C3)

		NUMBER OF PUPILS IN NON-SCHOOL EDUCATION-ORIENTED INSTITUTIONS	NUMBER OF PUPILS IN SCHOOLS		NUMBER OF CHILDREN (POPULATION)	PARTICIPATION RATES IN NON-SCHOOL EDUCATION-ORIENTED INSTITUTIONS (%)	PARTICIPATION RATES IN SCHOOLS (%)	PARTICIPATION RATES IN COMPULSORY PRIMARY EDUCATION (%)
		(A)	(B)	(A)+(B)	(C)	(A)/(C) = (D)	(B)/(C) = (E)	1-(D)-(E)
EUROPEAN UNION								
B	7 YEARS		140	140	120 072		0	100
	6 YEARS		5 704	5 704	122 536		5	95
	5 YEARS		121 507	121 507	123 604		98	1
	4 YEARS		125 484	125 484	126 064		100	
	3 YEARS		125 363	125 363	127 317		98	
DK	7 YEARS	490	4 560	5 050	57 341	1	8	91
	6 YEARS	5 390	50 168	55 558	59 968	9	84	
	5 YEARS	50 398	880	51 278	62 336	81	1	
	4 YEARS	50 677		50 677	64 334	79		
	3 YEARS	39 008		39 008	65 063	60		
D	7 YEARS	12 300	11 556	23 856	930 550	1	1	97
	6 YEARS	352 500	54 972	407 472	953 911	37	6	57
	5 YEARS	715 900	19 935	735 835	928 821	77	2	
	4 YEARS	668 100		668 100	940 780	71		
	3 YEARS	398 500		398 500	855 019	47		
EL	7 YEARS				113 181			94
	6 YEARS				110 250			94
	5 YEARS		60 232	60 232	108 194		56	24
	4 YEARS		57 706	57 706	106 574		54	
	3 YEARS		13 200		104 138		13	
E	7 YEARS				412 881			100
	6 YEARS				398 680			100
	5 YEARS		411 753	411 753	396 926		100	
	4 YEARS		393 319	393 319	389 712		100	
	3 YEARS		225 779	225 779	393 459		57	
F	7 YEARS		500	500	766 557		0	100
	6 YEARS		8 700	8 700	766 593		1	99
	5 YEARS		757 700	757 700	758 865		100	
	4 YEARS		762 000	762 000	753 646		100	
	3 YEARS		743 500	743 500	747 238		99	
IRL	7 YEARS		1 230	1 230	58 300		2	98
	6 YEARS		29 964	29 964	55 100		54	46
	5 YEARS		53 527	53 527	54 600		98	
	4 YEARS		29 127	29 127	55 200		53	
	3 YEARS		466	466	54 200		1	

		NUMBER OF PUPILS IN NON-SCHOOL EDUCATION-ORIENTED INSTITUTIONS	NUMBER OF PUPILS IN SCHOOLS		NUMBER OF CHILDREN (POPULATION)	PARTICIPATION RATES IN NON-SCHOOL EDUCATION-ORIENTED INSTITUTIONS (%)	PARTICIPATION RATES IN SCHOOLS (%)	PARTICIPATION RATES IN COMPULSORY PRIMARY EDUCATION (%)
		(A)	(B)	(A)+(B)	(C)	(A)/(C) = (D)	(B)/(C) = (E)	1-(D)-(E)
					EUROPEAN UNION (CONTINUED)			
I	7 YEARS				548 904			100
	6 YEARS				561 220			100
	5 YEARS		553 818	553 818	559 623		99	
	4 YEARS		536 413	536 413	556 353		96	
	3 YEARS		492 107	492 107	551 782		89	
L	7 YEARS				4 787			100
	6 YEARS				5 144			100
	5 YEARS				5 109		98 (e)	
	4 YEARS				5 431		92 (e)	
	3 YEARS				5 256			
NL	7 YEARS		175	175	190 724		0	100
	6 YEARS		1 688	1 688	189 858		1	99
	5 YEARS		189 144	189 144	191 897		99	
	4 YEARS		194 464	194 464	200 100		97	
	3 YEARS		5	5	200 037		0	
A	7 YEARS	297	770 (e)	1 067	91 990	0	1 (e)	99
	6 YEARS	25 991	8 350 (e)	34 341	93 375	28	9 (e)	63
	5 YEARS	83 180		83 180	92 239	90		
	4 YEARS	66 118		66 118	93 577	71		
	3 YEARS	28 976		28 976	95 256	30		
P	7 YEARS				108 360			100
	6 YEARS				105 580			100
	5 YEARS	30 649	46 435	77 084	110 170	28	42	
	4 YEARS	24 596	34 642	59 238	107 810	23	32	
	3 YEARS	23 959	23 995	47 954	114 500	21	21	
FIN	7 YEARS		400	400	60 636		1	99
	6 YEARS	33 315	3 126	36 441	64 036	52	5	
	5 YEARS	22 390		22 390	63 938	35		
	4 YEARS	19 450		19 450	65 961	29		
	3 YEARS	17 615		17 615	65 526	27		
S	7 YEARS				109 692			97
	6 YEARS	99 862		99 862	116 538	86		7
	5 YEARS	75 912		75 912	119 742	63		
	4 YEARS	73 042		73 042	126 791	58		
	3 YEARS	64 162		64 162	125 819	51		
UK	7 YEARS				766 083			100
	6 YEARS				785 400			100
	5 YEARS				771 462			100
	4 YEARS		731 719	731 719	781 481		94	
	3 YEARS		355 434	355 434	793 546		45	
					EFTA/EEA			
IS	7 YEARS				4 157			100
	6 YEARS		39	39	4 604		1	99
	5 YEARS		3 548	3 548	4 488		79	
	4 YEARS		3 948	3 948	4 765		83	
	3 YEARS		3 522	3 522	4 545		77	
LI	7 YEARS				388			100
	6 YEARS	411		411	417	99		
	5 YEARS	400		400	380	100		
	4 YEARS	12		12	391	3		
	3 YEARS				416			
NO	7 YEARS	342	290	632	55 091	1	1	99
	6 YEARS	29 789	22 559	52 348	58 328	51	39	
	5 YEARS	42 728	200	42 928	60 073	71	0	
	4 YEARS	40 212		40 212	61 716	65		
	3 YEARS	33 619		33 619	61 695	54		
					CEEC			
BG	7 YEARS		4 547	4 547	104 570		4	96
	6 YEARS		66 389	66 389	104 728		63	
	5 YEARS		65 195	65 195	102 523		64	
	4 YEARS		58 858	58 858	97 454		60	
	3 YEARS		45 953	45 953	89 491		51	
CZ	7 YEARS				128 071			100
	6 YEARS		21 379	21 379	129 686		16	84
	5 YEARS		108 017	108 017	125 783		86	
	4 YEARS		95 104	95 104	127 574		75	
	3 YEARS		89 493	89 493	128 220		70	
HU	7 YEARS				123 009			100
	6 YEARS		78 981	78 981	121 615		65	35
	5 YEARS		115 817	115 817	120 895		96	
	4 YEARS		107 630	107 630	123 571		87	
	3 YEARS		82 432	82 432	125 087		66	

145

		NUMBER OF PUPILS IN NON-SCHOOL EDUCATION-ORIENTED INSTITUTIONS	NUMBER OF PUPILS IN SCHOOLS		NUMBER OF CHILDREN (POPULATION)	PARTICIPATION RATES IN NON-SCHOOL EDUCATION-ORIENTED INSTITUTIONS (%)	PARTICIPATION RATES IN SCHOOLS (%)	PARTICIPATION RATES IN COMPULSORY PRIMARY EDUCATION (%)
		(A)	(B)	(A)+(B)	(C)	(A)/(C) = (D)	(B)/(C) = (E)	1-(D)-(E)
CEEC (CONTINUED)								
PL	7 YEARS		10 206	10 206	591 924		2	98
	6 YEARS		551 913	551 913	576 265		96	
	5 YEARS				552 553			
	4 YEARS		424 041	424 041	536 024		26	
	3 YEARS				537 046			
RO	7 YEARS				358 730			100
	6 YEARS		227 730	227 730	350 579		65	
	5 YEARS		223 258	223 258	352 988		63	
	4 YEARS		168259	168 259	284 444		59	
	3 YEARS		96 267	96 267	258 333		37	
SK	7 YEARS				81 384			100
	6 YEARS		22 988	22 988	80 719		28	72
	5 YEARS		57 663	57 663	77 502		74	
	4 YEARS		47 787	47 787	77 307		62	
	3 YEARS		36 780	36 780	77 421		48	

Source: Eurostat, additional collection.

PARTICIPATION OF 3-YEAR-OLDS IN EDUCATION-ORIENTED PRE-PRIMARY PROVISION, BY NUTS 1 AND 2 REGIONS, 1994/95 (FIGURE C4)

			RATE (%)	NUMBER OF 3-YEAR-OLDS IN EDUCATION-ORIENTED PRE-PRIMARY PROVISION (*Source:* Eurydice)	TOTAL NUMBER OF 3-YEAR-OLDS IN THE POPULATION (*Source:* Eurostat)
EUROPEAN UNION					
B		BELGIQUE — BELGIË			
	BE1	BRUXELLES — BRUSSEL	98 (e)	N/A	N/A
	BE2	VLAAMS GEWEST	98 (e)	N/A	N/A
	BE3	RÉGION WALLONNE	98 (e)	N/A	N/A
DK		DANMARK	60	39 008	65 063
D		DEUTSCHLAND			
	DE1	BADEN-WÜRTTEMBERG	N/A	N/A	121 603
	DE2	BAYERN	N/A	N/A	138 426
	DE3	BERLIN	N/A	N/A	31 240
	DE4	BRANDENBURG	N/A	N/A	17 678
	DE5	BREMEN	N/A	N/A	6 564
	DE6	HAMBURG	N/A	N/A	16 246
	DE7	HESSEN	N/A	N/A	63 873
	DE8	MECKLENBURG-VORPOMMERN	N/A	N/A	13 496
	DE9	NIEDERSACHSEN	N/A	N/A	88 501
	DEA	NORDRHEIN-WESTFALEN	N/A	N/A	202 584
	DEB	RHEINLAND-PFALZ	N/A	N/A	45 093
	DEC	SAARLAND	N/A	N/A	11 328
	DED	SACHSEN	N/A	N/A	30 916
	DEE	SACHSEN-ANHALT	N/A	N/A	19 551
	DEF	SCHLESWIG-HOLSTEIN	N/A	N/A	30 158
	DEG	THÜRINGEN	N/A	N/A	17 778
GR		ELLADA			
	GR1	VOREIA ELLADA	54	18 198	34 012
	GR2	KENTRIKI ELLADA	49	11 874	23 993
	GR3	ATTIKI	40	13 958	34 958
	GR4	NISIA AIGAIOU. KRITI	55	6 135	11 175
ES		ESPAÑA			
	ES1	NOROESTE	74	25 176	34 047
	ES2	NORESTE	92	30 366	32 896
	ES3	COMUNIDAD DE MADRID	62	30 427	49 051
	ES4	CENTRO (E)	71	36 516	51 597
	ES5	ESTE	72	74 653	104 360
	ES6	SUR	22	22 982	103 267
	ES7	CANARIAS	31	5 659	18 241
FR		FRANCE			
	FR1	ÎLE-DE-FRANCE	100	155 795	156 444
	FR2	BASSIN PARISIEN	97	132 712	136 498
	FR3	NORD-PAS-DE-CALAIS	100	57 583	57 247
	FR4	EST	98	66 315	67 329
	FR5	OUEST	100	93 126	91 164
	FR6	SUD-OUEST	100	65 423	65 685
	FR7	CENTRE-EST	99	88 325	89 155
	FR8	MÉDITERRANÉE	100	84 237	83 716
	FR9	DÉPARTEMENTS D'OUTRE-MER			
IRL		IRELAND	1	466	54 183

			RATE (%)	NUMBER OF 3-YEAR-OLDS IN EDUCATION-ORIENTED PRE-PRIMARY PROVISION (Source: Eurydice)	TOTAL NUMBER OF 3-YEAR-OLDS IN THE POPULATION (Source: Eurostat.)
EUROPEAN UNION (CONTINUED)					
IT		ITALIA			
	IT1	NORD OVEST	89	40 823	45 709
	IT2	LOMBARDIA	93	70 462	75 487
	IT3	NORD EST	93	53 021	56 860
	IT4	EMILIA-ROMAGNA	91	25 742	28 401
	IT5	CENTRO (I)	96	43 496	45 388
	IT6	LAZIO	88	43 773	49 518
	IT7	ABRUZZO-MOLISE	97	15 337	15 869
	IT8	CAMPANIA	83	63 649	77 106
	IT9	SUD	95	75 563	79 334
	ITA	SICILIA	72	44 586	61 635
	ITB	SARDEGNA	88	14 497	16 475
LU		LUXEMBOURG (GRAND-DUCHÉ)	N/A	N/A	5 256
NL		NEDERLAND			
	NL1	NOORD-NEDERLAND	0 (e)	N/A	20 072
	NL2	OOST-NEDERLAND	0 (e)	N/A	42 950
	NL3	WEST-NEDERLAND	0 (e)	N/A	93 884
	NL4	ZUID-NEDERLAND	0 (e)	N/A	43 131
AT		ÖSTERREICH			
	AT1	OSTÖSTERREICH	49	18 507	37 651
	AT2	SÜDÖSTERREICH	16	3 371	20 442
	AT3	WESTÖSTERREICH	19	7 098	37 163
PT		PORTUGAL			
	PT11	NORTE	35	15 990	45 320
	PT12	CENTRO (P)	54	9 639	17 860
	PT13	LISBOA E VALE DO TEJO	46	16 273	35 230
	PT14	ALENTEJO	55	2 738	5 020
	PT15	ALGARVE	30	1 173	3 910
	PT2	AÇORES	28	1 068	3 760
	PT3	MADEIRA	32	1 073	3 400
FI		SUOMI/FINLAND			
	FI11	UUSIMAA	36	6 532	17 920
	FI12	ETELÄ-SUOMI	26	5 618	21 383
	FI13	ITÄ-SUOMI	21	1 810	8 510
	FI14	VÄLI-SUOMI	19	1 755	9 152
	FI15	POHJOIS-SUOMI	22	1 828	8 243
	FI2	AHVENANMAA/ÅLAND	23	73	318
SE		SVERIGE			
	SE01	STOCKHOLM	65	16 050	24 782
	SE02	ÖSTRA MELLYEARSVERIGE	48	10 264	21 554
	SE03	SMÅLAND MED ÖARNA	44	4 958	11 327
	SE04	SYDSERIGE	51	8 658	17 079
	SE05	VÄSTSVERIGE	46	11 816	25 717
	SE06	NORRA MELLYEARSVERIGE	46	5 648	12 204
	SE07	MELLERSTA NORRLAND	54	2 886	5 322
	SE08	ÖVRE NORRLAND	50	3 882	7 834
UK		UNITED KINGDOM			
	UK1	NORTH	77	31 652	40 967
	UK2	YORKSHIRE AND HUMBERSIDE	64	44 229	68 785
	UK3	EAST MIDLANDS	44	24 255	54 940
	UK4	EAST ANGLIA	21	5 858	27 422
	UK5	SOUTH EAST (UK)	37	91 085	245 391
	UK6	SOUTH WEST (UK)	22	12 772	58 905
	UK7	WEST MIDLANDS	55	40 854	73 631
	UK8	NORTH WEST (UK)	59	52 762	90 014
	UK9	WALES	73	27 851	38 313
	UKA	SCOTLAND	21	13 818	66 607
	UKB	NORTHERN IRELAND	39	10 298	26 397
EFTA/EEA					
IS	ÍSLAND		77	3 522	4 545
LI	LIECHTENSTEIN		0	0	416
NO	NORGE		54	33 619	61 695
CEEC					
BG	BĂLGARIJA		51	45 953	89 491
CZ	ČESKÁ REPUBLIKA		70	89 493	128 220
HU	MAGYARORSZÁG		66	82 432	125 087
PL	POLSKA		26 (e)	N/A	537 046
RO	ROMÂNIA		37	96 267	258 333
SK	SLOVENSKÁ REPUBLIKA		48	36 780	77 421

Source: Eurostat, additional collection.

PROPORTION OF MOTHERS WITH A 3-YEAR-OLD CHILD AND IN EMPLOYMENT AND PARTICIPATION OF 3-YEAR-OLDS IN EDUCATION-ORIENTED PRE-PRIMARY PROVISION, 1994/95 (FIGURE C5)

	NUMBER OF 3-YEAR-OLDS IN EDUCATION-ORIENTED PRE-PRIMARY PROVISION	TOTAL NUMBER OF 3-YEAR-OLDS IN THE POPULATION	PARTICIPATION RATES (%) IN EDUCATION-ORIENTED PRE-PRIMARY PROVISION	PROPORTION OF EMPLOYED MOTHERS (%)
B	125 363	127 317	98	60
DK	39 008	65 063	60	73 (e)
D	398 500	855 019	47	41
EL	57 706	106 574	54	44
E	225 779	393 459	57	35
F	743 500	747 238	99	54
IRL	466	54 200	1	40
I	492 107	551 782	89	41
L	N/A	5 256	N/A	41
NL	5	200 037	0	48
A	28 976	95 256	30	63
P	47 954	114 500	42	67
FIN	17 615	65 526	27	54
S	64 162	125 819	51	67
UK	355 434	793 546	45	45

Source: Eurostat, UOE and Labour force survey.

AVERAGE DURATION OF ATTENDANCE AT AN EDUCATION-ORIENTED PRE-PRIMARY INSTITUTION, 1994/95 (FIGURE C6)

		NUMBER OF PUPILS IN EDUCATION-ORIENTED PRE-PRIMARY PROVISION	NUMBER OF CHILDREN (POPULATION)	PARTICIPATION RATES (%) IN EDUCATION-ORIENTED PRE-PRIMARY PROVISION	AVERAGE DURATION	THEORETICAL DURATION OF ATTENDANCE (IN YEARS)
			EUROPEAN UNION			
B	7 YEARS	140	120 072	0		
	6 YEARS	5 704	122 536	5		
	5 YEARS	121 507	123 604	98		
	4 YEARS	125 484	126 064	100		
	3 YEARS	125 363	127 317	98		
	TOTAL			301	3.01	3
DK	7 YEARS	5 050	57 341	9		
	6 YEARS	55 558	59 968	93		
	5 YEARS	51 278	62 336	82		
	4 YEARS	50 677	64 334	79		
	3 YEARS	39 008	65 063	60		
	TOTAL			322	3.22	4
D	7 YEARS	23 856	930 550	3		
	6 YEARS	407 472	953 911	43		
	5 YEARS	735 835	928 821	79		
	4 YEARS	668 100	940 780	71		
	3 YEARS	398 500	855 019	47		
	TOTAL			242	2.42	3
EL	7 YEARS		113 181	0		
	6 YEARS		110 250	0		
	5 YEARS	60 232	108 194	56		
	4 YEARS	57 706	106 574	54		
	3 YEARS		104 138	0		
	TOTAL			110	1.10	2
E	7 YEARS	0	412 881	0		
	6 YEARS	0	398 680	0		
	5 YEARS	411 753	396 926	100		
	4 YEARS	393 319	389 712	100		
	3 YEARS	225 779	393 459	57		
	TOTAL			257	2.57	3
F	7 YEARS	500	766 557	0		
	6 YEARS	8 700	766 593	1		
	5 YEARS	757 700	758 865	100		
	4 YEARS	762 000	753 646	100		
	3 YEARS	743 500	747 238	99		
	TOTAL			301	3.01	3
IRL	7 YEARS	1 230	58 300	2		
	6 YEARS	29 964	55 100	54		
	5 YEARS	53 527	54 600	98		
	4 YEARS	29 127	55 200	53		
	3 YEARS	466	54 200	1		
	TOTAL			208	2.08	2

148

		NUMBER OF PUPILS IN EDUCATION-ORIENTED PRE-PRIMARY PROVISION	NUMBER OF CHILDREN (POPULATION)	PARTICIPATION RATES (%) IN EDUCATION-ORIENTED PRE-PRIMARY PROVISION	AVERAGE DURATION (IN YEARS)	THEORETICAL DURATION OF ATTENDANCE (IN YEARS)
		EUROPEAN UNION (CONTINUED)				
I	7 YEARS	0	548 904	0		
	6 YEARS	0	561 220	0		
	5 YEARS	553 818	559 623	99		
	4 YEARS	536 413	556 353	96		
	3 YEARS	492 107	551 782	89		
	TOTAL			285	2.85	3
L	7 YEARS		4 787			
	6 YEARS		5 144			
	5 YEARS		5 109	98 (e)		
	4 YEARS		5 431	92 (e)		
	3 YEARS		5 256			
	TOTAL			190	1.90	2.5
NL	7 YEARS	175	190 724	0		
	6 YEARS	1 688	189 858	1		
	5 YEARS	189 144	191 897	99		
	4 YEARS	194 464	200 100	97		
	3 YEARS	5	200 037	0		
	TOTAL			97	0.97	1
A	7 YEARS	1 067 (e)	91 990	1 (e)		
	6 YEARS	34 341 (e)	93 375	37 (e)		
	5 YEARS	83 180	92 239	90		
	4 YEARS	66 118	93 577	71		
	3 YEARS	28 976	95 256	30		
	TOTAL			229	2.29	3
P	7 YEARS	0	108 360	0		
	6 YEARS	0	105 580	0		
	5 YEARS	77 084	110 170	70		
	4 YEARS	59 238	107 810	55		
	3 YEARS	47 954	114 500	42		
	TOTAL			167	1.67	3
FIN	7 YEARS	400	60 636	1		
	6 YEARS	36 441	64 036	57		
	5 YEARS	22 390	63 938	35		
	4 YEARS	19 450	65 961	29		
	3 YEARS	17 615	65 526	27		
	TOTAL			149	1.49	4
S	7 YEARS	0	109 692	0		
	6 YEARS	99 862	116 538	86		
	5 YEARS	75 912	119 742	63		
	4 YEARS	73 042	126 791	58		
	3 YEARS	64 162	125 819	51		
	TOTAL			258	2.58	4
UK	7 YEARS	0	766 083	0		E/W: 2
	6 YEARS	0	785 400	0		NI:1
	5 YEARS	0	771 462	0		SC:2
	4 YEARS	731 719	781 481	94		
	3 YEARS	355 434	793 546	45		
	TOTAL			138	1.38	
		EFTA/EEA				
IS	7 YEARS	0	4 157	0		
	6 YEARS	39	4 604	1		
	5 YEARS	3 548	4 488	79		
	4 YEARS	3 948	4 765	83		
	3 YEARS	3 522	4 545	77		
	TOTAL			240	2.40	3
LI	7 YEARS	0	388	0		
	6 YEARS	411	417	99		
	5 YEARS	400	380	100		
	4 YEARS	12	391	3		
	3 YEARS	0	416	0		
	TOTAL			202	2.02	2
NO	7 YEARS	632	55 091	1		
	6 YEARS	52 348	58 328	90		
	5 YEARS	42 928	60 073	71		
	4 YEARS	40 212	61 716	65		
	3 YEARS	33 619	61 695	54		
	TOTAL			282	2.82	3

		NUMBER OF PUPILS IN EDUCATION-ORIENTED PRE-PRIMARY PROVISION	NUMBER OF CHILDREN (POPULATION)	PARTICIPATION RATES (%) IN EDUCATION-ORIENTED PRE-PRIMARY PROVISION	AVERAGE DURATION OF ATTENDANCE (IN YEARS)	THEORETICAL
		CEEC				
BG	7 YEARS	4 547	104 570	4		
	6 YEARS	66 389	104 728	63		
	5 YEARS	65 195	102 523	64		
	4 YEARS	58 858	97 454	60		
	3 YEARS	45 953	89 491	51		
	TOTAL			243	2.43	3
CZ	7 YEARS	0	128 071	0		
	6 YEARS	21 379	129 686	16		
	5 YEARS	108 017	125 783	86		
	4 YEARS	95 104	127 574	75		
	3 YEARS	89 493	128 220	70		
	TOTAL			247	2.47	3
HU	7 YEARS	0	123 009	0		
	6 YEARS	78 981	121 615	65		
	5 YEARS	115 817	120 895	96		
	4 YEARS	107 630	123 571	87		
	3 YEARS	82 432	125 087	66		
	TOTAL			314	3.14	3
PL	7 YEARS	10 206	591 924	2		
	6 YEARS	551 913	576 265	96		
	5 YEARS		552 553			
	4 YEARS	424 041	536 024	26		
	3 YEARS		537 046			
	TOTAL			124	1.24	4
RO	7 YEARS	0	358 730	0		
	6 YEARS	227 730	350 579	65		
	5 YEARS	223 258	352 988	63		
	4 YEARS	168 259	284 444	59		
	3 YEARS	96 267	258 333	37		
	TOTAL			225	2.25	3
SK	7 YEARS	0	81 384	0		
	6 YEARS	22 988	80 719	28		
	5 YEARS	57 663	77 502	74		
	4 YEARS	47 787	77 307	62		
	3 YEARS	36 780	77 421	48		
	TOTAL			212	2.12	3

Source: Eurostat, additional collection.

PRESCRIBED OR RECOMMENDED NUMBERS OF 4-YEAR-OLD CHILDREN PER ADULT IN SCHOOLS AND OTHER EDUCATION-ORIENTED PRE-PRIMARY INSTITUTIONS, 1995/96 (FIGURE C8)

	EUROPEAN UNION								
	B	DK	D	EL	E	F	IRL	I	L
MAXIMUM NUMBER OF CHILDREN			30	30	25			25	26
MINIMUM NUMBER OF CHILDREN			15	15				15	
NUMBER OF ADULTS	(*)	(*)	2	1	1	(*)	1	1	1

	NL	A	P	FIN	S	UK (E/W)	UK (NI)	UK (SC)
MAXIMUM NUMBER OF CHILDREN		25	25	7		26	25	20
MINIMUM NUMBER OF CHILDREN			20					
NUMBER OF ADULTS	(*)	1	1	1	(*)	2	2	2

	EFTA/EEA		
	IS	LI	NO
MAXIMUM NUMBER OF CHILDREN	8	20	18
MINIMUM NUMBER OF CHILDREN		10	14
NUMBER OF ADULTS	1	1	2-3

	CEEC					
	BG	CZ	HU	PL	RO	SK
MAXIMUM NUMBER OF CHILDREN	16	20	25	25	20	25
MINIMUM NUMBER OF CHILDREN	8	15			10	
NUMBER OF ADULTS	2	1	1	1	1	1

Source: Eurydice.

(*): No regulations exist on the maximum and/or minimum class or group size, nor on the number of adults per group.

PRIMARY EDUCATION

CLASS SIZE REGULATIONS OR RECOMMENDATIONS, 1995/96 (FIGURE D3)

	EUROPEAN UNION							
	B	DK	D	EL	E	F	IRL	I
MINIMA				15				20
MAXIMA	(*)	28	28	30	25	(*)	35	25

	L	NL	A	P	FIN	S	UK (E/W, NI)	UK (SC)
MINIMA	18		10	20				
MAXIMA	26	(*)	30	34	(*)	(*)	(*)	33

	EFTA/EEE			CEEC					
	IS	LI	NO	BG	CZ	HU	PL	RO	SK
MINIMA		12		17	10		25	10	
MAXIMA	30	24	28	26	30	26	35	25	35

Source: Eurydice.

(*): No recommendations.

ANNUAL NUMBER OF HOURS OF TAUGHT TIME (AROUND AGE 7), 1995/96 (FIGURE D5)

	WEEKLY LOAD	NUMBER OF DAYS PER WEEK	DAILY LOAD	NUMBER OF DAYS PER YEAR	ANNUAL LOAD
EUROPEAN UNION					
B	min. 28 x 50' = 1 400'	5	280'	182	min. 50 960' = 849h
DK	20 x 45' = 900'	5	180'	200	min. 36 000' = 600h max. = 720h
D	977'	5	195'	188	36 750' = 613h
EL	min. 23 x 45' = 1 035' max. 25 x 45' = 1 125'	5	min. 207' max. 225'	175	min. 31 500' = 525h max. 39 375' = 656h
E	(25 x 60') - (5 x 30') = 1 350'	5	270'	180	48 600' = 810h
F	(26 x 60') - (5 x 30') = 1 410'	5	282'	180	50 760' = 846h
IRL	23h20' = 1 400'	5	280'	183	min. 51 240' = 854h max. = 915h
I	(27 x 60') - (6 x 30') = 1 440'	6	240'	min.200	min.48 000' = 800h
L	(18 x 55') + (12 x 50') = 1 590'	6	265'	212	56 180'=936h
NL	22h = 1 320'	5	264'	200	52 800' = 880h
A	21 x 50' = 1 050'	5/6	210'/175'	180/214	37 800' = 630h
P	(25 x 60') - (5 x 30') = 1 350'	5	270'	175	47 250' = 788 h
FIN	min. 19 x 45' = 855' max. 21 x 45' = 945'	5	min. 171' max. 189'	190	min. 32 490' = 542h max. 35 910' = 599h
S				min. 178 max. 190	
UK E/W	22h06' = 1 326'	5	265'	190	50 388' = 840h
NI	17h30' = 1 050'	5	210'	190	39 900' = 665h
SC	25h = 1 500'	5	300'	190	57 000' = 950h
EFTA/EEA					
IS	27 x 40'= 1 080'	5	216	160	34 560' = 576h
LI	21 x 45' = 945'	5	189'	200	37 800' = 630h
NO	min. 20 x 45' = 900'	5	min.180'	190	min. 34 200' = 570h
CEEC					
BG	min. 22 (ou 25) x 40'= 880'/1 000'	5	min.176'/200'	160	min.28 160' = 470h/ 32 000'= 533h
	max. 22 (ou 25) x 45' = 990'/1 125'	5	max.198'/225'	160	max.31 680'= 528h/ 36 000'= 600h
CZ	min. 22 x 45'= 990'	5	min. 198'	184	min. 36 432' = 607h
	max. 23 x 45' = 1 035'	5	max. 207'	184	max. 38 088' = 635h
HU	20 x 45'= 900'	5	180'	185	33 300' = 555h
PL	18 x 45' = 810'	5	162'	185	29 970' = 499h
RO	min. 20 x 50' = 1 000'	5	200'	170	min. 34 000' = 567h
	max. 24 x 50' = 1 200'	5	240'	170	max. 40 800' = 680h
SK	min. 21 x 45'= 945'	5	min. 189'	186	min. 35 154' = 586h
	max. 23 x 45' = 1 035'		max. 207'		max. 38 502' = 642h

Source: Eurydice.

ANNUAL NUMBER OF HOURS OF TAUGHT TIME (AROUND AGE 10), 1995/96 (FIGURE D6)

	WEEKLY LOAD	NUMBER OF DAYS PER WEEK	DAILY LOAD	NUMBER OF DAYS PER YEAR	ANNUAL LOAD
EUROPEAN UNION					
B	min. 28 x 50' = 1 400'	5	280'	182	min. 50 960' = 849h
DK	24 x 45' = 1 080'	5	216'	200	43 200' = 720h
D	1 136'	5	227'	188	42 723' = 712h
EL	min. 29 x 45' = 1 305' max. 30 x 45' = 1 350'	5	min. 261' max. 270'	175	min. 45 675' = 761h max. 47 250' = 788h
E	(25 x 60') - (5 x 30') = 1 350'	5	270'	180	48 600' = 810h
F	(26 x 60') - (5 x 30') = 1 410'	5	282'	180	50 760' = 846h
IRL	23h20' = 1 400'	5	280'	183	min. 51 240' = 854h max. = 915h
I	(30 x 60') - (6 x 30') = 1 620'	6	270'	min.200	min.54 000' = 900h
L	(18 x 55') + (12 x 50') = 1 590'	6	265'	212	56 180' = 936h
NL	25h = 1 500'	5	300'	200	60 000' = 1 000h
A	25 x 50' = 1 250'	5/6	250'/208'	180/214	45 000' = 750h
P	min. 30 x 50' = 1 500' max. 31 x 50' = 1 550'	5/6	min. 300' max. 310'	175	min. 52 500' = 875h max. 54 250' = 904h
FIN	min. 23 x 45' = 1 035' max. 25 x 45' = 1 125'	5	min. 207' max. 225'	190	min. 39 330' = 656h max. 42 750' = 713h
S				min. 178 max. 190	
UK E/W NI SC	23h30' = 1 410' 25h = 1 500' 25h = 1 500'	5 5 5	282' 300' 300'	190 190 190	53 580' = 893h 57 000' = 950h 57 000' = 950h
EFTA/EEA					
IS	30 x 40' = 1 200'	5	240'	160	38 400' = 640h
LI	30 x 45' = 1 350'	5	270'	200	54 000' = 900h
NO	min. 29 x 45' = 1 305'	5	min. 261'	190	min.49 590' = 827h
CEEC					
BG	min.25 (ou 29) x 40'= 1 000'/1 160' max. 25 (ou 29) x 45' = 1 125'/1 305'	5 5	min.200'/232' max. 225'/261'	165 165	min. 33 000' = 550h/ 38 280' = 638h max. 37 125' = 619h/ 43 065' = 718h
CZ	min. 24 x 45' = 1 080' max. 25 x 45' = 1 125'	5 5	min. 216' max. 225'	184 184	min. 39 744' = 662h max. 41 400' = 690h
HU	25 x 45'= 1 125'	5	225'	185	41 625' = 694h
PL	23 x 45' = 1 035'	5	207'	185	38 295' = 638h
RO	min. 23 x 50'= 1 150' max. 32 x 50' = 1 600'	5 5	230' 320'	170 170	min. 39 100' = 652h max. 54 400' = 907h
SK	min. 28 x 45' = 1 260' max. 31 x 45' = 1 395'	5	min. 252' max. 279'	186	min. 46 872' = 781h max. 51 894' = 865h

Source: Eurydice.

DISTRIBUTION OF ANNUAL HOURS OF TEACHING OF COMPULSORY SUBJECTS AT AROUND AGE 7, 1995/96 (FIGURE D8)

	MOTHER TONGUE	MATHEMATICS	HUMAN AND NATURAL SCIENCES	FOREIGN LANGUAGES	SPORT	ARTISTIC ACTIVITIES	RELIGION AND ETHICS	FLEXIBLE TIMETABLE	TOTAL
EUROEAN UNION									
B fr	272 32%	153 18%	110 13%		59 7%	136 16%	59 7%	59 7%	848 100%
B de	272 32%	153 18%	110 13%	59 7%	59 7%	136 16%	59 7%		848 100%
B nl	212 25%	183 22%	187 22%		59 7%	149 18%	59 7%		849 100%
DK	270 45%	120 20%	30 5%		30 5%	60 10%	60 10%	30 5%	600 100%
D	147 24%	135 22%	81 13%		75 12%	102 17%	56 9%	17 3%	613 100%
EL	236 36%	131 20%	83 13%		52 8%	105 16%	22 3%	26 4%	629 100%
E	216 27%	144 18%	180 22%		108 13%	108 13%	54 7%		810 100%
F	293 35%	163 19%						390 46%	846 100%
IRL	342 40%	145 17%	94 11%		43 5%	137 16%	94 11%		854 100%
I	119 15%	89 11%	148 18%		60 7%	117 15%	60 7%	208 26%	800 100%
L	38 4%	187 20%	92 10%	251 27%	92 10%	92 10%	92 10%	92 10%	936 100%
NL								880 100%	880 100%
A	210 33%	120 19%	90 14%		60 10%	90 14%	60 10%		630 100%
P								788 100%	788 100%
FIN	152 24%	105 17%	86 14%	38 6%	57 9%	95 15%	38 6%	57 9%	628 100%
S								100%	100%
UK (EW)								840 100%	840 100%
UK (NI)								665 100%	665 100%
UK (SC)								950 100%	950 100%
EFTA/EEA									
IS	149 26%	64 11%	43 7%		64 11%	106 18%	22 4%	128 22%	576 100%
LI	263 42%	131 21%	53 8%		79 13%	79 13%	26 4%		631 100%
NO	190 33%	124 22%	66 12%	19 3%	38 7%	76 13%	57 10%		570 100%
CEEC									
BG	150 32%	75 16%	47 10%		65 14%	75 16%		56 12%	468 100%
CZ	276 45%	138 23%	55 9%		55 9%	83 14%			607 100%
HU	333 45%	185 25%	37 5%		111 15%	74 10%			740 100%
PL	194 39%	111 22%	28 6%		55 11%	111 22%			499 100%
RO	255 45%	114 20%			85 15%	85 15%	28 5%		567 100%
SK	251 43%	112 19%	56 10%		84 14%	84 14%			587 100%

Source: Eurydice.

Finland: The required number for artistic activities and sport is 209. The figures given refer to the absolute minimum per subject.

DISTRIBUTION OF ANNUAL HOURS OF TEACHING OF COMPULSORY SUBJECTS AT AROUND AGE 10, 1995/96 (FIGURE D9)

	MOTHER TONGUE	MATHEMATICS	HUMAN AND NATURAL SCIENCES	FOREIGN LANGUAGES	SPORT	ARTISTIC ACTIVITIES	RELIGION AND ETHICS	FLEXIBLE TIMETABLE	TOTAL
EUROPEAN UNION									
B fr	212 25%	152 18%	196 23%		61 7%	91 11%	61 7%	75 9%	848 100%
B de	212 25%	151 18%	184 22%	90 11%	61 7%	91 11%	61 7%		850 100%
B nl	212 25%	183 22%	187 22%		59 7%	149 18%	59 7%		849 100%
DK	180 23%	120 15%	90 12%	60 8%	90 12%	180 23%	30 4%	30 4%	780 100%
D	160 22%	135 19%	120 17%		85 12%	125 18%	62 9%	25 4%	712 100%
EL	211 28%	105 14%	184 24%	79 10%	52 7%	52 7%	52 7%	26 3%	761 100%
E	144 18%	144 18%	144 18%	108 13%	108 13%	108 13%	54 7%		810 100%
F	254 30%	175 21%		43 5%				373 44%	845 100%
IRL	342 40%	145 17%	94 11%		43 5%	137 16%	94 11%		854 100%
I	121 13%	90 10%	149 17%	90 10%	60 7%	119 13%	60 7%	211 23%	900 100%
L	29 3%	159 17%	66 7%	374 40%	93 10%	93 10%	93 10%	29 3%	936 100%
NL								1000 100%	1000 100%
A	210 28%	120 16%	90 12%	30 4%	90 12%	150 20%	60 8%		750 100%
P	145.8 17%	116.6 13%	175 20%	116.6 13%	58.3 7%	233.3 27%	29.1 3%		875 100%
FIN	152 24%	105 17%	86 14%	38 6%	57 9%	95 15%	38 6%	57 9%	628 100%
S								100%	100%
UK (EW)								893 100%	893 100%
UK (NI)								950 100%	950 100%
UK (SC)								950 100%	950 100%
EFTA/EEA									
IS	128 20%	85 13%	107 17%		64 10%	127 20%	22 3%	107 17%	640 100%
LI	205 23%	147 16%	264 29%		88 10%	117 13%	78 9%		899 100%
NO	152 18%	105 13%	171 21%	67 8%	57 7%	171 21%	57 7%	47 6%	827 100%
CEEC									
BG	152 28%	76 14%	114 21%		57 10%	76 14%		76 14%	551 100%
CZ	193 29%	138 21%	83 13%	83 13%	55 8%	110 17%			662 100%
HU	259 28%	148 16%	148 16%	74 8%	111 12%	148 16%	37 4%		925 100%
PL	167 26%	139 22%	111 17%		83 13%	55 9%		83 13%	638 100%
RO	198 30%	114 17%	113 17%	57 9%	57 9%	85 13%	28 4%		652 100%
SK	139 18%	139 18%	167 21%	112 14%	56 7%	112 14%	28 4%	28 4%	781 100%

Source: Eurydice.

Finland: The required number for artistic activities and sport is 209. The figures given refer to the absolute minimum per subject.

NUMBER OF PUPILS IN PRIMARY EDUCATION LEARNING ENGLISH AND FRENCH DURING THE SCHOOL YEAR 1994/95 (FIGURE D11 AND D12)

(1 000)

	NUMBER OF PUPILS LEARNING		ADJUSTED NUMBER OF TOTAL PUPILS
	ENGLISH	FRENCH	ENROLLED
EUROPEAN UNION			
EU	4 420.9 (e)	446.1 (e)	
B fr	3.1	not applicable	304.0
B nl	0.0	137.6	393.5
DK	107.0	0.0	330.1
D	213.8	83.0	3 588.1
EL	323.3	31.5	659.9
E	1 497.9	41.9	2 364.9
F	554.7	not applicable	3 947.6
IRL	not applicable	0.0	0.0
I	625.2	125.8	2 815.6
L	0.0	22.3	27.1
NL	374.0	0.0	1 122.0
A	N/A	N/A	N/A
P	266.5	58.6	902.0
FIN	247.2	3.7	387.3
S	289.3	0.0	600.4
UK	not applicable	N/A	N/A
EFTA/EEA			
IS	4.3	0.0	29.1
LI	0.0	0.0	N/A
NO	206.5	0.0	314.1

Source: Eurostat, UOE.

CEEC			
BG	27.6	0.8	425.3
CZ	N/A	N/A	N/A
HU	285.9	12.0	N/A
PL	913.2	95.5	5 178.2
RO	876.4	1 509.6	2 532.2
SK	164.8	15.2	690.2

Source: National statistics.

The figure for the total number of students enrolled used to calculate the percentages has in some cases been adjusted to correspond with the limited coverage of the language data.

**NUMBER OF PUPILS IN PRIMARY EDUCATION LEARNING NO, ONE OR TWO FOREIGN LANGUAGES
DURING THE SCHOOL YEAR 1994/95 (FIGURE D13)**

(1 000)

	NUMBER OF PUPILS LEARNING **NO** FOREIGN LANGUAGES	NUMBER OF PUPILS LEARNING **ONE** FOREIGN LANGUAGE	NUMBER OF PUPILS LEARNING **TWO** FOREIGN LANGUAGES
EUROPEAN UNION			
B fr	N/A	N/A	N/A
B nl	N/A	N/A	N/A
DK	223.1	107.0	0.0
D	N/A	N/A	N/A
EL	N/A	N/A	N/A
E	820.0	1544.9	0.0
F	3180.2	767.4	0.0
IRL	381.0	0.0	0.0
I	2036.2	779.5	0.0
L	0.0	4.8	22.3
NL	N/A	N/A	N/A
A	N/A	N/A	N/A
P	576.6	325.4	0.0
FIN	121.7	241.6	23.0
S	311.1	289.3	0.0
UK	N/A	N/A	N/A
EFTA/EEA			
IS	20.5 (e)	4.3 (e)	4.3 (e)
LI	1.8	0.0	0.0
NO	107.6	206.5	0.0

Source: Eurostat, UOE.

CEEC			
BG	387.0	38.3	0.0
CZ	N/A	N/A	N/A
HU	N/A	N/A	N/A
PL	N/A	N/A	N/A
RO	470.9	1 206.2	855.1
SK	270.5	419.7	0.0

Source: National statistics.

SECONDARY EDUCATION

NUMBER OF PUPILS IN GENERAL AND VOCATIONAL UPPER SECONDARY EDUCATION (ISCED 3), 1994/95 (FIGURE E3)

(1 000)

	NUMBER OF PUPILS IN GENERAL UPPER SECONDARY EDUCATION	NUMBER OF PUPILS IN VOCATIONAL UPPER SECONDARY EDUCATION
EUROPEAN UNION		
EU	8 069.6	11 229.0
B	219.8	459.2
DK	104.5	123.2
D	692.7	2 261.0
EL	277.7	131.9
E	1 789.1	1 180.4
F	1 175.8	1 347.2
IRL	143.9	37.9
I	793.9	1 746.6
L	4.4	7.8
NL	216.4	515.2
A	90.6	309.9
P	346.6	110.6
FIN	121.6	133.0
S	208.6	248.8
UK	1 898.3	2 615.6
EFTA/EEA		
IS	10.8	6.2
LI	0.2	0.9
NO	96.1	118.1

Source: Eurostat, UOE.

CEEC		
BG	245.4	216.6
CZ	97.9	529.0
HU	140.4	388.3
PL	648.6	1 557.8
RO	307.2	749.1
SK	63.7	245.6

Source: National statistics.

Liechtenstein: National statistics.

NUMBER OF UPPER SECONDARY PUPILS IN GENERAL EDUCATION BY **NUTS 1** AND **2** REGIONS, **1994/95** (FIGURE E4)

			RATE (%)	TOTAL NUMBER OF PUPILS IN UPPER SECONDARY EDUCATION (1 000)	NUMBER OF PUPILS IN GENERAL UPPER SECONDARY EDUCATION (1 000)
		EUROPEAN UNION			
B		BELGIQUE — BELGIË			
	BE1	BRUXELLES — BRUSSEL	36	75.5	27.5
	BE2	VLAAMS GEWEST	31	359.0	111.1
	BE3	RÉGION WALLONNE	33	236.7	78.1
DK		DANMARK	46	227.8	104.5
D		DEUTSCHLAND			
	DE1	BADEN-WÜRTTEMBERG	18	398.0	71.6
	DE2	BAYERN	19	405.9	76.4
	DE3	BERLIN	36	112.6	40.5
	DE4	BRANDENBURG	33	89.0	29.7
	DE5	BREMEN	23	32.1	7.4
	DE6	HAMBURG	27	69.3	18.6
	DE7	HESSEN	26	216.9	55.9
	DE8	MECKLENBURG-VORPOMMERN	22	71.0	15.3
	DE9	NIEDERSACHSEN	22	299.8	64.4
	DEA	NORDRHEIN-WESTFALEN	28	646.9	179.5
	DEB	RHEINLAND-PFALZ	24	131.3	30.9
	DEC	SAARLAND	21	38.3	7.9
	DED	SACHSEN	22	161.0	35.2
	DEE	SACHSEN-ANHALT	23	90.6	21.1
	DEF	SCHLESWIG-HOLSTEIN	20	99.9	19.8
	DEG	THÜRINGEN	20	91.3	18.5
GR		ELLADA			
	GR1	VOREIA ELLADA	N/A	N/A	N/A
	GR2	KENTRIKI ELLADA	N/A	N/A	N/A
	GR3	ATTIKI	N/A	N/A	N/A
	GR4	NISIA AIGAIOU. KRITI	N/A	N/A	N/A
ES		ESPANĀ			
	ES1	NOROESTE	60	344.5	205.8
	ES2	NORESTE	58	325.5	189.5
	ES3	COMUNIDAD DE MADRID	67	405.2	271.5
	ES4	CENTRO (E)	61	381.2	231.6
	ES5	ESTE	56	758.0	427.0
	ES6	SUR	63	624.3	391.7
	ES7	CANARIAS	55	129.9	71.2
FR		FRANCE			
	FR1	ÎLE-DE-FRANCE	52	439.3	229.5
	FR2	BASSIN PARISIEN	45	468.8	211.3
	FR3	NORD-PAS-DE-CALAIS	42	204.2	86.4
	FR4	EST	45	225.3	100.5
	FR5	OUEST	46	366.4	170.2
	FR6	SUD-OUEST	48	244.6	116.6
	FR7	CENTRE-EST	50	292.9	145.2
	FR8	MÉDITERRANÉE	50	261.1	130.4
	FR9	DÉPARTEMENTS D'OUTRE-MER	N/A	N/A	N/A
IRL		IRELAND	79	181.8	143.9
IT		ITALIA			
	IT1	NORD OVEST	29	256.9	74.0
	IT2	LOMBARDIA	27	398.2	106.1
	IT3	NORD EST	24	314.6	74.8
	IT4	EMILIA-ROMAGNA	24	170.3	40.2
	IT5	CENTRO (I)	27	277.5	74.9
	IT6	LAZIO	35	278.9	97.5
	IT7	ABRUZZO-MOLISE	28	316.1	89.6
	IT8	CAMPANIA	28	89.2	24.6
	IT9	SUD	28	387.6	109.1
	ITA	SICILIA	27	279.3	75.6
	ITB	SARDEGNA	26	106.7	27.5
LU		LUXEMBOURG (GRAND-DUCHÉ)	36	12.2	4.4
NL		NEDERLAND			
	NL1	NOORD-NEDERLAND	27	83.3	22.5
	NL2	OOST-NEDERLAND	29	153.9	43.8
	NL3	WEST-NEDERLAND	32	337.3	106.9
	NL4	ZUID-NEDERLAND	32	158.4	50.1
AT		ÖSTERREICH			
	AT1	OSTÖSTERREICH	24	152.7	36.5
	AT2	SÜDÖSTERREICH	23	92.6	20.9
	AT3	WESTÖSTERREICH	21	155.1	33.1

			RATE (%)	TOTAL NUMBER OF PUPILS IN UPPER SECONDARY EDUCATION (1 000)	NUMBER OF PUPILS IN GENERAL UPPER SECONDARY EDUCATION (1 000)
EUROPEAN UNION (CONTINUED)					
PT	**PORTUGAL**				
PT11		NORTE	72	133.9	96.6
PT12		CENTRO (P)	72	74.4	53.8
PT13		LISBOA E VALE DO TEJO	80	187.7	149.4
PT14		ALENTEJO	72	22.9	16.6
PT15		ALGARVE	72	17.4	12.6
PT2		AÇORES	81	9.7	7.9
PT3		MADEIRA	87	11.2	9.7
FI	**SUOMI/FINLAND**				
FI11		UUSIMAA	55	60.2	33.4
FI12		ETELÄ-SUOMI	48	84.4	40.2
FI13		ITÄ-SUOMI	47	35.7	16.7
FI14		VÄLI-SUOMI	47	36.1	17.1
FI15		POHJOIS-SUOMI	47	29.9	13.9
FI2		AHVENANMAA/ÅLAND	35	1.1	0.4
SE	**SVERIGE**				
SE01		STOCKHOLM	52	90.7	46.7
SE02		ÖSTRA MELLANSVERIGE	45	77.9	34.9
SE03		SMÅLAND MED ÖARNA	42	41.4	17.4
SE04		SYDSERIGE	46	65.5	30.0
SE05		VÄSTSVERIGE	44	92.4	40.8
SE06		NORRA MELLANSVERIGE	42	41.7	17.3
SE07		MELLERSTA NORRLAND	44	20.0	8.7
SE08		ÖVRE NORRLAND	45	27.8	12.6
UK	**UNITED KINGDOM**				
UK1		NORTH	41	238.1	96.8
UK2		YORKSHIRE AND HUMBERSIDE	35	440.9	155.9
UK3		EAST MIDLANDS	43	308.0	132.9
UK4		EAST ANGLIA	46	147.0	68.2
UK5		SOUTH EAST (UK)	41	1360.8	561.4
UK6		SOUTH WEST (UK)	43	359.4	153.9
UK7		WEST MIDLANDS	37	452.8	169.4
UK8		NORTH WEST (UK)	36	537.5	194.0
UK9		WALES	47	206.3	96.9
UKA		SCOTLAND	62	316.5	196.0
UKB		NORTHERN IRELAND	50	147.6	73.7
EFTA/EEA					
IS	**ÍSLAND**		64	17.0	10.8
LI	**LIECHTENSTEIN**		22	1.1	0.2
NO	**NORGE**		45	214.2	96.1
CEEC					
BG	**BĂLGARIJA**		53	462.0	245.4
CZ	**ČESKÁ REPUBLIKA**		16	626.9	97.9
HU	**MAGYARORSZÁG**		27	528.6	140.4
PL	**POLSKA**		29	2206.3	648.6
RO	**ROMÂNIA**		29	1056.3	307.2
SK	**SLOVENSKÁ REPUBLIKA**		21	309.3	63.7

Source: Eurostat, UOE. — National statistics.

TREND IN THE NUMBER OF GIRLS AND BOYS IN GENERAL UPPER SECONDARY EDUCATION, 1985-95 (FIGURE E5)

(1 000)

	1985/86		1986/87		1987/88		1988/89		1989/90		1990/91		1991/92		1992/93		1993/94		1994/95	
	F	M	F	M	F	M	F	M	F	M	F	M	F	M	F	M	F	M	F	M
EUROPEAN UNION																				
B	117.3	105.3	117.3	105.1	117.0	104.0	116.0	103.4	114.6	101.6	114.3	101.8	114.1	100.3	114.3	99.9	116.0	100.7	118.0	102.0
DK	43.1	30.5	40.8	29.4	41.2	29.5	42.5	30.2	44.0	30.6	44.0	30.3	44.7	30.7	57.4	42.5	58.6	43.7	59.0	45.0
D	330.7	332.6	314.7	319.6	301.5	304.9	289.2	289.6	277.7	272.9	293.0	276.3	302.9	276.8	336.2	298.5	354.5	308.9	372.0	320.0
EL	147.7	119.7	147.4	119.8	144.9	116.8	147.9	118.3	149.9	120.3	152.3	121.5	154.3	123.5	151.6	121.4	151.8	122.8	152.4	125.4
E	666.0	585.0	691.1	608.2	741.5	657.5	790.3	687.3	829.4	708.9	859.3	732.4	870.5	760.9	913.9	799.7	942.0	822.7	949.0	840.0
F	497.8	358.2	524.1	380.0	561.8	411.7	599.9	445.8	637.6	480.8	653.9	497.8	654.2	497.8	663.3	541.4	657.3	535.2	650.5	525.3
IRL	54.8	50.3	57.6	52.0	59.1	53.7	61.1	55.2	63.3	57.9	63.4	58.7	65.3	61.2	67.2	63.7	69.9	66.6	74.0	70.0
I	341.6	291.7	362.1	283.8	369.9	318.6	378.0	330.0	404.9	316.9	405.1	328.3	414.3	333.5	445.4	345.4	447.2	344.7	448.0	346.0
L	N/A	N/A	N/A	N/A	N/A	N/A	N/A	N/A	2.4	2.1	2.2	2.0	2.1	1.8	2.2	1.9	2.4	2.0	2.4	2.0
NL	N/A	N/A	N/A	N/A	N/A	N/A	138.1	117.7	133.0	114.2	128.5	111.0	124.0	107.5	120.2	105.3	119.4	103.9	115.0	101.0
A	50.0	56.0	47.0	53.0	45.0	50.0	43.0	47.0	43.0	46.0	42.0	44.0	42.0	43.0	43.0	43.0	44.0	44.0	46.0	45.0
P	N/A	N/A	N/A	N/A	N/A	N/A	N/A	N/A	N/A	N/A	N/A	N/A	197.2	143.1	193.5	154.0	185.7	153.1	188.4	158.3
FIN	65.5	42.7	63.1	42.1	60.6	41.6	58.7	40.9	58.6	40.6	59.8	41.0	65.1	44.3	65.3	46.4	69.0	49.4	71.0	51.0
S	N/A	N/A	N/A	N/A	N/A	N/A	N/A	N/A	N/A	N/A	N/A	N/A	N/A	N/A	90.4	55.3	96.4	67.0	125.0	84.0
UK	1 065	1 099	1 045	1 080	1 000	1 034	969.0	982.7	936.0	962.0	928.5	955.8	916.3	941.3	918.2	942.1	899.6	928.0	935.0	963.0

Source: Eurostat, UOE.

	1985/86		1986/87		1987/88		1988/89		1989/90		1990/91		1991/92		1992/93		1993/94		1994/95	
	F	M	F	M	F	M	F	M	F	M	F	M	F	M	F	M	F	M	F	M
EFTA/EEA																				
IS	4.0	3.2	4.0	3.3	4.1	3.2	4.3	3.3	4.6	3.6	5.0	3.8	5.5	4.2	5.7	4.3	5.9	4.5	6.1	4.7
LI	N/A	N/A	N/A	N/A	N/A	N/A	N/A	N/A	N/A	N/A	N/A	N/A	N/A	N/A	N/A	N/A	N/A	N/A	0.1	0.1
NO	N/A	N/A	N/A	N/A	N/A	N/A	N/A	N/A	N/A	N/A	N/A	N/A	N/A	N/A	N/A	N/A	N/A	N/A	53.0	43.0
CEEC																				
BG	101.6	57.3	101.8	57.9	104.1	59.0	99.8	54.8	100.4	52.8	98.7	57.4	99.3	46.5	100.9	47.3	102.0	49.9	107.0	51.7
CZ	56.0	33.0	56.0	33.0	56.0	35.0	59.0	37.0	61.0	39.0	62.0	40.0	59.0	38.0	56.0	43.0	54.0	33.0	52.0	37.0
HU	68.8	37.0	68.6	36.6	69.5	36.5	71.6	36.9	77.3	39.0	81.0	41.0	86.0	44.0	89.0	47.0	89.0	49.0	89.0	52.0
PL	246.0	92.0	N/A	N/A	270.0	103.0	285.0	109.0	300.0	114.0	323.0	122.0	362.0	138.0	401.0	155.0	427.0	175.0	449.0	200.0
RO	N/A	N/A	N/A	N/A	N/A	N/A	N/A	N/A	N/A	N/A	110.8	63.5	164.0	84.7	187.3	90.5	201.0	95.3	207.8	99.4
SK	N/A	N/A	N/A	N/A	N/A	N/A	29.0	19.1	30.8	20.7	33.2	22.1	35.4	22.8	37.4	23.9	38.9	24.9	39.2	25.7

Source: National statistics.

TREND IN THE NUMBER OF GIRLS AND BOYS IN VOCATIONAL UPPER SECONDARY EDUCATION, 1985-95 (FIGURE E5)

(1 000)

	1985/86		1986/87		1987/88		1988/89		1989/90		1990/91		1991/92		1992/93		1993/94		1994/95	
	F	M	F	M	F	M	F	M	F	M	F	M	F	M	F	M	F	M	F	M
EUROPEAN UNION																				
B	200.0	209.8	197.2	205.2	200.7	211.1	202.3	210.4	201.3	208.7	197.4	206.1	197.4	206.3	209.0	234.2	215.2	239.3	220.0	239.0
DK	64.6	86.2	68.3	88.2	69.6	87.2	69.1	86.7	68.2	82.7	65.6	82.2	65.2	80.4	54.0	68.5	53.2	67.4	54.8	68.4
D	1 153.7	1 408.9	1 131.9	1 367.1	1 091.0	1 309.4	1 046.9	1 239.2	974.3	1 163.6	1 026.8	1 291.7	1 011.7	1 282.2	1 003.1	1 296.1	1 002.1	1 284.3	987.9	1 273.1
EL	30.9	74.9	33.3	80.1	38.0	88.1	39.4	90.8	40.7	86.5	43.0	88.4	49.3	95.0	50.0	84.4	47.3	90.4	46.6	85.3
E	388.0	461.3	398.1	470.1	429.0	488.1	435.9	522.1	503.1	534.9	541.8	559.9	594.9	567.9	629.8	590.7	630.1	591.4	613.1	567.3
F	531.5	648.3	533.8	658.9	551.9	698.1	571.6	743.7	585.8	760.1	590.7	763.9	591.1	766.7	565.5	712.5	573.4	745.0	580.1	767.1
IRL	15.8	19.6	16.1	18.2	16.4	18.2	15.6	17.0	16.5	17.6	17.2	17.9	17.5	21.0	20.4	22.4	20.2	20.9	19.2	18.7
I	979.4	1 026.3	978.9	1 066.2	1 000.1	1 065.4	1 022.0	1 102.0	1 041.1	1 124.1	1 021.3	1 101.7	1 012.5	1 097.9	1 106.1	1 223.5	1 013.2	1 136.6	814.1	932.5
L	N/A	N/A	N/A	N/A	N/A	N/A	N/A	N/A	3.5	4.3	3.4	4.0	2.9	3.6	3.1	3.8	3.4	4.2	3.4	4.4
NL	N/A	N/A	N/A	N/A	N/A	N/A	207.9	291.9	209.1	297.9	208.4	300.3	237.1	304.5	N/A	N/A	221.7	303.8	226.0	289.2
A	155.0	199.0	151.0	194.0	148.0	188.0	145.0	178.0	144.0	180.0	142.0	177.0	139.0	175.0	138.0	172.0	137.0	171.0	137.0	172.0
P	N/A	N/A	N/A	N/A	N/A	N/A	N/A	N/A	N/A	N/A	N/A	N/A	N/A	N/A	N/A	N/A	45.0	54.5	50.6	60.0
FIN	62.0	58.4	62.0	56.9	62.3	55.6	61.6	55.4	62.7	53.1	65.1	53.0	68.8	55.8	70.5	59.1	72.5	64.1	68.8	64.2
S	N/A	N/A	N/A	N/A	N/A	N/A	N/A	N/A	N/A	N/A	N/A	N/A	N/A	N/A	140.1	143.2	141.6	141.8	121.5	127.3
UK	962.0	831.0	1 014.0	863.0	1 050.0	875.0	1 107.0	924.3	1 148.0	933.0	1 126.8	907.4	1 324.4	1 028.7	1 296.5	1 010.5	1 413.0	1 081.3	1 501.5	1 114.0

Source: Eurostat, UOE.

	1985/86		1986/87		1987/88		1988/89		1989/90		1990/91		1991/92		1992/93		1993/94		1994/95	
	F	M	F	M	F	M	F	M	F	M	F	M	F	M	F	M	F	M	F	M
EFTA/EEA																				
IS	2.7	4.6	2.8	4.6	2.7	4.6	2.8	4.8	2.9	5.0	3.1	5.2	3.0	5.1	2.3	4.6	2.4	4.4	2.1	4.1
LI	N/A	N/A	N/A	N/A	N/A	N/A	N/A	N/A	N/A	N/A	N/A	N/A	N/A	N/A	N/A	N/A	N/A	N/A	65.0	
NO	N/A	N/A	N/A	N/A	N/A	N/A	N/A	N/A	N/A	N/A	N/A	N/A	N/A	N/A	N/A	N/A	N/A	N/A	46.4	71.7
CEEC																				
BG	78.8	132.3	81.4	135.5	84.0	139.0	89.2	145.3	92.4	149.2	93.9	147.6	90.2	146.1	83.7	140.5	80.3	134.3	80.7	135.9
CZ	171.4	204.8	166.8	207.0	177.5	212.6	191.6	228.6	204.3	242.2	200.9	242.4	206.8	236.9	259.0	254.2	235.2	261.3	255.6	273.4
HU	131.9	180.4	132.9	179.3	135.2	181.2	142.9	189.5	155.8	209.6	N/A	N/A	175.5	225.4	176.1	221.9	174.5	216.7	172.2	210.5
PL	555.0	674.0	N/A	N/A	591.0	750.0	605.0	778.0	628.0	813.0	631.0	820.0	631.0	847.0	629.0	873.0	644.0	890.0	646.0	884.0
RO	N/A	N/A	N/A	N/A	N/A	N/A	N/A	N/A	N/A	N/A	547.7	639.6	402.4	502.6	332.0	437.7	312.5	414.0	317.2	421.9
SK	N/A	N/A	N/A	N/A	N/A	N/A	110.6	114.9	114.7	119.1	113.5	121.1	113.4	122.5	115.3	124.7	117.8	130.1	117.8	131.8

Source: National statistics.

ANNUAL NUMBER OF HOURS OF TAUGHT TIME
IN GENERAL LOWER SECONDARY EDUCATION, 1995/96 (FIGURE E6)

	WEEKLY LOAD (A)			NUMBER OF DAYS PER WEEK (B)	DAILY LOAD (MINUTES) (A) / (B) = (E)	NUMBER OF DAYS PER YEAR (F)	ANNUAL LOAD =(E) X (F)		
EUROPEAN UNION									
B fr. B de	min. 28 x 50'	=	1 400'	5	280'	182	min. 50 960'	=	849h
	max. 34 x 50'	=	1 700'	5	340'	182	max. 61 880'	=	1 031h
B nl	min. 28 x 50'	=	1 400'	5	280'	182	min. 50 960'	=	849h
	max. 33 x 50'	=	1 650'	5	330'	182	max. 60 060'	=	1 001h
DK	min. 26 x 45'	=	1 170'	5	234'	200	min. 46 800'	=	780h
	max. 40 x 45'	=	1 800'	5	360'	200	max. 72 000'	=	1 200h
D	min. 28 x 45'	=	1 260'	5	252'	188	min. 47 376'	=	790h
	max. 34 x 45'	=	1 530'	5	306'	188	max. 57 528'	=	959h
EL	35 x 45'	=	1 575'	5	315'	175	max. 55 125'	=	919h
E	min. 28 x 55'	=	1 540'	5	308'	175	min. 53 900'	=	898h
	max. 33 x 55'	=	1 815'	5	363'	175	max. 63 525'	=	1 059h
F	min. 25.5 x 55'	=	1 402.5'	5	280.5'	180	min. 50 490'	=	841.5h
	max. 30 x 55'	=	1 650'	5	330'	180	max. 59 400'	=	990h
IRL	45 x 40'	=	1 800'	5	360'	179	64 440'	=	1 074h
I	min. (30 x 60') - (6 j x 20') = 1 680'			6	280'	(min.) 200	56 000'	=	933h
	max.(40 x 60') - (6 j x 20') = 2 280'			6	380'	(min.) 200	76 000'	=	1 266h
L	30 x 50'	=	1 500'	6	250'	216	min. 54 000'	=	900h
NL	theoretical average 32 x 50'=		1 600'	5	320'	200	64 000'	=	1 067h
A	min. 31 x 50'	=	1 550'	5	310'	180	min. 55 800'	=	930h
	max. 34 x 50'	=	1 700'	5	340'	180	max. 61 200'	=	1 020h
P	min. 30 x 50'	=	1 500'	5/6	300'/250'	175/210	min. 52 500'	=	875h
	max. 31 x 50'	=	1 550'	5/6	310'/258'	175/210	max. 54 250'	=	904h
FIN	30 x 45'	=	1 350'	5	270'	190	51 300'	=	855h
S									
UK (E/W)	average actual taught time 24.5h	=	1 470'	5	294'	190	55 860'	=	931h
UK (NI)	min. 22.5h	=	1 350'	5	270'	190	51 300'	=	855h
UK (SC)	variable								
EFTA/EEA									
IS	35 x 40'	=	1 400'	5	280'	160	44 800'	=	747h
LI	min. 34 x 45'	=	1 530'	5	306'	200	61 200'	=	1 020h
	max. 38 x 45'	=	1 710'	5	342'	200	68 400'	=	1 140h
NO	30 x 45'	=	1 350'	5	270'	190	51 300'	=	855h
CEEC									
BG	min. 30 x 45'	=	1 350'	5	270'	170	min. 45 900'	=	765h
	max. 34 x 45'	=	1 530'		306'		max. 52 020'	=	867h
CZ	min. 28 x 45'	=	1 260'	5	252'	184	min. 46 368'	=	773h
	max. 31 x 45'	=	1 395'		279'		max. 51 336'	=	856h
HU	25 x 45'	=	1 125'	5	255'	185	41 625	=	694h
PL	min. 24 x 45'	=	1 080'	5	216'	185	min. 39 960'	=	666h
	max. 27 x 45'	=	1 215'	5	243'	185	max. 44 955'	=	749h
RO	min. 31 x 50'	=	1 550'	5	310'	170	min. 52 700'	=	878h
	max. 40 x 50'	=	2 000'		400'		max. 68 000'	=	1 133h
SK	min. 28 x 45'	=	1 260'	5	252'	186	min. 46 872'	=	781h
	max. 33 x 45'	=	1 485'	5	297'		max. 55 242'	=	921h

Source: Eurydice.

Germany: The annual number of class hours is an average, calculated using the recommendations for different schools and courses at lower secondary level made by the Standing Conference of the Ministers of Education and Cultural Affairs of the *Länder* on 3 December 1993. The annual hours of teaching vary between a set minimum and maximum as secondary education can last either 8 or 9 years, according to the *Land*. The total number of taught hours for the whole of secondary education is the same for all *Länder*.

Spain: Data are approximate. They may vary slightly from one Autonomous Community to another. A five-minute deduction is made per hour to allow for changing classes.

Italy: A deduction of twenty minutes per day is made to allow for changing classes.

Ireland: Secondary schools must be open for a minimum of 179 days a year of which they may devote a maximum of 12 days to certificate examinations. The statistics presented here have been calculated on the basis of the minimum of 167 days of education.

Austria: Most lower secondary schools follow a set timetable. An increasing number of schools, however, are setting curricula themselves, as authorized by the law.

Finland: This is an average based on 30 weekly periods of 45 minutes each. The law also authorizes 50-minute periods.

Sweden: Since the 1995 reform, schools can freely distribute the 6 665 compulsory periods over the nine years of the *Grundskola*. There is no fixed annual or weekly distribution.

United Kingdom: There is no legal requirement for minimum taught lesson time in England and Wales. School governing bodies and headteachers in state schools are, however, required to ensure that there is sufficient time to deliver the whole curriculum. The figures for England and Wales are based on average taught lesson time per week in 1995. Time spent on registration, the daily act of collective worship and all breaks is excluded. For Northern Ireland, figures are based on the set minimum of 22.5 hours per week; compulsory religious education is not included. For Scotland, figures represent the maximum taught time that teachers are contractually required to provide; the actual time pupils spend in school is more.

Iceland: The municipalities are free to add hours to this minimum.

**ANNUAL NUMBER OF HOURS OF TAUGHT TIME
IN GENERAL UPPER SECONDARY EDUCATION, 1995/96** (FIGURE E7)

		WEEKLY LOAD (A)		NUMBER OF DAYS PER WEEK (B)	DAILY LOAD (MINUTES) (A) / (B) = (E)	NUMBER OF DAYS PER YEAR (F)	ANNUAL LOAD =(E) X (F)		
EUROPEAN UNION									
B fr. B de	min.	28 x 50' =	1 400'	5	280'	182	min.	50 960' =	849h
	max.	34 x 50' =	1 700'	5	340'	182	max.	61 880' =	1 031h
B nl	min.	28 x 50' =	1 400'	5	280'	182	min.	50 960' =	849h
	max.	33 x 50' =	1 650'	5	330'	182	max.	60 060' =	1 001h
DK	min.	30 x 45' =	1 350'	5	270'	200	min.	54 000' =	900h
	max.	32 x 45' =	1 440'	5	288'	200	max.	57 600' =	960h
D	min.	30 x 45' =	1 350'	5	270'	188	min.	50 760' =	846h
	max.	33 x 45' =	1 485'	5	297'	188	max.	55 836' =	931h
EL	min.	30 x 45' =	1 350'	5	270'	175	min.	47 250' =	788h
	max.	34 x 45' =	1 530'	5	306'	175	max.	53 550' =	893h
E	min.	29 x 55' =	1 595'	5	319'	175	min.	55 825' =	931h
	max.	32 x 55' =	1 760'	5	352'	175	max.	61 600' =	1 027h
F	min.	29 x 55' =	1 595'	5	319'	180	min.	57 420' =	957h
	max.	31 x 55' =	1 705'	5	341'	180	max.	61 380' =	1 023h
IRL		45 x 40' =	1 800'	5	360'	167	min.	60 120' =	1 002h
I	min.	(25 x 60') - (6 j x 20') = 1 380'		6	230'	(min.) 200	min.	46 000' =	767h
	max.	(30 x 60') - (6 j x 20') = 1 680'		6	280'	(min.) 200	max.	56 000' =	933h
L	min.	30 x 50' =	1 500'	6	250'	216	min.	54 000' =	900h
	max.	31 x 50' =	1 550'	6	258'	216	max.	55 800' =	930h
NL	theoretical average 30 x 50' =		1 500'	5	300'	200		60 000' =	1 000h
A	min.	32 x 50' =	1 600'	5	320'	180	min.	57 600' =	960h
	max.	38 x 50' =	1 900'	5	380'	180	max.	68 400' =	1 140h
P	min.	23 x 50' =	1 150'	5/6	230'/2'	160/2	min.	36 800' =	613h
	max.	33 x 50' =	1 650'	5/6	330'/275'	160/2	max.	52 800' =	880h
FIN		28.5 x 45' =	1 282.5'	5	256.5'	190		48 735' =	812h
S	theoretical average 20 x 60' =		1 200'	5	240'	178		42 720' =	712h
UK (E/W)	Average actual taught time 24.6 x 60' =		1 476'	5	295.2'	190		56 088' =	935h
UK (NI)	min.	22.5 x 60' =	1 350'	5	270'	190		51 300' =	855h
UK (SC)	variable								
EFTA/EEA									
IS		35 x 40' =	1 400'	5	280'	160		44 800' =	747h
LI	min.	34 x 45' =	1 530'	5	306'	200	min.	61 200' =	1 020h
	max.	38 x 45' =	1 710'	5	342'	200	max.	68 400' =	1 140h
NO	min.	30 x 45' =	1 350'	5	270'	190	min.	51 300' =	855h
	max.	35 x 45' =	1 575'	5	315'	190	max.	59 850' =	998h
CEEC									
BG	min.	31 x 45' =	1 395'	5	279'	180	min.	50 220' =	837h
	max.	35 x 45' =	1 575'		315'		max.	56 700' =	945h
CZ		31 x 45' =	1 395'	5	279'	184		51 336' =	856h
HU		30 x 45' =	1 350'	5	270'	185		49 950' =	833h
PL	min.	25 x 45' =	1 125'	5	225'	185	min.	41 625' =	694h
	max.	28 x 45' =	1 260'	5	252'	185	max.	46 620' =	777h
RO	min.	30 x 50' =	1 500'	5	300'	170	min.	51 000' =	850h
	max.	34 x 50' =	1 700'		340'		max.	57 800' =	963h
SK	min.	30 x 45' =	1 350'	5	270'	186	min.	50 220' =	837h
	max.	37 x 45' =	1 665'	5	333'	186	max.	61 938' =	1 032h

Source: Eurydice.

Germany: The annual number of class hours was calculated on the basis of the 'Agreement on the reorganisation of the *Gymnasiale Oberstufe*' made by the Standing Conference of the Ministers of Education and Cultural Affairs on 7 July 1972, as amended on 11 April 1988. The annual hours of teaching vary between a set minimum and maximum as secondary education can last either 8 or 9 years, according to the *Land*. The total number of taught hours for the whole of secondary education is the same for all *Länder*.

Greece: Data only refer to the general *Lykeio*.

Spain: Data are approximate. They may vary slightly from one Autonomous Community to another.

Italy: A deduction of twenty minutes per day is made to allow for changing classes.

Ireland: Secondary schools must be open for a minimum of 179 days a year of which they may devote a maximum of 12 days to certificate examinations. The statistics presented here have been calculated on the basis of the minimum of 167 days of education.

Portugal: In 1995/96, a new system of evaluation was established. Final tests and examinations introduced by this system effectively lead to a three-week reduction in taught time.

Finland: Data refer to a theoretical average. In practice, there are considerable differences between individual pupils and between the three years of upper secondary education.

Sweden: The theoretical average is based on the equal distribution of 2 150 periods over three years

United Kingdom (E/W and NI): Data are for the last two years of compulsory education (14- to 16-year-olds) For **England** and **Wales**, they are based on statistics of average taught lesson time per week in 1995. For **Northern Ireland**, figures are based on the prescribed minimum of 22.5 hours per week (not including religious education which must be provided in state and grant-aided schools). In post-compulsory education (16- to 18-year-olds), there is no prescribed annual number of taught hours as each pupil has an individual programme. Individual examining bodies may, however, provide guidance on the number of lessons which might be required to cover the syllabus. Attendance requirements are determined by the individual institution. In **Scotland**, the number of hours for post-compulsory education (16- to 18-year-olds) is the same as for compulsory secondary education but pupils have the choice of a number and kinds of courses.

Iceland: For a normal four-year course, the average is 747 hours per year.

NUMBER AND PERCENTAGES OF MINIMUM ANNUAL TIMETABLE ALLOCATED TO COMPULSORY SUBJECTS AROUND AGE 13 IN GENERAL LOWER SECONDARY EDUCATION, 1995/96 (FIGURE E9)

	MOTHER TONGUE	MATHE-MATICS	NATURAL SCIENCES	HUMAN SCIENCES	FOREIGN LANGUAGES	PHYSICAL EDUCATION	ARTISTIC ACTIVITIES	OPTIONAL COMPULSORY SUBJECTS	FLEXIBLE TIMETABLE	OTHER	TOTAL
EUROPEAN UNION											
B fr, B de	152 18%	152 18%	61 7%	121 14%	121 14%	91 11%	30 4%	121 14%			849 100%
B nl	121 14%	121 14%	30 4%	61 7%	121 14%	61 7%	61 7%	152 18%		121 14%	849 100%
DK	180 20%	120 13%	120 13%	120 13%	180 20%	60 7%	90 10%			30 3%	900 100%
D	115 13%	114 13%	115 13%	115 13%	210 24%	71 8%	57 7%			77 9%	874 100%
EL	105 11%	105 11%	79 9%	105 11%	131 14%	79 9%	53 6%			266 29%	923 100%
E	96 10%	96 10%	96 10%	96 10%	96 10%	64 6%	64 6%	64 6%	96 10%	225 23%	994 100%
F	153 16%	136 15%	119 13%	119 13%	102 11%	102 11%	68 7%	68 7%		68 7%	935 100%
IRL									1 074 100%		1 074 100%
I	187 20%	93 10%	93 10%	156 17%	93 10%	63 7%	124 13%			124 13%	933 100%
L		90 10%	30 3%	90 10%	480 53%	60 7%	90 10%			60 7%	900 100%
NL	111 10%	111 10%	89 8%	144 14%	144 14%	100 9%	78 7%	233 22%		56 5%	1 067 100%
A	120 12%	165 16%	180 18%	120 12%	90 9%	90 9%	90 9%			165 16%	1 020 100%
P	117 13%	117 13%	117 13%	175 20%	87 10%	58 7%	87 10%	87 10%		29 3%	874 100%
FIN	76 9%	86 10%	123 14%	57 7%	133 16%	57 7%	29 3%	190 22%		104 12%	855 100%
S	95 12%	95 12%	119 15%	173 21%	71 9%	71 9%	97 12%	86 11%			807 100%
UK (E/W)									912 100%		912 100%
UK (NI)									855 100%		855 100%
UK (SC)									893 100%		893 100%
EFTA/EEA											
IS	107 14%	85 11%	64 9%	64 9%	129 17%	64 9%	149 20%		85 11%		747 100%
LI	150 15%	150 15%	60 6%	120 12%	120 12%	120 12%	120 12%			180 18%	1 020 100%
NO	144 17%	114 13%	85 10%	85 10%	85 10%	57 7%	114 13%			171 20%	855 100%
CEEC											
BG	128 17%	102 13%	153 20%	102 13%	102 13%	51 7%	102 13%			26 3%	765 100%
CZ	110 14%	110 14%			83 10%	55 7%			414 52%	28 3%	800 100%
HU	148 14%	148 14%	257 25%	74 7%	74 7%	111 11%	110 11%	74 7%		37 4%	1 033 100%
PL	139 21%	111 17%	111 17%	29 4%	55 8%	55 8%	111 17%		55 8%		666 100%
RO	113 13%	113 13%	227 26%	85 10%	113 13%	57 6%	57 6%	28 3%		85 10%	878 100%
SK	112 12%	112 12%	167 18%	167 18%	56 6%	56 6%	83 9%	112 12%	56 6%		921 100%

Source: Eurydice.

Belgium (B fr): The number of hours for mathematics, sciences, a foreign language and other subjects are the minima which pupils can complete according to their chosen options. The time can rise to four times the set minimum once these options have been added.

Denmark: The distribution of hours per subject are only set by Ministry guidelines based on an estimated 30 periods per week. However, in practice, the municipalities and the schools decide on the minimum and maximum number of hours per week.

Germany: The annual number of hours per subject is an average based upon the number of lesson hours per week for a class in the eighth year of education in the various types of school and different *Länder*. The category 'Other' groups together religious education and other subjects, according to the *Land*.

Greece: This corresponds to the curriculum for the second year of the *gymnasio*.

Spain: These data are approximate due to the slight variations that can exist between the different Communities. The number of lesson hours in the flexible curriculum includes learning a language other than Castilian for those Autonomous Communities with their own mother tongue.

Ireland: Curricula and directives give full school autonomy for allocating the time spent on each subject.

Netherlands: Greek and Latin are included under optional subjects.

Austria: Refers to the fourth year of the *Hauptschule*.

Portugal: The number of hours attributed to sport depends on the available human resources and infrastructure in each school. It can rise to 105 hours.

Finland: The numbers of hours have been calculated on the basis of a 30-hour week. Figures therefore show a theoretical average based on the assumption that the subjects are spread equally throughout the three years. Differences exist between schools.

Sweden: The 1995 reform also establishes the number of lesson hours per subject throughout compulsory education and schools are free to decide at what moment they introduce a discipline and how the hours for this subject are distributed over the nine years. As the reform is implemented, the situation will tend towards a flexible timetable.

United Kingdom: Schools are substantially free to decide the amount of time to allocate to each subject.

Czech Republic: The flexible hours concern the following subjects: geography, history, biology, music, arts, physics, practical work and other options. The headteacher sets the number of taught hours per subject, as long as all the curriculum subjects are taught, the minimum number of hours is adhered to and the set maximum is not exceeded.

Poland: The category 'Artistic activities' includes technology and computer science. 'Natural sciences' includes geography. Flexible timetables contain these options.

NUMBER AND PERCENTAGES OF MINIMUM ANNUAL TIMETABLE ALLOCATED TO COMPULSORY SUBJECTS AROUND AGE 16 IN THE SCIENCE SECTION OF GENERAL UPPER SECONDARY EDUCATION, 1995/96 (FIGURE E10)

	MOTHER TONGUE	MATHE-MATICS	NATURAL SCIENCES	HUMAN SCIENCES	FOREIGN LANGUAGES	PHYSICAL EDUCATION	ARTISTIC ACTIVITIES	OPTIONAL COMPULSORY SUBJECTS	FLEXIBLE TIMETABLE	OTHER	TOTAL
EUROPEAN UNION											
B fr, B de	152 / 18%	121 / 14%	152 / 18%	91 / 11%	182 / 21%	61 / 7%		30 / 4%		61 / 7%	850 / 100%
B nl	121 / 14%	91 / 11%	61 / 7%	91 / 11%	152 / 18%	61 / 7%		212 / 25%		61 / 7%	850 / 100%
DK	90 / 10%	120 / 13%	270 / 29%	90 / 10%	210 / 23%	60 / 6%	90 / 10%				930 / 100%
D								282 / 33%	564 / 67%		846 / 100%
EL	105 / 13%	131 / 17%	184 / 23%	53 / 7%	53 / 7%	39 / 5%				223 / 28%	788 / 100%
E	96 / 9%	128 / 13%	257 / 25%	96 / 9%	96 / 9%	64 / 6%		128 / 13%	96 / 9%	64 / 6%	1 026 / 100%
F	132 / 14%	198 / 21%	231 / 24%	99 / 10%	99 / 10%	66 / 7%		99 / 10%	33 / 3%		957 / 100%
IRL								1 002 / 100%			1 002 / 100%
I	122 / 16%	92 / 12%	154 / 20%	122 / 16%	92 / 12%	62 / 8%	30 / 4%			92 / 12%	767 / 100%
L		120 / 13%	90 / 10%	90 / 10%	420 / 47%	60 / 7%	30 / 3%	30 / 3%		60 / 7%	900 / 100%
NL	100 / 10%			22 / 2%	89 / 9%	33 / 3%	22 / 2%	734 / 73%			1 000 / 100%
A	90 / 9%	120 / 11%	210 / 20%	180 / 17%	180 / 17%	60 / 6%	60 / 6%	90 / 9%		60 / 6%	1 050 / 100%
P	80 / 10%	107 / 13%	213 / 27%	80 / 10%	80 / 10%	53 / 7%				187 / 23%	800 / 100%
FIN									812 / 100%		812 / 100%
S									712 / 100%		712 / 100%
UK (E/W)									912 / 100%		912 / 100%
UK (NI)									855 / 100%		855 / 100%
UK (SC)									893 / 100%		893 / 100%
EFTA/EEA											
IS	128 / 17%	128 / 17%	128 / 17%	85 / 11%	213 / 29%	33 / 4%		32 / 4%			747 / 100%
LI	120 / 11%	120 / 11%	210 / 20%	90 / 8%	240 / 23%	60 / 6%	60 / 6%			160 / 15%	1 060 / 100%
NO	119 / 14%	147 / 17%	147 / 17%		265 / 31%	59 / 7%				119 / 14%	855 / 100%
CEEC											
BG	81 / 10%	81 / 10%	216 / 26%	162 / 19%	108 / 13%	54 / 6%		135 / 16%			837 / 100%
CZ	83 / 10%	83 / 10%	165 / 19%	138 / 16%	166 / 19%	55 / 6%	55 / 6%		110 / 13%		855 / 100%
HU	150 / 14%	96 / 9%	352 / 34%	64 / 6%	150 / 14%	64 / 6%	64 / 6%	64 / 6%		32 / 3%	1 036 / 100%
PL	111 / 16%	83 / 12%	83 / 12%	29 / 4%	139 / 20%	55 / 8%	55 / 8%		139 / 20%		694 / 100%
RO	85 / 10%	142 / 17%	255 / 30%	113 / 13%	113 / 13%	57 / 7%		57 / 7%		28 / 3%	850 / 100%
SK	84 / 8%	84 / 8%	195 / 19%	56 / 6%	167 / 17%	84 / 8%		167 / 17%	167 / 17%		1 004 / 100%

Source: Eurydice.

Germany: Optional subjects (564 hours a year) are grouped into three fields (languages, literature and arts; human sciences; mathematics, natural sciences and technology) to which religion and sport are added. Amongst these subjects, emphasis is placed on mother tongue, mathematics and a foreign language. Each of these subjects is allocated 10% of the weekly timetable. The compulsory optional subjects (282 hours a year) are intended for individual specialization in these fields.

Ireland: Curricula and directives give full school autonomy for allocating the time spent on each subject.

Luxembourg: This timetable shows the scientific branch of general secondary education within the 'modern humanities' section.

Finland: The curriculum gives schools and pupils considerable autonomy, but there are still compulsory subjects at this level of education.

United Kingdom: Schools are substantially free to decide the amount of time to allocate to each subject.

Czech Republic: The flexible hours concern the following subjects: geography, history, biology, music, arts, physics, practical work and other options. The headteacher sets the number of taught hours per subject as long as all the curriculum subjects are taught, the minimum number of hours is adhered to and the set maximum is not exceeded.

NUMBER OF PUPILS LEARNING FOREIGN LANGUAGES IN GENERAL SECONDARY EDUCATION (ISCED 2+3) DURING THE SCHOOL YEAR 1994/95 (FIGURE E12)

(1 000)

	TOTAL NUMBER OF PUPILS LEARNING FOREIGN LANGUAGES	ADJUSTED NUMBER OF TOTAL PUPILS ENROLLED
EUROPEAN UNION		
EU	31 033 (e)	24 605 (e)
B fr	297.7	215.9
B nl	504.0	263.6
DK	594.8	321.1
D	7 302.4	5 884.6
EL	N/A	N/A
E	3 706.5	3 557.9
F	7 399.4	4 612.1
IRL	354.2	350.9
I	3 075.5	2 744.3
L	26.0	9.0
NL	1 614.0 (e)	666.0
A	N/A	N/A
P	921.5	714.1
FIN	736.4	301.5
S	538.0	322.3
UK	N/A	N/A
EFTA/EEA		
IS	N/A	N/A
LI	3.0	2.0
NO	N/A	N/A
CEEC		
BG	417.7	245.4
CZ	160.2	89.0
HU	252.0	140.0
PL	N/A	N/A
RO	1 224.9	757.7
SK	129.0	68.0

Source: Eurostat, UOE. — National statistics.

NB: The figure for the total number of pupils enrolled used to calculate the percentages has in some cases been adjusted to correspond with the limited coverage of the language data.

NUMBER OF PUPILS LEARNING ENGLISH, FRENCH, GERMAN AND SPANISH IN GENERAL SECONDARY EDUCATION (ISCED 2+3) DURING THE SCHOOL YEAR 1994/95 (FIGURES E13, E14, E15 AND E16).

(1 000)

	NUMBER OF PUPILS LEARNING				ADJUSTED NUMBER OF TOTAL PUPILS ENROLLED
	ENGLISH	FRENCH	GERMAN	SPANISH	
EUROPEAN UNION					
EU	18448 (e)	6330 (e)	3274 (e)	1806 (e)	
B fr	128.6	NOT APPLICABLE	11.3	5.6	215.9
B nl	184.5	258.9	59.9	0.6	263.6
DK	302.2	52.7	219.2	17.3	321.1
D	5 483.1	1 395.2	NOT APPLICABLE	58.7	5 884.6
EL	N/A	N/A	N/A	N/A	N/A
E	3 395.7	295.9	8.1	NOT APPLICABLE	3 557.9
F	4 394.3	NOT APPLICABLE	1 293.4	1 472.6	4 612.1
IRL	NOT APPLICABLE	246.5	92.8	13.2	350.9
I	2 004.4	940.3	96.4	12.1	2 744.3
L	6.9	8.9	8.9	0.9	9.0
NL	659.0	435.0	520.0	0.0	666.0
A	N/A	N/A	NOT APPLICABLE	N/A	N/A
P	531.3	373.7	16.8	0.8	714.1
FIN	298.4	33.4	98.5	N/A	301.5
S	320.6	53.5	145.2	7.6	322.3
UK	NOT APPLICABLE	N/A	N/A	N/A	N/A
EFTA/EEA					
IS	N/A	N/A	N/A	N/A	N/A
LI	1.3	1.4	NOT APPLICABLE	0.0	1.8
NO	156.7	13.1	49.3	0.2	156.7

Source: Eurostat, UOE.

NB: The figure for the total number of pupils enrolled used to calculate the percentages has in some cases been adjusted to correspond with the limited coverage of the language data.

(1 000)

	NUMBER OF PUPILS LEARNING				ADJUSTED NUMBER OF TOTAL PUPILS
	ENGLISH	FRENCH	GERMAN	SPANISH	ENROLLED
	CEEC				
BG	145.5	67.4	59.8	7.5	245.4
CZ	113.8	15.4	88.5	3.0	126.5
HU	107.0	20.0	83.0	3.0	140.0
PL	421.0	118.0	334.0	N/A	602.0
RO	424.9	574.0	73.9	148.6	757.7
SK	59.0	7.0	47.0	1.0	68.0

Source: National statistics.

PERCENTAGE OF THOSE AGED 22 HAVING COMPLETED AT LEAST UPPER SECONDARY EDUCATION (ISCED 3), 1995
(FIGURE E17)

(%)

	EUROPEAN UNION							
	EUR 15	B	DK	D	EL	E	F	IRL
PERCENTAGE OF PUPILS	71	79	90	83	73	60	79	72

	I	L	NL	A	P	FIN	S	UK
PERCENTAGE OF PUPILS	60	53	83	84	46	84	92	66

Source: Eurostat, labour force survey.

NUMBER OF GIRLS AND BOYS OBTAINING A GENERAL UPPER SECONDARY EDUCATION QUALIFICATION, 1994/95
(FIGURE E18)

(1 000)

	NUMBER OF GIRLS AND BOYS	NUMBER OF GIRLS	NUMBER OF BOYS
	EUROPEAN UNION		
EU	1 326 (e)	733 (e)	593 (e)
B	41.5	22.7	18.8
DK	36.1	20.9	15.3
D	214.4	116.7	97.7
EL	74.3	42.0	32.3
E	289.3	159.9	129.4
F	281.0	159.2	121.8
IRL	66.7	34.6	32.0
I	146.0	82.0	64.0
L	1.0	0.5	0.4
NL	61.9	32.5	29.5
A	13.8	7.9	5.9
P	N/A	N/A	N/A
FIN	32.1	18.8	13.3
S	27.9	18.1	9.8
UK	N/A	N/A	N/A
	EFTA/EEA		
IS	N/A	N/A	N/A
LI	0.055	0.027	0.028
NO	22.4	12.6	9.8

Source: Eurostat, UOE.

	CEEC		
BG	92.1	47.2	44.9
CZ	19.2	11.8	7.4
HU	31.0	11.0	20.0
PL	141.0	101.0	40.0
RO	68.3	48.4	19.9
SK	15.3	9.3	5.9

Source: National statistics.

Liechtenstein: National statistics.

HIGHER EDUCATION

HIGHER EDUCATION STUDENTS AS A PERCENTAGE OF ALL PUPILS AND STUDENTS,
BY NUTS 1 AND 2 REGIONS, 1994/95 (FIGURE F4)

			TOTAL (1 000)	ISCED 5 à 7 (1 000)	%
		EUROPEAN UNION			
B		BELGIQUE — BELGIË			
	BE1	BRUXELLES — BRUSSEL	311.3	73.7	24
	BE2	VLAAMS GEWEST	1 353.4	142.5	11
	BE3	RÉGION WALLONNE	869.3	106.1	12
DK		DANMARK	1 144.9	169.8	15
D		DEUTSCHLAND			
	DE1	BADEN-WÜRTTEMBERG	2 069.31	267.1	13
	DE2	BAYERN	2 271.92	298.3	13
	DE3	BERLIN	744.74	159.3	21
	DE4	BRANDENBURG	571.03	23.2	4
	DE5	BREMEN	135.85	28.0	21
	DE6	HAMBURG	333.82	75.9	23
	DE7	HESSEN	1 150.63	170.6	15
	DE8	MECKLENBURG-VORPOMMERN	433.33	20.3	5
	DE9	NIEDERSACHSEN	1 509.80	189.7	13
	DEA	NORDRHEIN-WESTFALEN	3 561.92	604.4	17
	DEB	RHEINLAND-PFALZ	752.95	98.1	13
	DEC	SAARLAND	197.80	29.0	15
	DED	SACHSEN	984.17	75.6	8
	DEE	SACHSEN-ANHALT	566.59	30.2	5
	DEF	SCHLESWIG-HOLSTEIN	502.61	55.5	11
	DEG	THÜRINGEN	537.92	30.7	6
EL		GREECE			
	GR1	VOREIA ELLADA	N/A	N/A	N/A
	GR2	KENTRIKI ELLADA	N/A	N/A	N/A
	GR3	ATTIKI	N/A	N/A	N/A
	GR4	NISIA AIGAIOU, KRITI	N/A	N/A	N/A
ES		ESPAÑA			
	ES1	NOROESTE	1 007.5	148.9	15
	ES2	NORESTE	936.1	155.3	17
	ES3	COMUNIDAD DE MADRID	1 318.9	271.1	21
	ES4	CENTRO (E)	1 229.8	156.4	13
	ES5	ESTE	2 509.6	361.4	14
	ES6	SUR	2 204.0	281.1	13
	ES7	CANARIAS	421.3	48.2	11
FR		FRANCE			
	FR1	ÎLE-DE-FRANCE	2 899.7	569.0	20
	FR2	BASSIN PARISIEN	2 632.3	275.7	10
	FR3	NORD-PAS-DE-CALAIS	1 158.6	142.8	12
	FR4	EST	1 311.9	177.6	14
	FR5	OUEST	1 954.7	248.8	13
	FR6	SUD-OUEST	1 395.7	226.6	16
	FR7	CENTRE-EST	1 743.4	252.7	14
	FR8	MÉDITERRANÉE	1 625.0	227.6	14
	FR9	DÉPARTEMENTS D'OUTRE-MER	490.3	25.4	5
IRL		IRELAND	1 011.7	121.7	12
IT		ITALIA			
	IT1	NORD OVEST	930.4	155.0	17
	IT2	LOMBARDIA	1 512.4	252.8	17
	IT3	NORD EST	1 126.5	166.7	15
	IT4	EMILIA-ROMAGNA	645.0	163.4	25
	IT5	CENTRO (I)	965.5	214.4	22
	IT6	LAZIO	1 106.0	265.9	24
	IT7	ABRUZZO-MOLISE	320.3	43.7	14
	IT8	CAMPANIA	1 339.0	150.7	11
	IT9	SUD	1 476.1	143.0	10
	ITA	SICILIA	1 135.3	147.9	13
	ITB	SARDEGNA	368.2	51.3	14
LU		LUXEMBOURG (GRAND-DUCHÉ)			
NL		NEDERLAND			
	NL1	NOORD-NEDERLAND	389.1	51.4	13
	NL2	OOST-NEDERLAND	740.7	79.3	11
	NL3	WEST-NEDERLAND	1 640.3	241.7	15
	NL4	ZUID-NEDERLAND	802.6	140.0	17
AT		ÖSTERREICH			
	AT1	OSTÖSTERREICH	679.1	138.0	20
	AT2	SÜDÖSTERREICH	353.2	49.8	14
	AT3	WESTÖSTERREICH	595.1	57.1	10

			TOTAL (1 000)	ISCED 5 à 7 (1 000)	%
	EUROPEAN UNION (CONTINUED)				
PT	**PORTUGAL**				
PT1		CONTINENTE	2 227.0	300.6	13
PT11		NORTE	815.6	89.5	11
PT12		CENTRO (P)	399.3	50.9	13
PT13		LISBOA E VALE DO TEJO	818.0	138.1	17
PT14		ALENTEJO	113.0	10.4	9
PT15		ALGARVE	81.1	7.0	9
PT2		AÇORES	62.3	2.5	4
PT3		MADEIRA	62.0	2.2	4
FI	**SUOMI/FINLAND**				
FI1		MANNER-SUOMI			
FI11		UUSIMAA	268.4	67.7	25
FI12		ETELÄ-SUOMI	348.0	67.1	19
FI13		ITÄ-SUOMI	143.6	22.4	16
FI14		VÄLI-SUOMI	149.6	25.2	17
FI15		POHJOIS-SUOMI	129.4	22.5	17
FI2		AHVENANMAA/ÅLAND	3.8	0.1	3
SE	**SVERIGE**				
SE01		STOCKHOLM	386.0	52.5	14
SE02		ÖSTRA MELLANSVERIGE	344.9	50.7	15
SE03		SMÅLAND MED ÖARNA	171.9	14.4	8
SE04		SYDSERIGE	280.7	36.3	13
SE05		VÄSTSVERIGE	390.7	45.8	12
SE06		NORRA MELLANSVERIGE	177.7	14.8	8
SE07		MELLERSTA NORRLAND	85.2	8.6	10
SE08		ÖVRE NORRLAND	128.1	22.7	18
UK	**UNITED KINGDOM**				
UK1		NORTH	749.5	76.5	10
UK2		YORKSHIRE AND HUMBERSIDE	1 284.6	149.5	12
UK3		EAST MIDLANDS	959.9	107.3	11
UK4		EAST ANGLIA	455.8	49.4	11
UK5		SOUTH EAST (UK)	4 260.0	602.6	14
UK6		SOUTH WEST (UK)	1 049.7	103.7	10
UK7		WEST MIDLANDS	1 344.4	148.0	11
UK8		NORTH WEST (UK)	1 635.4	177.3	11
UK9		WALES	693.3	79.6	11
UKA		SCOTLAND	1 164.4	198.3	17
UKB		NORTHERN IRELAND	467.0	42.0	9

Source: Eurostat, UOE.

		TOTAL (1 000)	ISCED 5 à 7 (1 000)	%
	EFTA/EEA			
IS	ÍSLAND	80.6	7.4	9
LI	LIECHTENSTEIN		0.3	
NO	NORGE		173.0	17
	CEEC			
BG	BĂLGARIJA	1 666.7	223.0	13
CZ	ČESKÁ REPUBLIKA	2 256.4	179.2	8
HU	MAGYARORSZÁG		116.0	6
PL	POLSKA	8 996.5	682.0	8
RO	ROMÂNIA	4 594.5	300.5	7
SK	SLOVENSKÁ REPUBLIKA		82.2	8

Source: National statistics.

NUMBER OF STUDENTS IN HIGHER EDUCATION BETWEEN 1975 AND 1994 (FIGURE F5)

MEN AND WOMEN

(1 000)

EUROPEAN UNION							
	EU	B	DK	D	EL	E	F	IRL
1975/76	5 648	176	97	1 334	117	548	1 053	46
1980/81	6 553	217	115	1 515	121	698	1 176	55
1985/86	7 991	248	125	1 842	182	934	1 358	70
1990/91	9 655	276	151	2 082	195	1 222	1 698	90
1994/95	11 791	353	170	2 156	296	1 527	2 073	122

	I	L	NL	A	P	FIN	S	UK
1975/76	977	N/A	291	97	89	90	N/A	733
1980/81	1 126	N/A	364	125	90	113	N/A	828
1985/86	1 192	N/A	405	173	118	128	183	1 033
1990/91	1 452	N/A	479	206	186	166	193	1 258
1994/95	1 792	2	503	234	301	205	246	1 813

Source: Eurostat, UOE.

	EFTA/EEA			CEEC					
	IS	LI	NO	BG	CZ	HU	PL	RO	SK
1975/76	3	N/A	N/A	130	103	64	565	199	67
1980/81	4	N/A	N/A	101	126	64	580	221	79
1985/86	5	N/A	N/A	114	117	64	431	182	62
1990/91	5	N/A	N/A	189	126	76	512	222	65
1994/95	7	0.2	173	223	137	116	682	300	82

Source: National statistics.

168

WOMEN

(1 000)

	EUROPEAN UNION							
	EU	B	DK	D	EL	E	F	IRL
1975/76	2 297.9	69.0	45.0	568.8	43.0	198.0	500.0	16.0
1980/81	2 877.6	93.0	54.0	680.3	50.0	305.0	594.0	22.0
1985/86	3 777.2	113.0	60.0	829.3	89.0	458.0	708.7	30.0
1990/91	4 683.3	133.3	77.0	880.4	97.9	623.9	901.9	41.4
1994/95	5 972.0	174.3	88.0	935.4	146.5	802.0	1 138.4	59.8

	I	L	NL	A	P	FIN	S	UK
1975/76	381.0	N/A	94.0	36.5	42.0	40,6	N/A	264.0
1980/81	482.0	N/A	144.0	53.1	44.0	53.2	N/A	303.0
1985/86	551.0	N/A	166.0	78.6	65.0	62.5	96.1	470.0
1990/91	720.5	N/A	212.4	94.0	103.5	86.5	103.5	607.0
1994/95	940.0	0.8	237.3	111.8	170.2	108.5	135.0	923.9

Source: Eurostat, UOE.

	EFTA/EEA		
	IS	LI	NO
1975/76	1.0	N/A	N/A
1980/81	1.6	N/A	N/A
1985/86	2.5	N/A	N/A
1990/91	3.1	N/A	N/A
1994/95	4.3	N/A	94.5

Source: Eurostat, UOE.

CEEC					
BG	CZ	HU	PL	RO	SK
74.0	40.5	N/A	309.0	89.7	29.0
57.0	49.8	N/A	326.0	83.9	34.4
62.0	47.3	N/A	244.0	73.1	27.0
97.0	53.6	N/A	286.0	102.1	30.3
135.0	59.4	59.5	374.7	142.6	40.3

National statistics.

MEN

(1 000)

	EUROPEAN UNION							
	EU	B	DK	D	EL	E	F	IRL
1975/76	3 349.8	107.0	52.0	765.0	74.0	350.0	553.0	30.0
1980/81	3 675.5	124.0	61.0	834.8	71.0	393.0	582.0	33.0
1985/86	4 213.6	135.0	65.0	1 013.0	93.0	476.0	649.2	40.0
1990/91	4 971.4	142.9	74.0	1 201.3	97.3	598.2	796.8	48.9
1994/95	5 818.7	178.3	81.8	1 220.3	149.8	725.0	934.2	61.9

	I	L	NL	A	P	FIN	S	UK
1975/76	596.0	N/A	197.0	60.2	47.0	49,4	N/A	469.0
1980/81	644.0	N/A	220.0	71.8	46.0	60.0	N/A	525.0
1985/86	641.0	N/A	239.0	94.6	53.0	65.5	86.6	563.0
1990/91	731.8	N/A	266.4	111.8	82.3	79.2	89.1	651.1
1994/95	851.7	0.8	265.6	122.1	130.4	96.6	111.0	889.4

Source: Eurostat, UOE.

	EFTA/EEA		
	IS	LI	NO
1975/76	2.1	N/A	N/A
1980/81	2.1	N/A	N/A
1985/86	2.3	N/A	N/A
1990/91	2.3	N/A	N/A
1994/95	3.1	N/A	78.4

Source: Eurostat, UOE.

CEEC					
BG	CZ	HU	PL	RO	SK
56.0	62.8	N/A	256.0	110.1	37.9
44.0	75.8	N/A	254.0	137.3	45.1
52.0	69.3	N/A	187.0	109.5	35.4
92.0	72.1	N/A	226.0	120.0	34.4
88.0	77.2	56.9	307.5	157.9	41.9

National statistics.

NUMBER OF STUDENTS IN HIGHER EDUCATION BY MEMBER STATE BY AGE AND BY SEX, 1994/95 (FIGURE F6)

MEN

(1 000)

	EUROPEAN UNION							
	EU	B	DK	D	EL	E	F	IRL
16 YEARS	0.9	0.0	0.0	0.0	0.0	0.0	0.2	0.0
17 YEARS	17.1	0.4	0.0	0.6	0.0	0.0	6.0	0.0
18 YEARS	276.2	16.9	0.1	3.6	26.7	52.8	70.3	2.1
19 YEARS	430.9	23.3	1.5	16.4	30.1	76.8	118.1	8.6
20 YEARS	516.5	27.5	4.2	44.0	26.2	85.9	147.1	10.6
21 YEARS	505.0	25.8	6.7	67.4	21.0	77.3	143.7	9.4
22 YEARS	467.1	21.4	8.3	91.2	12.7	77.3	117.2	4.3
23 YEARS	412.3	15.3	8.7	112.1	9.6	67.2	80.8	3.9
24 YEARS	337.1	9.8	7.8	120.5	4.7	50.0	45.9	3.3
25 YEARS	301.0	6.2	7.0	129.6	5.9	38.0	34.6	2.9
26 YEARS	257.5	4.5	6.1	124.1	4.0	28.9	26.1	N/A
27 YEARS	222.6	3.5	5.2	108.4	2.8	23.8	19.4	N/A
28 YEARS	181.2	3.0	4.3	85.9	1.8	18.5	16.5	N/A
29 YEARS	162.6	2.4	3.4	66.8	1.5	15.2	14.0	N/A

	EUROPEAN UNION (CONTINUED)							
	I	L	NL	A	P	FIN	S	UK
16 YEARS	N/A	N/A	0.0	0.0	0.0	0.1	0.0	0.6
17 YEARS	N/A	N/A	1.6	0.0	0.3	0.1	0.0	6.2
18 YEARS	N/A	N/A	10.8	1.8	6.8	0.5	0.2	74.1
19 YEARS	N/A	N/A	19.9	5.0	12.3	3.6	5.2	105.5
20 YEARS	N/A	N/A	26.9	7.7	14.6	6.1	9.1	107.7
21 YEARS	N/A	N/A	30.2	8.5	14.8	8.1	9.9	86.8
22 YEARS	N/A	N/A	31.7	9.4	14.2	8.9	10.9	61.1
23 YEARS	N/A	N/A	30.2	9.6	12.3	9.1	10.8	46.4
24 YEARS	N/A	N/A	24.4	9.6	10.0	8.4	9.1	35.7
25 YEARS	N/A	N/A	18.5	9.7	7.6	7.4	7.8	29.5
26 YEARS	N/A	N/A	12.3	9.1	5.8	6.3	6.8	25.8
27 YEARS	N/A	N/A	9.1	7.7	4.5	5.4	5.7	23.6
28 YEARS	N/A	N/A	6.9	6.2	3.7	4.4	4.7	22.2
29 YEARS	N/A	N/A	5.9	5.3	3.1	3.5	3.7	21.3

Source: Eurostat, UOE.

	EFTA/EEA				CEEC					
	IS	LI	NO		BG	CZ	HU	PL	RO	SK
16 YEARS	0.0	N/A	0.0		0.0	N/A	N/A	N/A	N/A	N/A
17 YEARS	0.0	N/A	0.0		1.0	N/A	N/A	N/A	N/A	N/A
18 YEARS	0.0	N/A	0.1		5.1	8.8	N/A	N/A	10.0	N/A
19 YEARS	0.0	N/A	3.8		8.6	16.3	N/A	22.7	16.7	N/A
20 YEARS	0.2	N/A	5.9		12.0	14.0	N/A	39.5	18.9	N/A
21 YEARS	0.4	N/A	7.7		10.7	13.3	N/A	39.3	17.2	N/A
22 YEARS	0.5	N/A	8.6		9.5	9.7	N/A	34.8	16.5	N/A
23 YEARS	0.4	N/A	8.5		8.5	6.7	N/A	29.2	14.9	N/A
24 YEARS	0.3	N/A	7.3		7.1	3.1	N/A	20.6	11.8	N/A
25 YEARS	0.3	N/A	6.4		5.8	1.6	N/A	N/A	8.6	N/A
26 YEARS	0.2	N/A	5.1		3.5	1.1	N/A	N/A	5.5	N/A
27 YEARS	0.1	N/A	3.8		2.4	0.9	N/A	N/A	3.4	N/A
28 YEARS	0.1	N/A	3.1		1.8	0.9	N/A	N/A	1.9	N/A
29 YEARS	0.1	N/A	2.5		1.6	0.8	N/A	N/A	1.4	N/A

Source: Eurostat, UOE.   National statistics.

WOMEN

(1 000)

	EUROPEAN UNION							
	EU	B	DK	D	EL	E	F	IRL
16 YEARS	0.9	0.0	0.0	0.0	0.0	0.0	0.2	0.0
17 YEARS	28.4	0.5	0.0	6.5	0.0	0.0	9.2	2.3
18 YEARS	363.4	23.6	0.1	19.2	25.8	75.3	102.0	9.2
19 YEARS	546.1	29.9	1.2	52.0	30.0	100.8	154.6	11.0
20 YEARS	628.8	31.2	4.3	80.9	24.8	111.4	180.7	9.2
21 YEARS	577.6	25.9	7.5	80.5	20.7	100.8	171.5	4.8
22 YEARS	487.4	18.9	9.8	82.3	13.0	91.7	137.0	3.6
23 YEARS	388.9	11.8	10.0	85.2	9.6	68.0	96.6	3.2
24 YEARS	295.9	7.1	8.9	78.4	5.6	48.2	62.7	2.3
25 YEARS	236.4	4.5	7.5	74.8	6.4	34.6	40.6	N/A
26 YEARS	190.7	3.1	6.2	66.4	4.8	25.6	28.2	N/A
27 YEARS	160.2	2.3	5.0	56.0	2.4	19.9	21.1	N/A
28 YEARS	129.5	1.9	4.0	45.1	1.7	15.8	17.1	N/A
29 YEARS	129.3	1.5	3.2	36.6	1.1	12.5	13.7	N/A

	I	L	NL	A	P	FIN	S	UK
16 YEARS	N/A	N/A	0.0	0.0	0.0	0.0	0.0	0.6
17 YEARS	N/A	N/A	2.7	0.0	0.6	0.2	0.0	6.8
18 YEARS	N/A	N/A	13.7	3.3	10.6	0.6	0.3	76.1
19 YEARS	N/A	N/A	23.7	6.9	18.4	5.4	6.9	105.0
20 YEARS	N/A	N/A	28.1	8.4	22.1	9.4	12.6	108.5
21 YEARS	N/A	N/A	28.9	8.3	22.0	10.4	13.4	85.7
22 YEARS	N/A	N/A	28.5	8.5	20.0	10.2	12.6	54.9
23 YEARS	N/A	N/A	23.9	8.4	16.6	9.5	11.1	39.8
24 YEARS	N/A	N/A	18.0	7.9	12.1	8.2	8.6	31.5
25 YEARS	N/A	N/A	12.8	7.6	8.5	6.7	6.9	27.6
26 YEARS	N/A	N/A	8.6	6.9	6.3	5.9	5.8	24.9
27 YEARS	N/A	N/A	6.1	5.5	4.8	4.9	4.9	23.0
28 YEARS	N/A	N/A	4.7	4.5	3.9	4.0	4.0	21.6
29 YEARS	N/A	N/A	4.0	3.5	3.3	3.4	3.5	20.4

Source: Eurostat, UOE.

WOMEN

(1 000)

	EFTA/EEA				CEEC					
	IS	LI	NO	BG	CZ	HU	PL	RO	SK
16 YEARS	0.0	N/A	0.0	0.1	N/A	N/A	N/A	N/A	N/A
17 YEARS	0.0	N/A	0.0	2.1	N/A	N/A	N/A	N/A	N/A
18 YEARS	0.0	N/A	0.2	12.6	6.2	N/A	N/A	9.2	N/A
19 YEARS	0.0	N/A	5.4	20.2	11.7	N/A	38.5	15.6	N/A
20 YEARS	0.2	N/A	8.7	19.4	11.5	N/A	43.3	19.2	N/A
21 YEARS	0.5	N/A	9.6	17.2	9.7	N/A	40.4	18.0	N/A
22 YEARS	0.6	N/A	10.0	14.0	8.3	N/A	35.3	15.9	N/A
23 YEARS	0.5	N/A	9.4	11.3	6.1	N/A	29.6	13.5	N/A
24 YEARS	0.4	N/A	7.4	8.6	2.7	N/A	14.2	10.8	N/A
25 YEARS	0.3	N/A	6.0	6.2	1.1	N/A	N/A	7.1	N/A
26 YEARS	0.2	N/A	4.4	5.0	0.7	N/A	N/A	4.3	N/A
27 YEARS	0.2	N/A	3.6	3.6	0.6	N/A	N/A	2.4	N/A
28 YEARS	0.1	N/A	2.9	2.8	0.5	N/A	N/A	1.1	N/A
29 YEARS	0.1	N/A	2.4	2.1	0.3	N/A	N/A	0.8	N/A

Source: Eurostat, UOE.   National statistics.

NUMBERS OF STUDENTS SELECTED TO PARTICIPATE IN AN ERASMUS EXCHANGE PROGRAMME 1988 TO 1995 (FIGURES F9 AND F10)

	B	DK	D	EL	E	F	IRL	I	L	NL	A	P	FIN	S	UK
1988/89	684	230	2 859	309	1 647	3 677	398	1 380	1	1 077	N/A	239	N/A	N/A	3 515
1989/90	1 385	600	4 502	583	3 008	5 907	688	2 610	15	1 887	N/A	609	N/A	N/A	5 658
1990/91	2 732	1 079	6 894	1 194	5 057	8 979	1 175	4 052	18	3 309	N/A	1 138	N/A	N/A	8 857
1991/92	3 973	1 626	9 843	1 798	7 282	12 651	1 744	5 658	12	4 791	N/A	1 850	N/A	N/A	12 109
1992/93	5 029	2 236	13 058	2 207	9 619	16 360	2 299	7 309	8	6 063	822	2 559	374	1 417	16 688
1993/94	8 105	2 734	17 084	3 005	12 185	20 421	2 890	9 409	11	7 268	1 580	3 432	1 083	2 509	21 105
1994/95	7 374	3 102	20 470	3 992	15 316	24 406	3 754	11 483	11	8 406	2 371	4 136	2 444	3 390	24 295
1995/96	8 111	3 747	23 927	4 726	18 101	27 263	4 422	13 444	21	9 491	3 193	4 753	3 917	4 534	26 825

Source: Erasmus, Time series statistics 1988/89 to 1995/96.

NUMBER OF HIGHER EDUCATION STUDENTS SELECTED TO BE SENT AND RECEIVED UNDER THE COMMUNITY PROGRAMME, 1994/95 (FIGURE F11)

(1 000)

	EUROPEAN UNION							
	B	DK	D	EL	E	F	IRL	I
NUMBER OF STUDENTS	322.4	169.8	2 155.7	296.4	1 527.0	2 072.6	121.7	1 791.7
NUMBER OF STUDENTS RECEIVED	6.9	2.9	18.8	3.1	15.1	24.8	4.5	10.3
NUMBER OF STUDENTS SENT	7.4	3.1	20.5	4.0	15.3	24.4	3.8	11.5

	L	NL	A	P	FIN	S	UK
NUMBER OF STUDENTS	1.8	502.9	234.0	298.1	205.0	245.9	1 813.3
NUMBER OF STUDENTS RECEIVED	0.005	8.4	2.2	3.5	2.1	3.2	29.1
NUMBER OF STUDENTS SENT	0.01	8.4	2.4	4.1	2.4	3.4	24.3

	EFTA/EEA		
	IS	LI	NO
NUMBER OF STUDENTS	7.4	5.0	173.0
NUMBER OF STUDENTS RECEIVED	0.05	0.001	1.3
NUMBER OF STUDENTS SENT	0.07	0.0	1.6

Source: Erasmus, Time series statistics 1988/89 to 1995/96.

STUDENTS IN HIGHER EDUCATION BY FIELD OF STUDY, 1994/95 (FIGURE F13)

MEN AND WOMEN

(1 000)

	EUROPEAN UNION							
	EU	B	DK	D	EL	E	F	IRL
HUMANITIES, APPLIED ARTS, THEOLOGY	1 263.8	32.5	31.7	328.7	N/A	145.6	N/A	26.4
SOCIAL SCIENCE	2 505.4	97.5	45.1	522.9	N/A	391.1	N/A	25.9
LAW	861.8	15.7	5.9	107.5	N/A	269.0	N/A	1.9
NATURAL SCIENCE	563.3	8.5	6.5	137.0	N/A	96.4	N/A	16.5
MATHEMATICS, COMPUTER SCIENCE	447.0	10.4	6.8	116.9	N/A	82.2	N/A	3.6
MEDICAL SCIENCE	1 006.2	43.5	19.1	218.2	N/A	114.5	N/A	5.3
ENGINEERING, ARCHITECTURE	1 580.1	53.2	23.2	427.2	N/A	257.5	N/A	15.9
OTHER	1 211.1	61.1	31.7	297.5	N/A	170.9	N/A	26.5
TOTAL	9 438.8	322.4	169.8	2 155.7	N/A	1 527.0	2 072.6	121.7

(1 000)

	EUROPEAN UNION (CONTINUED)							
	I	L	NL	A	P	FIN	S	UK
HUMANITIES, APPLIED ARTS, THEOLOGY	250.3	0.1	42.8	44.6	25.3	28.0	37.4	270.2
SOCIAL SCIENCE	448.4	0.5	206.2	82.7	102.5	36.6	54.9	491.2
LAW	294.8	0.1	33.3	27.7	23.0	4.2	10.9	68.0
NATURAL SCIENCE	107.5	0.0	15.7	16.1	9.2	10.4	11.2	128.4
MATHEMATICS, COMPUTER SCIENCE	51.2	0.0	8.2	17.9	12.8	12.6	14.4	110.2
MEDICAL SCIENCE	159.6	0.1	45.1	21.8	16.5	36.1	32.7	293.9
ENGINEERING, ARCHITECTURE	300.5	0.3	58.9	38.9	56.5	46.7	41.3	260.1
OTHER	179.8	0.4	91.7	31.9	54.8	30.5	43.1	191.4
TOTAL	1 792.0	1.6	501.9	281.7	300.6	205.1	245.9	1 813.3

Source: Eurostat, UOE.

	EFTA/EEA			CEEC					
	IS	LI	NO	BG	CZ	HU	PL	RO	SK
HUMANITIES, APPLIED ARTS, THEOLOGY	1.5	N/A	21.4	51.6	19.4	20.3	95.6	35.2	7.1
SOCIAL SCIENCE	1.4	N/A	42.4	70.4	32.3	11.7	168.2	54.8	12.7
LAW	0.5	N/A	8.3	12.8	6.1	5.0	44.6	15.4	3.7
NATURAL SCIENCE	0.4	N/A	10.2	5.2	4.9	7.9	21.3	11.9	2.5
MATHEMATICS, COMPUTER SCIENCE	0.3	N/A	1.3	3.4	2.0	28.0	16.0	15.3	0.8
MEDICAL SCIENCE	1.1	N/A	18.8	18.1	10.1	11.7	34.1	36.4	6.9
ENGINEERING, ARCHITECTURE	0.6	N/A	19.6	55.0	37.7	0.0	146.1	113.6	27.6
OTHER	1.6	N/A	51.1	6.5	24.0	31.8	156.4	17.8	20.8
TOTAL	7.4	N/A	173.0	223.0	136.6	116.4	682.2	300.5	82.2

Source: Eurostat, UOE.   National statistics.

NUMBER OF WOMEN STUDENTS IN HIGHER EDUCATION BY FIELD OF STUDY, 1994/95 (FIGURE F14)

(1 000)

	EUROPEAN UNION							
	EU	B	DK	D	EL	E	F	IRL
HUMANITIES, APPLIED ARTS, THEOLOGY	828.5	19.1	21.7	201.0	N/A	93.1	N/A	16.6
SOCIAL SCIENCE	1 240.7	49.3	17.5	222.1	N/A	217.8	N/A	14.2
LAW	464.4	8.1	3.2	46.0	N/A	155.1	N/A	1.0
NATURAL SCIENCE	249.9	3.3	2.6	45.7	N/A	48.6	N/A	8.4
MATHEMATICS, COMPUTER SCIENCE	123.4	2.4	1.8	26.7	N/A	26.1	N/A	1.1
MEDICAL SCIENCE	685.7	28.3	15.3	136.7	N/A	78.5	N/A	3.2
ENGINEERING, ARCHITECTURE	296.0	10.3	5.1	62.2	N/A	62.7	N/A	1.9
OTHER	810.0	38.3	20.8	195.0	N/A	120.1	N/A	13.3
TOTAL	4 698.7	159.1	88.0	935.4	N/A	802.0	N/A	59.8

	I	L	NL	A	P	FIN	S	UK
HUMANITIES, APPLIED ARTS, THEOLOGY	197.6	0.1	26.4	27.8	18.0	19.7	24.0	163.4
SOCIAL SCIENCE	224.2	0.3	97.5	39.5	60.5	20.6	31.3	246.0
LAW	166.7	0.1	16.1	11.9	13.9	2.1	5.7	34.6
NATURAL SCIENCE	55.9	0.0	5.1	6.4	5.5	5.3	5.3	57.8
MATHEMATICS, COMPUTER SCIENCE	22.1	0.0	0.8	3.9	6.0	2.3	3.9	26.4
MEDICAL SCIENCE	85.1	0.1	31.6	12.9	12.0	30.2	24.5	227.4
ENGINEERING, ARCHITECTURE	70.5	0.0	7.5	6.7	16.0	7.1	8.3	37.7
OTHER	127.8	0.3	52.3	20.0	38.4	21.3	31.9	130.6
TOTAL	949.8	0.8	237.3	129.0	170.2	108.5	135.0	923.9

Source: Eurostat, UOE.

	EFTA/EEA			CEEC					
	IS	LI	NO	BG	CZ	HU	PL	RO	SK
HUMANITIES, APPLIED ARTS, THEOLOGY	0.9	N/A	13.7	40.3	7.2	N/A	67.5	25.0	4.0
SOCIAL SCIENCE	0.7	N/A	21.4	45.0	19.8	N/A	97.0	33.7	7.3
LAW	0.2	N/A	4.3	7.7	4.2	N/A	23.9	5.0	1.9
NATURAL SCIENCE	0.2	N/A	4.1	3.2	1.7	N/A	14.0	8.5	1.3
MATHEMATICS, COMPUTER SCIENCE	0.0	N/A	0.4	1.8	0.3	N/A	8.7	8.4	0.2
MEDICAL SCIENCE	0.8	N/A	14.9	12.2	7.1	N/A	21.5	25.4	4.4
ENGINEERING, ARCHITECTURE	0.1	N/A	3.7	24.3	7.9	N/A	29.2	29.6	7.9
OTHER	1.2	N/A	32.0	0.4	11.1	N/A	112.8	9.8	13.3
TOTAL	4.3	N/A	94.5	135.0	59.4	N/A	374.7	145.4	40.3

Source: Eurostat, UOE.   National statistics.

PROPORTION OF PEOPLE WITH HIGHER EDUCATION QUALIFICATIONS, BY AGE GROUP, 1995
(FIGURES F15 AND F16)

(%)

AGE	EU	B	DK	D	EL	E	F	IRL	I	L	NL	A	P	FIN	S	UK
30-34	21	30	30	24	21	23	22	25	9	18	24	10	13	25	31	24
35-39	21	26	31	26	18	19	21	22	11	17	25	12	16	26	31	24
40-44	21	25	33	27	16	16	18	20	11	17	24	10	14	22	34	25
45-49	18	22	32	25	13	12	18	17	9	17	21	7	11	20	30	22
50-54	16	20	25	23	10	10	15	14	7	16	18	7	10	23	29	19
55-59	13	14	21	19	8	7	10	12	5	12	15	5	7	17	21	16

Source: Eurostat, Labour force survey, 1995.

NUMBER OF HIGHER EDUCATION STUDENTS STUDYING IN ANOTHER EU MEMBER STATE OR EFTA/EEA COUNTRY, BY NATIONALITY, 1994/95 (FIGURE F12)

	B	DK	D	EL	E	F	IRL	I	L	NL	A	P	FIN	S	UK	IS	LI	NO	Total of national students inside the country AND in another Member State or EFTA/EEA country	Total of national students in another Member State or EFTA/EEA country
Belgian		11	1 002	N/A	632	1 577	42	185	N/A	660	58	26	7	15	1 505	11	N/A	25	323 520	5 763
Danish	54		710	N/A	195	389	32	45	N/A	58	71	2	28	620	1 003	33	N/A	663	165 373	3 924
German	655	544		N/A	2 458	5 332	445	1 282	N/A	843	5 195	204	135	635	9 518	15	N/A	436	2 028 889	27 765
Greek	928	20	8 231	N/A	177	2 806	38	7 046	N/A	102	369	3	12	155	10 374	0	N/A	27	326 645	30 303
Spanish	1 542	61	4 241	N/A		3 263	187	189	N/A	278	184	203	13	89	4 983	7	N/A	54	1 528 655	15 307
French	5 137	80	5 872	N/A	2 895		297	575	N/A	156	291	537	28	167	8 936	2	N/A	130	1 932 305	25 125
Irish	67	27	541	N/A	263	547		18	N/A	29	47	3	8	32	9 799	0	N/A	15	127 950	11 393
Italian	4 421	54	5 890	N/A	1 767	3 372	81		N/A	238	5 767	60	32	103	3 107	2	N/A	41	1 792 918	24 965
Luxembourg	1 605	1	1 193	N/A	17	1 048	10	37		6	298	11	1	0	273	0	N/A	1	6 114	4 502
Dutch	2 949	80	2 564	N/A	698	841	43	106	N/A		91	21	16	118	2 009	0	N/A	138	505 269	9 720
Austrian	30	29	6 686	N/A	402	392	16	93	N/A	62		5	13	113	497	2	N/A	35	217 189	8 372
Portuguese	504	17	1 330	N/A	545	3 492	9	33	N/A	84	36		6	27	1 090	0	N/A	26	299 148	7 201
Finnish	32	58	1 126	N/A	108	575	18	63	N/A	47	126	4		2 131	630	5	N/A	175	207 571	5 143
Swedish	69	289	1 079	N/A	216	708	53	104	N/A	86	178	8	229		943	13	N/A	803	237 110	4 778
United Kingdom	321	324	3 535	N/A	1 948	4 217	2 034	392	N/A	418	248	59	58	436		6	N/A	479	1 670 778	14 476
Icelandic	7	400	283	N/A	7	66	1	23	N/A	10	11	0	21	361	120		N/A	175	8 711	1 473
Liechtenstein	N/A	N/A	N/A	N/A	N/A	N/A	N/A	N/A	N/A	N/A	N/A	N/A	N/A	N/A	N/A	N/A		N/A	N/A	N/A
Norwegian	33	745	1 274	N/A	104	392	13	53	N/A	93	77	4	28	861	2 094	14	N/A		167 594	5 921

Source: Eurostat, UOE.

Greece and **Luxembourg**: There are no data on foreign students by nationality.
France: Data on the distribution of foreign students only account for about 80% of those enrolled in France.
Ireland and **United Kingdom**: Data refer only to foreign students studying full-time.
Netherlands and **Austria**: Data on foreign students refer only to university institutions.

NUMBER OF PEOPLE WITH HIGHER EDUCATION QUALIFICATIONS BY SEX, 1994/95 (FIGURE F17)

	EU	B	DK	D	EL	E	F	IRL
WOMEN	763 791	N/A	15 308	153 214	17 558	101 320	N/A	12 475
MEN	691 733	N/A	14 935	185 083	13 602	76 417	N/A	13 066

	I	L	NL	A	P	FIN	S	UK
WOMEN	102 783	N/A	40 639	9 697	22 916	16 158	19 970	251 753
MEN	80 274	N/A	40 754	9 079	13 494	11 872	14 862	218 295

Source: Eurostat, UOE.

	EFTA/EEA			CEEC					
	IS	LI	NO	BG	CZ	HU	PL	RO	SK
WOMEN		N/A	27 832	N/A	9 973	30 192	10 000	N/A	N/A
MEN	N/A	N/A	22 449	N/A	9 512	35 005	10 410	N/A	N/A

Source: Eurostat, UOE.   National statistics.

NUMBER OF PEOPLE WITH HIGHER EDUCATION QUALIFICATIONS BY FIELD OF STUDY, 1994/95 (FIGURE F18)

(1 000)

	EUROPEAN UNION							
	EU	B	DK	D	EL	E	F	IRL
HUMANITIES, APPLIED ARTS, THEOLOGY	158.7	N/A	2.7	28.1	N.D.	17.5	N/A	1.5
SOCIAL SCIENCE	344.8	N/A	7.9	71.3	N.D.	42.9	N/A	12.3
LAW	82.4	N/A	0.7	11.7	N.D.	25.7	N/A	0.6
NATURAL SCIENCE	78.5	N/A	0.7	19.8	N.D.	8.2	N/A	4.2
MATHEMATICS, COMPUTER SCIENCE	57.8	N/A	0.4	12.3	N.D.	7.5	N/A	1.8
MEDICAL SCIENCE	212.6	N/A	4.9	57.4	N.D.	20.1	N/A	1.1
ENGINEERING, ARCHITECTURE	218.8	N/A	6.5	79.1	N.D.	22.6	N/A	5.3
OTHER	274.1	N/A	6.5	58.6	N.D.	33.2	N/A	2.9
TOTAL	1 427.8	N/A	30.2	338.3	0.0	177.7	N/A	29.7

	I	L	NL	A	P	FIN	S	UK
HUMANITIES, APPLIED ARTS, THEOLOGY	16.7	N/A	6.5	2.5	3.3	1.7	2.0	76.1
SOCIAL SCIENCE	27.7	N/A	30.0	4.0	12.4	2.6	7.3	126.2
LAW	16.0	N/A	3.7	1.6	2.2	0.5	1.0	18.7
NATURAL SCIENCE	7.4	N/A	2.1	1.0	0.7	0.7	1.2	32.6
MATHEMATICS, COMPUTER SCIENCE	4.0	N/A	2.0	0.8	1.1	1.6	1.6	24.8
MEDICAL SCIENCE	26.8	N/A	10.0	2.1	3.3	8.4	6.3	72.3
ENGINEERING, ARCHITECTURE	14.9	N/A	9.9	2.5	4.5	6.4	6.3	60.9
OTHER	69.5	N/A	16.5	4.2	8.9	6.1	9.2	58.6
TOTAL	183.1	N/A	80.7	18.8	36.4	28.0	34.8	470.0

Source: Eurostat, UOE.

	EFTA/EEA			CEEC					
	IS	LI	NO	BG	CZ	HU	PL	RO	SK
HUMANITIES, APPLIED ARTS, THEOLOGY	N/A	N/A	11.1	7.8	5.5	N/A	10.2	7.2	N/A
SOCIAL SCIENCE	N/A	N/A	17.5	5.4	4.1	N/A	13.8	8.5	N/A
LAW	N/A	N/A	1.8	0.4	0.9	N/A	2.8	3.2	N/A
NATURAL SCIENCE	N/A	N/A	1.2	0.5	0.6	N/A	1.4	3.0	N/A
MATHEMATICS, COMPUTER SCIENCE	N/A	N/A	0.6	0.5	0.3	N/A	1.7	2.8	N/A
MEDICAL SCIENCE	N/A	N/A	4.5	4.9	2.0	N/A	6.7	8.1	N/A
ENGINEERING, ARCHITECTURE	N/A	N/A	4.6	9.2	4.4	N/A	12.5	31.6	N/A
OTHER	N/A	N/A	9.9	1.7	1.6	N/A	20.1	6.2	N/A
TOTAL	N/A	N/A	51.2	30.4	19.5	N/A	69.3	70.4	N/A

Source: Eurostat, UOE.   National statistics.

PARTICIPATION RATE IN HIGHER EDUCATION BY EDUCATIONAL LEVEL OF PARENTS (19- TO 24-YEAR-OLDS), 1995 (FIGURE F19)

(%)

EDUCATIONAL LEVEL OF PARENTS:	EU	B	DK	D	EL	E	F	IRL
PRIMARY OR LOWER SECONDARY	17	26	12	N/A	10	22	22	12
UPPER SECONDARY	26	44	13	N/A	28	49	35	30
HIGHER	48	61	30	N/A	53	63	68	54

EDUCATIONAL LEVEL OF PARENTS:	I	L	NL	A	P	FIN	S	UK
PRIMARY OR LOWER SECONDARY	17	9	16	N/A	20	8	15	N/A
UPPER SECONDARY	46	24	26	N/A	51	12	25	N/A
HIGHER	61	45	43	N/A	73	37	55	N/A

Source: Eurostat, Labour force survey, 1995.

Denmark, Finland and **Sweden**: National surveys.

174

TEACHERS

PUPILS, ISCED LEVELS 1 TO 3, AND TOTAL POPULATION, 1994/95 (FIGURE G5)

(1 000)

	NUMBERS OF STUDENTS, ISCED 1 TO 3	TOTAL POPULATION
EUROPEAN UNION		
EU	61 167.4	371 330.9
B	1 790.3	10 101.0
DK	773.6	5 215.7
D	11 879.5	81 538.6
EL	1 552.4	10 442.9
E	7 109.7	39 177.4
F	10 075.4	58 020.4
IRL	771.7	3 579.6
I	7 306.5	57 268.6
L	52.5	401.0
NL	2 697.9	15 424.1
A	1 167.5	8 039.9
P	1 865.6	9 912.1
FIN	842.0	5 098.8
S	1 451.9	8 816.4
UK	11 886.8	58 294.4
EFTA/EEA		
IS	59.4	267.0
LI	3.5	30.6
NO	685.0	4 348.4

Source: Eurostat, UOE and population statistics.

	CEEC	
BG	1 210.6	8 427.4
CZ	1 731.9	10 333.2
HU	1 550.1	10 245.7
PL	7 230.6	38 580.6
RO	4 388.5	22 712.4
SK	1 024.5	5 356.2

Source: National statistics.

NUMBER OF TEACHERS, BY SEX, WORKING EITHER FULL-TIME OR PART-TIME AT PRIMARY LEVEL, 1994/95
(FIGURES G7, G8 AND G10)

(1 000)

	ISCED 1						
	FULL-TIME				PART-TIME		
	MEN	WOMEN	TOTAL		MEN	WOMEN	TOTAL
EUROPEAN UNION							
B	15.3	32.9	48.2		1.8	10.7	12.5
DK	10.2 (e)	13.9 (e)	24.1 (e)		3.7 (e)	5.3 (e)	9.0 (e)
D	27.8	79.5	107.3		4.1	102.1	106.2
EL	19.9	24.2	44.1		not applicable	not applicable	not applicable
E	38.0	94.6	132.6		negligible	negligible	negligible
F	47.3	156.1	203.4		0.7	12.9	13.6
IRL	3.6	12.6	16.2		0	0.1	0.1
I	17.6	238.9	256.5		0	0.4	0.4
L	0.8	1.1	1.9		N/A	N/A	N/A
NL	20.5	19.1	39.6		2.1	22.1	24.2
A	5.3	27.4	32.7		N/A	N/A	N/A
P	3.2 (e)	32.3 (e)	35.5		N/A	N/A	N/A
FIN	13.4	28.0	0		0.5	1.9	2.4
S	6.7	31.5	38.2		6.2	16.7	22.9
UK	45.3	180.4	225.7		6.2	49.3	55.5
EFTA/EEA							
IS	0.8	1.6	2.4		0.1	0.8	0.9
LI	0.055	0.070	0.125		N/A	N/A	N/A
NO	N/A	N/A	N/A		N/A	N/A	N/A

Source: Eurostat, UOE.

	CEEC						
BG	2.9	22.2	25.0		N/A	N/A	N/A
CZ	4.6 (e)	20.8 (e)	25.4		N/A	N/A	N/A
HU	2.7	38.5	41.2		N/A	N/A	N/A
PL	50.4	297.2	347.6		11.9	30.7	42.6
RO	9.8	51.2	61.0		0.2	0.8	1.0
SK	1.3	14.2	15.5		N/A	N/A	N/A

Source: National statistics.

NB: **Liechtenstein**: National statistics.

NUMBER OF TEACHERS, BY SEX, WORKING EITHER FULL-TIME OR PART-TIME AT SECONDARY LEVEL, 1994/95
(FIGURES G7, G9 AND G10)

(1 000)

	ISCED 2						ISCED 3					
	FULL-TIME			PART-TIME			FULL-TIME			PART-TIME		
	MEN	WOMEN	TOTAL	MEN	WOMEN	TOTAL	MEN	WOMEN	TOTAL	MEN	WOMEN	TOTAL
EUROPEAN UNION												
B							47.1	40	87.1	12.4	27.5	39.9
DK	7.7 (e)	10.6 (e)	18.3 (e)	2.5 (e)	4.0 (e)	6.5 (e)	10.2 (e)	8.2 (e)	18.4 (e)	3.8 (e)	3.1 (e)	6.9 (e)
D	140.1	101.7	241.8	28.4	87.6	116.0	96.0	30.3	126.3	22.5	34.7	57.2
EL	11.7	20.1	31.8	negligible	negligible	negligible	17.8	14.9	32.7	negligible	negligible	negligible
E	42.9	58.9	101.8	negligible	negligible	negligible	89.8	81.6	171.4	13.4 (e)	12.5 (e)	25.9 (e)
F							172.8	217	389.8	22.3	61.6	83.9
IRL							9.7 (e)	11.4 (e)	21.1 (e)	2.5 (e)	2.7 (e)	5.2 (e)
I	55.7	139.6	195.3	0.6	1.4	2	126.8	153	279.8	1.7	2.5	4.2
L							1.6	0.9	2.5	N/A	N/A	N/A
NL	25.5	2.9	28.4	10.9	12.5	23.4	16.8	2.0	18.8	8.1	9.6	17.7
A	17.2	29.2	46.4	N/A	N/A	N/A	19.0	18.2	37.2	N/A	N/A	N/A
P				N/A	N/A	N/A	32.9	73.9	106.8	N/A	N/A	N/A
FIN							9.5	12.4	21.9	0.9	1.2	2.1
S	8.7	10.4	19.1	7.4	11.4	18.8	7.6	5.3	12.9	16.9	19.0	35.9
UK	59.6	64.9	124.5	5.0	19.0	24.0	65.7	71.9	137.6	5.7	21.6	27.3
EFTA/EEA												
IS							0.6	0.4	1.0	0.1	0.1	0.2
LI	0.104	0.019	0.123	N/A	N/A	N/A	N/A	N/A	N/A	N/A	N/A	N/A
NO	N/A	N/A	N/A	N/A	N/A	N/A	N/A	N/A	N/A	N/A	N/A	N/A

Source: Eurostat, UOE.

	ISCED 2						ISCED 3					
CEEC												
BG	9.3	26.1	35.4	N/A	N/A	N/A	10.6	20.8	31.4	N/A	N/A	N/A
CZ	6.8 (e)	30.6 (e)	37.4	N/A	N/A	N/A	13.5 (e)	21.5 (e)	35.0	N/A	N/A	N/A
HU	11.9	36.7	48.6	N/A	N/A	N/A	10.6	17.3	27.9	N/A	N/A	N/A
PL							44.7	75.5	120.2	24.4	24.8	49.2
RO	30.4	57.2	87.6	4.1	7.7	11.8	24.1	32.7	56.8	3.9	5.2	9.1
SK	5.5	17.9	23.4	N/A	N/A	N/A	12.2	15.4	27.6	2.3	3.0	5.3

Source: National statistics.

Belgium, France, Ireland and **Luxembourg**: Figures for teachers at ISCED level 2 are included in the figures for teachers at ISCED level 3.

Portugal: Figures for teachers at ISCED level 1 are those for the first stage of *ensino básico* whereas figures for teachers at ISCED level 3 include the second and third stages of *ensino básico* as well as upper secondary education.

Finland: Figures for teachers at ISCED level 2 are included in those for teachers at ISCED level 1. Figures for teachers at ISCED level 3 include those at ISCED level 5.

Iceland and **Poland**: Figures for teachers at ISCED level 2 are included in those for teachers at ISCED level 1.

NUMBER OF HEADTEACHERS, BY SEX, PRIMARY AND SECONDARY, PUBLIC AND PRIVATE SECTORS, 1994/95
(FIGURE G11)

	ISCED 1		ISCED 2 and 3	
	WOMEN	MEN	WOMEN	MEN
EUROPEAN UNION				
B	1 498	2 535	527	1 641
DK	400	2 000	N/A	N/A
D	N/A	N/A	N/A	N/A
EL	N/A	N/A	N/A	N/A
E	N/A	N/A	N/A	N/A
F	33 450	18 353	1 649	5 380
IRL	1 527	1 792	237	557
I	1 999	2 310	2 506	6 335
L	not applicable	not applicable	5	22
NL	N/A	N/A	N/A	N/A
A	1 768	1 878	386	1 816
P	N/A	N/A	N/A	N/A
FIN	554	1 552	86	322
S	971	955	696	1 006
UK	13 058	11 437	1 568	4 602
EFTA/EEA				
IS	73	136	10	42
LI	2	13	1	8
NO	957	2 184	134	542
CEEC				
BG	N/A	N/A	N/A	N/A
CZ	N/A	N/A	N/A	N/A
HU	1 633	1 606	216	481
PL	N/A	N/A	N/A	N/A
RO	N/A	N/A	N/A	N/A
SK	N/A	N/A	804	1 327

Source: Eurostat, additional collection.

NUMBER OF TEACHERS BY AGE BAND, PRIMARY EDUCATION, PUBLIC AND PRIVATE SECTORS, 1994/95
(FIGURES G13 AND G14)

(1 000)

	< 30	30-39	40-49	>=50	Age unknown
EUROPEAN UNION					
EU	147.8 (e)	371.1 (e)	542.3 (e)	326.7 (e)	34.5 (e)
B	15.4	25.4	23.9	13.2	
DK	1.1 (e)	8.2 (e)	15.3 (e)	8.5 (e)	
D	11.7	43.4	89.2	69.2	0.0
EL	N/A	N/A	N/A	N/A	N/A
E	N/A	N/A	N/A	N/A	N/A
F	38.2	99.6	124.0	56.3	
IRL	3.1	6.9	6.2	4.7	0.1
I	15.7 (e)	78.6 (e)	85.9 (e)	74.7 (e)	34.4 (e)
L	0.4	0.3	0.7	0.5	
NL	N/A	N/A	N/A	N/A	N/A
A	6.4	11.8	10.8	3.6	
P	5.8	20.0	25.2	12.7	
FIN	2.7	5.4	4.7	4.1	
S	4.4	9.7	25.6	21.5	
UK	42.9	61.9	130.9	57.7	
EFTA/EEA					
IS	0.4	1.1	1.1	0.7	
LI	0.08	0.07	0.05	0.02	
NO	5.5	10.5	20.6	16.3	0.9
CEEC					
BG	5.5	8.9	6.1	4.5	
CZ	N/A	N/A	N/A	N/A	N/A
HU	N/A	N/A	N/A	N/A	N/A
PL	N/A	N/A	N/A	N/A	N/A
RO	N/A	N/A	N/A	N/A	N/A
SK	N/A	N/A	N/A	N/A	N/A

Source: Eurostat, additional collection.

NUMBER OF TEACHERS BY AGE BAND, SECONDARY EDUCATION, PUBLIC AND PRIVATE SECTORS, 1994/95
(FIGURES G13 AND G15)

(1 000)

	< 30	30-39	40-49	>=50	Age Unknown
EUROPEAN UNION					
EU	135.4 (e)	504.0 (e)	820.7 (e)	575.8 (e)	149.2 (e)
B	10.8	28.7	39.5	30.5	
DK	1.5 (e)	12.4 (e)	23.1 (e)	13.1 (e)	
D	12.1	112.7	234.6	165.6	16.4
EL	N/A	N/A	N/A	N/A	N/A
E	N/A	N/A	N/A	N/A	N/A
F	55.9	112.7	195.2	109.9	
IRL	3.1	6.5	7.8	4.6	4.3
I	4.7 (e)	108.8 (e)	175.9 (e)	144.3 (e)	128.5 (e)
L	0.2	0.7	1.0	0.6	
NL	N/A	N/A	N/A	N/A	N/A
A	11.1	35.3	26.2	11.0	
P	16.3	25.0	15.0	6.9	
FIN	3.9	11.8	17.3	13.8	
S	4.7	14.2	30.7	37.1	
UK	11.1	35.1	54.4	38.3	
EFTA/EEA					
IS	0.07	0.3	0.5	0.4	
LI	0.04	0.1	0.09	0.03	
NO	2.0	5.6	10.5	8.4	1.9
CEEC					
BG	7.2	16.2	14.7	8.3	
CZ	N/A	N/A	N/A	N/A	N/A
HU	N/A	N/A	N/A	N/A	N/A
PL	N/A	N/A	N/A	N/A	N/A
RO	N/A	N/A	N/A	N/A	N/A
SK	N/A	N/A	N/A	N/A	N/A

Source: Eurostat, additional collection.

GDP PER CAPITA 1995. (FIGURES G16, G17 AND G18)

	GDP IN NATIONAL CURRENCY AT CURRENT PRICES, (000 MILLION), 1995	NUMBER OF INHABITANTS, 1995 (1 000)
EUROPEAN UNION		
B	7 936.0	10 130.6
DK	970.8	5 215.7
D	3 457.4	81 538.6
EL	26 486.1	10 442.9
E	69 778.9	39 177.4
F	7 674.8	58 020.4
IRL	40 136.5	3 579.6
I	1 770 949.0	57 268.6
L	244.0	406.6
NL	635.0	15 424.1
A	2 272.3	8 039.9
P	15 073.2	9 912.1
FIN	545.7	5 098.8
S	1 665.0	8 816.4
UK	697.5	58 294.4
EFTA/EEA		
IS	416.0	267.0
LI	1 564 377.0	30.6
NO	925.9	4 348.4

Source: Eurostat, National Accounts ESA and population statistics.

	CEEC	
BG	871.0	8 427.4
CZ	1 212.0	10 333.2
HU	5 500.0	10 245.7
PL	600.0	38 580.6
RO	72 559.7	22 712.4
SK	518.0	5 356.2

Source: European Bank for Reconstruction and Development and Eurostat population statistics.

Ireland, Luxembourg and **Iceland**: GDP in national currency and at current prices, in millions, 1995.
Liechtenstein: GDP calculated on the basis of Swiss GDP, 1995.
Bulgaria: GDP in national currency and at current prices, in millions, 1995.
Romania: National statistics.

TEACHERS' GROSS ANNUAL SALARIES IN NATIONAL CURRENCY, PRIMARY, LOWER AND UPPER SECONDARY LEVELS, 1994/95. (FIGURES G16, G17 AND G18)

	PRIMARY		LOWER SECONDARY		UPPER SECONDARY	
	MINIMUM	MAXIMUM	MINIMUM	MAXIMUM	MINIMUM	MAXIMUM
EUROPEAN UNION						
B	786 392	1 273 386	818 505	1 416 319	1 020 392	1 794 272
DK	194 000	250 000	194 000	250 000	225 000	322 000
D	59 033	78 387	66 296	87 195	67 870	88 769
EL	3 027 380	4 361 034	3 151 738	4 495 392	3 151 738	4 495 392
E	2 873 484	N/A	2 873 484	N/A	3 622 938	5 180 964
F	125 202	234 073	142 867	252 828	142 867	331 346
IRL	14 400	26 300	14 600	26 500	14 600	26 500
I	28 011 808	42 891 514	30 397 932	47 624 018	30 397 932	49 873 390
L	1 302 000	2 525 250	1 680 000	2 940 000	1 680 000	2 940 000
NL	47 148	70 658	49 624	77 617	50 064	103 421
A	279 930	607 229	279 930	607 229	309 148	750 995
P	1 829 800	4 391 520	2 653 210	5 672 380	2 653 210	5 672 380
FIN	96 121	172 127	96 121	172 127	98 592	180 268
S	145 000	186 000	161 500	202 500	161 500	207 000
UK (E/W)	11 883	20 145	11 883	20 145	11 883	20 145
UK (NI)	11 883	20 145	11 883	20 145	11 883	20 145
UK (SC)	12 147	22 008	12 147	26 568	12 147	26 568
EFTA/EEA						
IS	822 516	1 529 724	822 516	1 529 724	806 856	1 529 724
LI	59 000	93 700	67 300	101 200	86 200	119 800
NO	165 059	263 941	178 583	263 941	200 339	284 619
CEEC						
BG	3 799	N/A	4 426	N/A	4 426	N/A
CZ	91 504	135 367	91 504	135 367	105 951	156 952
HU	252 000	441 000	252 000	441 000	288 000	504 000
PL	2 688	6 144	2 688	6 144	2 688	6 144
RO	1 297 200	2 298 000	1 482 000	3 038 400	1 519 200	3 038 400
SK	62 280	96 480	62 280	96 480	69 000	96 480

Source: Eurydice.

SPECIAL EDUCATION

NUMBER OF PUPILS WITH **SEN** IN SEPARATE SPECIAL SCHOOLS AND TOTAL NUMBER OF PUPILS
AT THE **ISCED** LEVELS **1, 2** AND 3, **1994/95** (FIGURE H6)

(1 000)

	PUPILS IN SPECIAL SCHOOLS[1]	Total number of pupils[2]
EUROPEAN UNION		
B	64.7	1 790.3
DK	3.5	773.6
D	390.9	11 879.5
EL	14.1 (e)	1 552.4
E	31.9	7 109.7
F	265.0	10 075.4
IRL	7.8	771.7
I	12.8	7 306.5
L	0.5	50.9
NL	116.5	2 697.9
A	18.5	1 167.5
P	5.5	1 408.4
FIN	13.9	842.0
S	0.7	1 240.2
UK	116.8	11 886.8

Source: Eurostat, UOE.

EFTA/EEA		
IS	0.2	42.2
LI	0.04	3.5
NO	3.3	685.0
CEEC		
BG	17.4	1 210.6
CZ	65.8	1 732.0
HU	41.7	1 550.1
PL	106.0	7 230.6
RO	49.1	4 388.5
SK	20.4	1 024.4

Source: National statistics.

[1] The numbers of pupils in separate special schools are the numbers indicated in the UOE questionnaire ENRLSUP1a, column 11.

[2] The numbers of pupils in mainstream schools are the total numbers of pupils and students at the ISCED levels 1, 2 and 3 (Eurostat/UOE statistics, 1994/95, ENRL1).

SOURCES

A. Context

	EUROPEAN UNION
FIN	A5: Statistics Finland
	EFTA/EEA
IS	A9, A10, A11, A14: Statistics Iceland
LI	A6, A8, A9: Ministry of Education
NO	A9, A10, A11, A14: Labour Force Survey Norway
	CEEC
BG	
CZ	A6, A7, A8, A9, A10, A11, A14: Institute for Information on Education
HU	A6, A9: Hungarian Statistical Yearbook, 1996, Budapest, Central Statistical Agency A7, A8: Data on Educational Statistics 1995/96, Budapest, Central Statistical Agency
PL	A6, A7, A8: A9, A10, A11, A14: Labour Force Survey Poland
RO	A6, A7, A8: Documentaire statistique pour l'année scolaire 1994/1995 A9, A10, A11, A14: Commission Nationale de Statistique
SK	A6, A7, A8, A9, A10, A11, A14: Statistical Office of the Slovak Republic

B. Structures and schools

	EFTA/EEA
LI	B2: Ministry of Education
	CEEC
BG	
CZ	
HU	B2: Annual Report on Hungarian School Education - 1995, National School Educational Research Institute
PL	
RO	B2: Commission Nationale de Statistique - L'Enseignement en Roumanie, données statistiques, 1996
SK	B2: Institute of Information and Prognoses of Education

C. Pre-primary education

	EUROPEAN UNION
S	C5: Statistics Sweden

D. Primary education

	CEEC
BG	
CZ	D11, D12: Institute for Information on Education
HU	D11, D12: Hungarian Ministry of Culture and Education - Dept. of School Educational Development, Annual Report on Primary School Education, 1996
PL	D11, D12: Statistical yearbook of Education 1993/94 - Central Statistical Office 1994
RO	
SK	D11, D12, D13: Institute of Information and Prognoses of Education

E. Secondary education

EFTA/EEA	
IS	E5: Statistics Iceland
LI	E3, E4, E5, E18: Ministry of Education
CEEC	
BG	E3, E4, E5: National Statistic Institute E12, E13, E14, E15, E16: Institute for Educational Research
CZ	E3, E4, E5, E12, E13, E14, E15, E16, E18: Institute for Information on Education
HU	E3, E4, E5: Hungarian Ministry of Culture and Education - Dept. of School Educational Development, Annual Report on Secondary School Education, 1996 E12, E13, E14, E15, E16, E18: Annual Report on Hungarian School Education 1996, National School Educational Research Institute, Budapest
PL	E3, E4: Education in 1994/95, Central Statistical Office E5, E13, E14, E15, E18: Statistical Yearbook on Education, Central Statistical Office, 1994
RO	E3, E4, E5, E18: Commission Nationale de Statistique - Annuaire Statistique 1996 E12, E13, E14, E15, E16: Commission Nationale de Statistique - L'Enseignement en Roumanie, données statistiques, 1996; Ministère de l'Enseignement - Documentaire statistique 1994/95
SK	E3, E4, E5, E12, E13, E14, E15, E16: Institute of Information and Prognoses of Education

F. Higher education

EFTA/EEA	
IS	F4, F5, F7, F8, F13, F15: Statistics Iceland F12, F16-18, F20: not available
LI	
NO	F4: Eurostat
CEEC	
CZ	F2, F4, F5, F7, F8, F13, F14, F15, F18, F19, F20: Institute for Information on Education F17: Czech Statistical Office (national census 1991) F6: Institute for Information on Education and Czech Statistical Office F14, F16: NA F12: Centre for Higher Education Studies, 1995
BG	F2: Higher Education Act 95 (chapter 5, articles 42 and 44) F3, F4, F5, F6, F7, F8, F9, F10, F13, F14, F15, F18, F20: National Statistical Institute F12, F14, F16, F17, F18: NA
HU	F1: 1993 No LXXIX Act on School Education and its 1996 Amendments F2, F3: Annual Report on Higher Education 1996, Hungarian Ministry of Culture and Education F4, F5, F7, F8: Hungarian Statistical Yearbook, 1996, Budapest, Central Statistical Agency F6: data not available
PL	F4, F5, F6, F7, F8, F13, F14, F15, F17, F18: Central Statistical Office, Warsaw
RO	F3, F4, F6, F7, F8, F13, F15: Commission nationale de Statistique - L'enseignement en Roumanie, données statistiques 1996 F5: Ministère de l'Enseignement - Documentaire statistique 1994/95 F10, F20: Ministère de l'Enseignement - Documentaire statistique 1994/95; La Commission Nationale de Statistique - L'Enseignement en Roumanie, données statistiques 1996 F14, F18: Commission nationale de Statistique - L'enseignement en Roumanie, données statistiques 1996 + Ministère de l'enseignement - Documentaire statistique 94/95
SK	

G. Teachers

	EFTA/EEA
LI	G5, G10: Ministry of Education

	CEEC
BG	G5, G7, G8, G9, G10, G14, G15: National Statistic Institute G16, G17, G18: European Bank for Reconstruction and Development
CZ	G5, G7, G8, G9, G10: Institute for Information on Education G16, G17, G18: European Bank for Reconstruction and Development
HU	G5: Annual report of Hungarian Statistical Agency G7, G8, G9, G10: Ministry of Culture and Education G16, G17, G18: European Bank for Reconstruction and Development
PL	G5, G7, G8, G9, G10: Statistical Yearbook 1995; EWIKAN 1994/95 (Statistical Information on Teachers) G16, G17, G18: European Bank for Reconstruction and Development
RO	G5:
SK	G5: Institute of Information and Prognoses of Education; Statistical Yearbook of the Slovak Republic - 1996 G7, G8, G9, G10, G11: Institute of Information and Prognoses of Education G16, G17, G18: European Bank for Reconstruction and Development

H. Special education.

	EUROPEAN UNION
F	H6: Unité française Eurydice
L	H6: Unité luxembourgeoise Eurydice
A	H6: Unité autrichienne Eurydice
FIN	H6: National Board of Education

	EFTA/EEA
IS	H6: Fjöldi nemenda í grunnskólum 1994-95, Menntamálaráðuneypið des. 1994
LI	H6: Ministry of Education
NO	H6: Ministry of Education

	CEEC
BG	H6: National Statistic Institute
CZ	H6: Institute for Information on Education
HU	
PL	H6: Central Statistical Office, Statistical Yearbook on Education
RO	
SK	H6: Institute of Information and Prognoses of Education

BIBLIOGRAPHY – EURYDICE PUBLICATIONS
(Eurydice web site:http://www.eurydice.org)

- Eurydice, Cedefop. *Structures of the Education and Initial Training Systems,* Second edition, Luxembourg, Office for Official Publications of the European Communities, 1995, p. 458, ISBN 92-826-9319-8.

  For anyone trying to understand the education systems in Europe, this is a basic work, with many unique features. It covers the 15 Member States of the European Union and the three EFTA/EEA countries and brings out the diversity of their individual education situations. As each monograph is structured on the basis of a common framework, the document facilitates comparison between the different countries. The analysis deals with not only the education systems but also the organisation of initial vocational training. Produced by the European Unit of Eurydice, this is the result of close collaboration between the National Units of Eurydice and the members of the Cedefop documentary network.

  A supplement to this second edition will be published at the end of 1997 covering the six associated central and eastern European countries (Bulgaria, the Czech Republic, Hungary, Poland, Romania and Slovakia) which have been participating in the activities of the Eurydice network since 1996. The three Baltic States, Slovenia and Cyprus will be included in 1998.

- Eurydice. *School Heads,* Brussels, Eurydice European Unit, 1996, p. 96, ISBN 2-87116-252-2.

  This study concentrates on the management of schools and in particular on the main tasks of headteachers at primary and secondary level in the 15 Member States of the European Union and the three EFTA/EEA countries. Detailed information is provided on the administrative and educational responsibilities of school heads as well as on entry to the profession, the teaching load, and appraisal procedures. A terminological glossary is also provided to facilitate understanding of the many designations in use.

- Eurydice. *Organisation of School Time,* Second edition, Brussels, Eurydice European Unit, 1995, p. 44, ISBN 2-87116-229-8.

  This second edition of the study on the organisation of school time in the European Union now embraces the three EFTA/EEA countries and examines the situation in both primary and secondary education in considerable detail. A broad spectrum of information is presented, covering the duration of compulsory education, the organisation of the school year, the placing of holidays, daily and weekly timetables etc.

- Eurydice. *Organisation of School Time,* Brussels, Eurydice European Unit, 1997, p. 20, ISBN 2-87116-270-0.

  Data on an annual basis have been updated in 1997. These relate to the dates of the start of the school year and the length and placing of school holidays. The 1997 update also includes the situation in the associated central and eastern European countries which have been participating in the Eurydice network since 1996, the three Baltic States and Slovenia.

- Eurydice. *Secondary Education in the European Union: Structures, Organisation and Administration,* Brussels, Eurydice European Unit, 1997, p. 160, ISBN 2-87116-263-8.

  The main areas covered by this document include the structural organisation of secondary education, its administration and educational organisation, and the initial and in-service training of teachers. Diagrams illustrate the place of secondary education and its various branches in relation to the overall education system of each country. Pupil assessment and the organisation of school time are also subjected to detailed analysis. The document also attempts to establish the relative importance of the professional training of teachers (educational theory and practice) relative to their academic education (knowledge of the subject matter to be taught). Several indicators have been constructed on this point and these represent an original analysis. The study presents a comparative analysis of the situation in the 15 Member States of the European Union and the three EFTA/EEA countries.

- Eurydice. *The Role of Parents in the Education Systems,* Brussels, Eurydice European Unit, 1997, p. 128, ISBN 2-87116-260-3.

  The theme of this study is the participation of parents in the management of the education systems in the 15 Member States of the European Union and the three EFTA/EEA countries. The patterns of representation of parents and the powers and responsibilities they have in the various participatory bodies are described country by country. A comparative overview brings out both the diversity of the national situations and also the convergences found in Europe in this area.

- Eurostat. *Education across the European Union – Statistics and Indicators*, 1996
  Office for Official Publications of the European Communities, 1997, p. 327,
  Catalogue No. CA-91-96-090-3A-C, ISBN 92-827-9631-0

  This statistical document provides comparable data for the 15 Member States of the European Union on pupils, students, and teaching staff, as well as on educational attainment levels of the population. It focuses largely on the academic year 1993/94, supplemented by a time series for certain variables 1975/76 to 1993/94. Indicators range from the proportion of the population in education to the most popular modern foreign languages taught at school, and from the age structure of new entrants to higher education to the proportion of students attending university abroad. A number of these indicators are provided for the regions of the EU. Finally, drawing on data from the Community labour force survey, the document contains a special section on the levels of educational attainment of the population.

- Eurostat. *Youth in the European Union — From education to working life*
  Office for Official Publications of the European Communities, 1997, p. 111,
  Catalogue No. CA-98-96-267-C, ISBN 92-828-0438-0

  Today, those aged 15 to 24 in the 'Europe of the Fifteen' number approximately 50 million people, a figure which increases to 80 million if we include 25 to 29 year olds. Two points emerge from the present study: first, regardless of how youth is defined, the percentage of 'young' people in the population is slowly but surely falling in every Member State of the European Union. Secondly, the characteristic stages in the transition from full-time education to employment are slowing down: young people are staying longer in education, taking more time to cross over from training to work, and waiting longer before starting families of their own. While following this common path, the stages of transition to adulthood tend to be shaped by national characteristics and policies. In this study, we attempt to describe the major trends, similarities and contrasts which exist between Member States in such areas as education, training, transition to the labour market, family life and living conditions.

- Eurostat. *Demographic Statistics 1997*
  Office for Official Publications of the European Communities, 1997, p. 275,
  Catalogue No. CA-05-97-600-C, ISBN 92-828-0737-1

  While all European Union countries possess highly developed systems of demographic statistics, the wide diversity of practice with regard to the statistical documentation and presentation of results makes it very difficult to obtain the comparable and up-to-date information required to study trends within the Union. This document is designed to make good this deficiency. All the principal series of demographic statistics are covered, namely population by sex and age group, births, deaths, migration, marriages, divorces, fertility, life expectancy and population projections. Both absolute numbers and rates are given in considerable detail for each country in the Union.

- Eurostat. *Labour Force Survey — Results 1995*
  Office for Official Publications of the European Communities, 1996, p. 277,
  Catalogue No. CA-96-96-433-C, ISBN 92-827-8360-X

  The labour force sample survey was carried out in spring 1995 in all the Member States of the European Union, in application of Council Regulation (EEC) No 3711/91 of 16 December 1991. In this statistical document, Eurostat presents the main results of the survey. The data cover, in particular the total population of private households, the labour force and unemployed persons by sex and age group; employed persons by sex, professional status and branch of activity; weekly working hours; the main groups of persons seeking employment, by sex, reason for seeking employment, duration of search and methods used.

- Eurostat. *Education and Job Prospects: What can we expect today? (Statistics in Focus – Population and social conditions – 1995/12)*
  Office for Official Publications of the European Communities, 1995, p. 12,
  Catalogue No. CA-NK-95-012-C

- Eurostat. *Education in the European Union: Opportunities and choices (Statistics in Focus – Population and social conditions – 1997/4)*
  Office for Official Publications of the European Communities, 1997, p. 4,
  Catalogue No. CA-NK-97-004-C

ACKNOWLEDGEMENTS

We wish to thank the Eurydice National Units and the Eurostat national contact points for their essential contribution to this report.

THIS REPORT HAS BEEN COORDINATED AND PRODUCED BY THE EURYDICE EUROPEAN UNIT

Texts drafted by

Arlette Delhaxhe

Anne Godenir

Annick Sacré

Preparation of graphics and layout

Patrice Brel

Translation and revision of English version

Anne O'Brien

Technical assistance for printing and secretarial support

Gisèle De Lel

Athena Papas

Helga Stammherr

STATISTICAL CONTRIBUTIONS WERE PROVIDED BY THE STATISTICAL OFFICE OF THE EUROPEAN UNION, EUROSTAT

Laurent Freisson

Rachel Harris

Bettina Knauth

THE FOLLOWING PROVIDED EXPERT SUPPORT IN THE PREPARATION OF THE REPORT

Service de Pédagogie Expérimentale, University of Liège, Belgium

Institut des Sciences et Pratiques d'Éducation et de Formation,
Lumière University, Lyon 2, France

EURYDICE NETWORK

**Eurydice European Unit
Rue d'Arlon 15
B-1050 Brussels
(http://www.eurydice.org)**

National Units which have contributed to the preparation of the report

E U R O P E A N   U N I O N

BELGIQUE / BELGIË
Unité francophone d'Eurydice
Ministère de l'Éducation, de la Recherche et de la Formation
Secrétariat Général
Cité Administrative de l'État
Boulevard Pachéco 19, Bte 0, 7e étage
1010 Bruxelles
Contribution: joint responsibility

Vlaamse Eurydice-Eenheid
Ministerie van de Vlaamse Gemeenschap
Departement Onderwijs
Afdeling Beleidsgerichte Coördinatie
RAC Arcadengebouw – 3de verd.
1010 Brussel
Contribution: joint responsibility

Agentur Eurydice
Ministerium der deutschsprachigen Gemeinschaft
Agentur für Europäische Programme
Gospertstrasse 1-5
4700 Eupen
Contribution: joint responsibility

DANMARK
Eurydice's Informationskontor i Danmark
Undervisningsministeriet
Frederiksholms Kanal 21D
1220 København K
Contribution: joint responsibility

BUNDESREPUBLIK DEUTSCHLAND
Eurydice - Informationsstelle beim
Bundesministerium für Bildung, Wissenschaft,
Forschung und Technologie
Heinemannstrasse 2
53175 Bonn
Contribution: joint responsibility

Eurydice - Informationsstelle der Länder
im Sekretariat der Kultusministerkonferenz
Lennéstrasse 6
53113 Bonn
Contribution: joint responsibility

ELLADA
Eurydice Unit
Ministry of National Education and Religious Affairs
Direction CEE / Section C
Mitropoleos 15
10185 Athens
Contribution: Antigoni Faragoulitaki

ESPAÑA
Unidad de Eurydice
Ministerio de Educación y Cultura
CIDE – Centro de Investigación y Documentación Educativa
c/General Oráa 55
28006 Madrid
Contribution: Mercedes Muñoz-Repiso, Javier Murillo,
Irene Arrimadas, Begoña Arias, Ana Isabel Martín,
Elisa Gavari

FRANCE
Unité d'Eurydice
Ministère de l'Éducation nationale, de la Recherche et de la
Technologie
Délégation aux Relations internationales et à la Coopération
Bureau de l'information sur les systèmes éducatifs et la
reconnaissance des diplômes
Rue de Grenelle 110
75357 Paris
Contribution: joint responsibility

IRELAND
Eurydice Unit
Department of Education and Science
International Section
Floor 1 – Block 4
Irish Life Centre – Talbot Street
Dublin 1
Contribution: joint responsibility

ITALIA
Unità di Eurydice
Ministero della Pubblica Istruzione
Biblioteca di Documentazione Pedagogica
Via Buonarroti 10
50122 Firenze
Contribution: Daniela Nenci, Antonelle Turchi

LUXEMBOURG
Unité d'Eurydice
Centre de Psychologie et d'Orientation Scolaire
Route de Longwy 280
1940 Luxembourg
Contribution: Raymond Harsch

NEDERLAND
Eurydice Eenheid Nederland
Bibliotheek en Documentatie
Ministerie van Onderwijs, Cultuur en Wetenschappen
Postbus 25000 – Europaweg 4
2700 LZ Zoetermeer
Contribution: joint responsibility

EUROPEAN UNION (continued)

ÖSTERREICH
Eurydice - Informationsstelle
Bundesministerium für Unterricht und
kulturelle Angelegenheiten
Abt. I/6b
Minoritenplatz 5
1014 Wien
Contribution: joint responsibility

PORTUGAL
Unidade de Eurydice
Ministério da Educação
Departamento de Avaliação, Prospectiva e Planeamento
(DAPP)
Av. 24 de Julho 134
1350 Lisboa
Contribution: joint responsibility

SUOMI / FINLAND
Eurydice Finland
National Board of Education
Hakaniemenkatu 2
00530 Helsinki
Contribution: joint responsibility

SVERIGE
Eurydice Unit
Ministry of Education and Science
Drottninggatan 16
10333 Stockholm
Contribution: joint responsibility

UNITED KINGDOM
Eurydice Unit London
National Foundation for Educational Research
The Mere, Upton Park
Slough, Berkshire SL1 2DQ
Contribution: joint responsibility

Eurydice Unit Scotland
International Relations Branch
The Scottish Office Education and Industry Department
Floor 1 Area B Victoria Quay
Edinburgh EH6 6QQ
Contribution: joint responsibility

EFTA/EEA COUNTRIES

ÍSLAND
Eurydice Unit
Ministry of Education, Science and Culture
Sölvholsgata 4
150 Reykjavik
Contribution: joint responsibility

LIECHTENSTEIN
National Unit of Eurydice
Schulamt
Herrengasse 2
9490 Vaduz
Contribution: joint responsibility

NORGE
Eurydice Unit
Royal Norwegian Ministry of Education,
Research and Church Affairs
P.O. Box 8119 Dep.
Akersgaten 42
0032 Oslo
Contribution: joint responsibility

CENTRAL AND EASTERN EUROPEAN COUNTRIES (CEEC)

BĂLGARIJA
Eurydice Unit
International Relations Department
Ministry of Education, Science and Technology
2A, Knjaz Dondukov Bld
1000 Sofia
Contribution: joint responsibility

ČESKÁ REPUBLIKA
Eurydice Unit
Institute for Information on Education – ÚIV/IIE
Senovážné nám. 26
Praha 1, 111 21
Contribution: joint responsibility

MAGYARORSZÁG
Eurydice Unit
Ministry of Education
Szalay u. 10-14
1054 Budapest
Contribution: Zoltán Zarándy, Zoltán Loboda,
Zsuzsanna Tuska, Áron Ecsedy, Mária Némedi

POLSKA
Eurydice Unit
Institute for Educational Research
Documentation and Information Unit
Górczewska 8
01-180 Warszawa
Contribution: Prof. Rafat Piwowarski (expertise),
Anna Smoczyńska (coordination)

ROMÂNIA
Eurydice Unit
Socrates National Agency
1 Schitu Magureanu – 2nd Floor
70626 Bucharest
Contribution: Alexandru Modrescu

SLOVENSKÁ REPUBLIKA
Eurydice Unit
Slovak Academic Association for International Cooperation
Staré grunty 52
842 44 Bratislava
Contribution: joint responsibility

EUROSTAT CONTACT POINTS

Statistical Office of the European Communities
Bâtiment Jean Monnet
L-2920 Luxembourg

National contact points that have taken part in preparing this report

E U R O P E A N   U N I O N

BELGIQUE / BELGIË
Service des Statistiques
Communauté française de Belgique
Boulevard Pachéco 19 - Bte 0
1010 Bruxelles
Contribution: Jean-Claude Roucloux

Ministerie van de Vlaamse Gemeenschap
Dept. Onderwijs - Rijksadministratief Centrum
Afdeling Begroting en gegevensbeheer
Arcadengebouw, Blok F, 3e verdieping, Bur. 3084
1010 Brussel
Contribution: Ann Van Driessche

DANMARK
Ministry of Education
Data Division
Frederiksholms Kanal 26
1220 Kobenhavn OE
Contribution: Brigitte Bovin

BUNDESREPUBLIK DEUTSCHLAND
Statistisches Bundesamt
65180 Wiesbaden
Contribution: Walter Hörner

Ständige Konferenz der Kultusminister der Länder
in der Bundesrepublik Deutschland
Lennéstrasse 6
53113 Bonn
Contribution: Katharina Schumacher

ELLADA
Ministry of Education
Director of Planning and Operational
Mitropoleos Street 15
10185 Athens
Contribution: Gregory Kafetzopoulos, Christos P. Kitsos

National Statistical Service of Greece
Syngrou Ave. 56
11742 Athens
Contribution: Panayota Korilaki

ESPAÑA
Education Statistics
Instituto Nacional de Estadistica
Paseo de la Castellana 183
28046 Madrid
Contribution: Fernando Celestino Rey

Ministerio de Educación y Cultura
Oficina de planificación y estadistica
C/Alfonso XII, 3 - 5
28014 Madrid
Contribution: Mr Jesús Ibáñez Milla

FRANCE
Ministère de l'Education nationale
Boulevard du Lycée 58
92170 Vanves
Contribution: Paul Esquieu

IRELAND
Department of Education
Statistics Section
Irish Life Center, Block 1
Lower Abbey Street
Dublin 1
Contribution: Mary Dunne

ITALIA
Servizio Statistico
Ministero della Pubblica Istruzione
Viale Trastevere 76A
00153 Roma
Contribution: Gemma De Sanctis

Capo Servizio F.I.L.
(Formazione, Istruzione, Lavoro)
Istituto Nazionale di Statistica
Viale Liegi 11
00198 Roma
Contribution: Giovanni Cariani

LUXEMBOURG
Ministère de l'Education nationale et de la Formation
Professionnelle
29, rue Aldringen
2926 Luxembourg
Contribution: Jérôme Levy

NEDERLAND
Ministerie van Onderwijs en Wetenschappen
Europaweg 4 - POB 25000
1700 LZ Zoetermeer
Contribution: Ruud Abeln

Centraal Bureau voor de Statistiek
Prinses Beatrixlaan 428
2270 AZ Voorburg
Contribution: Max Van Herpen

ÖSTERREICH
Österreichisches Statistisches Zentralamt
Hintere Zollamtstrasse 2b
1030 Wien
Contribution: Wolfgang Pauli

EUROPEAN UNION (continued)

PORTUGAL
Ministerio da Educaçao
DEPGEF
Av. 24 de Julho 134
1350 Lisboa
Contribution: Ruth Gomes

SUOMI / FINLAND
Statistics Finland
00022 Helsinki
Contribution: Timo Ertola

SVERIGE
Statistics Sweden
Department of Labour and Education
23 Klostergatan
701 89 Örebro
Contribution: Ronnie Andersson

UNITED KINGDOM
Department for Education and Employment
Room 113
Mowden Hall
Staindrop Road
Darlington DL3 9BG
Contribution: David Sorensen

EFTA/EEA COUNTRIES

ÍSLAND
Statistics Iceland
Skuggasundi 3
150 Reykjavik
Contribution: Hjalti Kristgeirsson

NORGE
Statistics Norway
Oterveien 23
P.b. 1260
2201 Kongsvinger
Contribution: Elisabetta Vassenden

European Commission

Key data on education in the European Union — 1997

Luxembourg: Office for Official Publications of the European Communities

1997-206 p. — 21x29,7 cm

ISBN 92-828-1884-5

Price (excluding VAT) in Luxembourg: ECU 25